COLLINS

Complete

GARDEN
MANUAL

COLLINS

Complete

GARDEN MANUAL

CONSULTANT
ADAM PASCO

CONTRIBUTORS
DAVID STEVENS
ANNE SWITHINBANK
SUE PHILLIPS
ANDI CLEVELY
ADAM PASCO

HarperCollins*Publishers*
London

HarperCollins*Publishers*
London

First published in 1998 by HarperCollins*Publishers*

Design and layout © HarperCollins*Publishers* 1998
Text: *Introduction* © Adam Pasco 1998
Text: *Garden Planning and Design* © David Stevens 1998
Text: *Best Plants for Every Site* © Anne Swithinbank 1998
Text: *Gardening in Practice* © Sue Phillips 1998
Text: *The Kitchen Garden* © Andi Clevely 1998
Text: *The Gardener's Calendar* © Adam Pasco 1998

The Authors assert their moral rights to be identified
as the authors of this work

A catalogue record for this book is available
from the British Library.

ISBN 000 414010 9

Designed and produced for HarperCollins*Publishers* by
Cooling Brown, Middlesex, England
Editorial: Carole McGlynn, Ann Kay
Design: Alistair Plumb, Tish Mills
Photography: Peter Anderson, Steve Gorton, Matthew Ward
Illustrations: Nicola Gregory, Vanessa Luff, Des Fox

Colour origination: Colourscan

Printed in Italy by Rotolito Lombarda SpA.

Contents

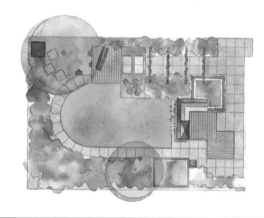

Best Plants for Every Site

Gardening in Practice
Part 3

❖

The Kitchen Garden
Part 4

❖

The Gardener's Calendar

Part 5

❖

QUICK SUBJECT REFERENCE

❖

INTRODUCTION

❖

WHAT BETTER WAY to learn about gardening than in the company of a trusted friend, who is passionate about gardening and prepared to show you the shortcuts to success? Well, that is exactly what this book sets out to do, by combining the horticultural knowledge and experience of four of my gardening friends, all experts in their field, who will share with you their ideas and advice on all aspects of gardening.

△ **A SMALL GREENHOUSE** *will open up a world of opportunities, especially for more tender subjects.*

Throughout the Complete Garden Manual *our team will help you tackle your garden from scratch, with*

advice on planning and design, on choosing the best plants, on growing crops in the kitchen garden and on a host of techniques that will show you how to plant, prune and propagate almost anything. They can all be seen in action, often in their own gardens, so you will soon get to know them personally. At the end of the book you will find my tips and ideas, a complete gardening calendar telling you what to do and how to do it, month by month.

This book will soon be a constant gardening companion, guiding you through every job step-by-step. Use it for reference, to look up plants and get practical advice, or read it to gain inspiration from the wealth of ideas and beautiful colour

◁ **GOOD PLANNING** *forms the backbone to a great design, whether simply sprucing up your front garden or tackling a complete makeover of your outdoor space.*

▷ **WITH THOUSANDS OF PLANTS** *to choose from, follow our guide to select the very best for every site and situation in your garden.*

photographs inside. Our team takes nothing for granted and won't baffle you with jargon, so, as you tackle gardening tasks and master new techniques, your confidence will build and you will soon be sure of success every time.

Never feel daunted by your garden, even if it is a new or overgrown plot: with a little time and careful planning, everyone can create an attractive and productive space. The most important thing is to have a go, enjoy it at every stage, and never be put off by the mystique that some experts build up around plants and gardening techniques. The more you put in, the more you will get out of your garden, of course, but even if you can spare only a few hours a week, little by little your garden will be transformed. Keep a diary of your successes and failures, both equally important in the great gardening game. Learn from your failures and next year will be even better, more productive and more rewarding than the last.

I hope the Complete Garden Manual will serve you well as both friend and guide to help you get the most from your plot. Gardening should always be fun, so I wish you an enjoyable time ahead as you read, consult and explore this book.

△ **GROWING YOUR OWN** *fruit and vegetables is easier than you might think, creating a garden that is both ornamental and productive.*

ADAM PASCO

GARDEN PLANNING AND DESIGN

GARDEN DESIGN is an essentially simple subject and one people should not be afraid of. It can appear daunting due to the vast amount of information in the form of books, magazines, on television programmes and at flower shows, added to which is a nursery and garden centre trade hungry to sell their wares. The choice available serves only to confuse us and it is no wonder that many gardens become a jumble of unrelated features that do little to serve their owners or make the most of the location.

Another problem is that we tend to think of house and garden as separate entities when, in fact, the best gardens work as an extension of the home. Most of us are more than capable of planning the rooms inside the house, but all too often our confidence and sound common sense are lost when we move outside. The real secret is to link our inside and outside living spaces as seamlessly as possible, both to each other and to the surrounding location, through the choice of style, materials, colour and, of course, planting, all of which should be tuned to your needs and reflect the personality of you and your family.

Your garden is an extremely valuable space, giving you somewhere to relax, play, dine, entertain, grow plants and escape from the pressures of everyday life. The planning and maintenance of that space should be challenging, enjoyable and endlessly satisfying.

DAVID STEVENS

What is good design?

A good garden design is, above all, simple yet practical. It should reflect the needs of those that use it, provide a link with the adjoining house, blend with the surrounding environment and provide colour and interest throughout the year. No two gardens are ever alike, because the requirements of each person or family are different, which in turn shapes the finished layout.

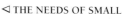

12 △ **CONTRASTING MATERIALS** *produce a strong design feature in this paved garden.*

WHY DESIGN A GARDEN?

Design is all about control and it is this that sets any garden apart from a natural environment. Even the most seemingly random wildlife area will have been as carefully planned as a formal garden, albeit to suit a very different set of circumstances.

Working out a design allows you to create a garden that fits you like a glove, allocates a sensible budget that can be spread over a period of time and lessens the chances of over-complication from those frequent and expensive visits to the local garden centre.

◁ **IN THIS ENCLOSED** *city courtyard, a raised timber deck supports table and chairs, while the central area of the garden is laid as stone flags. The raised pool adds interest and brings soothing sounds to mask city noises. A small shed tucked into the corner is stained dark to make it unobtrusive.*

Apart from the pleasure gained from enjoying a tailor-made space, a well-planned garden will, in all probability, add value to your home should you wish to move.

SETTING A THEME

While it is attractive to think of, say, a cottage- or an oriental-style garden, such a rigid approach can be dangerous, particularly in the initial stages of working out a design. By far the most important consideration is you and the needs of your family. There is little point in dreaming of an idyllic cottage garden then finding that you have to contend with boisterous youngsters playing football, riding bikes and generally having a good time romping through your prize delphiniums.

Remember that a garden can change its style and character over a period of time and what may start off as a tough, but hopefully good-looking, family environment, could end up a few years later as a peaceful, idyllic haven dedicated to plants.

◁ **THE NEEDS OF SMALL CHILDREN** *have been catered for by cleverly integrating a sandpit into a paved area. It would need to be covered when not in use.*

FORM FOLLOWS FUNCTION

A good garden is therefore one that reflects the needs of its owners in a simple and straightforward way. It should be practical but full of interest and surprises and hopefully give a real impression of space. The best designs offer mystery and surprise by dividing the area into a number of separate 'outside rooms', each one of which can have a different theme or purpose.

None of this is expensive or difficult to achieve. Most professional garden designers work to a well-tried and tested set of rules that they know will work in the majority of situations. There is nothing mysterious about these 'tricks of the trade', so observe the guidelines given in the following pages and you will achieve a garden design that really works.

▷ **BRICK STEPS** *separate the two tiers of this garden but lawned areas on both levels give continuity. The geometric design is softened by the abundant planting.*

• *see also:* STARTING FROM SCRATCH p14; DESIGN CONSIDERATIONS p18

Starting from scratch

There are advantages and disadvantages to starting with a brand new plot. The positive aspect is having a clean canvas, allowing you to plan everything exactly as you want. The down side will often be that you inherit a barren space, surrounded by stark fences and offering little in the way of screening from neighbouring windows.

14

ASKING THE RIGHT QUESTIONS

The first stage of any planning is to ask two simple questions – what do you have and what do you need? If you can answer these honestly and accurately, you will be well on the way to creating a successful garden. But first of all, if your plot is a new development, take a look at what the builders have left you. Developers usually provide a minimal amount of paving – often a few paving slabs and a path to the back door – and they may also have laid a lawn.

This is the time to check the quality of the soil, to ensure the builders have provided ample clean topsoil. The difference between topsoil and subsoil lies in its fertility: the former should be rich in organic matter, easily workable and able to support healthy plant growth. The subsoil, which lies beneath the topsoil, is unable to support plant growth and is usually impossible to work. But irresponsible builders may have simply dumped subsoil from the house foundations over the garden, in which case you should ask them to remove this layer of subsoil and replace it with clean topsoil.

WHAT DO YOU HAVE?

This can be assessed by carrying out a simple survey. While we shall be dealing with how to measure your garden a little later, there are a number of important factors to consider at the outset.
• Check out any existing features, including the type of fences and walls, and look at the building materials of the house itself, all of which could suggest materials for the new garden.
• See if there are any good views of which you could take advantage or – rather more common – any bad views that would need screening. Check out any changes in level that could determine the position of steps.
• Check the orientation of your plot by noting the position of the sun throughout the day. It will rise in the east and set in the west, being due south at midday, and the path it takes across your garden will suggest the best place to site a patio, pool, summer house or greenhouse, as well as where to grow vegetables and position planting that enjoys bright or shady conditions. If in doubt, use a compass.
• Find out just what kind of soil you have, whether it is acid or alkaline, as this will

△ **TAKE A CRITICAL LOOK AT THE BOUNDARIES,** *noting the condition of fences and walls. You may decide to replace them in the final design.*

△ **USE A SOIL TESTING METER** *to check what type of soil you have. Be sure to take samples in several places, as the soil can vary in different areas around the garden.*

• *see also:* DRAWING UP A PLAN p22; DEALING WITH PROBLEM SITES p24; FENCING AND TRELLIS p26; PAVING AND PATIOS p34; STARTING A NEW LAWN p192

△ LAYING OUT THE BONES OF A GARDEN *and constructing it in stages helps you to realize its full potential.*

determine the type of plants that will flourish in your garden. This assessment is best carried out over some months; if you are prepared to take a full year, you will see changes wrought by the seasons and the pattern of shadows cast by buildings or trees, and will start to get a feel for your own space that will be invaluable when you come to prepare the design.

WHAT DO YOU WANT?

Assemble a list of your needs and desires over a period of time, throwing the discussion open to the whole family: after all, everyone will use the space in one way or another. Your wish list will, of course, depend on the available space but a typical list might include lawn, patio, pool, barbecue, swing, slide, shed, greenhouse, salad crops, fruit, shrub and herbaceous planting and rockery. If the list seems too long, you can reduce it later: the important thing is not to leave anything out at the planning stage.

THE ORDER OF WORK

Only once you have completed the design can you plan the construction of the garden, but it is as well to consider a logical order of work at this stage. The creation of the garden will be divided between the 'hard landscape', comprising paving, walls, fences, paths and any other permanent features, and the 'soft landscape', including lawn and planting.

The hard landscape is generally tackled first. It makes sense to work out from the house ends, initially laying the patio or terrace, which may incorporate raised beds, overhead beams, built-in barbecue and seating. Electric cables, run through conduit, should be set below the paved area before work starts; enlist the help of a professional electrician first. Think also about the provision of an outside tap for taking water down the garden.

In a sloping garden a terrace can link into steps, which in turn will give way to any paths that lead down the garden. If a

new fence or wall is needed, make this a priority, to provide shelter and screening.

If no lawn was laid by the developer, this will be the next job, with any island beds accurately cut out and cultivated. You can then erect an arch or pergola and install any garden buildings. Besides a patio, think about providing a simple concrete or paved work area round a shed or greenhouse: it will be invaluable for parking a wheelbarrow, organizing tools and allowing you to carry out a multitude of outdoor jobs. Paving is also practical in front of a summer house or beneath an arbour. Finally, you can think about the inclusion of other major features, such as a rockery or a pool.

In terms of the soft landscape, place trees first, securely staked and tied, followed by shrubs, herbaceous plants and ground cover. Mulch beds with bark to preserve moisture while plants establish. Use boards to protect a new lawn from both feet and barrows.

Developing an existing garden

Moving into an established garden means that, instead of starting with a clean canvas, you will inherit features built to suit circumstances entirely different from your own. It is important not to feel constrained by this but, on the other hand, think carefully before getting rid of established trees and shrubs that have taken a long time to grow. Maturity is not something you can instantly replace.

16

ASSESSING WHAT IS THERE

When a garden has been designed for another family it may initially seem fine, but does it really suit you? If it has been well looked after, the temptation is to leave things the way they are, or simply to tack new features on to the existing layout in an attempt to make it more appropriate for you. But compromise rarely works: your first job should be to take a good, hard look at what is there and decide exactly what you would like to keep and what you want to remove.

Classic examples of existing elements you need to re-consider might include a vegetable plot that you do not have the time to maintain, borders that are either too big for you to manage or too small for the plants you want to grow, a pool that could be a hazard for young children or simply the lack of a big enough patio for your family to eat outdoors.

It makes sense to carry out the basic survey in exactly the same way as for a brand new garden, but there will be many more features to measure and take note of. It is important to check the position of existing trees and other large plants, identifying them if you can. You may want to keep some and move others, supplementing them with plants of your own choice. List all the additional features you wish to include.

ADDING AND SUBTRACTING

The most radical measures may involve removing a tree that has outgrown its position or that casts too much shade; rebuilding or extending of a patio or breaking up paving to establish a lawn in its place; laying new paths to provide better access around the garden and to double as a hard surface for wheeled toys. If you have young children, you may need to install securely fixed play equipment where it can be clearly seen from the house.

If you wish to introduce a summer house, a greenhouse or a shed, their position will depend on the layout of the garden and, in the case of a greenhouse, the course of the sun throughout the day. You may want to

▽ IN THIS INFORMAL, *low-maintenance design, sun-loving plants flop out over the gravel surface, while the sundial acts as a focal point.*

△ ADVANTAGE IS TAKEN *of a sloping site to create a series of pools, linked by a soothing waterfall. Lush planting along the banks, including irises, ligularias and euphorbias, softens the pool edges and reinforces the garden's watery feel.*

• *see also:* STARTING FROM SCRATCH p14; PAVING AND PATIOS p34; PLANTING AND MOVING SHRUBS p204

◁ A GENTLE TRANSITION is provided in this garden, from the hard-surfaced patio to the softly planted borders at the far end. The mature apple trees have great character and have been left as a feature of the lawn.

Often the first view of an existing garden is one of an overgrown wilderness; however tempting it may be, never adopt a 'slash and burn' policy, as there will almost certainly be some trees and shrubs that are well worth keeping. While it makes sense to root out brambles and other invaders as soon as possible, take your time over everything else and get to know the garden before embarking on drastic reshaping. If possible, leave it for several seasons to see what plants come up.

RENOVATING

As with a new garden, it is sensible to renovate any hard landscaping first and to embark on a programme of getting everything back into condition. Paving can be re-laid or simply re-pointed, fences and walls should be checked over for sturdiness and weather-proofing and pools must cleaned out if they are badly silted up. Beds can then be tidied and the soil improved by the addition of well-rotted organic matter. At the appropriate time of year, shrubs can be pruned, hardy perennials divided, climbers thinned and neatly tied into trellis or horizontal wires and lawns started on their own renovation programme.

Leave some framework plants in a border to give the impression of maturity while your new plants develop. You can take them out later if you do not want them. Or, to provide a young border with an established look, plant fast-growing species like buddleja, broom and mallow; remove these in due course if you wish.

ON THE MOVE

❖

Rather than getting rid of plants that are in the wrong place, move them to a better one. Take out a large, deciduous shrub in the winter by carefully digging around its base and sliding it on to a polythene sack with as much root as possible. Slide the sack across the lawn or paving and place the shrub into a well-prepared hole so that the new soil level matches the old. Water well, staking it if it is in a windy position, and cut the stems back by about half.

incorporate, or to remove, a vegetable or herb garden, site a rock garden on a sunny slope, or perhaps include a pool. You might decide to set a pergola over an existing path or tuck a gazebo into a distant corner. And you can reduce, increase or simply re-organize existing planting. All new features must be positioned in relation to the existing layout, unless you conclude that the layout simply will not work for you, in which case the design must be modified in order to incorporate your new ideas.

If a small lawn is in poor condition, consider paving it over to reduce maintenance and increase sitting space. On the other hand, if there is too much paving, you may want to replace it with lawn and planting, in which case you must remove all the old surface and the foundations beneath raised beds or other features. You will have to break up and thoroughly cultivate the underlying soil to improve drainage, forking in well-rotted manure or compost. For shrubs and general planting you need to import 45cm (18in) of clean topsoil; for a lawn this depth can be reduced to a minimum of 15cm (6in).

Design considerations

The checklist which you and your family drew up will now be invaluable in working out just what you can fit in and putting the various features in order of importance. A patio might well be top of the list, with a lawn, particular types of planting, a barbecue and a pool following on. Some items at the end of the list may have to be left out but prioritizing your needs in this way will help to focus your design more clearly.

18

△ **A KITCHEN GARDEN** *need not be tucked out of sight: it may be more practical near the house.*

SIZE

The size of the garden will obviously have a bearing on just how many or how few features you can include. A large space could be sub-divided into separate garden 'rooms' or areas, separated by walls, hedges or trellis, each space having a different style, purpose or type of planting. A garden compartmentalized in this way will display the classic elements of mystery and surprise, leading you to wonder just what is around the corner or in the next room, and this naturally provides a sense of greater space.

Small plots effectively concentrate the mind on just what you want to include, as there will definitely not be room for everything. While most people consider a patio or sitting area essential, it does diminish the area available for planting, unless you incorporate raised beds. Think carefully about how important a lawn is in a small space; you may decide that the area will have more unity if it is entirely paved, with plant-filled containers, raised beds and climber-clad boundary walls providing the essential softening elements.

BUDGET

One of the great advantages of working to a plan is that you can allocate a sensible budget over a period of time, by building the garden in stages over several seasons or even years. The hard landscape elements of paving, fencing, walling and paths will take the lion's share of the budget, representing up to 75 per cent of the total cost. This means that it is essential to get the design right in the first place, since mistakes could be expensive to rectify. Plants and planting are a relatively inexpensive part of the finished garden and, if you are a keen gardener, can be propagated or grown from seed at minimal cost.

THE FUNCTION OF A GARDEN

The prime function of a garden is to meet the needs of you and your family and the secret is to allocate space logically so that one activity does not disrupt another. This means having ample room for sitting and dining, preferably close to the house, possibly divided by a low wall or planting from the lawn, where ball games and all kinds of play can take place. Space permitting, this might in turn give way to fruit, vegetables and space for a working or utility area. One of the most important aspects of garden design is to ensure that all areas are linked by paths that give access in all weathers, leading the eye in a pleasing way from one part of the garden to another.

◁ **IN THIS FORMAL DESIGN**, *trellis and low hedging are the elements used to divide up the garden. The box hedges provide a crisp edge, framing the planting as well as separating the 'rooms'.*

• *see also:* CHANGES OF LEVEL p40; SCREENS WITHIN THE GARDEN p46; GARDEN BUILDINGS p54

AGE AND ABILITY
No garden need remain unchanged throughout its life. The key is to build a garden that can be added to and modified as your lifestyle alters, without changing the underlying structure. This might mean that a toddler's sandpit becomes a raised bed or pool, while tough 'ball-proof' planting could be replaced by more delicate species once young children have grown up. A lawn could give way to an area of loose cobbles, gravel and planting, requiring little maintenance for busy people.

19

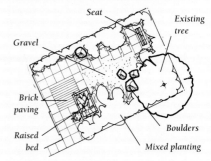

WORKING PERSON WITH NO CHILDREN

Seat

Existing tree

Gravel

Brick paving

Raised bed

Boulders

Mixed planting

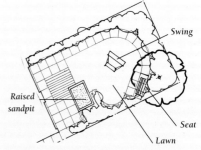

COUPLE WITH GROWING CHILDREN

Swing

Raised sandpit

Seat

Lawn

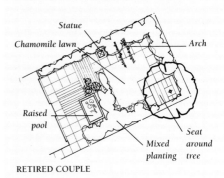

RETIRED COUPLE

Statue

Chamomile lawn

Arch

Raised pool

Seat around tree

Mixed planting

PRACTICALITIES
Remember that a garden has to include the utilitarian as well as the beautiful. It makes sense to group certain practical items together, such as a shed, greenhouse, compost and incinerator, and contain them within a hard-surfaced working area of ample size. They could then be neatly screened from the rest of the garden with trellis or hidden behind a 'wing' of planting.

Washing lines are usually essential and will need easy access by a path; some can be housed in a reel attached to the house wall so that they can be neatly stored when not in use. Dustbins can be kept in a purpose-built store with hinged doors and top. Remember to fit a sandpit with a removable cover that could double as a play surface as well as discouraging nocturnal visitors.

△ **CLEVERLY POSITIONED** *wall mirrors, perhaps framed by a false arch or trellis, can dramatically increase the feeling of space.*

SMALL-SCALE SOLUTIONS
❖
- Garden buildings such as sheds take up a lot of space but you may be able to incorporate storage alongside or beneath a built-in barbecue, or design overhead beams, smothered with climbers, to frame a potting bench that doubles as a tool store.

- Raised beds maximize the planting area while their retaining walls can double as built-in seating.

- If the sound and movement of water is a priority, bear in mind that a wall-mounted or millstone water feature takes up far less space than a pool.

Garden styles

Style should never be confused with fashion, which is a passing fad, usually with little substance. It can be dangerous to simply 'lift' a style which was born in another country or set of circumstances and superimpose it on your garden because it can all too easily end up a pastiche. But if you are influenced by a particular garden style, it is possible to make a sensitive but practical interpretation of it. The essential point about style is that it should be your own.

△ **A CRISP WOODEN DECK** *is the perfect link between indoors and out in this modern garden.*

FORMAL STYLES

Strictly formal gardens rely on symmetry of design, where one side mirrors the other, using planting, lawns, clipped hedges, pools, screens and other elements in a geometric layout. Such designs often look their best adjoining a period home with a formal facade. They can be equally appropriate in small town gardens whose design becomes like that of a stage set, to be viewed from the front. Formal gardens have a naturally 'static' feel and you are guided through them by the position of the various features. While they can be extremely elegant, and are ideal for dividing into 'rooms', they are unlikely to suit a young family needing plenty of open space for play and other activities.

INFORMAL STYLES

Informal gardens come in all guises and while the best are well laid out to suit a wide range of needs, the worst are a haphazard jumble of features. In a good design there is a logical progression through the space, from a terrace or patio that has a unity with the house to the more distant areas of the garden. There should be a feeling of movement that detracts from the garden's rectangular boundaries. Features and focal points should be carefully placed to draw you through the garden and the planting should have a soft, naturalistic feel to it. Above all, this is a family-friendly style of garden.

THE PLANT LOVER'S GARDEN

A plant enthusiast's garden can take any form but most of its space will be devoted to planting beds. It is a mistake to think that such gardens favour planting at the expense of everything else, as many elegantly architectural designs, with a strong structure provided by hard landscaping, provide the perfect foil for plant form and for the texture and colour of foliage and flowers. Nor do such gardens need to contain a huge range of species, since many plant lovers are specialist growers, revelling in the characteristics of a single or limited number of plant families, such as alpines or roses. Into this same category come colour-themed gardens, foliage gardens or those devoted to sun- or shade-loving plants. Such gardens can be large or small, rural or urban, but by their very nature they tend to be places for tending and viewing rather than for boisterous play.

COTTAGE GARDENS

This romantic style of English garden, evocative of past traditions, needs more maintenance than many people imagine. And, because it relies heavily on herbaceous plants that die down in the winter, it can look very thin for half the year. But if you want a cottage garden, try framing the beds with low, evergreen hedges, such as box, to provide winter structure and include some evergreens, such as euphorbias and hellebores, among the perennials to add form and extend the display.

△ **THE SYMMETRY** *of this formal garden is used to divide it into 'rooms'. Trellis panels and clipped box frame the entrance to the lawn area while the focal statue is flanked by box spheres.*

• *see also:* ALPINE AND ROCK GARDEN PLANTS p120; WILDFLOWERS p124; ARCHITECTURAL PLANTS p126

◁ IN THIS COTTAGE-STYLE *garden, a rich combination of plants spill out profusely from the borders in a wonderfully informal display. The paths impose some structure on the design.*

GARDENS FOR WILDLIFE

❖

Over recent years there has been a trend towards growing native species of trees, shrubs and wildflowers in order to encourage wildlife into the garden. This environmentally-oriented garden is always informal in style, tending towards the wild, as it involves letting grass grow longer and leaving plants to develop seedheads and hips rather than cutting them down when they finish flowering. Provided you match species carefully to the soil type and local conditions, the planting will need little irrigation and mean lower maintenance.

◁ THIS SUNNY, MEDITERRANEAN *garden is based on a Moorish theme. Container-grown citrus trees frame the rill that drops into the pool, while ceramic tiles decorate a whitewashed wall.*

ORIENTAL STYLE

A Japanese style of garden is probably the hardest to copy, partly because it looks deceptively simple. Unless you are fully versed in the deeply religious philosophy involved, which invests each plant or rock with meaning and its placing with great significance, there is a danger that your oriental-style garden will end up a pastiche of the real thing.

By all means, gain inspiration by looking at the simple yet exquisite detailing of the surfaces and structures of Japanese gardens, such as a raked gravel floor or the beautifully tied knots on fence panels. You will learn the vital lesson that simplicity is everything in terms of design. You could use elements like well-placed, smooth boulders or a 'river' of loose stones to simulate a dry stream bed and find pleasure in creating a simple but perfect composition.

MEDITERRANEAN STYLE

There is an intimacy to Mediterranean gardens that has to do with sunny courtyards, shade-giving overhead beams clad with climbers and warm terracotta tiles. And with the effects of global warming, such gardens are starting to look and feel right in many other parts of the world too. The most appropriate planting is fragrant and drought-tolerant, including aromatic herbs like rosemary, lavender and thyme. Suitable plant species include many with grey, felted leaves, such as senecio and phlomis, or with the sword-like form of yuccas and phormiums, all of which have a low rate of transpiration that makes them ideal in hot, dry conditions.

MODERNIST AND MINIMAL STYLES

Since garden design is about simplicity, if you have a fondness for modernist styles, why not think in minimalist terms? A swathe of gravel, with a few architectural plants piercing through, adjoining an area of crisp paving or decking, could look superb. With large-foliage plants, such as *Vitis coignetiae* or *Fatsia japonica*, or the delicate tracery of Japanese maples against a white-painted wall, nothing more would be needed.

Drawing up a plan

Despite what you may have heard, it is quite impossible to design a garden on the back of an envelope. The plan is the foundation for all that follows, allowing you to work out the construction in stages, to give an accurate estimate of the materials needed or to brief one or more contractors to quote in competition. At a later stage it will provide you with the basis of your planting plan.

22

MEASURING UP

Surveying the garden is a simple job and one that is quite fun to do. You need some basic equipment, including a 30m (100ft) tape measure (this can be hired if necessary), a pad of paper, a pencil and a clipboard, a skewer or metal pin and a magnetic compass to check the orientation. First sketch a rough outline of the house and garden on a sheet of paper. Then start measuring as shown below, transferring the dimensions clearly to your sketch.

TAKING MEASUREMENTS

Fix the tape to a fence or boundary close to the building, unreeling it across the width of the garden to the opposite fence.

Lay the tape on the ground and take 'running' measurements across the building: include all windows, doors, drains and manholes.

Reel in the tape, then repeat the operation, this time running down the length of the garden, away from and at right angles to the house, noting the position of any features, trees or planting.

△ **CHECK THE HEIGHT** *of existing steps or retaining walls. You can also get a rough idea of the fall on sloping land using a tape measure – and your eye.*

△ **UNLESS YOU HAVE A HELPER** *use a skewer to fix the end of a tape in the ground. Then take running measurements, starting with one corner of the house.*

• *see also:* STARTING FROM SCRATCH p14; DESIGN CONSIDERATIONS p18

CHANGES OF LEVEL

A slope away or up from the house will need measuring as this may determine the position of steps, a ramp or other features such as a split-level pool. If you have an architect's drawing of the house and garden, this will clearly show levels; otherwise existing steps or retaining walls can easily be measured and added together. On downward-sloping land, you could run out a tape at right angles, and horizontally, from a fixed point and measure the distance down to ground level to get a rough idea of the fall. In a large garden you may need the help of a professional surveyor.

PREPARING A SCALE DRAWING

When you have finished measuring up, transfer the information to a scale drawing that will become the basis for

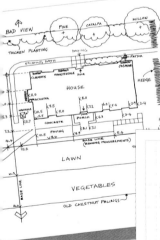

△ **START WITH A ROUGH SKETCH**
and mark on all the measurements. Transfer these onto graph paper, reduced to a convenient scale of 1:100 or 1:50; mark on all the existing features you will keep.

TRIANGULATION

If a feature, such as a tree, is in a freestanding position that is not easily measured by running a tape down or across the garden, you can employ a technique called triangulation to plot its position; this can also be used to plot the line of boundaries that are out of square. Triangulation involves running out a tape from two previously measured points (which could be either end of the house) to the feature and noting the distances on your survey drawing. Transfer these distances to a scale drawing using a pair of compasses extended to the scaled-down measurements: the position of the tree is where the two arcs intersect. Note also the position of any trees overhanging from a neighbour's garden: their shade could influence where you site a feature.

23

your design. This is made easier if you use squared graph paper, taking one or more squares to represent each metre or foot. Draw in the exact shape of the house and the line of garden boundaries and plot the position of existing plants and other features you intend to retain.

DRAWING UP THE DESIGN

The benefit of taking your time over preparing the survey is that it allows you to assess just what you have and to form an idea of what you want. You will

start to get a real feeling for your garden and may also begin to formulate an approximate layout in your head.

Once you are ready to commit yourself to paper, do not crystallize your ideas too soon: at this stage just sketch in roughly what features will go where. If, for example, the rear of the house gets the sun for most of the day, this will be the obvious place to site a patio, with possibly a built-in barbecue and maybe some raised beds or a pool. A path could then sweep away down the garden, running across or curving around a lawn, pausing at a seat before leading to the more distant parts of the garden, which might well include the utility or working area. Make sure that paths connect and give access to all parts of the garden. Other features on your priority list, such as a play area, a summer house, an arch or a pergola, can be roughly positioned at this stage, together with any steps or walls.

It is usually a good idea to do several alternative layouts to show the family. Once everyone is happy with a layout, firm it up by making a final working drawing. Do not overwork the design or try to fit too many things in: simplicity is the key to a successful design.

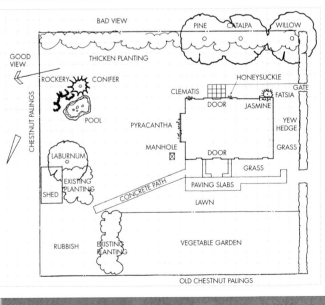

Dealing with problem sites

24

Not all gardens are a simple rectangle: like people, they come in all shapes and sizes. This often gives them an individual character and what can at first seem like an awkward or uncompromising shape may have the potential, with the right treatment, to be turned into a garden of real distinction.

The key to an interesting garden is our ability to move through the space so that not everything is visible at a single glance. While it is possible to divide up a garden that is longer than it is broad into individual areas, other shapes of plot can present real problems.

SQUARE PLOTS
Square plots tend to be completely static, with the surrounding boundaries seeming particularly dominant. The first job will be to soften and screen the boundaries and one way this can be done is with climbing plants. A good design solution is to base the whole garden on a bold, circular pattern that sets up a real feeling of space and movement. Another 'trick of the trade' is to design the garden on diagonal lines, which provides the greatest distance across the plot. It can therefore be very effective to turn the whole design at 45° to the house and the boundaries.

WIDE PLOTS
Gardens that are wider than they are long can feel very restrictive, even when they are of a reasonable size, because of the closeness of the opposite boundary. Never place a focal point on this boundary as the eye will immediately be drawn to it, which foreshortens the space. Sit in your

△ **A CIRCULAR DESIGN** *makes the most of a square space, opening it up and leading the eye out to its perimeter.*

favourite chair in the living room, look out into the garden and assess how far down the garden you can see to either side. This is the place for a focal point as it will draw the eye away from the nearest boundary and down the garden.

DOG-LEG
Gardens that disappear around a corner are fun, but the reality is that most people ignore the valuable extra space, concentrating simply on the part they can see. The trick is to encourage movement into the area, by sweeping a path or pergola from one section to the other. This provides that vital ingredient of mystery, of wondering what lies beyond, and once you are in the new 'room' a whole new garden opens up.

DEALING WITH A SLOPE
While a gentle bank has all kinds of possibilities, a steep slope can be both daunting and expensive to deal with. If you wish to have level planting areas, you could create a series of terraces but building the necessary retaining walls is a skilled job, best left to a specialist

contractor. The design possibilities are increased, however, as such walls can be built to include steps, water features and split-level beds.

SCREENING BAD VIEWS
In town gardens it is all too common to have a bad view or to be overlooked by neighbours' windows. A carefully positioned tree, garden building or planting on the boundary will often provide the perfect screen or privacy. Remember too the screening potential of a pergola, archway or overhead beams.

△ **TRELLIS PANELS** *can be used to boost the height of a fence or wall in order to obliterate unwelcome views or mask urban surroundings.*

▷ **CLEVER USE** *has been made of the change in level in a tiny garden by creating a series of gravel-paved terraces ornamented by pots. Brick steps lead down from the ground floor of the house.*

• *see also:* DESIGN SOLUTIONS FOR INDIVIDUAL GARDENS pp66–85

Fencing and trellis

While timber fences form the boundaries of most gardens, trellis is used more as a divider, to separate different 'rooms' or to screen a utility area. There are many styles of fence, from robust panels to more open kinds that can be tailored to a specific design or situation. Trellis is either square- or diamond-patterned, in various sizes. Rot is the enemy of timber in the garden, so treat fences regularly with a non-toxic preservative.

26

CHOOSING A STYLE

Boundaries should provide shelter, security, privacy and screening, without being too imposing; more often than not they are quickly obscured by planting. Think about the overall design of the garden and its surroundings and choose a style of fence or trellis accordingly. A crisp, ranch-style fence will look fine adjoining a modern house, while close-board is more suitable in a traditional setting and wattle hurdles or a picket fence would be ideal around a cottage garden. Although the range of fence styles is wide, you could still design your own, using vertical boards in varying widths and heights to build up an elegant and durable pattern. If necessary, use re-cycled timber and paint the fence, to keep the cost down.

If you are lucky enough to have a good view you will want to retain this by keeping the fence low, or using an open style such as post and rail, but in most town gardens you will be looking for a solid boundary at a reasonable cost (see box, opposite).

More expensive, close-boarded fences are built on site, using vertically set, overlapping, 'feather-edged' boards nailed to horizontal arris rails that are morticed into posts set about 1.8m (6ft) apart. The bottom of the fence often stops 15cm (6in) above ground level with a replaceable gravel-board set beneath. Close-boarded fences will last for about 20 years.

Other options include traditional picket fences, which are most appropriate for cottage front gardens, and vertically- or diagonally-slatted ranch-style fences that have a modern, more architectural feel. All use slats fixed to horizontal rails, morticed into posts. The gaps left between the slats and the varied width of the slats themselves set up an interesting rhythm.

▷ **NEAT TRELLIS PANELS** *can become a focal point in their own right.*

◁ **CRISP PICKET FENCES** *always associate well with planting.*

Wattle or osier hurdles, originally used for penning livestock, can create an excellent low-key boundary and an ideal background for developing plants. They come in panels of varying widths and heights up to 1.8m by 1.8m (6ft by 6ft), wired to round posts; their maximum life is about ten years.

TRELLIS

The basic trellis design uses an open framework of wooden strips to form see-through boundaries or internal

◁ **HAND-WOVEN WATTLE HURDLES** *have a wonderful texture and create a suitably natural-looking background for plants in a rural garden, seen here covered with* Hedera helix *'Goldheart'.*

METAL SPIKES

You can buy square metal sleeves, fitted with a spike, to hold fence posts. Drive the spike into the ground, ensuring sleeves are upright, and slot the posts into them, setting out the run as described opposite.

• *see also:* PLANTS TO COVER FENCES p114

garden screens. It is often used in conjunction with another boundary, such as on top of a fence or wall to increase its height. Trellis panels come in a wide range of sizes and the tops may be flat or curved, or sometimes a more interesting shape. The more expensive styles of trellis use a more complex combination of slats of different thicknesses and spacing, in square or diagonal patterns. Trellis is available in natural form or painted or stained in different colours, in a wide range of non-toxic finishes.

The top of trellis can be finished with finials and cappings but always beware of over-complicating the end result. Fix freestanding trellis panels or those on the top of walls and fences to vertical posts. Trellis can also be fixed against a wall, using spacers such as cotton reels to keep it clear of the surface in order to minimize rot; use brass or stainless steel screws to prevent rust. All forms of trellis make a good host for climbing plants, offering them support.

△ **TRELLIS MAKES** *a great garden divider: it provides low-cost screening, support for climbers and allows light through to plants on either side.*

BUDGET BOUNDARIES

❖

A fence is one of the more expensive items in a garden so it makes sense to choose carefully. The cheapest option is strands of wire stretched between metal or concrete posts, but this offers nothing in the way of privacy or shelter and will be of little use in containing youngsters or pets.

The most economic solid fence uses panels, usually 1.8m (6ft) long and in various heights up to 1.8m (6ft), set between timber or concrete posts. Made up of interwoven or overlapping laths of thin timber (*see right*), they come complete with a protective top rail. The panels are ready-treated against rot but often need toning down with a darker, non-toxic stain to prevent them looking too garish. If well maintained they should last up to 20 years.

ERECTING A FENCE PANEL

Panels can be either fixed between timber posts 7.5cm (3in) square or slotted between ready-made concrete posts, the latter being more durable. The process of erection is similar for both.

Work out the spacing of posts before you start, then clear the ground along the fence line and dig the first post hole 30cm (1ft) square and 60cm (2ft) deep. Fill the bottom of the hole with compacted hardcore so that for a 1.8m (6ft) fence the post stands 1.9m (6ft 2in) out of the ground. This will allow the bottom of the fence to sit slightly proud of ground level to prevent rot. Put in the post and fill around it with a semi-dry concrete mix, bringing the mix slightly above ground level to shed water away from the post. Check that the post is vertical and fix it with a temporary strut.

Once the first post is in position, mark out the rest of the run with a builder's line and repeat the operation.

△ **CONCRETE FENCE POSTS** *have a long life and are slotted to accept ready-made wooden fence panels.*

Boundary and retaining walls

28

Walls are the most permanent and expensive of all garden boundaries. Built properly from materials that are in keeping with their immediate surroundings, they can look very handsome. Walls provide excellent security, need little maintenance and will last a lifetime. Keep their design as simple as possible.

△ **DRY STONE WALLS** *have a naturally strong local character but building them is a skilled job.*

STYLES AND HEIGHT

The best walls are built from local materials, usually brick or stone. But you should not ignore the potential of crisp concrete blocks that may be cement-rendered, colour-washed or neatly pointed to produce a more contemporary style of wall that would be just right for a modern home built from similar materials. As walls are a long-term investment, choose your materials carefully, ensuring they are appropriate to the surroundings, of the best quality and built to the highest possible standards. The folly of using brick or concrete outside an old stone cottage should be obvious. There are many imitation stone walling products and they are much cheaper than the real thing, but while some of these look reasonable, many do not.

Decide on the wall's height, to offer either complete privacy or to allow a view. Certain materials, such as stone, laid dry, should only be used on walls up to a maximum of 1m (3ft) high. Brick is the most versatile material for most situations, coming in many colours from a soft yellow to terracotta. As long as you are reasonably competent, you can build a brick wall yourself; if in any doubt, or when dealing with retaining walls over 1m (3ft) high, enlist the professional help of a landscape designer or structural engineer.

△ **CONCRETE IS** *the stone of the twentieth century and can be used in numerous innovative ways. Its beauty lies in its strength and its ability to be cast to virtually any shape.*

◁ **TO PREVENT MOISTURE** *penetrating a wall, lay a 'coping' on top. The simplest, and often the best looking for a double brick wall, is a coping of bricks on edge. Pre-cast concrete copings are available in various patterns while ridge tiles, shown here, can also be effective.*

• *see also:* CLIMBERS FOR WALLS pp110–113

❖

In order to make a double brick wall as strong as possible, lay the bricks in a 'bond', so they interlock with one another. Flemish bond is the most common bond for brick walls but English and garden wall bonds are slightly stronger and look more attractive. If building a double brick wall in stretcher bond, use galvanized butterfly ties to ensure its strength.

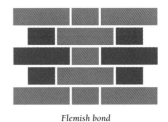

Flemish bond

Garden wall bond

English bond

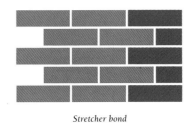

Stretcher bond

△ **BRICK HAS A CRISP, ARCHITECTURAL FEEL** *which can help to furnish a visual link with an adjoining building. In this situation it has been used to build retaining walls for the raised beds as well as for the step and mowing edge, providing overall continuity in the garden.*

HOW A BRICK WALL IS BUILT

Walls can be built either one or two bricks thick. While the former will be quicker to build and use less bricks, it will not be as strong as a 'bonded' brick wall of double thickness. Never build a single-thickness wall more than 1m (3ft) high unless you incorporate single or double brick piers every 1.8m (6ft). Any wall, of whatever type, should be built on top of a suitable foundation or 'footing', which must be absolutely level. Its depth will vary, depending on the type of soil and the height of the wall, but it should be at least 25cm (10in) deep and twice as wide as the finished wall.

MORTAR PRECAUTION

❖

Use a suitable mortar mix of four parts soft sand to one part cement with the addition of a 'plasticizer'. Remember that the cement used in mortar is alkaline (chalky) and if any is left at the base of a wall, it will raise the pH of the soil, making it different from elsewhere in the garden and, quite possibly, unsuitable for plant growth. This also applies to lime mortar that may be raked out of an old wall before repointing. Lay boards at ground level to catch any dropped mortar, which can then be removed.

Hedges as boundaries and features

30

Hedges usually form the most cost-effective boundary. They take time to establish but, once mature, they look superb. The style of hedge should take its cue from the surrounding garden: whereas precision-clipped yew will look right in a formal layout, the much looser habit of Rosa rugosa *would be ideal for a softly planted country garden.*

△ HEDGES HAVE *a naturally softer outline than walls and can be formally clipped or allowed to grow in a looser manner. Depending on the plant used, they may be squared, scalloped or easily trained into arches, like the beech hedge shown here.*

FORMAL OR INFORMAL?

Formal hedges are clipped to produce a crisp and regular outline, producing an architectural feature in a geometric layout. They can be either high, using species such as yew, beech or hornbeam to enclose the site, or low, including box, lavender and *Lonicera nitida*, acting as a framework for a geometric pattern at ground level.

Informal hedges are allowed to grow naturally, remaining unclipped, or at most loosely trained, to reveal their informal character. Many species make ideal candidates for such a treatment, though they take up rather more room than a clipped hedge. *Rosa rugosa, R. eglanteria* and many shrub roses are suitable, along with a wide selection of flowering shrubs that include choisya, potentilla, escallonia and berberis. In a rural garden you can plant a mixed hedge, using species native to the area, which might include hawthorn, blackthorn, wild dogwood and viburnum as well as hazel and elder. Such a field hedge would provide an excellent habitat for wildlife.

EVERGREEN OR DECIDUOUS?

Evergreen hedges, such as yew, holly, escallonia and laurel not only make excellent boundaries but also act as efficient windbreaks. Beech, although deciduous, holds on to its dead leaves throughout the winter, also providing a year-round screen. Although deciduous hedges are at their best in the summer, the framework of branches still provides protection and security during the winter.

▽ IN A 'COUNTRY' HEDGE *like this hawthorn boundary, you can allow the odd sapling to grow out into a tree.*

HEDGE CLIPPING
❖

When clipping a formal hedge, make it slightly wedge-shaped, with the top just narrower than the bottom. This will ensure that ample light reaches the base and that the foliage is thick right down to ground level.

• *see also:* PLANTING A HEDGE p198; TRIMMING HEDGES p200

△ **THIS PRIVET SEAT** *shows that hedges can be tightly clipped to all sorts of shapes as well as providing the garden with a touch of wit.*

SPEED OF GROWTH

Given the right planting conditions and good aftercare, most hedges will establish quickly but some are quicker than others. The fastest of all are the conifers, *Chamaecyparis lawsoniana* and X *Cupressocyparis leylandii*, which can easily put on 30–45cm (12–18in) a year. They are greedy feeders, take enormous amounts of nutrients from the ground and, if left unclipped, grow to a huge height very quickly. The secret is to keep them rigorously clipped once they have reached the height you want. Plant these hedges only if you need to establish a boundary quickly and are prepared for the consequences and maintenance involved. Privet is another thug of the hedging world and exactly the same rules apply – use with caution!

Medium-fast growers include beech and hornbeam, while escallonia and

DWARF HEDGES

❖

Low-growing hedges are ideal for framing beds at ground level. They can be clipped to heights of 15–45cm (6–18in) and may be either evergreen or flowering. Lavender is a good example of a flowering hedge and the low-growing *Berberis thunbergii* 'Atropurpurea Nana' also makes an attractive edger. Box (*see below*) forms the classic, formally clipped low hedge, while *Lonicera nitida* can create a neat border at heights up to 1m (3ft).

BUDGET HEDGES

The cost of any plant is usually related to its size at the time of planting, its speed of growth and the ease or difficulty of propagating it. Relatively slow growers, such as box or yew, are therefore at the top end of the price range. If you go direct to a nursery you can often buy 'bare-root' hedging plants which can be planted only during the dormant season. These are usually small, but correspondingly cheap. Container-grown varieties can be planted at any time of year but are generally more expensive.

griselinia are an excellent choice for gardens close to the sea. Most informal hedges, using shrubs like osmanthus or viburnum, are relatively fast developers. Yew is not as slow-growing as people think, although it is not always the best choice for a hedge because it has toxic berries and foliage. The secret of success is thorough ground preparation before planting: dig a trench, 30cm (12in) deep, then fill it with a mix of good topsoil and organic material such as well-rotted manure or compost. This planting technique applies to all hedges.

Making the most of grass

Grass forms the most important surface of English-style and country gardens. Pleasing to the eye, it is also tough, easy to shape and relatively straightforward to maintain. It provides a soft background for the widest possible range of activities. Quality is a matter of choice, from a near-perfect bowling green to a utility-grade that takes children's play and ball games in its stride.

SHAPE AND SIZE

In gardens where the lawn occupies the largest area, it will also be the most dominant element visually. It will play an important part in the overall design and, depending on its shape, has the ability to lead the eye away from geometric boundaries, sweep through an area in a series of strong, flowing curves or act as a classic rectangular space in a formal layout. Keep lawn shapes simple and, if using curves, never resort to the practice of hurling a hosepipe on the ground, kicking it around 'until you have a pleasing shape', then cutting out the resulting mess. Draw curves with a compass when preparing a design, one flowing into another and all the better for being generous. Transfer the outline to the garden by using a spike to act as

SPECIAL FEATURE

❖

Why not build a seat of chamomile or thyme? Construct a raised bed 45cm (18in) high, with stone or brick sides. Fork over the bottom of the bed, put in a 15cm (6in) layer of broken stone or hardcore, top this with a layer of geo-textile membrane and fill with topsoil. Plant the top with small species at the recommended distance apart. Once established, the feature will look delightful and be fragrant in use.

a radius from which you swing a line to produce the finished curve.

LAWNS FOR PLAY

Grass is a soft surface and lawns were made for play, so make sure your lawn is of ample size and of a quality that will take regular cup finals and test matches. If turf was laid by a builder it will probably be fairly tough, with a proportion of hard-wearing rye grass; if you are seeding a lawn from scratch, make sure your seed mix includes rye grass.

△ **THERE IS NOTHING BETTER** *than a sweep of lawn to lead your eye around the garden. Generous curves make mowing easier.*

PRACTICALITIES

Regular lawn maintenance is not onerous if you incorporate a number of features and factors to make life easier. The first is to keep the shape simple, so the area can be easily mown without having to back in and out of awkward corners. Edging by hand can be time-consuming, so consider laying a mowing edge (a paved strip set just below the turf – see inset) so the machine can run smoothly over the top.

This may take the form of a narrow path, laid as slabs or brick, to prevent border plants from flopping out on to the lawn, where they would also impede mowing.

Stepping stones across a lawn should also be set just below the turf level, as should an edge to a terrace or patio. If the terrace is raised, lay a mowing strip between the grass and the upstand so that the mower misses the raised area.

◁ **GRASS CAN CREATE** *a most interesting juxtaposition with paving slabs, in this case helping to break up the expanse of a path.*

▷ **A CURVED PATH** *around this garden is set into the lawn in the form of irregularly shaped stepping stones to prevent wear to the grass.*

• *see also:* LAWN TOOLS p188; CHOOSING A LAWN p190; STARTING A NEW LAWN p192; ROUTINE LAWN CARE p194; DEALING WITH LAWN PROBLEMS p196

Paving and patios

Paved areas form a major part of the garden's hard landscaping and will take the lion's share of your budget, so their design and construction are crucial. Having hundreds of different paving materials and styles to choose from makes decisions difficult but remember that simplicity, and a visual link with the surroundings, are the keys to good design. Paving forms the background to a wide range of activities, such as outdoor eating, so it must be integrated into the garden, preferably through plants.

Random-sized cobbles

34

PAVED GARDENS

'Patio' is the correct name for a paved and walled garden, although the word is now used to describe any hard-surfaced area. There are certain situations, where space is limited or where grass is unnecessary, in which a completely paved area, together with planting at ground level or in raised beds or containers, will form the perfect courtyard garden. If you add a well-designed water feature, some overhead beams, a barbecue and built-in

furniture, you have an outside room of the highest order. Such gardens may be found at ground level, in town or country, or even perched high above the city as a stunning rooftop living space.

SITING A PATIO

Most people automatically think of siting a patio in the sun, which makes sense for many cooler climates. But shade is a vital element in gardens in those parts of the world where the sun rises high in the sky, with correspondingly soaring temperatures. It is important to be aware of the aspect of your garden so that you know where its sunny and shady areas fall throughout the day and can site your patio accordingly, perhaps to catch the evening sun. Consider whether you might need to screen a patio from the prevailing wind. It is usually best to select a position that has easy access from the house, perhaps adjacent to it. You may also be able to provide a secret sitting area, tucked away in a secluded corner of the garden, perhaps shaded by an arbour

◁ **COLOURED COBBLES** *lend themselves to being laid in intricate patterns to enliven a paved area. Pack them closely together to leave no gaps.*

smothered in fragrant climbers, enabling you to get away from the clamour of house and family for a while.

PAVING MATERIALS

Different materials bring varied qualities to a paved area. Look at the range of materials on offer at any garden centre and assess their relative costs. Always try to link paving materials with those used in the house or elsewhere in the garden. While a single surface may look bland, three or more will be too busy.

Brick

Brick paving is small-scale, providing an intimate, often mellow surface that can form an obvious link with an adjoining brick-built house if the same colour and texture of bricks are used. It acts as an excellent foil to another surface, such as pre-cast concrete slabs or natural stone, when used in panels or a 'grid'. To make an interesting surface when used on their own, bricks can be laid in a number of patterns that include stretcher bond (like bricks in a wall), herringbone, basketweave and soldier courses.

Bricks vary in durability and some are too soft for paving, so make sure

THE IDEAL SIZE

❖

There is nothing worse than a terrace or patio whose dimensions are mean and, as a general rule, you should think of building something no smaller than a good-sized room inside the house. A minimum size of 3.6m by 3.6m (12ft by 12ft) will allow for eating comfortably. Keep the design simple, with a geometric pattern close to the house and more fluid, rounded shapes further away. A patio built up from a series of overlapping rectangles might offer opportunities for incorporating raised beds, seating and possibly water and a barbecue.

◁ **GRANITE SETTS** *have a slightly irregular and textured surface, making them ideal for paths and drives where grip is important. They also make an excellent edging to contain gravel.*

those you choose are hard enough to withstand frosty conditions. Today a wide range of frostproof paving bricks is available in all colours and textures; to be sure of quality, visit a good builder's yard or landscape centre. Check with the supplier or scrape the surface with a hard object. If it flakes away, do not use the bricks as a paving material. Engineering bricks, although hard, are not ideal for paving as they are slippery when wet.

Stone

Natural stone is the most expensive material available but looks superb and will last a lifetime. Random rectangular slabs are best for a terrace but need skilled laying. Because such paving is often recycled

from old mill floors or pavements, make sure the slabs are as clean as possible and not impregnated with oil, which can sweat out in hot weather. The

thickness varies, so the base foundation will have to take account of this. When laying, start with a small 'keystone' and radiate the pattern outwards, staggering

Engineering bricks

Brick patterned paving slab

Irregular-shaped paving slab

Riven concrete paving slab

Stable pavers

Precast concrete paving slab

the joints so that no more than two slabs line up with each other. New stone paving, of uniform thickness, is available, but the cost is usually prohibitive.

Both natural stone and concrete slabs are available in broken form, which can be used to lay 'crazy paving'. Visually, this can be a busy and potentially messy pattern, hard to lay effectively, and it could conflict with the clean lines of an adjoining house. It looks better laid within a framework of bricks but is generally best used in an informal part of the garden.

Reconstituted stone and concrete

The widest range of paving is essentially pre-cast concrete slabs, of various finishes. Some are exceptionally good substitutes for natural stone, the original moulds being taken from the real thing, complete with chisel marks and surface

INCORPORATING PLANTS

When laying 'random' paving, leave out the odd slab and remove any underlying hardcore. Break up the ground below and fill with clean soil, then plant low-growing species such as helianthemum or thyme that will sprawl over the surrounding paving.

irregularities. Other slabs are sharply architectural, with a smooth surface and regular edges. Let your choice be influenced by the prevailing design style of the adjoining house or wider location. Regular architectural slabs would look out of place in front of a country cottage but second-hand natural weathered stone, or a good imitation, could be just right. Colour is an important consideration: while grey

and the pale stone hues are fine, the more garish colours tend to look out of place. Size is also variable: use paving units all the same size to form a grid or random sizes to create a staggered pattern.

Granite setts and cobbles

Granite setts are either brick-shaped (full setts) or cubed (half setts). They were originally used as street paving and form a slightly uneven surface, making them ideal for drives or as an edge 'trim' around trees or another feature, but unsuitable for a terrace where tables and chairs are used. They are expensive and extremely durable. They have to be professionally laid over consolidated hardcore on a mortar bed.

Cobbles are egg-shaped, water-worn stones in a wide range of sizes. Like setts, they can be laid in beautifully complex patterns, either in large areas for driveways or in a more intimate setting. There is a delightful fashion for creating floor pictures in cobbles of different colours, the only limitation being your imagination. Cobbles should be packed tightly together and laid on a bed of mortar over well-consolidated hardcore.

Decking

Raised wooden decks are becoming ever more popular as a flooring material: they are lightweight, warm underfoot, shed water easily and cover up ugly surfaces. They are especially suitable for roof gardens, where weight is a consideration, as they can be suspended from the edges over much, or all, of the area. It is important to ensure adequate

◁ TIMBER DECKING MAKES *a wonderfully versatile surface. It can be quickly constructed and fits easily into a wide range of situations.*

36

• see also: DESIGNING WITH PATHS p38

⊲ **TILES ARE USED** *to create an imaginative floorscape on this roof terrace. Diagonal lines distract the eye from the squareness of the area.*

37

bed bricks on wet mortar and carefully point the joints with mortar afterwards, being careful not to dirty their surface.

Laying concrete block pavers

Block pavers are the size of bricks but made from concrete. Available in a range of colours, they are ideal for paving drives and other areas of hard wear; the whole area must be contained within a fixed edge, preferably of blocks set in concrete. A well-consolidated base of hardcore is essential and the blocks are butt-jointed on sand before being 'vibrated' into position with a hired plate vibrator. More sand is brushed into the surface and the area vibrated again.

ventilation below the deck to minimize rotting. The basic construction is much the same as a floor inside the house, the boards being nailed to joists which in turn are bolted to posts set in concrete. Use pressure-treated softwood or hardwood from a renewable source. The widths of the boards can be varied, to set up an interesting surface pattern, and stains in a wide range of colours can be used to link decking with a colour scheme on the exterior of the building or inside the home.

Decks are a useful solution on sloping sites where they can be built as a series of interlocking terraces, framed by railings or built-in seating and linked by steps.

LAYING PAVING

The unseen preparation is all-important to ensure a long and durable life; paving laid on poor foundations or with an uneven surface will quickly deteriorate and may become unsafe. Any paved area should finish below the damp-proof course of the house to prevent moisture working its way through the wall into your home. And give paving a slight

'fall' of not less than 1:100, to allow water to run away from the building.

The depth of foundations for paving will vary, depending on the type of ground. Remove all topsoil first as it is organic and can rot down over time, causing subsidence. Bearing in mind that the finished paving level should be 15cm (6in) below the damp-proof course, excavate to allow for a layer of well-compacted hardcore or crushed stone 10cm (4in) thick, topped with a layer of sharp sand and small stones (ballast) so that all gaps in the hardcore are filled in.

Laying brick pavers

Special paving bricks are about the thickness of a paving slab, but if you are using a conventional house brick for a paved area remember to adjust the foundation level accordingly. Lay bricks on a 5cm (2in) bed of semi-dry mortar, consisting of four parts soft sand to one part cement. Once the bricks are in position, brush more dry mortar into the joints and leave to set with the aid of water absorbed from the ground by capillary action. Alternatively you can

---

LAYING PAVING SLABS

❖

Prepare a good foundation and position each slab on five spots of mortar, one at each corner and one in the centre, then carefully tamp them down to achieve the right level. Slabs can either be butt-jointed, to fit tightly together, or laid with joints, using wooden spacers that are removed before pointing.

Designing with paths

While a patio or terrace is a static feature, paths provide movement, allowing access to all parts of the garden by taking the most interesting route around it. They define and often separate the major areas such as lawn, planting and utility. Not only practical, garden paths are a major design element that need to be sited carefully in relation to the overall layout.

38

Gravel

Ornamental stone chippings

THE ROLE OF PATHS

While the prime function of a path is to take you from A to B, paths should also blend into the garden and may not necessarily take the most direct route. When working out a design, professionals refer to 'desire lines': these are the most logical, and often the shortest, route between two different points in the garden.

When you are formulating your garden plan, take account of where various features are positioned and link them with paths that take a pleasing and practical course through the garden. A vegetable garden or area for salad crops will need all-weather access from the kitchen rather than a tramp over a soggy lawn in the depth of winter. Similarly, to reach a shed set diagonally on the other side of the lawn from the back door, you might need to lay a line of carefully positioned stepping stones set into the lawn. And, leading up to a gate or an entrance, there should ideally be a path that

allows two people to pass each other easily. The width of a path is important. While stepping stones can be laid with a single row of paving slabs, a route that is regularly used by wheelbarrows and wheeled toys should be approximately 90cm (3ft) wide.

Besides fulfilling a practical role, paths should be given visual continuity with the rest of the garden. Try to use bricks or paving slabs similar to those laid in a terrace or patio.

△ **BRICK IS AN IDEAL** *material for paths in a traditional garden setting. Fringed by Sedum spectabile, this herringbone path has been softened by letting moss grow between the bricks.*

▷ **REMEMBER THAT** *paths and paving should form a simple background and not detract from planting or other features on either side of them.*

• *see also:* PAVING AND PATIOS p34

◁ GRAVEL OFFERS *a neat, practical and low-cost surface that is ideal for paths and drives on a level site. As gravel is a mobile material, it needs to be given an edging, in this case of brick, to retain it.*

gravel, small cobbles, bark chips and tarmac are fluid and can be more easily laid in sweeping curves and irregular shapes. Slabs, bricks and concrete blocks should be laid in exactly the same way as a terrace, over a well-consolidated base of hardcore.

Concrete

Concrete is the stone of the twentieth century, elegant and durable. It can be laid over a hardcore base and finished in numerous ways that will include trowelling smooth, tamping to formed a ribbed effect, 'seeding' with gravel when still wet, or brushing with a stiff or soft broom to produce yet more finishes.

Gravel

Gravel is an excellent low-cost material, both for an informal path and to create a flowing surface over a larger area. There are wide regional variations in colour and texture. The correct laying of gravel is crucial as thorough compaction is essential at all stages. It requires a well-consolidated hardcore base not less than 10cm (4in) thick, topped with a 5cm (2in) layer of coarse gravel, again well compacted. Finish with a 2.5cm (1in) layer of fine gravel mixed with 'hoggin', which is a clay binder, usually from the same gravel pit. Roll a final, thin top-dressing of washed shingle into the hoggin to finish the job neatly. Gravel drives should have a camber to shed water easily and all gravel surfaces need 'edge restraints', which could be bricks set in concrete, or boards pegged firmly in place, to stop it spreading everywhere.

STEPPING STONES

When laying stepping stones across a lawn, position them on the turf and walk over them to get the spacing right. Leave slabs in place, cut round them with a sharp spade, remove the turf and bed the slabs on a weak concrete mix so the finished level is just below the lawn.

Log slices, 15cm (6in) thick, make an excellent woodland or informal path through planting. In a shady area, staple chicken wire to their surface to provide added grip.

▷ THIS PATH *running through a lawn is made up of setts. They have been bedded on the soil, just below the level of the grass, so that a mower can run smoothly over the top.*

SHAPES AND MATERIALS

While a straight path looks fine in a formal layout, it naturally encourages faster movement than a route which gently meanders, perhaps disappearing from view with a feeling of mystery. The materials you choose and the way in which you lay them will also have a visual impact. Slabs or bricks laid in a staggered bond down the length of a path tend to lead the eye on, encouraging movement, whereas the same materials laid across the path slow things down visually.

Bricks and slabs are 'modular' materials, having a fixed size and lending themselves to rectangular paving patterns, but surfaces like

Changes of level

Sloping gardens can often provide greater interest than a flat plot, as areas created at different levels may become individual spaces with their own theme. Such spaces will need to be linked with the rest of the garden in some way, either by the inclusion of steps or by making a ramp, both of which can become important features in their own right.

40

INTEGRATING STEPS

The design of steps should always take its cue from the immediate surroundings. If you are stepping down from a terrace precisely laid with brick or with pre-cast slabs, use similar materials for the steps. If, on the other hand, the change of level is some way from the house, in an informal part of the garden, the steps can be built from logs, railway sleepers or natural stone, to reflect this. As a general rule, it is a good idea to keep to a more 'architectural' treatment close to the house and more informal further away. A change of level also offers the opportunity to incorporate other features, such as a well-planned rocky outcrop, or a series of pools that drops down the slope, in association with the steps. Steps need not necessarily occupy only one part of the garden; if you make them large enough – big circles or overlapping hexagons, for example – they become more like a series of terraces and could form virtually the whole of a sloping site. If you make the edge or outline of brick or stone, the 'treads' forming the main garden areas could be laid with paving of various kinds or with gravel, grass or even planting.

STEPS: THE PRACTICALITIES

Make steps as broad and generous as possible as there is nothing worse – or more dangerous – than a mean and narrow flight. It is important to get the proportions right, both visually and for comfort: each step should have a 'rise' of 15cm (6in) and a tread of 45cm (18in).

⊲ IN AN INFORMAL SITUATION, planting can be introduced to soften the line of steps.

There are no set rules about their width, but a wide flight looks more restful, and will be easier to negotiate than a narrow one. In a long flight of steps, you might incorporate a landing every 10–15 treads: this could provide a platform for a group of pots or other garden ornaments. Remember that steps need not necessarily go straight up a slope; they could change direction to take a zig-zag course up a steep change of level.

The construction of steps up a shallow slope can become a straightforward DIY project; if you use logs or railway sleepers, these are simply pegged firmly into the slope. But steep changes in level and complex step structures will need specialist input in terms of both building and their design. Always seek professional help if you are in any doubt at all.

Steps can be built from virtually any of the usual hard landscape materials; where stone or pre-cast concrete slabs are used for the treads, let them overhang the risers by just under 5cm (2in) to create a discreet shadow line that will visually soften the flight. In

⊲ BRICKWORK PROVIDES continuity (far left) between the raised beds and the wide flight of steps.

A CO-ORDINATING PAINT SCHEME and crisp detailing (left) tie in these wooden steps with the decking and balustrades in a contemporary garden on two levels.

• *see also:* BOUNDARY AND RETAINING WALLS p28; A SLOPING SITE p80

△ **A TIMBER EDGING** *perfectly integrates these brick steps with the built-in raised beds from which planting cascades from level to level.*

order to emphasize a change of level from terrace to steps, lay a course of bricks, or other contrasting material, flush with the edge of the paving. This gives an indication of the position of the first step to someone who is unfamiliar with the garden layout.

MAKING A RAMP

If steps were used to link every level in a garden, it would be virtually impossible to move mowers, barrows, wheelchairs or wheeled toys from place to place. To give easy access for wheeled vehicles and for elderly or disabled gardeners or visitors, it makes sense to incorporate a ramp, or a series

of slopes. Be sure you have enough space: a comfortable gradient of 1:25 or 1:50 makes a ramp two to three times the length of a flight of steps.

RAISED BEDS

While raised beds can be a freestanding feature within a paved area or other area of the garden, they can also become part of a flight of steps or change of level. If they are also helping to retain the slope, they should be built with this in mind, with suitable drainage incorporated at regular intervals. Since the walls of built-in raised beds have to take pressure, it is advisable to seek professional advice for any such wall over 60cm (2ft) high.

Freestanding raised beds can be rectangular or curved; always design them to fit in with the surroundings or underlying paving pattern. The walls

STEP SAFETY

Both steps and ramps should be lit for safety at night. The neatest solution is to build lighting into the flanking walls or the step risers, otherwise you can position low-level lights to flank a flight of steps. If there is a steep drop, or if elderly people will use the garden, it is a good idea to incorporate a handrail too: make sure it is sturdy.

can be built from virtually any material, as well as timber and railway sleepers. Their construction is similar to that of boundary walls, with a suitable concrete foundation and a coping at the top. A height of about 45cm (18in) will allow the wall of the raised bed to double as an occasional seat.

Fork over the bottom of the raised bed and fill it with approximately 15cm (6in) of clean hardcore. Top this with a layer of geo-textile membrane (available at your local garden centre) and fill the bed up with clean topsoil.

△ **RAILWAY SLEEPERS** *make ideal shallow steps for an informal part of the garden. The repetition of pots emphasizes the rhythm of the flight.*

Arches, arbours and pergolas

Garden features such as arches and pergolas bring a vertical dimension to the garden and often act as a major focal point. As well as drawing the eye they can also be invaluable for providing shade or screening a bad view; they also act as hosts for climbing plants.

42

△ **ARCHES AND ENTRANCES** *provide the classic garden elements of tension, mystery and surprise. This brick-built arch is covered by honeysuckle to entice the visitor with its fragrance.*

THE ROLE OF VERTICAL FEATURES

Both arches and pergolas encourage movement through the garden. Arches are usually set over a gateway or entrance and serve as an entry point into the garden or into one area of it from another, or they can be positioned as a focal point, flanked by trellis, planting or hedges that separate different garden areas. Pergolas are like a series of arches joined together to form a single structure, providing a linking element that leads you from one distinct point to another. They often span a paved path, though the ground-level surface may well be grass. Arches induce a feeling of tension as you approach them, coupled with that essential element of mystery as you try to glimpse what is beyond.

Pergolas, while also creating tension, draw you into a soft, green tunnel of flower and foliage, dappled with sunlight and allowing tantalizing views of the garden to either side, framed by the upright posts. Part of the essential function of a pergola is that it leads to

△ **A SQUARE-TOPPED ARCH** *provides support for Rosa 'Albertine'. Timber is easy to work with and offers versatility, ideal for a do-it-yourself project.*

somewhere positive, which might be another part of the garden or a well-positioned focal point or seat; it should not simply lead to the incinerator or the compost heap!

An arbour, on the other hand, is a static feature. It is an open-sided structure, usually set over a quiet sitting area and often situated in an informal part of the garden. Arbours can also be smothered with climbers, which should preferably be fragrant.

Another feature, sometimes erroneously called a pergola, uses an open framework of overhead beams built out from the house or a wall. It is often positioned directly above a patio, where it will cast light shade when covered with climbing plants, and will also be useful for masking a view from neighbouring windows.

A HARMONIOUS DESIGN

The design of arches, pergolas and arbours should be in keeping with the overall style of the garden and their position within it. Close to the house the design might be crisply architectural, constructed from planed timber or metal hoops. In a more distant part of a garden the character could be distinctly informal, using piers of old brick and cross-beams of solid

43

WHICH CLIMBERS?

Climbers grown over a freestanding structure often do better than when planted against a wall or fence because they receive plenty of light and moisture. If an arch or pergola is of ample size, virtually any climbing plant will be suitable, but if the gap is narrow you should avoid roses with sharp thorns, or other bushy plants. While the choice of a single species can be fine, a combination of climbers would extend the flowering season and provide an attractive mix. You might grow laburnum, trained over the structure, together with wisteria or the large-leafed vine *Vitis coignetiae* with the late-flowering *Clematis tangutica*. For fragrance, think of planting summer jasmine, honeysuckle or scented roses.

timber. It is important that these features are simply designed, in proportions that are as bold and generous as possible, and they should be amply planted. Flimsy metal and timber structures will deteriorate quickly and can look appalling. Each of these vertical features is one of the easier garden projects to build yourself: for inspiration, look at traditional designs in many older gardens.

If bought off the peg, these garden features are usually easy enough to assemble by slotting components together and fixing them into spiked metal sockets driven into the ground or concreting posts into position. Timber posts will generally have been pressure-treated to prevent rot, but it will be worth applying additional non-toxic preservative every two or three years; bear in mind that climbers will have to be taken down in order to do this, however. Metal hoops are usually plastic-coated and will need little maintenance. You could paint or stain a pergola or arch to match with a colour scheme used elsewhere in the garden; paints and stains formulated for outdoor woodwork come in a wide range of colours; shades of blue and green blend into the garden but primary colours can have a bold impact.

▷ SHADE IS IMPORTANT *in a garden and may have to be created. Here, vine-covered overhead beams built out from a boundary and supported by wooden posts make a sheltered sitting area.*

• *see also:* STARTING FROM SCRATCH p14; DESIGN CONSIDERATIONS p18; FENCING AND TRELLIS p26

BUILDING AN ARCH

Timber is an ideal material for a self-build feature and a simple arch can be built from 10 x 10cm (4 x 4in) uprights and 10 x 5cm (4 x 2in) cross-pieces. All timber should be treated with non-toxic preservative before erecting and touched up on completion. Both the height and width should be ample for people passing beneath, particularly as the strcture will be planted with climbers that can reduce the effective dimensions considerably. Since a garden path is generally 1m (3ft) wide, you should add another 30cm (1ft) to either side to allow room for climbers, making a total width of 1.5m (5ft).

The height should also allow for climbing plants hanging down; a comfortable height would be 2.1m (7ft). The posts can be slotted into metal sockets, spiked into the ground, or concreted in position. A pergola is quite simply a series of arches joined together with timber top rails, so the construction is essentially exactly the same as that of an arch.

Screw-eyes or galvanized nails can be fixed to the uprights of an arch or pergola after construction to carry wires that offer support for climbers. Plants can then be encouraged to climb by winding them around the wires.

▷ PAINTED METAL can be imaginatively used in all kinds of vertical features and is particularly successful in this delightful apple tunnel, shown to its best at blossom time.

◁ SOLID BRICK PIERS and stout overhead beams are appropriate materials for a traditional pergola that will last a lifetime. It offers support to climbing roses 'Aloha' and 'Compassion'.

BUILDING AN ARBOUR

Arbours can be built from similarly dimensioned timber and a simple rectangular shape is usually most successful, with four corner posts and a simple cross-braced top. The sides can also be cross-braced to increase stability and purchase for climbers, or filled in

◁ THIS SELF-CONTAINED little arbour provides an intimate seat for one person. It is shaded by the rose 'Alister Stella Gray'.

with slats or trellis panels to produce a more intimate and enclosed feel, leaving the front open.

A more ambitious design could use brick or stone piers, if these or similar materials are used elsewhere in the garden, built over suitably solid and stable concrete foundations with heavy timber cross-pieces to form the top. Designs on this scale would look best in a larger garden.

Overhead beams that run out from a building can be slotted into proprietary joist hangers or a horizontal 'wall plate' fixed into the wall. These can be bought from good garden suppliers or DIY stores. Their other end will be supported by a metal or timber post.

45

Screens within the garden

A garden that can be divided into separate areas, perhaps having their own theme, will always be more interesting than a space that can be taken in at a single glance. The way in which you divide a garden depends on its size and shape as well as the budget available. Solid divisions can be created by a wall or hedge or can be more minimal, using trellis screens or a limited number of well-chosen shrubs. Sensitive manipulation of the space can help you to introduce the elements of mystery and surprise.

46

OUTDOOR ROOMS

If you have taken over an established garden, the bones of internal divisions may already exist or they can be strengthened to break your view from one area through to another. An existing 'wing' of planting to one side of a plot could be echoed by a new bed, either directly opposite, to achieve a balanced and formal effect, or offset, to create a more informal sense. Hedges, on the other hand, will have a far more architectural feel and can be clipped either to form a simple rectangular outline or with their ends curved down. If a hedge is set within a bed, allow

room for clipping by laying a simple path with slabs or stepping stones to either side.

Trellis is a favourite divider, but instead of buying standard panels from a garden centre, why not think of making your own, taking your inspiration from screens created by interior designers? You will see endless variations in restaurants and other public places that use different patterns, widths of timber and colours, all of which could be adapted for outdoor use. At the end of a run of trellis you might position a timber obelisk that will provide a positive full stop or focal point.

Slim vertical slats set between a top and bottom rail will form a delicate wooden screen, as will bamboo poles, perhaps with the tops at slightly different heights to set up a fascinating rhythm.

SOLID SCREENS

Walls are the most expensive option and make an opaque screen; always use walling materials that link with the house or other features. A solid wall can create a good deal of turbulence on the lee side of it, however, whereas a

▽ HEDGES ARE A *versatile living screen and most species develop rapidly in well-prepared soil. This hedge of purple-leaved prunus encloses an intimate garden room.*

△ SCREENS NEED NOT *be expensive and a little imagination can work wonders. This simple bamboo blind provides privacy by hiding the house and garden behind.*

• *see also:* FENCING AND TRELLIS p26, BOUNDARY AND RETAINING WALLS p28; HEDGES AS BOUNDARIES AND FEATURES p30

BUDGET OPTIONS

❖

The cheapest screen is created by using a few well-chosen plants that simply break your line of vision. If a path curves away past this it will naturally encourage a sense of movement and some expectation as to just what lies beyond. You can make an elegant and attractive screen by constructing a timber frame of top and bottom rails, approximately 1.8m (6ft) high, and stretching vertical wires between them. The wires will act as a host to climbing plants and soften your screen with vegetation.

△ OUT OF SIGHT . . . *A well-positioned shrub provides a simple but effective screen to this compost heap.*

▷ **TRELLIS CAN BE BOUGHT** *in a wide range of patterns. In this garden the sturdy trellis with elaborate finials makes a handsome feature as well as an ideal host for climbing plants. You could design and make your own panels, which will be cheaper as well as more original.*

screen that is pierced or has gaps in it makes a far better windbreak because it filters the flow of air, rather than blocking it. One such screen is the 'honeycomb' brick wall in which gaps are left between every other brick so that you catch a glimpse of what lies beyond the wall.

Focal points

Focal points are the exclamation marks of a garden – they draw the eye, bringing surprise and adding interest. The primary rule is to choose and use them sparingly: too many will over-complicate a design but one or two, carefully positioned, will give it a focus. Make sure that not more than one focal point is visible at any one time, otherwise your eye will be diverted from one place to another, weakening their impact.

48

▽ **A STRONG EYE-CATCHER,** *like this urn mounted on a stone plinth, needs to be positioned with care: if it is too dominant, it could foreshorten a view.*

THE CHOICE

The choice of a focal point will be up to you but it should be something that commands attention. In a small garden it might be a large container, an urn or a sculpted figure, perhaps placed at the end of a pergola, or positioned to draw the eye diagonally across a lawn, helping to open up the space. It might be a sculptural group of plants, a flowering tree against an undemanding background or the simple plume of a fountain set in the middle of a circular lawn. Larger focal points could take the form of a summer house or gazebo, a rock outcrop or a major water feature.

As any such element, large or small, is an attractive part of the garden, you are naturally drawn to walk towards it. Once there, you are bound to turn round and take in the reverse view, which you should ensure is equally pleasing; there will be little point in looking at the back of someone's garage or an unsightly building.

Apart from containers, sculpture and statuary that can be bought off the shelf, do not ignore the potential charm and eye-catching qualities of found objects. These are generally more personal and might include a gnarled log set beside an informal path or a piece of sun-bleached driftwood on an architectural terrace. Groups of smooth stones or boulders can be carefully placed to draw the eye and topiary, strategically positioned, will provide interest throughout the year. All such *objets trouvés* will cost you virtually nothing but they can add immeasurably to the overall design of the garden.

FORMAL OR INFORMAL?

As a general rule, classical urns, bowls and statues will sit most comfortably in a formal layout and should be placed geometrically on one of the garden's main axes. Planted containers and all kinds of found object, on the other hand, make useful focal points in a more informal or free-flowing layout.

△ **LOOKING GOOD** *at all times of year, this pale bust stands out in sharp relief against the dark background of yew. It is surrounded in winter by the frosted spikes of rosemary.*

• *see also:* DESIGN CONSIDERATIONS p18

Sometimes the degree of formality lies mainly in the materials: a stone obelisk will demand attention in an architectural setting, while a similar feature made from trellis and smothered in plants makes an altogether softer outline, or that which is more appropriate in an informal setting.

FOCAL POINTS IN SMALL GARDENS

In small gardens, the choice of focal points has to be carefully controlled, otherwise the garden will become hopelessly busy. Much has to do with compatibility and in a small town garden a collection of terracotta containers at the foot of a wall might form a composition that is sufficiently unified to serve as a focal point. Always remember the precept 'less is more' in a small space and be sparing in your choice. At the same time you should not be afraid to ring the changes by moving ornaments or other focal points around, in much the same way as you might do inside the house.

Painted scenes on the walls of a small garden can be both humorous and exotic and they certainly draw the eye. You might paint a false doorway, slightly ajar to give a glimpse of an imaginary landscape beyond. Mirrors can also be an invaluable way of drawing the eye at the same time as increasing the feeling of space; be sure not to position them at the end of a path or you will simply see yourself approaching and there will be no sense of mystery. Angling a mirror into planting, so that it appears to recede into the distance, is generally a much better solution.

△ **GENEROUS-SIZED CONTAINERS,** *like this olive jar, always draw the eye and often look far better left unplanted. Set them among foliage which will enhance and just temper their architectural line.*

Pools and other water features

Water is one of the most attractive elements in any garden, bringing movement and sound as well as being a cooling influence and a haven for many kinds of wildlife. Water features can be large or small, formal or informal and, with most garden centres selling a huge range of equipment and suitable plants, there should be something to suit all tastes and type of plot.

50

△ **THE CLASSIC** *garden elements of paving, planting and water are perfectly combined in this simple but striking geometric design.*

FORMAL OR INFORMAL?

Water features divide quite clearly into the formal and the informal and your choice will be influenced by the feature's position within the garden and, of course, by the character of the garden design. In general terms the areas closer to the house will be planned in a more architectural way, very often with a crisp paving pattern based on a series of overlapping rectangles. A geometric-shaped pool will fit readily into this pattern. In a totally formal garden you might have a pair of rectangular or square pools balancing each other on opposite sides of a courtyard garden.

In the more distant parts of a garden, where the design can be less formal, using strong, flowing curves, the water feature can take a more informal outline. Taking this to the extreme, you could create a natural wildlife pool, flanked by marginal and bog planting and set within gently undulating ground.

Naturally sloping ground may provide the perfect opportunity for a series of pools set one above the other, with a linking stream or cascade; this could be designed in either a formal or an informal way, to match the style of garden.

▷ **THE CRISP FORMALITY** *of this pool is echoed by the symmetrical placing of iris and water lilies. Raising the feature slightly gives it greater importance, allowing the outline to stand out in sharp relief.*

△ **AN INFORMAL POOL** *needs balanced planting to attract wildlife. A pebble beach will allow birds, frogs and many other creatures to visit the pool.*

▽ **WATER CAN PROVIDE** *movement, sound and interest in even the smallest garden. Here, a water feature on two levels allows the fish to gush water into a pool below.*

SUNKEN OR RAISED?

The question of whether water should be set at, or above, ground level will depend on the character of the surrounding area. While a raised pool, its sides crisply constructed from bricks or stone, may be the perfect complement to a formal terrace, such a feature would look out of place in the further reaches of a garden, which is altogether less formal; in this case a free-form shape, flush with the ground, may be called for.

A raised pool should always look comfortable: if built too high, it will simply look incongruous. A good height is 45cm (18in), which allows people to sit on the edge, doubling as an occasional seat. A raised pool may well have started life as something else; for safety reasons, open water in the garden is not a good idea while toddlers are growing up, but a raised bed or a sandpit could easily be converted to water at a later date.

WILDLIFE POOLS

In reality, any body of water will encourage wildlife and even a formal pool will be attractive to a range of species from fish and aquatic plants to all kinds of insects, frogs and toads as well as visitors such as birds. Most people's perception of a wildlife pool, however, is an informal pond, set some way from the house (though not in shade). Planting can and should be incorporated both in the water itself and around the margins; the pool could also include a boggy area which in turn leads into drier shrub and mixed planting. In this way you will offer a wide range of habitats for wildlife and if you can also provide a log pile, leaf litter and a nearby hedge, so much the better. Beauty is always in the eye of the beholder and such an area should be truly informal, rather than a mess, so do not be tempted to clean it up too often or you may well damage sensitive ecosystems.

52 BOG GARDENS

There are many superb plants that grow naturally in the marshy or boggy conditions that occur around a natural pool. Many of these have handsome foliage and striking flowers. In an artificial situation you will have to create a boggy area and this can be done by allowing water to seep over the edge of a pool constructed from a pond liner, into another lined area that is filled with soil. The liner must be perforated to prevent the garden from becoming waterlogged.

MOVING WATER

While a still sheet of water can set up wonderful reflections, movement will bring a new dimension to the garden. Moving water will also provide a degree of aeration that is beneficial for fish, particularly during hot summer days. There are numerous ways in which you can introduce moving water, from a simple bubble jet set in the middle of a small pool to the most elaborate fountains, cascades and water slides, but the golden rule is to keep things simple.

Moving water features divide into the informality of natural streams and cascades and more formal jets and fountains. Position them appropriately within the overall garden layout. There is a wide range of perfectly safe submersible pumps to drive the largest waterfall or the smallest bubble jet. Exceptionally durable, pumps can be bought at any good garden centre or nursery that specializes in water gardening; they will also advise you on the correct size of pump for the water feature in question.

SMALL WATER FEATURES

Even the smallest patio or courtyard can incorporate a water feature, ranging from a 'millstone' with water flowing over its surface, to a classical mask that spouts into a trough below. Most such water features are positioned over a concealed sump, where a submersible small pump recirculates water around the system. The advantage of millstones, or features where water cascades out of a container into a bed of stones or cobbles, is that they are far safer for young children than an open stretch of water. Many such features can be bought off the peg or, with a little imagination and practical know-how, can be constructed as a uniquely personal focal point.

◁ IN A SLOPING GARDEN *the possibilities for creating streams, cascades and pools are endless. Hostas and salix, seen here, are among the many plants that will thrive in damp soils.*

• *see also:* PLANTS FOR POOLS p158; MARGINALS AND BOG GARDEN PLANTS p160; POND CARE p222

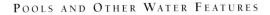

△ **THERE IS NO NEED FOR A FOUNTAIN** *to create interest in a tiny garden: a simple mask and spout pouring water into a brimming stone tank bring all the soothing qualities of water.*

PRACTICALITIES

The success of a pool lies in getting the right balance of wildlife; this includes plants as well as fish and a myriad other tiny creatures that will be drawn to the pool. This means that, within reason, the larger the pool the better; it will certainly be difficult to achieve a balanced ecosystem in a pool that is less than 1.8m (6ft) square. Depth is another important consideration, as is the shape below the water level, known as the profile. While a garden pool need be no more than 45cm (18in) deep, it should include a 'marginal shelf', extending around approximately two-thirds of the pool; this will allow you to grow aquatic plants that enjoy just having their toes in the water. The shelf should be about 22cm (9in) below the water level; if it is built in two sections, bays will be left that form ideal breeding areas for fish.

A pond or pool should always be positioned in an open situation, away from deep shade or overhanging trees. Neither fish nor aquatic plants will thrive in total shade and fish can be harmed by dead leaves or other vegetation falling into the water and rotting.

CONSTRUCTION OPTIONS

In recent years the use of plastics and glass fibre has transformed pool construction into an easy, home-build option. The real choice is between a rigid, preformed pool and one that uses a 'liner' of some kind. Preformed pools are easy to install but can only be bought in a limited range of sizes, mostly small. They are simply bedded on sand in a suitable excavation; always make sure that the rim is absolutely level by using a long straightedge and a spirit level.

Larger pools can be constructed using a tough liner made of laminated PVC or butyl rubber. Liners can be bought from any good garden centre; they come with full instructions for their installation. Since liners can easily be punctured by sharp stones, their excavation must take this into account and the liner should be bedded on a 5cm (2in) layer of sand. The 'profile' of the pool excavation should include marginal shelves and the liner can be continued to form a bog garden around part of the perimeter.

Water features involving streams and changes of level are more difficult to construct yourself and may well need to be left in the hands of a professional with the necessary expertise and equipment. Such features will almost certainly use submersible pumps and may also need a filtration unit.

WATER SAFETY

❖

- An open body of water is dangerous for young children, so always bear this in mind when choosing and siting any feature.

- Electricity is potentially lethal and, although most water-feature kits are easy to use and install, make sure you follow the instructions and safety codes to the letter.

- All pumps are completely sealed and many run off a 12-volt power supply through a transformer safety device that will automatically switch off the system in the event of failure.

- There is a wide range of exterior light and power fittings designed for safe garden use.

- If in any doubt about anything electrical in the garden, be sure to enlist the help of a qualified electrician.

△ **IF YOU HAVE** *young children and are worried about open water in the garden, build something entirely safe that recirculates water from a concealed sump, through a pot or similar feature.*

Garden buildings

Your garden is both a practical and a decorative space and has to cater for a wide range of activities as well as storage. It is inevitable that you will have to find room for at least one utilitarian building, but with a little imagination and modification these can be dressed up, camouflaged or screened, or built from scratch and integrated as an attractive feature of the design.

54

SHEDS

With houses on the whole becoming smaller and more cars standing on the drive, there is usually a real need to provide storage space in the garden. At the very least this will be needed for garden tools and equipment, but it often has to cater also for children's bikes and outdoor toys as well as garden furniture. A good-sized shed is usually the answer and it is generally good advice to buy one that is large rather than small for your immediate needs. Durability is also important: make sure the building is constructed from good quality timber and is soundly put together. You can then either hide the shed from view or dress it up to make it look more attractive.

As an alternative you can construct your own shed, tailoring it to your needs exactly, making it either

◁ **THIS PAN-TILED** *shed is pretty enough to suit any traditional garden. It is partially screened by roses 'Mme. Plantier' and 'New Dawn' smothering the wall.*

free-standing or a lean-to structure against a wall. To prevent rot, always stand a building on a firm, dry base which can either be concrete, paving slabs or well-laid gravel. Since the roof will have the potential to collect rainwater, always fit a gutter and run this via a downpipe into a water butt.

GREENHOUSES

Make sure that a greenhouse, like a shed, is big enough for your needs. Many people who start off with a small glasshouse soon get the bug for growing exotic plants or raising seeds and wish they had bought a bigger model. Position a greenhouse in an open position that receives plenty of sun throughout the day. If you are considering using a propagator or electric heater, it will be essential to have a safe supply of electricity laid on by a qualified electrician.

Greenhouses can be made of metal (usually aluminium), which has a longer, maintenance-free life, or timber, which is traditional and blends into the garden well but which needs regular applications of a non-toxic preservative. They may be glazed down to the ground or have brick sides a third of the way up. Greenhouse bases usually come as pre-cast concrete strips and the floor can either be solid

△ **WITH CAREFUL ORGANIZATION** *you can grow a surprising amount in a tiny greenhouse.*

throughout or have earth beds on either side for cultivation, with a central path.

SUMMER HOUSES

These are simply small garden buildings designed for leisure. They will inevitably become a focal point of the garden and should be carefully positioned to draw the eye in a particular direction. Remember that when you are sitting in or outside the building, the view back from the summer house is equally important, so make sure it has a pleasing prospect. There is a wide range of different styles of building available, but bear in mind that the summer house should be in keeping with the rest of the garden and the adjoining house. You would not put a rustic, timbered summer house alongside a crisp glass and concrete building, for example. A simple design will look comfortable in most garden surroundings.

• *see also:* CHOOSING A GREENHOUSE p218; USING A GREENHOUSE p220

TONING DOWN NEW BUILDINGS

❖

Many new timber buildings look garish and stark when new, standing out like a sore thumb. If you tone them down with a suitable shade of non-toxic preservative, or even a wood stain, they will settle far more comfortably and discreetly into their outdoor surroundings.

◁ A SUMMER HOUSE CAN *fulfil several roles in a small town garden. This one acts as a focal point, offering a shady place to sit while helping to screen the adjoining buildings from view.*

▽ THIS WOODEN GAZEBO *acts a a linking element and offers views into two garden rooms. The blue woodwork makes a bold statement and serves as a host to Rosa 'Aloha'.*

INTEGRATION AND ACCESS

Any garden building should be integrated into the design in its initial stages, which really comes down to sensible planning. If space permits, it makes sense to incorporate a hard-surfaced work area into the garden that could accommodate shed, greenhouse, incinerator and compost bins. It could be neatly screened off from the rest of the garden but linked to the house, or other parts of the garden, by means of a path or other paving. A summer house, being a fair-weather building, could simply sit on the far side of a lawn, where it would act as a large-scale focal point; it need not necessarily have a direct path leading to it.

Garden security

Garden security is becoming increasingly important, not just as a deterrent for house burglary but also against the theft of ornaments and features from the garden itself. There are many ways in which intruders can be discouraged and the methods should always be as unobtrusive as possible, for both practical and aesthetic reasons.

56

△ **SPIKY AND THORNY** *plants on a boundary provide a real deterrent to intruders. This holly (Ilex aquifolium 'Argentea Marginata') is a superb evergreen for year-round interest.*

▽ **LIGHTING CAN** *be both practical and good-looking. These simple glass globes make a positive contribution to this small garden.*

LIGHTING

Garden lighting can serve either a practical or a decorative purpose, although there is considerable overlap between the two roles. On a practical level, garden lights are used to illuminate entrances, driveways, paths, patios, steps and general areas around the house and garden buildings. All too often such lighting is provided by extremely bright halogen floodlights, which are surrounded by deep pools of shadow in which people are practically invisible. Security lighting is often far more effective, using a lower-powered light with a more diffused beam so that pools of illumination merge together. The effect created also looks much less harsh.

EFFECTIVE SOLUTIONS

Lighting along a drive needs to be both effective and aesthetically pleasing at the same time. Avoid the ostentation of imitation 'street lamps' up the drive and instead use lower-level fittings that can cast light across the surface of the drive or path. The pupose is to illuminate where you are going, not the top of your head. Exactly the same principle applies to lighting steps: special fittings can either be built into the risers, so that light is cast directly onto the treads, or well designed fittings positioned to either side of the flight.

There are many forms of decorative outdoor lighting, varying in sophistication from easily installed, low-voltage kits that you can position

• *see also:* CHANGES OF LEVEL p40

△ **SURFACES THAT CRUNCH** *underfoot can be a surprisingly effective burglar deterrent and gravel is an ideal material in this respect for both paths and drives. Even if the crunch of an intruder is not immediately heard by people, it quickly attracts the attention of a dog.*

yourself to sophisticated schemes planned by a professional lighting installation company. Techniques such as floodlighting, spotlighting and backlighting are fairly obvious, but try moonlighting, where a light is suspended in the branches of a tree to cast delicate shadows on the ground, or 'grazing', where the beam is shone directly up or down a wall or other feature, picking out its surface pattern and texture.

BOUNDARIES AND PLANTING

Keeping your boundaries in good condition is an essential aspect of garden maintenance. Whereas a sound fence, whose gates are securely locked or bolted, will deter the casual thief, a broken one might do just the opposite. The type of boundary obviously comes into it too and you may have to decide between a low boundary that embraces a view and something higher that provides a physical barrier. This may be a situation where an electronic alarm could be used, but their installation is a specialist business if they are not to be continually tripped by passing animals.

Do not under-estimate the deterrent value of spiky, thorny or really dense planting, especially on the boundaries. A hedge of mature holly can provide a prickly formal boundary or you could equally well plan an informal border to include thorny shrubs like pyracantha, berberis, crataegus and mahonia, as well as yucca and other 'aggressive' species. The effect works both ways, however, and stout clothes and gloves will be needed for maintenance.

5   60

△ **THE COMBINATION**
of different heights,
colours and leaf textures
produces an interesting
and well-balanced border.
The plants descend in
tiered heights from the
tall yellow spires of
golden rod (Solidago)
and the flat heads of
achillea to the low-
growing ground cover
provided by geraniums
and Stachys byzantina
at the front of the border.

FAST-MATURING SHRUBS
❖

As shrubs are usually relatively small when planted, use a number of faster growing species such as buddleja, lavatera or broom. These will mature quickly and can be removed once the slower framework plants have started to become established.

Much framework planting will be set against a boundary and it is worth remembering that large, bold leaves tend to draw the eye and diminish the space – something to avoid on a fence or wall close to the house. Fine, feathery foliage, on the other hand, has just the opposite effect and can help to make a boundary recede visually.

FILLING IN

Once the framework is in position you can begin to fill in with lower, more colourful material. This should be a combination of shrubs and herbaceous planting, the shrubs providing structure and support to the herbaceous perennials, which will in turn give the necessary colour and delicacy. Numbers in a group or drift of plants can be greater than the background framework and should reinforce a sweeping curve or soften a sharp angle by using the same material on either side to lead the eye past.

THE GROUND FLOOR

At the lowest level, towards the front of a border, ground cover can be used in still greater numbers to create a carpet, link the various taller plants together and provide visual continuity. Such planting is usually permanent, using low-growing shrubs or hardy perennials, but annual

GOOD INFILL PLANTS
❖

Acanthus

Cytisus

Cistus

Delphiniums

Deutzia

Hydrangea

Lupins

Potentilla

Rosemary

Roses

Rudbeckia

Spiraea

GOOD GROUND FLOOR PLANTS
❖

Alchemilla

Bergenia

Cistus x dansereaui

Cotoneaster dammeri

Epimedium

Hebe pinguifolia

Hedera (ivy)

Hypericum calycinum

Geraniums

Lamium

Pachysandra

Vinca

• *see also:* BEST PLANTS FOR EVERY SITE pp86–175

plants can be very effective on a temporary basis, particularly when a border is developing and needs bulking up with instant flower and foliage.

When planting a border and grading it from taller plants at the back to lower-growing species towards the front, you can always add interest by drifting a number of taller species forward into the middle ground. This applies particularly to lofty hardy perennials such as delphiniums and lupins.

Spring bulbs and low-growing annuals, including half-hardy summer bedding, may be classed as ground cover and they can be invaluable in providing instant colour at different times of year, as well as for filling in gaps between slower-growing plants in a developing border.

MAKING THE MOST OF COLOUR

In many respects it is the overall form or outline of plants, together with the shape and texture of their foliage, that is the real worth of a well-planned border. Flowers are almost a bonus and, in many cases, on show for only a limited time. It is nevertheless important to understand how colour works in the garden.

The hot colours – red, orange and yellow – are always dominant, drawing the eye. If these are placed at the bottom of a garden or view they will demand your attention and tend to foreshorten the space. Pastels, on the other hand, are far less demanding. In principle, if you group the hot colours close to the house or main viewpoint and the pastel colours further away, this will enhance the feeling of space as the eye is drawn more slowly down the garden. Grey, present in the foliage of many plants, is a great harmonizer, softening the hot colours and drawing colour ranges together.

61

▽ **THE BEAUTY OF** *a herbaceous border lies in the tiered effect of plants at different heights, furnishing colour and interest all summer. The pergola is clothed with climbing roses,* R. 'New Dawn' *and* R. multiflora, *while tall delphiniums provide impact in the middle of the border*

SUITING THE SOIL

❖

Remember that certain types of plant enjoy quite different kinds of soil. There is little point growing ericaceous plants, such as azaleas, rhododendron and pieris (*see picture below*) or summer-flowering heathers in alkaline or chalky soil as they will never be happy. Some plants prefer moist soil and others like dry conditions, so always check the soil type and conditions into which you will be planting. Bear in mind too that any soil benefits from the addition of organic material such as well-rotted compost and manure, so add this at the time of planting to ensure your plants have a good start.

A border for year-round interest

Everybody's ideal border is one that looks good for 365 days of the year and this is a true test of the skill of your planting. Although it is difficult to make a border as colourful in winter as it is in high summer, with careful planning there is no reason why a winter border should lack interest. The secret is a balance of evergreen and deciduous plants, carefully selected for different flowering times, strong shapes and leaf texture.

THE BORDER IN SUMMER

When you plan for summer, think of the richness of the planting palette and the overall character of individual plants rather than going for brash flower colours. Put together plants whose habit or leaf texture complement each other and regard their flowers as a bonus. This border relies at one end on the contrasting leaves of acanthus and *Vitis coignetiae,* with the stunning blue flowers of ceanothus and *Hebe* 'Midsummer Beauty' providing extra impact. Towards the other end, the netted gold leaves of the honeysuckle offset the delicate, upright grass, *Miscanthus sinensis* 'Nippon'.

▷ **WINTER IS THE SEASON** *when the shape of plants and evergreen foliage come into their own. At the back of this border the honeysuckle retains most of its leaves, softening the fence. Spiky yuccas look good at any time of year, while escallonia, broom,* Euphorbia polychroma *and* Stachys olympica *are all evergreen.*

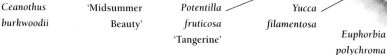

Delphinium

Hibiscus syriacus 'Woodbridge'

Crambe cordifolia

Vitis coignetiae

Acanthus spinosus

Spiraea japonica 'Goldflame'

Ceanothus burkwoodii

Hebe 'Midsummer Beauty'

Potentilla fruticosa 'Tangerine'

Yucca filamentosa

Euphorbia polychroma

see also: SHRUBS FOR YEAR-ROUND INTEREST p100; SHRUBS FOR SEASONAL INTEREST p102–108; GROUND COVER PLANTS p118; THE SUMMER FLOWER GARDEN p138

62

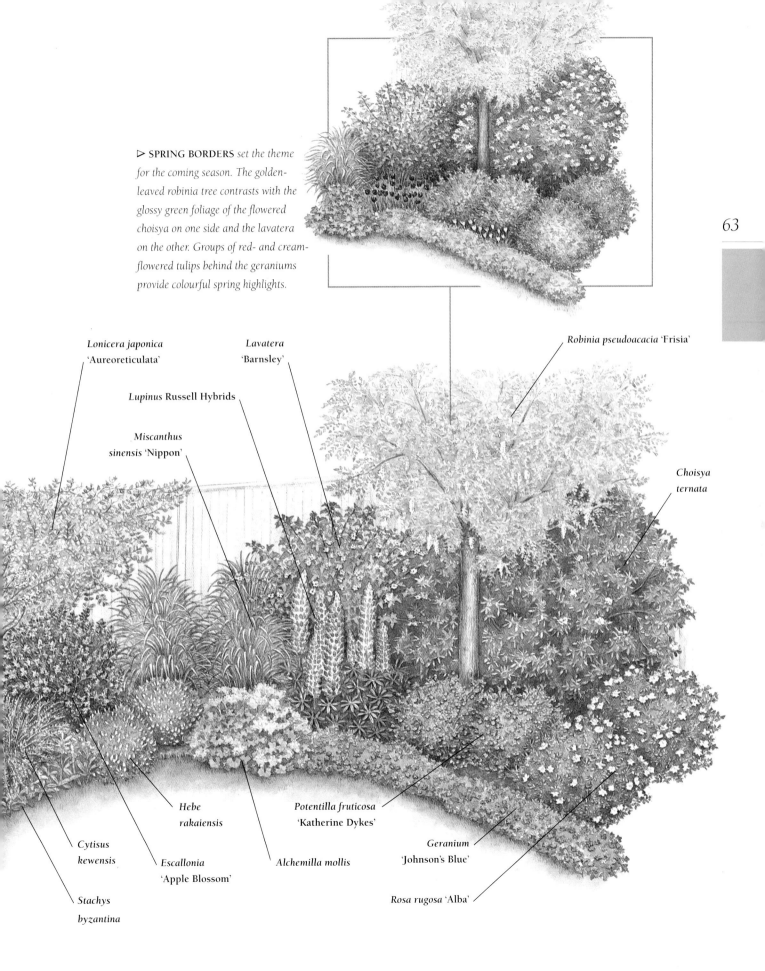

▷ **SPRING BORDERS** *set the theme for the coming season. The golden-leaved robinia tree contrasts with the glossy green foliage of the flowered choisya on one side and the lavatera on the other. Groups of red- and cream-flowered tulips behind the geraniums provide colourful spring highlights.*

Lonicera japonica 'Aureoreticulata'

Lavatera 'Barnsley'

Robinia pseudoacacia 'Frisia'

Lupinus Russell Hybrids

Miscanthus sinensis 'Nippon'

Choisya ternata

Hebe rakaiensis

Potentilla fruticosa 'Katherine Dykes'

Cytisus kewensis

Escallonia 'Apple Blossom'

Alchemilla mollis

Geranium 'Johnson's Blue'

Stachys byzantina

Rosa rugosa 'Alba'

Creating a theme

While the divisions and hard landscape of a garden provide its structure and its framework, it will be plants that animate it and the overall feel of your garden will be determined by the species you choose. As there is a variety of different environments in most gardens, it makes sense to select plants whose cultural needs suit their situation as well as keeping to a clear design theme.

64

PLANTING FOR A SHADY WALL

Many people despair of the shady areas in their garden, but there are many species that will thrive in such a situation. This shady wall is almost completely obscured by evergreens: the rhododendron, with its handsome flowers and foliage, is flanked by hypericum and winter jasmine, both yellow-flowered although blooming at different times of year, and *Viburnum tinus* has deliciously fragrant flowers in winter. Spring-flowering hellebores and bergenias sprawl closer to ground level.

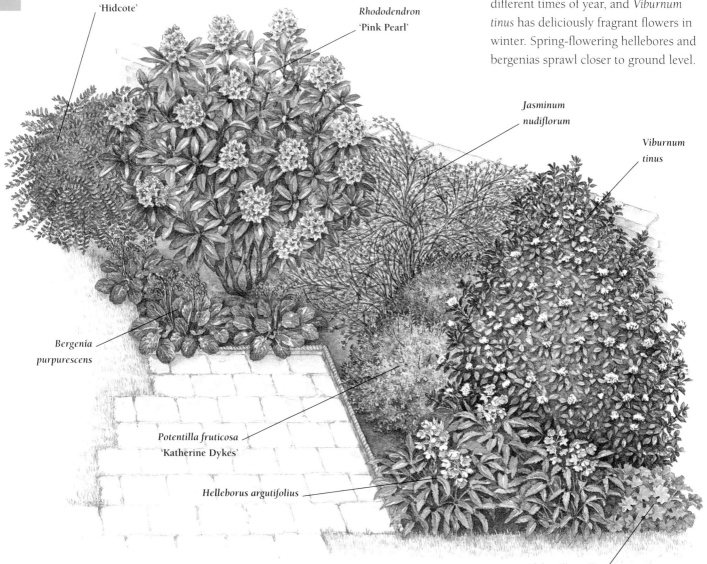

Hypericum 'Hidcote'

Rhododendron 'Pink Pearl'

Jasminum nudiflorum

Viburnum tinus

Bergenia purpurescens

Potentilla fruticosa 'Katherine Dykes'

Helleborus argutifolius

Alchemilla mollis

see also: SCENTED PLANTS p130; PLANTS FOR DRY SHADE p164

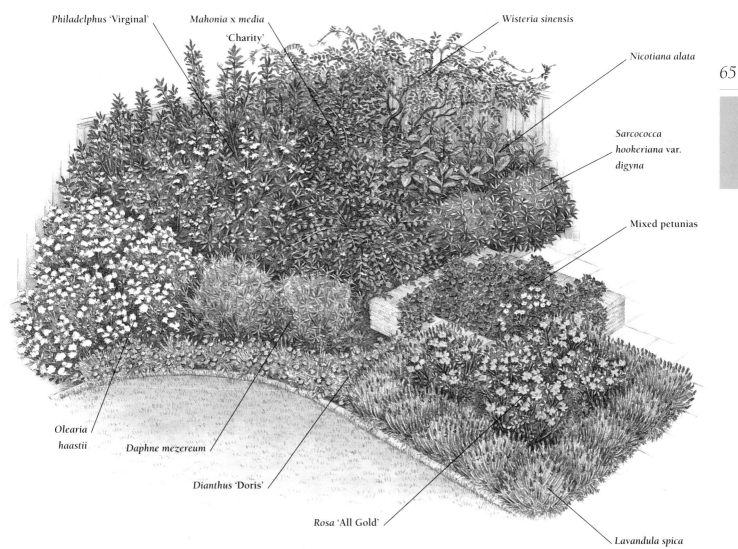

Philadelphus 'Virginal'

Mahonia x media 'Charity'

Wisteria sinensis

Nicotiana alata

Sarcococca hookeriana var. *digyna*

Mixed petunias

Olearia haastii

Daphne mezereum

Dianthus 'Doris'

Rosa 'All Gold'

Lavandula spica 'Hidcote'

A FRAGRANT BORDER

I try always to plan fragrant areas into my gardens, choosing places that will most benefit from scented flower and foliage. A bed like this would be ideal close to French doors opening on to a generous terrace or flanking a summer house in a more distant part of the garden. The scent of lavender is released as you brush past it, while philadelphus (mock orange) is one of the most strongly perfumed of all garden plants. Evenings would bring the fragrance of wisteria and night-scented tobacco plants. Daphne, sarcococca and the daisy bush (*Olearia haastii*) all exude more unusual scents.

Three treatments

There are unlimited ways in which to design a garden but to be successful any plot should reflect the owner's personality and lifestyle, which is why it is never a good idea to simply copy a garden from a book, a television programme or a flower show. Use such gardens as inspiration by all means, but always try to give your design a personal hallmark. The three designs for the same plot shown here reflect individual approaches.

66

SIMPLE CURVES

In this simple, naturalistic layout, the design is built up from a series of strong, flowing curves. The surface is mainly lawn, with a path sweeping up to the top of the garden where it terminates at the seat, which also acts as a focal point. A successful device is the wing of planting that divides up the space so that not everything is visible at a single glance. The creation of a feeling of mystery and surprise is effective even in a small space.

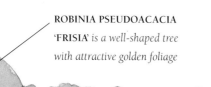

ROBINIA PSEUDOACACIA *'FRISIA' is a well-shaped tree with attractive golden foliage*

SHRUB PLANTING *softens the rectangular boundaries. Evergreen species include bamboo, elaeagnus and skimmia, combined with deciduous shrubs like philadelphus and with smaller herbaceous subjects*

LAWNS *have a strongly curved outline which lends continuity to the design*

PATH *is made up of large, precast concrete slabs set just below the surface of the lawn to facilitate mowing*

MIXED PLANTING *has been planned to provide colour and interest through the year and uses drifts and groups rather than a medley of individual species*

SUMACHS, *with their architectural outline and brilliant autumn colour, are one of my favourite shrubs despite their tendency to sucker*

SEAT *draws the eye across the garden and acts as a positive focal point*

• *see also:* DESIGN CONSIDERATIONS p18

THE ESSENTIAL GARDEN

This slightly more structured design, with a central lawn, again uses curves to suggest movement but allows more room for sitting and dining as well as space for a utility area, or shed, in the far corner. This is a fairly basic garden design that is flexible enough to have other features 'bolted on' to it at a later date.

MIXED PLANTING *screens next door's garage, using Viburnum tinus,* holly, miscanthus *and* Elaeagnus ebbingii *'Limelight'*

APPLE TREE

COMPOST/ UTILITY

ROBINIA

LAWN

ROSES *are a perennial favourite in any garden: keep to one colour range*

POTS PLANTED *with silver-leaved plants including* Convolvulus cneorum, *artemisia, stachys and* Hebe pinguifolia

PAVING IN MIXED MATERIALS

DEVELOPING THE THEME

This more sophisticated design is a logical progression of the garden above, introducing a path that sweeps away from the extended terrace to pause at the seat placed on the brick paving. Stepping stones cross the pool and return to the house, passing under the pergola flanked by planting.

APPLE TREE

A POOL *is a delightful element in any garden. Stepping stones are set just above the water's surface*

MIXED PLANTING *clothes the boundaries: there are plants for interest in all seasons*

COMPOST HEAP

SEAT

PERGOLA *clothed with climbing roses and clematis*

PAVING

HERBS *surrounded with lavender*

WALL, *1.2m (4ft) high, contains the terrace area and backs a built-in seat and barbecue*

STATUE

LAWN

ROBINIA

RAISED BED *has a collection of miniature conifers that look effective grouped together*

Low-maintenance garden

Maintenance, or lack of it, is often in the eye of the owner. There is a fine distinction between just pottering and more serious work in a garden and the key to minimizing the upkeep required is a sensible balance between hard and soft landscape. A good combination of shrubs, herbaceous perennials and ground cover will knit together to keep maintenance to a minimum once the planting is established.

68

HIGH INTEREST, LOW UPKEEP

This garden, for a hard-working couple with limited leisure time, was designed to look interesting but need minimum maintenance. The rectangular site, typical of the plots behind thousands of newly built homes, measures 10m by 7m (33ft by 23ft) and slopes gently up, away from the house. As the garden is small, the whole design has been turned on the diagonal to help create a feeling of greater space.

The generous terrace is paved in simulated natural stone flags with inserts of brick to give a visual link with the house. A small, raised pool adds interest and steps climb up to the strongly curved lawn, its outline emphasized by a brick edging, that provides visual movement in the centre of the garden. Planting, consisting of low-maintenance shrubs with flowering bulbs and perennials, wraps all around the lawn.

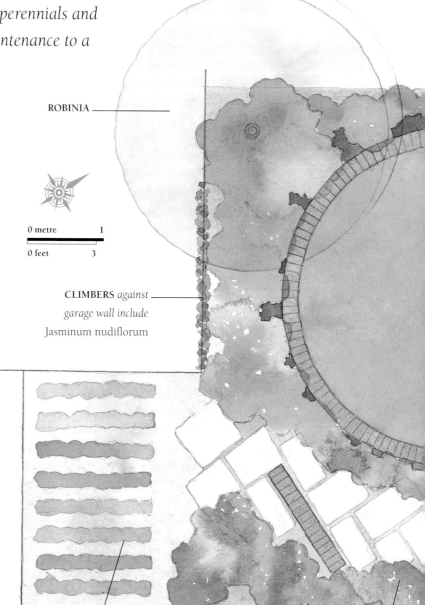

ROBINIA

0 metre 1
0 feet 3

CLIMBERS *against garage wall include* Jasminum nudiflorum

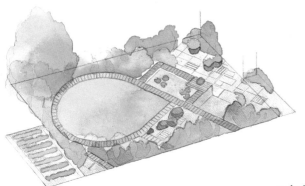

SALAD CROPS *are tucked away in an awkward corner of the garden*

MIXED PLANTING *softens the boundary with* potentilla, Spiraea japonica *'Goldflame'*, Alchemilla mollis; Clematis montana *clothes the fence*

• *see also:* STARTING FROM SCRATCH p14; DESIGN CONSIDERATIONS p18

PLANTING *includes a mix of shrubs and herbaceous perennials, with sweeps of* Geranium endressii *and* G. x riversleaianum *'Russell Prichard' at the front of the border*

FORMAL POOL *is raised 45cm (18in) above terrace level and fitted with a simple bubble fountain. One corner is formed into a plinth for a large pot*

CLIMBERS INCLUDE Clematis tangutica *and* Vitis vinifera *'Purpurea'*

BRICK EDGING *makes mowing easier*

POTS PLANTED *with a collection of alpines such as arabis, saxifrages, sedum and gentians*

IMITATION STONE SLABS *are interspersed with random brick paving*

STEPS UP

PLANTING *by the house consists of a fragrant sarcococca, underplanted with ground-covering periwinkle*

IN THIS SHADY *part of the garden, planting includes euonymus, hostas and bergenias, with* Hydrangea petiolaris *on the fence*

SMALL LAWN *takes little time to mow*

GRAVEL AND SMOOTH BOULDERS *bring sculptural interest by the side of the path while low, sprawling plants introduce colour*

RETAINING WALL

Family garden

Children, grandchildren or just friends' children will all appreciate a garden that really works for them. This will usually involve the provision of enough hard surfacing close to the house, a lawn that is hard-wearing enough for boisterous play and, if possible, a path running right around the garden for wheeled toys and vehicles. If you can add to this colourful flowers and foliage and a bed set aside for child-orientated planting, you may well have budding young gardeners on your hands.

CATERING FOR ALL NEEDS

This amply sized family garden was designed to provide for a wide range of different activities. Moving away from the house, the terrace is generous enough for play as well as for relaxation and outdoor meals. The raised sandpit has a removable cover and could be replaced later by a raised bed for planting or by a raised pool. A path sweeps away around the garden, leading the eye away from the rectangular boundaries and giving access to the salad crops and the slide, set in rougher grass. Planting softens the whole area and a predominance of tough species will still look good, notwithstanding the ravages of the odd football or errant tricycle.

The main play areas and equipment are in view from the house windows, an important safety aspect. Planting in front of the windows has been kept low, using small shrubs, so it does not obscure the view.

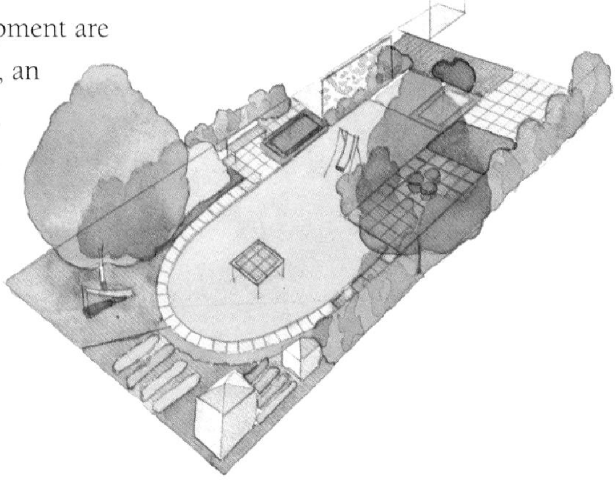

SLIDE

SHED

APPLE TREE *set in longer grass, naturalized with bulbs*

SALAD CROPS *take up less space than a vegetable plot but ensure fresh produce. Many salads are also ideal crops for children to grow, giving quick returns*

COMPOST HEAP *screened by beech hedge*

BEECH HEDGE

SORBUS ARIA 'LUTESCENS' *is an excellent small garden tree whose silvery-grey leaves look wonderful in spring*

• *see also:* DESIGN CONSIDERATIONS p18

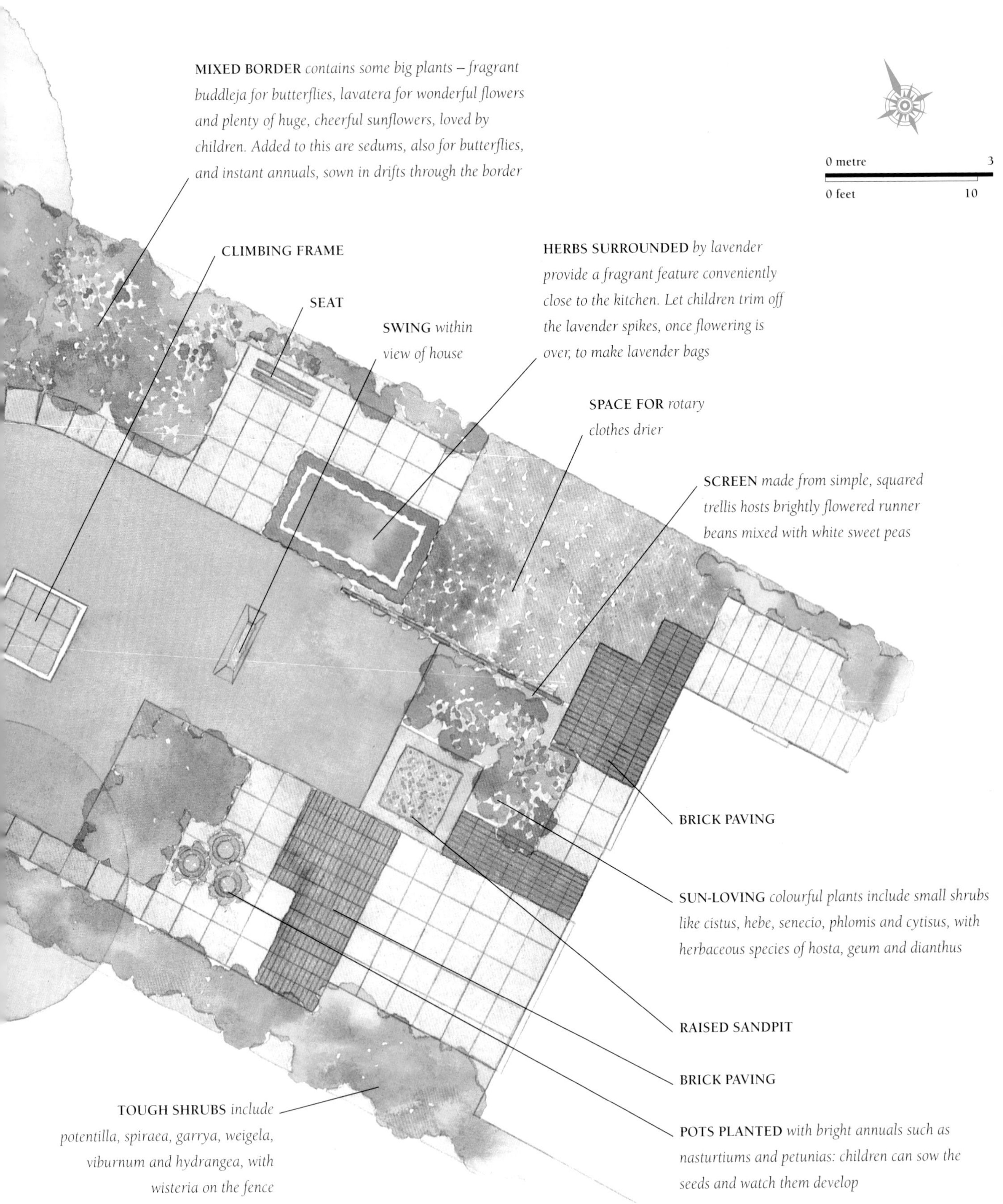

MIXED BORDER *contains some big plants – fragrant buddleja for butterflies, lavatera for wonderful flowers and plenty of huge, cheerful sunflowers, loved by children. Added to this are sedums, also for butterflies, and instant annuals, sown in drifts through the border*

CLIMBING FRAME

SEAT

SWING *within view of house*

HERBS SURROUNDED *by lavender provide a fragrant feature conveniently close to the kitchen. Let children trim off the lavender spikes, once flowering is over, to make lavender bags*

SPACE FOR *rotary clothes drier*

0 metre   3
0 feet   10

SCREEN *made from simple, squared trellis hosts brightly flowered runner beans mixed with white sweet peas*

BRICK PAVING

SUN-LOVING *colourful plants include small shrubs like cistus, hebe, senecio, phlomis and cytisus, with herbaceous species of hosta, geum and dianthus*

RAISED SANDPIT

BRICK PAVING

TOUGH SHRUBS *include potentilla, spiraea, garrya, weigela, viburnum and hydrangea, with wisteria on the fence*

POTS PLANTED *with bright annuals such as nasturtiums and petunias: children can sow the seeds and watch them develop*

Two front gardens

First impressions count, which is why the front garden is an important space that should look good throughout the year. There is no excuse for a front garden to look drab and neglected, as is all too often the case. In constant use, front gardens often have to cater for car parking as well as access by people. Since this space is usually of limited dimensions whether or not it includes car parking, simplicity is generally the key to a successful design.

72

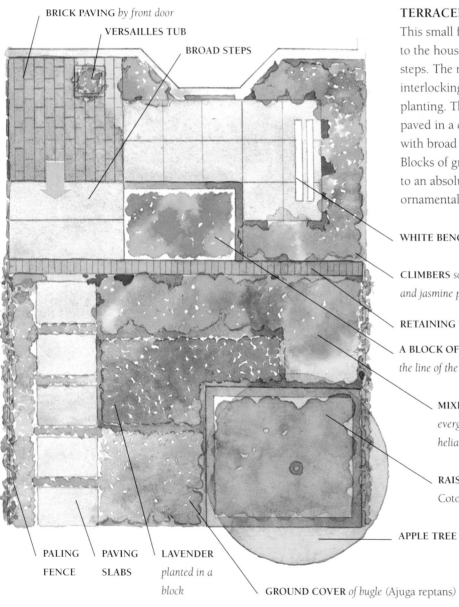

BRICK PAVING *by front door*

VERSAILLES TUB

BROAD STEPS

PALING FENCE

PAVING SLABS

LAVENDER *planted in a block*

GROUND COVER *of bugle* (Ajuga reptans)

TERRACED HOUSE

This small front garden originally sloped down to the house, with poorly designed and dangerous steps. The new layout is conceived as a series of interlocking rectangles created by paving and planting. The lower level, close to the house, is paved in a combination of brick and pre-cast slabs, with broad steps giving access to the upper garden. Blocks of ground-cover planting keep maintenance to an absolute minimum, the raised bed and the ornamental apple tree providing the focal points.

WHITE BENCH SEAT

CLIMBERS *soften the tall dividing wall: honeysuckle and jasmine provide fragrance close to the front door*

RETAINING WALL

A BLOCK OF *white marguerite daisies mask the line of the retaining wall*

MIXED PLANTING *includes sun-loving evergreens such as hebe, cistus and helianthemums for year-round interest*

RAISED BED *is planted with* Cotoneaster dammeri

APPLE TREE

0 metre — 1

0 feet — 3

• *see also:* STARTING FROM SCRATCH p14; DESIGN CONSIDERATIONS p18

FRONT GARDEN WITH DRIVE

As this front garden incorporates a driveway for cars, minimal maintenance was
called for so either side of the drive is surfaced with gravel and smooth boulders,
laid over a permeable 'weed mat'. Paving gives access to both the front and side
of the house, with plants in pots and the raised bed supplying colour and
interest. Planting elsewhere softens the garden, the purple-leaved birches casting
dappled shade and providing a vertical emphasis.

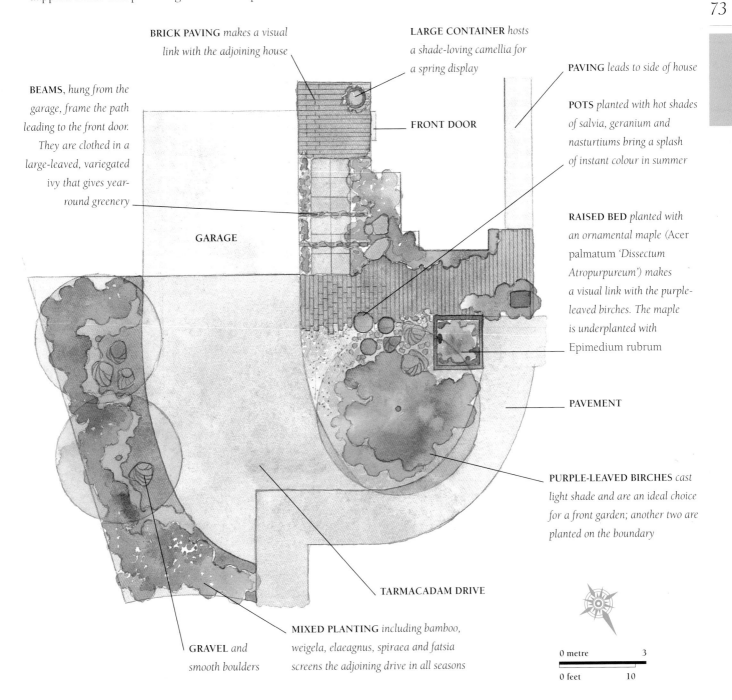

BRICK PAVING *makes a visual
link with the adjoining house*

LARGE CONTAINER *hosts
a shade-loving camellia for
a spring display*

PAVING *leads to side of house*

BEAMS, *hung from the
garage, frame the path
leading to the front door.
They are clothed in a
large-leaved, variegated
ivy that gives year-
round greenery*

FRONT DOOR

POTS *planted with hot shades
of salvia, geranium and
nasturtiums bring a splash
of instant colour in summer*

GARAGE

RAISED BED *planted with
an ornamental maple (Acer
palmatum 'Dissectum
Atropurpureum') makes
a visual link with the purple-
leaved birches. The maple
is underplanted with
Epimedium rubrum*

PAVEMENT

PURPLE-LEAVED BIRCHES *cast
light shade and are an ideal choice
for a front garden; another two are
planted on the boundary*

TARMACADAM DRIVE

GRAVEL *and
smooth boulders*

MIXED PLANTING *including bamboo,
weigela, elaeagnus, spiraea and fatsia
screens the adjoining drive in all seasons*

0 metre 3

0 feet 10

Roof terrace

Roof gardens, terraces and balconies make delightful gardens, often with spectacular views, but they have their own particular difficulties, chiefly concerned with load-bearing, high winds and problems of access. Since this is the only outdoor space available to many city dwellers, it is worth undertaking any structural work required to make the garden safe; the reward will be a verdant oasis perched high above the streets.

74

```
0 metre                    1
0 feet                     3
```

A GARDEN IN THE SKY

This tiny roof garden measures just 5m by 5m (16ft by 16ft) and nestles between two sides of the building and a dividing wall that separates it from the house next door. The fourth side is open, looking across a skyscape of roof tiles and chimneys.

As this was a relatively new building, the sub-structure of the roof had been designed to support a living space as well as to provide access, but anyone contemplating this kind of project should *always check the roof's load-bearing capacity with an architect or structural engineer before proceeding.* As the strongest part of most roofs is around the edges, this is where the main weight is distributed, in this case in the form of raised beds and a small pool. The raised beds are built from lightweight blocks that were rendered and painted a warm, earthy colour. They are filled with lightweight compost and watered by automatic irrigation. The pool is fitted with a butyl liner.

The floor is paved in a combination of lightweight, square tiles and thin terracotta tiles, the latter forming a grid that ties the composition together visually. Decking would be another lightweight alternative. The front of the garden has a glass screen to provide shelter while making the most of the view.

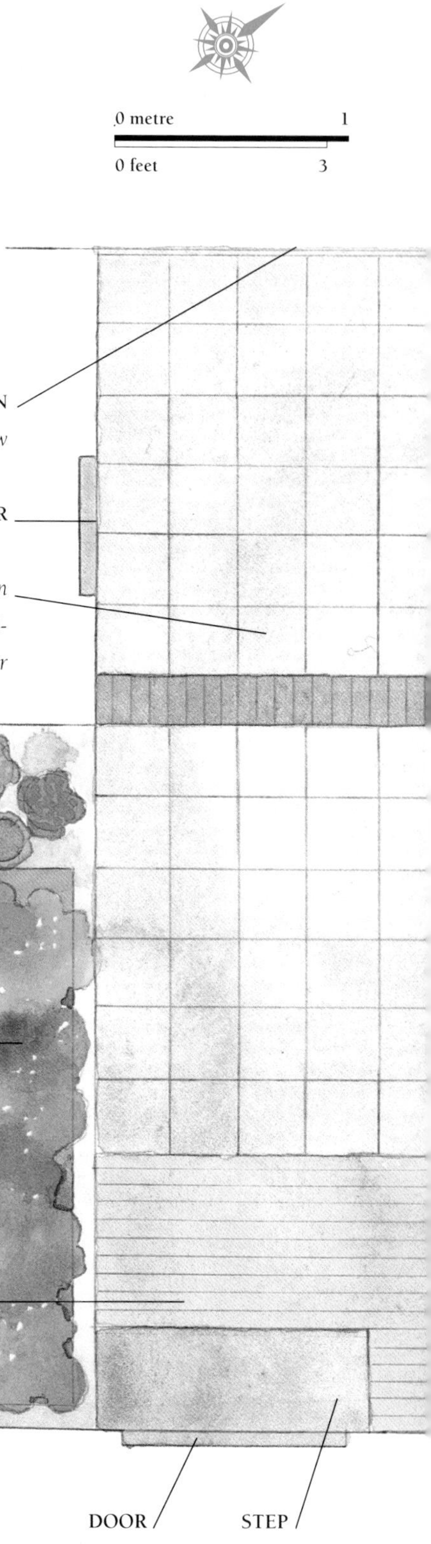

TOUGHENED GLASS SCREEN *provides shelter while retaining the view*

DOOR

LIGHTWEIGHT TILES *are bedded on waterproof mastic to provide a hard-wearing and quick-draining floor*

POTS ON TILED PLINTH *are planted with herbs that enjoy sunny conditions, like rosemary, thyme and marjoram*

RAISED BED, *45cm (18in) deep, is planted with senecio, cistus, Festuca glauca and Genista hispanica, all of which tolerate wind and thrive in hot conditions*

THIN TILES *of terracotta match the level of the adjacent square tiles and provide a visual link with flooring inside the apartment and the wall colour of the raised beds*

DOOR   **STEP**

• *see also:* STARTING FROM SCRATCH p14; DESIGN CONSIDERATIONS p18

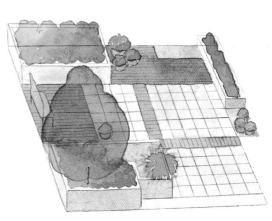

RAISED POOL *is built from lightweight blocks*
and lined with a butyl sheet; aquatic plants
and fish thrive here. A small submersible pump
provides a bubble fountain

APPLE TREE *grown on a dwarfing rootstock is*
ideal in a limited space; it is planted in the
raised bed and secured to the adjoining wall

LARGE RAISED BED *contains sun-loving shrubs*
such as helianthemum, phlomis, Convolvulus
cneorum *and Hebe pinguifolia* 'Pagei'

LARGE CONTAINER *planted with yellow*
marguerite daisies in summer

SEAT *placed to enjoy the pool*

HIGH BOUNDARY WALL

RAISED BED *contains Ceanothus thyrsiflorus*
var. repens, Salvia officinalis, Cytisus
battandieri *and yucca. All these plants will need*
regular feeding

TERRACOTTA POTS *host a collection of colourful bulbs*
in spring and annual bedding in summer

Dog-leg garden

Gardens that run around two sides of a house, or where one part of the plot is not visible from the house, are quite common and the challenge in design terms is to provide continuity. All too often this results in a missed opportunity because only one section of the garden is developed or drawn together into an overall composition. The appeal of a 'dog-leg' shaped plot is the feeling of mystery and surprise as you are encouraged from one area of the garden into another, where a whole range of features and opportunities opens up.

76

EXISTING CONIFERS

SEAT WITH ARBOUR

MIXED PLANTING softens the hard fence line with a combination of shrubs and herbaceous perennials, including weigela, spiraea, potentilla, lupins, geum and euphorbias

LAWN

PLANTING INCLUDES *fragrant species such as roses, lilies and Choisya ternata*

HERBS SURROUNDED *with lavender*

POT PLANTED *with marguerite daisies and trailing pelargoniums*

BRICK PANELS *set between natural stone slabs*

DOOR

• *see also:* STARTING FROM SCRATCH p14; DESIGN CONSIDERATIONS p18

SUNNY BORDER *uses sweeps of ground-covering shrubs and herbaceous perennials, including* Geranium *'Johnson's Blue',* Stachys byzantina *and* Hebe pinguifolia *'Pagei' to keep maintenance low*

A TOUR ROUND THE GARDEN

In this plot, the 'side' garden is a narrow passage that opens out from a conservatory attached to the house and in full view from it. Pine trees filled the space and, once these were thinned, a delightful walkway of stepping stones through ground cover was created to lead naturally to the more open garden at the rear of the house. When you turn the corner, a clematis-covered arch provides a sense of expectation as the view through to the main garden opens out. Once in the larger garden area, with access from both the dining and sitting rooms of the house, there is a real feeling of space and movement, with a flowing area of lawn and well-stocked flower borders. There is ample room for sitting and dining on the terrace, which is paved with a mixture of brick and natural stone slabs. Herbs provide fragrance and easy pickings close to the kitchen.

77

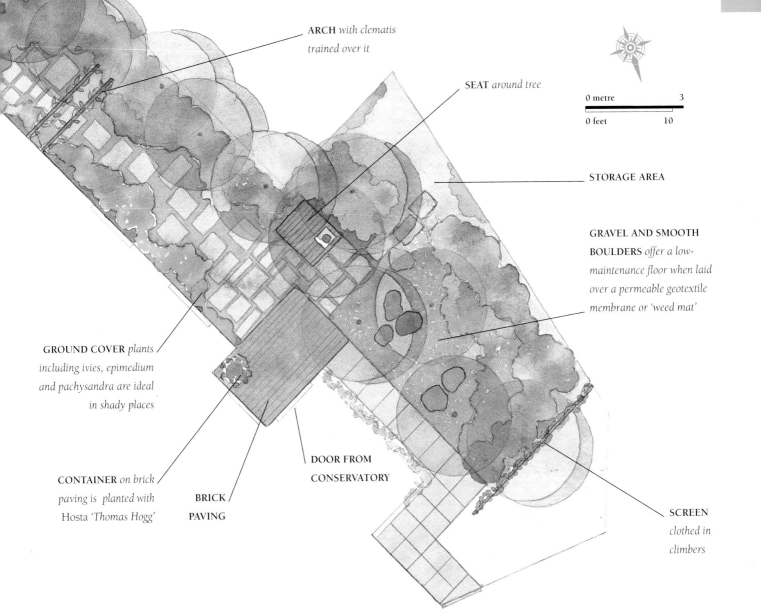

ARCH *with clematis trained over it*

SEAT *around tree*

0 metre — 3
0 feet — 10

STORAGE AREA

GRAVEL AND SMOOTH BOULDERS *offer a low-maintenance floor when laid over a permeable geotextile membrane or 'weed mat'*

GROUND COVER *plants including ivies, epimedium and pachysandra are ideal in shady places*

CONTAINER *on brick paving is planted with* Hosta *'Thomas Hogg'*

BRICK PAVING

DOOR FROM CONSERVATORY

SCREEN *clothed in climbers*

Long, narrow garden

Town gardens are often long and thin, particularly those outside older properties that interlock with one another to produce awkwardly aligned boundaries. Such gardens can frequently be shady and overlooked but they form perfect outdoor rooms with plenty of shelter. Given a design that aims to break up the length visually, and with carefully chosen hard surfacing, architectural plants and minimal maintenance, small can often mean beautiful.

78

TINY TOWN PLOT

This restricted site is barely 13m long by 6m wide (43ft by 20ft) in the main part of the garden. Access is from the kitchen door on to a lower terrace, floored in old York stone and courses of brick that aim to widen the space visually. A change of level is used as a means of dividing up the space and adding interest. A single, broad step leads to the upper garden level, where you pass beneath an arch and up to a compact little painted shed. Planting along the boundaries is vitally important to soften the line of the surrounding walls and prevent the garden from being overlooked or feeling too closed in.

FONT, *found at an antique sale, makes a wonderful plant container*

ARCH *provides spatial division between the two garden levels and leads to the shed*

SMALL TREE

POTS

SPACE *for rotary clothes drier*

POT PLANTED *with large-leaved hosta*

MIXED PLANTING *on this sunny side of the garden includes ceanothus, senecio, hibiscus, datura and summer-flowering jasmine*

SMALL SHED *is brightly painted*

COMPOST HEAP OR STORAGE

0 metre 1

0 feet 3

MULTI-STEMMED BIRCH *as a screen*

• *see also:* STARTING FROM SCRATCH p14; DESIGN CONSIDERATIONS p18

MIXED PLANTING *includes*
hellebores, astilbes, hemerocallis
and Euphorbia wulfenii

SEAT

POT PLANTED
with variegated ivies

CLEMATIS

POTS PLANTED *with annuals*

CLEMATIS *'Nelly Moser'*

POT PLANTED
with camellia

DOOR

MIXED PLANTING
includes ferns and hostas

BRICK *courses laid within*
the York stone helps to relieve
the overall expanse

GATE

PAVING *of random*
old York stone slabs

CLEMATIS TANGUTICA *looks*
wonderful on a shady wall, with its
bell-shaped yellow flowers and
feathery seedheads that last into winter

POTS FILLED *with*
ericaceous compost and
planted with pieris, camellia
and Japanese azalea

RAISED BED *holds a collection of hellebores*
and hostas, beneath Garrya elliptica

RETAINING WALL *and top step*

POTS WITH *a collection of ferns*

SHADE PLANTING *includes aucuba, bamboos, skimmia,*
sarcococca, Viburnum davidii and Fatsia japonica.
All are evergreen and provide year-round interest

A sloping site

Sloping gardens can provide far greater interest than a flat site but they may also cost a good deal more to construct. Creating a series of changes of level involves the building of retaining walls, steps, ramps and terracing in order to provide several flat, usable areas. Always bear in mind that a garden which slopes up, in front of you, tends visually to foreshorten the space, while one that drops away from you has the opposite effect.

80

CHANGES IN LEVEL

The slope in this garden is just under 2m (6ft) from the top end of the garden to the bottom and the space has been organized into a flat terrace close to the house and a level lawn in the middle. Steps climb the bank to the left, terminating by an arbour at the highest point of the garden; the seat enclosed within the arbour looks out over the pool, with its rocky outcrops and tumbling waterfall. Planting softens and surrounds the garden, detracting the eye from those awkward boundaries.

ARBOUR *clothed in scented roses provides informal seating that looks back towards the house*

ROCKERY WITH *waterfall acts as a focal point from the house and hosts an alpine collection*

BANK

STEPPING STONES *lead the way up the bank*

GENTLE SLOPE

PERGOLA WITH *fragrant climbing plants links the more formal areas around the house with the altogether softer garden close to the arbour*

PAVING

MIXED PLANTING *throughout the garden is a combination of shrubs and herbaceous perennials, with evergreens for winter interest*

• *see also:* STARTING FROM SCRATCH p14, DESIGN CONSIDERATIONS p18

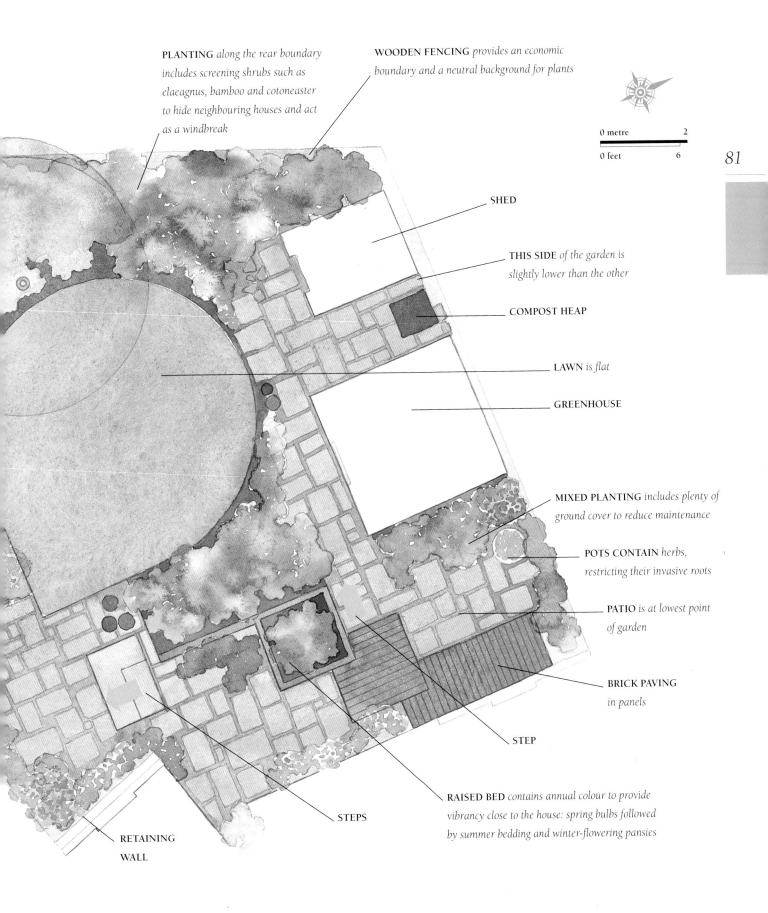

PLANTING along the rear boundary includes screening shrubs such as elaeagnus, bamboo and cotoneaster to hide neighbouring houses and act as a windbreak

WOODEN FENCING provides an economic boundary and a neutral background for plants

0 metre 2
0 feet 6

81

SHED

THIS SIDE of the garden is slightly lower than the other

COMPOST HEAP

LAWN is flat

GREENHOUSE

MIXED PLANTING includes plenty of ground cover to reduce maintenance

POTS CONTAIN herbs, restricting their invasive roots

PATIO is at lowest point of garden

BRICK PAVING in panels

STEP

RAISED BED contains annual colour to provide vibrancy close to the house: spring bulbs followed by summer bedding and winter-flowering pansies

STEPS

RETAINING WALL

A formal garden

Formal gardens have a naturally static, traditional feel and offer a controlled sense of space based on symmetry. They have a balance from one side of the design to the other and rely on a single axis or a number of well-defined axes to divide the area up into a pattern of compartments or rooms that can be given over to different individual themes. Formal designs tend to look best adjoining a period or modern house that has a regular, classical, often somewhat plain facade that is formal in character.

82

MIRROR IMAGE

This garden adjoins a small modern town house with a single French window giving access to a slightly raised terrace. The terrace is paved in a combination of bricks and pre-cast concrete slabs, the brick paving in the middle providing a visual link with the building. Broad steps lead down to the central lawn, flanked by two inward-facing seats.

The rectangular plot is divided lengthways into two halves, with two 'wings' of wall or trellis separating the first from the second. The central path that forms the main axis passes beneath a pergola and ends at the summer house situated at the far end of the garden. Two smaller lawns and identical trees strengthen the sense of formality, at the same time providing balance and visual stability.

CORNER TREES: *two symmetrically planted, golden-leaved catalpas provide a glorious backdrop, their large leaves softening the line of the summer house*

CLASSICAL SUMMER HOUSE *acts as a focal point, drawing the eye*

A PAIR OF CONTAINERS *is identically planted with purple-leaved cordylines*

MIXED PLANTING *includes mixed shrubs and herbaceous perennials in cool colours*

• *see also:* DESIGN CONSIDERATIONS p18; GARDEN STYLES p20; DRAWING UP A PLAN p22

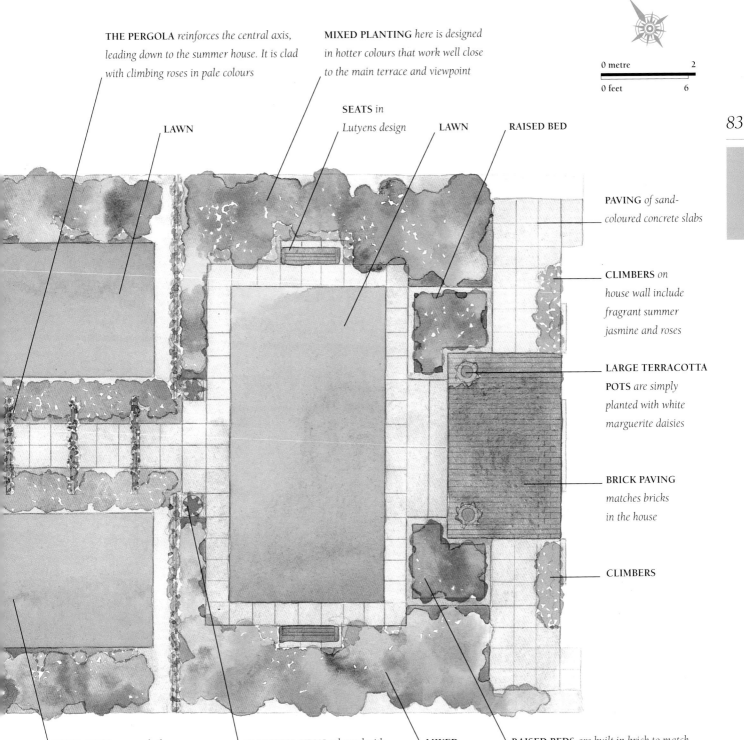

THE PERGOLA *reinforces the central axis, leading down to the summer house. It is clad with climbing roses in pale colours*

MIXED PLANTING *here is designed in hotter colours that work well close to the main terrace and viewpoint*

SEATS *in Lutyens design*

LAWN

LAWN

RAISED BED

0 metre 2
0 feet 6

PAVING *of sand-coloured concrete slabs*

CLIMBERS *on house wall include fragrant summer jasmine and roses*

LARGE TERRACOTTA POTS *are simply planted with white marguerite daisies*

BRICK PAVING *matches bricks in the house*

CLIMBERS

THE LAWNS *are made from the highest quality lawn seed, as this garden is not subject to heavy wear*

CLASSICAL URNS, *planted with trailing pelargoniums in summer, are set on pedestals to increase their height and visual importance*

MIXED PLANTING

RAISED BEDS *are built in brick to match adjoining paving and house. Both are 45cm (18in) high and planted with aromatic herbs*

Wrap-around garden

In many situations, a detached house may stand right in the middle of its plot, with the garden forming an envelope of spaces that flow from one to another. A successful design will not only reinforce this feeling of continuity but at the same time also allow each area to have its own identity or specific purpose. This can present a challenge, especially if the dimensions of each section of garden are limited, but it should still be possible to harness the sense of flowing space.

84

SMALL SIDE LAWN
has a strong shape

LARGE CONTAINER
gives a focus in entrance to first garden area

MIXED PLANTING
includes shade-loving plants

A FLUID DESIGN

The beauty of this garden unfolds as you move around the house. The simple semi-circle of the side lawn is screened from the main garden by a trellis and arch. Once you have passed through this, the strongly formed composition provides real movement as the curved path sweeps beneath the pergola and leads round to the seat and arbour in the far corner of the main garden. The sitting area with water is paved with random, rectangular slabs, the water feature bringing sound, movement and interest. Moving on again, the overhead beams give way to a formal herb bed and vegetable garden. So while each area has its own character and purpose, the design links them seamlessly together.

GREENHOUSE

CLIMBERS *are trained against fence*

COMPOST HEAP

A VEGETABLE PLOT *fills the awkward shape between house and boundary. Greenhouse, compost heap and shed all have a practical function; runner beans are trained against fence*

• *see also:* STARTING FROM SCRATCH p14; DESIGN CONSIDERATIONS p18

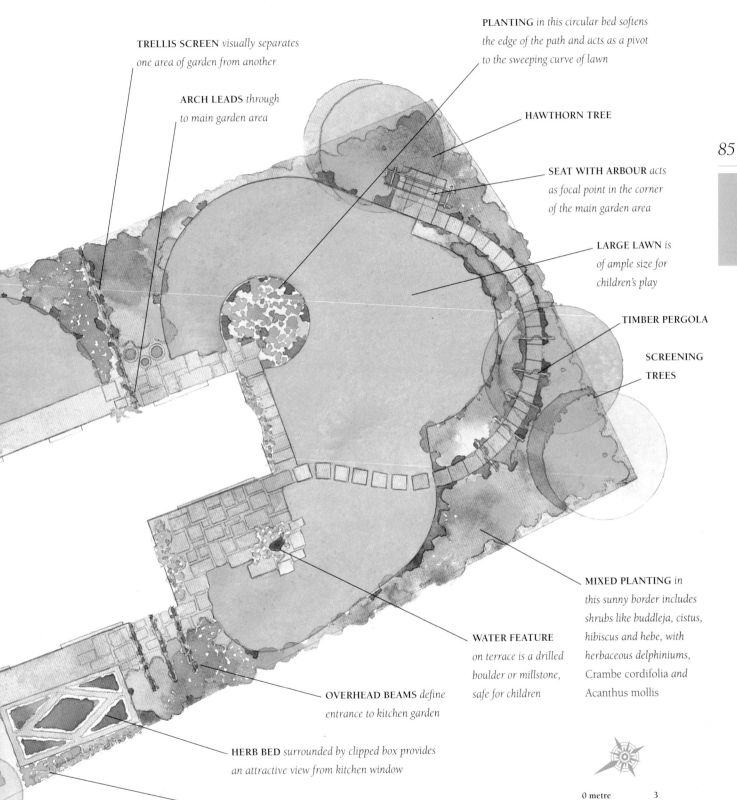

TRELLIS SCREEN *visually separates one area of garden from another*

ARCH LEADS *through to main garden area*

PLANTING *in this circular bed softens the edge of the path and acts as a pivot to the sweeping curve of lawn*

HAWTHORN TREE

SEAT WITH ARBOUR *acts as focal point in the corner of the main garden area*

LARGE LAWN *is of ample size for children's play*

TIMBER PERGOLA

SCREENING TREES

MIXED PLANTING *in this sunny border includes shrubs like buddleja, cistus, hibiscus and hebe, with herbaceous delphiniums, Crambe cordifolia and Acanthus mollis*

WATER FEATURE *on terrace is a drilled boulder or millstone, safe for children*

OVERHEAD BEAMS *define entrance to kitchen garden*

HERB BED *surrounded by clipped box provides an attractive view from kitchen window*

CLIMBER *against fence is Clematis tangutica*

STANDARD FRUIT *trees act as screen*

0 metre 3

0 feet 10

BEST PLANTS FOR EVERY SITE

WITH THOUSANDS of cultivated plants from which to choose, selecting those to suit us and our gardens presents a real challenge. This section identifies different sites and situations for which I suggest some of my favourite plants. Many of these subjects thrive in my own garden, or they are plants I would love to have the space, soil or climate to try. You will find a good many for sale at your local garden centre but those that are less common are rewarding enough to justify the effort of ordering by mail-order from specialist nurseries.

Each plant description is accompanied by symbols, some of which refer to the plant's hardiness. Those awarded three stars (❋ ❋ ❋) should be fully hardy and able to tolerate temperatures down to -15°C (5°F). Those with two stars (❋ ❋) could be described as frost-hardy and will withstand temperatures to about -5°C (23°F). One star (❋) indicates only half-hardiness, with plants rarely surviving temperatures below 0°C (32°F). The few tender plants included have no star but are given a minimum temperature. The leaf symbols tell you whether a plant is evergreen (❀) or deciduous (❍).

Some plants sport a cup-shaped symbol (♆) next to their name. This indicates that they have been awarded the Royal Horticultural Society's Award of Garden Merit. To achieve this, their display must represent good value in the garden, they should be easy to care for, readily available and not especially prone to pests and diseases.

ANNE SWITHINBANK

Trees for small gardens

Where space is restricted it makes sense to choose a tree with as many attributes as possible. Expect them to pay double or triple rent for their space and offer, perhaps, spring blossom, colourful fruits and autumn colour or beautiful foliage and attractive bark. Trees like birches make very suitable contenders, despite their height, because they cast comparatively little shade.

Acer japonicum 'Aconitifolium'

Acer japonicum 'Aconitifolium' ♛
Fernleaf maple

☼ ☀ ❋ ❋ ❋ ○ **H/S** 3m /10ft

88

This delightful cultivar bears rounded yet deeply lobed leaves, toothed around the edges. Fresh lime green spring foliage accompanies clusters of small red flowers, pale seedpods appear in summer and its autumn tints are rich crimson. Give all Japanese maples a moist but well-drained soil in a sheltered position as they dislike waterlogging and exposure to wind.

Amelanchier lamarckii ♛
Snowy mespilus

☼ ☀ ❋ ❋ ❋ ○ **H/S** 8m /25ft

Delicate white spring blossom contrasts prettily with silky, copper-tinged young leaves and is followed by black fruits.

The leaves turn orange-red in autumn. To encourage a tree-like shape, buy a standard-trained plant or select one or more main stems and prune out others. Plant in well-drained, lime-free soil.

Betula albosinensis var. septentrionalis ♛
Chinese red birch

☼ ☀ ❋ ❋ ❋ ○ **H** 18m /60ft **S** 6m /20ft

Although tall, most birches are slender and their dainty leaves cast little shade. In smaller gardens, those with beautiful trunks will give year-round pleasure. This choice Chinese birch bears a rich orange-pink peeling bark, pale and satiny when newly exposed. It also has spring catkins and yellow autumn leaves.

Cornus controversa 'Variegata' ♛
Table dogwood

☼ ☀ ❋ ❋ ❋ ○ **H/S** 6m /20ft

Although slow-growing, the wait is worthwhile for this delightful small tree, grown for its foliage. Tiered branches bear narrow, pointed leaves with irregular creamy margins. Tiny white flowers appear in early summer in large, flat clusters, followed by blue-black fruit. Plant in humus-rich, neutral to acid soil and shelter from spring frosts.

Genista aetnensis ♛
Mount Etna broom

☼ ❋ ❋ ❋ ❋ ○ **H/S** 8m /25ft

Few flowering trees match the display of fragrant, pea-like yellow flowers that this tall broom makes in early summer. The weeping, almost leafless, bright green stems are attractive too. Choose a free-draining soil and sheltered site as wind rock will shorten a plant's life. It tolerates poor, drought-prone, stony soils.

Malus floribunda ♛
Japanese crab apple

☼ ☀ ❋ ❋ ❋ ○ **H/S** 10m /30ft

Surely the most stunning of crab apples when its fleeting display of red buds opens to pale pink blooms that smother the canopy. Small fruits make little impact. Choose *M. x robusta* 'Red Sentinel' ♛ for white blossom and red fruits which last well past midwinter.

Prunus serrula ♛
Tibetan cherry

☼ ❋ ❋ ❋ ❋ ○ **H/S** 6–10m /20–30ft

One of my favourite trees, this makes a fine lawn specimen when sited to catch winter sun. There is year-round beauty in the rich

Amelanchier lamarckii

Prunus serrula

Eucalyptus pauciflora subsp. *niphophila*

• *see also:* PLANTING AND CARING FOR TREES p202

red-brown bark, constantly peeling away to reveal brighter patches beneath. A smattering of small white flowers in spring is followed by dainty, narrow leaves. Grow as a standard tree or buy a stooled specimen with several trunks.

Pyrus salicifolia 'Pendula' ♀
Weeping silver pear

☼ ❉ ❉ ❉ ◌ **H** 5m/15ft **S** 4m/12ft

Weeping branches sweep down to the ground, making a waterfall of long, narrow silvery leaves all summer. Use to fill a corner or as a backdrop to other plants in a wide border. Creamy-white

---

△ **MALUS FLORIBUNDA** *The spreading branches of this small tree are smothered by such a wealth of spring blossom that the emerging leaves almost disappear.*

flowers in early spring are a bonus. If specimens become too wide, prune some stems back to the top in winter.

Robinia pseudoacacia 'Frisia' ♀
Golden false acacia

☼ ❉ ❉ ❉ ◌ **H** 9m/30ft **S** 6m/20ft

This small to medium tree is widely used where its leaves, composed of many rounded leaflets, bring a welcome splash of golden-yellow. Provide shelter from strong winds, especially while young plants are establishing. To restrict height, weigh down the ends of young branches to create a slight weeping habit.

Salix caprea 'Kilmarnock' ♀
Kilmarnock willow

☼ ❉ ❉ ❉ ◌ **H** 2–3m/6–10ft **S** 2m/6ft

This miniature weeping willow offers a good winter outline of yellow-brown stems, studded by silvery catkins with yellow anthers in late winter. Oval, toothed leaves are grey-green beneath. Trees mature into a wide umbrella shape.

SMALL TREE SELECTION
❖

Acer griseum (paperbark maple) ♀ ◌

Betula utilis var. *jacquemontii* ♀ ◌

Cornus alternifolia 'Argentea' (silver pagoda dogwood) ♀ ◌

Eucalyptus pauciflora subsp. *niphophila* (snow gum) ♀ ●

Gleditsia triacanthos 'Sunburst' (honey locust) ♀ ◌

Prunus x *subhirtella* 'Autumnalis' (winter cherry) ♀ ◌

SUPPORTING TREES
❖

There are two basic approaches to tree staking; rely on common sense to judge which is best for your tree. For most sturdy young trees, drive a short stake into the ground at an angle (*see below*). For trees with weak trunks unable to stand upright on their own, a better method involves driving a taller stake into the ground, parallel to the tree, some 15cm (6in) away from the trunk, so it reaches the point at which the branches start. Attach the stem to the stake in one or two places, using tree ties.

For some specimens I prefer to create a support 45cm (18in) high by making a cross-piece out of two uprights, 30cm (12in) away from the trunk on each side, with a horizontal piece of wood between them. Tie the stem into the horizontal, using a flexible material that will not rub (like nylon tights). Guide stakes close to the stems of bare-rooted trees between roots in the planting hole, but avoid driving stakes through the rootball of containerized trees.

STAKING A TREE *Insert a short stake in the ground at a 45° angle, on the side of the tree from which the wind mostly blows. Using a tree tie, attach the stem to it, about 45cm (18in) above ground.*

KEY: ♀ *Award of Merit* ☼ *sun* ❉ *semi-shade* ❅ *shade* ❉ *half-hardy* ❉❉ *frost-hardy* ❉❉❉ *fully hardy* ◌ *deciduous* ● *evergreen* ◐ *semi-evergreen* **H** *height* **S** *spread*

Columnar trees

One way of coping with small spaces is to choose trees with a narrow growth habit. Many favourites, like oak, mountain ash and yew, have narrow or columnar forms, which add height but not spread. Look out for the word fastigiata in their name, which means they have close, erect branches. With their strong, vertical shapes, some slim trees make great architectural statements.

Cupressus arizonica var.
arizonica 'Blue Ice'

90 *Abies pinsapo* 'Glauca' ♀
Spanish fir
☼ ❄ ❄ ❄ ● **H** 25m /80ft **S** 6m /20ft
This selection of the Spanish fir is a delight for its pleasing habit and striking, blue-green needles. By no means small, it remains slim for its height. Cylindrical cones 12cm (5in) long are brown when ripe. Originating from a limestone region of S E Spain, this fir tolerates chalk, yet flourishes on all soils.

Betula pendula 'Laciniata' ♀
Swedish birch
☼ ☼ ❄ ❄ ❄ ♡ **H** 22m /70ft **S** 1.8m /6ft
Plant a stand of several slender Swedish birches as an interesting alternative to a single spreading tree. The peeling white bark is attractive and both the branches and the pretty, deeply cut leaves are pendulous, creating a tall but weeping effect. Leaves turn an attractive yellow before falling in autumn.

Cupressus arizonica var. *arizonica*
'Blue Ice'
Smooth Arizona cypress
☼ ❄ ❄ ❄ ● **H** 12m /40ft **S** 4.5m /15ft
Choose this conifer to provide a slender, hazy, blue-green cone of loose, informal shape. My specimen tolerates poor soil

well and has grown to 4.5m (15ft) in seven years, recently making an ideal nesting site for birds. Its bark is reddish brown and its aromatic, sage-green cones are covered with white bloom.

Cupressus sempervirens 'Totem Pole'
Italian cypress
☼ ❄ ❄ ❄ ● **H** 20m /70ft **S** 2.2m /7ft
One of the classic, pencil-thin cypresses reminiscent of Mediterranean hillsides, this conifer will add height and

---

KEEP OUT THE WEEDS
❖

Where trees, such as this Irish yew, are grown as a lawn specimen, keep the planting area around the trunk free of weeds to avoid competition for water and nutrients.

---

authenticity to groups of other plants able to tolerate well-drained soils and sunny positions. Neat, green, scale-like leaves show up well against the orange-brown stems. Site in a sheltered position, as frost and cold winds can cause damage to new growth.

Fagus sylvatica 'Dawyck Purple' ♀
Purple Dawyck beech
☼ ❄ ❄ ❄ ♡ **H** 22m /70ft **S** 4.5m /15ft
Guaranteed to make a statement in any garden, this narrow, columnar beech with deep purple foliage needs careful placing – it works well as a focal point, where it will show up against plain green foliage. In common with other beeches, the Dawyck tolerates many soil types, including chalk.

Prunus 'Amanogawa' ♀
Upright Japanese cherry
☼ ❄ ❄ ❄ ♡
H 4.5–7.5m /15–25ft **S** 2.5–3.7m /8–12ft
This tree offers the opportunity to enjoy a fleeting display of cherry blossom without having to surrender much garden space. Its upright branches are decked with clusters of semi-double, pale pink, lightly fragrant flowers in spring and there is a moderate flush of leaf colour in the autumn.

• *see also:* PLANTING AND CARING FOR TREES p202

Fagus sylvatica
'Dawyck Purple'

Prunus 'Amanogawa'

Taxus baccata
'Fastigiata Aureomarginata'

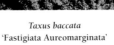

91

THE ROLE OF SLIM TREES

❖

Examine the motive behind choosing a slim or columnar tree to be sure of planting the right one.

- Create an Italianate or Mediterranean atmosphere by choosing narrowly columnar trees such as *Cupressus sempervirens* or *Chamaecyparis lawsoniana* 'Columnaris'.

- Enjoy trees like oak, rowan, pines and firs in a restricted space by opting for *Quercus robur* 'Fastigiata', *Sorbus aucuparia* 'Fastigiata', *Pinus sylvestris* 'Fastigiata' and *Abies pinsapo* 'Glauca'.

- Use slender trees as living sculpture or as focal points at the end of short vistas, by planting lovely Dawyck beech (*Fagus sylvatica* 'Dawyck').

- For lawns, choose good specimen trees like *Taxus baccata* 'Fastigiata' or *Betula pendula* 'Laciniata'.

Quercus robur 'Fastigiata Koster' ♀
Cypress oak

☼ ☀ ❄ ❄ ❄ ○ **H** 22m/70ft **S** 2.2m/7ft

This selected form of the English oak grows upwards rather than ouwards, casting less shade and making it suitable for restricted spaces. The shallowly lobed leaves and acorns remain similar to those of the species. The young growth of this tree sometimes springs disconcertingly out of shape, but it bends back as the tree matures.

Sorbus aucuparia 'Fastigiata'
Upright mountain ash

☼ ☀ ❄ ❄ ❄ ○ **H** 6m/20ft **S** 2.7m/9ft

Retaining the attributes of a regular mountain ash, this columnar tree bears erect stems crowded with pinnate leaves, usually turning yellow and red in autumn. Heads of white flowers open in late spring, followed by clusters of ripe red berries that are much-loved by birds. Prefers cool, moist situations, becoming prone to fireblight when under stress due to drought conditions.

Taxodium distichum var. *imbricatum* 'Nutans' ♀
Pond cypress

☀ ❄ ❄ ❄ ❄ ○ **H** 15m/50ft **S** 4.5m/15ft

Green, upright shoots of awl-shaped leaves burst from the bare branches of this tree in spring, eventually becoming pendent as they mature. The autumn colour of this form is a rich orange-brown, after which whole shoots are shed. Despite being suited to wet soils, this choice columnar tree will also thrive in most other soils, although it dislikes chalk.

Taxus baccata 'Fastigiata Aureomarginata' ♀
Golden Irish yew

☼ ☀ ❄ ❄ ❄ ● **H** 5.5m/18ft **S** 1.2m/4ft

Choose this slimline tree as a lawn specimen for a small garden on any well-drained soil. My own plant has grown from 90cm (3ft) to 4.5m (15ft), with a spread of 60cm (2ft) in seven years. The gold-edged leaves and the bright yellow-orange of new stems are attractive features. Being a male form, there will be small clouds of pollen, but no fruits.

KEY: ♀ *Award of Merit* ☼ *sun* ☀ *semi-shade* ❄ *shade* ❄ *half-hardy* ❄❄ *frost-hardy* ❄❄❄ *fully hardy* ○ *deciduous* ● *evergreen* ◐ *semi-evergreen* **H** *height* **S** *spread*

Trees with fruit and berries

Planting trees that bear attractive fruits not only brings colour to the garden during autumn, but provides a valuable natural larder for birds in the colder weather. Make sure you position berrying trees where you can watch the birds from a house window.

Mespilus germanica

92

Arbutus x andrachnoides ♥
Strawberry tree
☼ ❄ ❄ ❄ ● **H/S** 8m/25ft

This hybrid between *A. andrachne* and *A. unedo* is found naturally in Greece and offers much to a garden. Its attributes include peeling cinnamon bark, evergreen leaves and small, white, bell-shaped flowers that appear during spring or autumn. They usually coincide with the ripening of last season's rounded fruits as they turn through orange to red. Although strictly edible, the fruits are barely palatable. *Arbutus* tolerates chalk, but needs a sheltered position away from cold winds.

Catalpa bignonioides ♥
Indian bean tree
☼ ❄ ❄ ❄ ○ **H/S** 4.5–15m/25–50ft

The spreading canopy of this North American tree is impressive enough, due to the exotic appearance of the large, roughly heart-shaped leaves. The effect is compounded by panicles of flowers like chubby white foxgloves spotted with yellow and purple. These appear in summer, followed by a display of curious, bean-like pods to 38cm (15in) long. Plant in good, well-drained soil and avoid exposed positions.

Cotoneaster frigidus
Himalayan tree cotoneaster
☼ ☼ ❄ ❄ ❄ ○● **H/S** 6m/20ft

Trees sold under this common name may be the true species or one of the hybrids more correctly described as *C. x watereri*. Either way, you can expect a robust, deciduous or semi-evergreen tree bearing long, oval leaves and flat clusters of small white flowers in early summer, followed by a splendid crop of bright red berries that last into winter.

Ilex aquifolium
'Handsworth New Silver' ♥
Holly
☼ ❄ ❄ ❄ ● **H** 8m/25ft **S** 4.5m/15ft

My favourite among the variegated hollies, this beauty eventually grows to a small, vaguely columnar tree. Prickly, mottled leaves have distinct, creamy-white margins and grow from attractive purple stems. Being a female form, bright red berries will be produced if there is a male holly in the vicinity.

Juglans regia ♥
Common walnut
☼ ❄ ❄ ❄ ○ **H** 18m/60ft **S** 9m/30ft

Walnuts make beautiful trees which, with their long history of cultivation, lend great character to a garden. Their pinnate leaves are attractive and their edible nuts develop inside greenish fruits. Plant selected clones such as 'Buccaneer' for earlier, better crops of nuts. Current breeding programmes are in the process of creating improved trees. Avoid frost pockets when planting.

Ilex aquifolium
'Handsworth New Silver'

HOW TO CHOOSE?
❖

- Some trees, like rowans (*Sorbus*) make a mess when their berries drop, or are thrown about by birds. Avoid siting these near paths and patios, which might become stained and slippery.

- Some fruits and berries, such as those of yew and ivy, are poisonous and a hazard to young children.

- Wildlife enthusiasts may wish to plant fruiting trees to supply birds with food in winter. Hawthorn (*Crataegus*), rowan (*Sorbus*) and red-berried hollies (*Ilex*) are best value.

- Those who make their own jams, jellies and wines will welcome fruiting trees as a source of natural ingredients: damsons, crab apples and medlar are good choices.

• *see also:* SHRUBS FOR AUTUMN COLOUR p106

> ## BEAT THE BIRDS
> ❖
>
> In general, birds tend to go first for red and orange berries, leaving pink or white ones until last. The fruits of *Malus* 'Red Sentinel', *M.* 'Golden Hornet', *M.* 'Joseph Rock' and *Sorbus cashmiriana* therefore tend not to be the birds' first choice.

◁ **SORBUS CASHMIRIANA** *Sorbus like this pretty Kashmir rowan are easy to raise from seed. Simply squash the ripe berries, extract their seed and sow into pots. Cover lightly with grit and set them outdoors to germinate.*

Koelreuteria paniculata ♀
Golden rain tree, Pride of India
☼ ❋ ❋ ❋ ◯ **H/S** 9m / 30ft

The chief features of this excellent tree are its fine, pinnate foliage and the panicles of yellow flowers produced in summer, followed later by the pink-flushed, bladder-like fruit capsules. Yellow leaf tints provide its finale for the year. This Chinese native can be tricky to establish, but thrives on a fertile, loamy soil and, given plenty of sun, it will flower and fruit even when young.

Malus 'John Downie' ♀
Crab apple
☼ ❋ ❋ ❋ ◯ **H** 7.5m / 25ft **S** 5m / 16ft

Clusters of the luminous orange and red fruits of this tree appearing against a blue, late-summer sky is one of my favourite sights as the season draws to a close. These oval crab apples are edible and can be used to make jelly. There is also a good display of white blossom, opening from pink buds during late spring. The crab apple thrives in any fertile, well-drained soil.

Mespilus germanica
Medlar
☼ ☼ ❋ ❋ ❋ ◯ **H** 6m / 20ft **S** 8m / 26ft

This tree of great character blooms in early summer, producing a sprinkling of large, solitary white flowers. These are followed by distinctive brown fruits

Malus 'John Downie'

that make a good jelly but can be eaten raw only when left until half-rotten. Trees generally take on a low, gnarled shape and often bear spines on their mature branches.

Prunus insititia 'Prune Damson'
Damson
☼ ❋ ❋ ❋ ◯ **H/S** 3–6m / 10–20ft

White spring blossom and good crops of oval, blue-black fruits are features of this damson. The greeny yellow-fleshed fruits are superb in tarts and jams. Damsons are robust and grow well on most soils, including poor ones.

Sorbus cashmiriana ♀
Kashmir rowan
☼ ☼ ❋ ❋ ❋ ◯ **H/S** 6m / 20ft

In contrast to its size and daintiness, this tree bears comparatively large heads of pink-flushed flowers in late spring. By autumn, these have developed into beautiful white fruits. Birds are not fond of these, so they are usually left, hanging by red stalks, long after the leaves have fallen. Plant in moist, well-drained soil.

KEY: ♀ *Award of Merit* ☼ *sun* ☼ *semi-shade* ☀ *shade* ❋ *half-hardy* ❋ ❋ *frost-hardy* ❋ ❋ ❋ *fully hardy* ◯ *deciduous* ● *evergreen* ◑ *semi-evergreen* **H** *height* **S** *spread*

Flowering and fruiting hedges

The leafy backdrop created by a good hedge makes a pleasing boundary. Hedges also play a role as living screens and dividers within gardens, with their good looks and natural appearance. As well as acting as barriers, hedges filter noise and wind and can be used to obscure unsightly views. To match the style of a garden, choose plants carefully, taking into account their size and whether a formal or informal hedge will suit the design. Heights and spreads are given for the plants when grown (and clipped) as a hedge.

94

Berberis x *stenophylla* ♔
Barberry

☼ ☼ ❄ ❄ ❄ ◗

H 1.2–1.8m /4–6ft **S** 75–90cm /2ft 6in–3ft

This evergreen hybrid makes a dense, spiny, virtually impenetrable hedge of generally formal appearance. Arching shoots bear golden-yellow flowers in spring, followed by purple berries that are often removed by trimming. Plant in autumn or early spring, 50cm (20in) apart, immediately pruning off the top quarter of growth to promote bushiness. Trim annually after flowering.

Cotoneaster simonsii ♔

☼ ❄ ❄ ❄ ◗ **H** 1.2–1.5m /4–5ft **S** 90cm /3ft

Choose this cotoneaster for an informal, semi-evergreen hedge decorated with bright orange-red berries as the leaves turn red in autumn. There is a display of pink-tinged, white flowers in early summer. Plant from autumn to spring, setting them 35cm (14in) apart. If possible, use secateurs to prune back long stems after flowering, leaving developing berry clusters. Tidy up again during late summer and autumn.

Escallonia 'Apple Blossom' ♔

☼ ❄ ❄ ◗ **H** 1.5m /5ft **S** 90cm /3ft

Although escallonias are slightly tender, they make good, dense hedges of quite formal appearance in sheltered areas. Being salt-tolerant, they thrive near mild coastlines. The glossy, evergreen leaves of this variety are joined by pale pink flowers during summer. E. 'Langleyensis' ♔ is hardier and a good dark pink. Plant in spring or autumn, 45cm (18in) apart. Trim the top third back after planting to encourage bushiness. Prune lightly after flowering.

Forsythia x *intermedia* 'Lynwood' ♔

☼ ❄ ❄ ❄ ⟳ **H** 2.5m /8ft **S** 90cm–1.2m /3–4ft

Forsythias form rather gangly, informal hedges but they certainly make their presence felt in spring when smothered with bright yellow flowers. Their ability to thrive almost everywhere has ensured them great popularity. Plant in the autumn at 45cm (18in) intervals, pruning by one third to promote growth. Remove older stems after flowering.

Garrya elliptica
Silk tassel bush

☼ ☼ ❄ ❄ ◗

H 1.5–2.2m /5–7ft **S** 90cm /3ft

Choose this evergreen for a stylish informal hedge. Set against a backdrop of leathery, grey-green leaves from winter to spring is a display of beautiful, pale green catkins. Males (the showiest) and females are

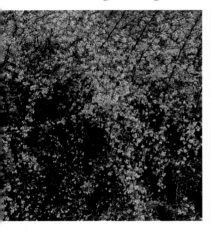

Berberis x *stenophylla*

Forsythia x *intermedia* 'Lynwood'

Garrya elliptica

• *see also:* HEDGES AS BOUNDARIES AND FEATURES p30; PLANTING A HEDGE, p198; TRIMMING HEDGES p200

◁ ROSA RUGOSA

The hedgehog rose should not be dead-headed as this would rob the garden of its plump hips which are such a welcome feature in late summer and into autumn.

borne on separate plants, so it pays to select a male clone like 'James Roof' ⚘, whose silvery catkins are 20cm (8in) long. Plant 45cm (18in) apart in autumn or spring and prune hedges back with secateurs after the tassels have faded.

Osmanthus x burkwoodii ⚘
☼ ◐ ❋ ❋ ❋ ♠

H 1.5–1.8m /5–6ft **S** 75–90cm /2ft 6in–3ft

A neat but informal hedge of glossy, dark green leaves sprinkled liberally with clusters of small, white, sweetly-scented flowers in spring. Plant 45cm (18in) apart during winter, trimming any spreading plants back by up to one third in spring to encourage a bushy shape. Tackle regular pruning after flowering in late spring.

Pyracantha 'Watereri' ⚘
Firethorn
☼ ◐ ❋ ❋ ❋ ♠

H 2–2.5m /6–8ft **S** 75–90cm /2ft 6in–3ft

This glossy-leaved shrub will make a good informal hedge; it bears clusters of small white flowers in spring and bright red berries during late summer and autumn. Tough and reliable, it grows well on most soils but can be susceptible to fireblight. Plant 60cm (2ft) apart between autumn and spring. Prune carefully after flowering, leaving the developing berries to ripen.

Ribes sanguineum 'Pulborough Scarlet' ⚘
Flowering currant
☼ ❋ ❋ ❋ ❋ ⟲ **H** 1.5–1.8m /5–6ft **S** 90cm–1.2m /3–4ft

Despite their somewhat acrid smell, flowering currants make splendid informal floriferous hedges in spring. This cultivar bears racemes of red flowers, but there are those with white (*R.s.* 'Tydeman's White' ⚘), pink and pale pink blooms. Set young plants 45cm (18in) apart from autumn to spring and prune back directly after flowering.

Rosa rugosa
Hedgehog rose
☼ ❋ ❋ ❋ ❋ ⟲ **H** 1.5m /5ft **S** 1.2m /4ft

Choose this rose to make a delightful informal hedge for the boundary of a large garden. Its growth may be a little unruly, but the fragrant, single, pinkish-red roses, followed by a display of bold hips, more than compensate for it. Look for white-flowered *R.r.* 'Alba' ⚘ and strongly scented, purple-red, double-flowered *R.* 'Roseraie de l'Häy' ⚘. Plant 45cm (18in) apart from autumn to spring and prune in early spring by removing weak and unwanted growth.

Rosmarinus officinalis
Rosemary
☼ ❋ ❋ ❋ ❋ ♠

H 1.3–1.5m /4–5ft **S** 75–90cm /2ft 6in–3ft

Rosemary makes a fragrant and beautiful informal hedge, and will even produce some flowers during mild spells in winter. The flowers vary from purple-blue to white and contrast well with the needle-like, grey-green leaves. The habit of this shrub is naturally upright, but to accentuate this, choose *R.o.* 'Miss Jessopp's Upright' ⚘. Plant 38cm (15in) apart in spring or autumn and prune during midsummer.

THORNY BOUNDARIES
❖

Some gardens need a tough, impenetrable, thorny barrier. Hedges have a lot to offer here, as many hedging plants are armed with spines or thorns. There are instances where a fence or wall might seem tame by comparison with a hedge of berberis, holly, rose, hawthorn or even *Poncirus trifoliata*. The latter is the Japanese bitter orange often used as a stock for cultivated orange and lemon varieties; it will make a deciduous hedge, around 1.5m (5ft) tall, of rigid green shoots armed with vicious spines; fragrant white flowers are followed by small, inedible, orange-like fruit.

Foliage and dwarf hedges

Hedges that are vital for privacy and screening tend to have a dense, leafy nature. Conifers are often the first choice because some species have rapid growth rates and, when well cared for and trimmed regularly from the start, will make quick, reliable living barriers. There is also often a need for low-growing hedges composed of dwarf plants that can be used most effectively to provide a neat edging for garden paths and beds.

Taxus baccata

96

Buxus sempervirens ♀
Box
☼ ◐ ❋ ❋ ❋ ❧

H 30cm–1.2m / 1–4ft **S** 23–45cm / 9–18in

To create formal enclosures for informal planting schemes, box is virtually unsurpassable. The neat, dense hedges, with their distinct aroma, fit neatly into small and large gardens alike. For the best compact hedges, the slower-growing *B.s.* 'Suffruticosa' ♀ is preferred. Space 25cm (10in) apart in spring or autumn. Clip two to three times during the growing season as necessary, or once in midsummer.

Chamaecyparis lawsoniana 'Pembury Blue' ♀
Lawson cypress
☼ ❋ ❋ ❋ ❧

H 1.5–3m / 5–10ft **S** 75–90cm / 2ft 6in–3ft

The gently draping sprays of blue-grey foliage make this quick-growing conifer ideal for bringing both colour and texture to a garden. The result will be a classy, formal hedge. Use on its own or mix with similar conifers of slightly different colour for a less strictly formal effect. Plant 50cm (20in) apart from autumn to spring. Trim in early summer and again in early autumn, but never cut into old wood.

X Cupressocyparis leylandii 'Robinson's Gold' ♀
Leyland cypress
☼ ◐ ❋ ❋ ❋ ❧

H 1.8–3.7m / 6–12ft **S** 75–90cm / 2ft 6in–3ft

Use a formal golden hedge as a contrast to a plain green backdrop. This choice, quick-growing conifer bears bronze-yellow foliage in spring, changing to gold and lime green as it matures. Plant 60cm (2ft) apart in spring. For neat

---

MIXED HEDGES

❖

In an open, rural setting where a garden is surrounded by fields and wild places, a natural-looking hedge is most appropriate. Choose a mixture of any of the following for an attractive, wildlife-friendly and productive hedge: *Prunus spinosa* (sloe or blackthorn), *Prunus insititia* (bullace), *Crataegus monogyna* (hawthorn or May), *Corylus avellana* (hazelnut), *Acer campestre* ♀ (field maple), *Sorbus aria* (whitebeam), *Salix caprea* (pussy willow), *Rosa rubiginosa* (sweet briar), *Sambucus nigra* (elder) and *Viburnum lantana* (wayfaring tree). Plant and prune when young, setting plants about 45–60cm (18–24in) apart, add a few native honeysuckle or woodbine and stand back.

---

conifer hedges, remove tops when the desired height is reached and trim two to three times a growing season, ending in autumn. Never cut into old wood.

Fagus sylvatica ♀
Beech
☼ ◐ ❋ ❋ ❋ ♡

H 1.2–6m / 4–20ft **S** 75–90cm / 30–36in

Apart from the six weeks during spring when it drops its leaves, beech is a superb formal hedge. Making a solid wall of bronze-tinged, lime green new growth against a deep green background, the leaves then turn russet in autumn and hang in place all winter. For purple foliage, choose *F.s.* 'Riversii' ♀. Tolerates chalk well. Plant from autumn to spring 45cm (18in) apart. Clip in late summer.

Ilex aquifolium ♀
Holly
☼ ◐ ❋ ❋ ❋ ❧ **H** 1.5–3m / 5–10ft **S** 90cm / 36in

Holly makes a smart, formal evergreen barrier. Red berries form on female plants when males are grown in proximity for pollination. One of the best variegated cultivars for hedges is *I.a.* 'Argentea Marginata' ♀. This female type has spiny leaves marked with broad white margins. Plant in spring or autumn 45cm (18in) apart. Trim in summer.

• *see also:* HEDGES AS BOUNDARIES AND FEATURES p30; PLANTING A HEDGE, p198; TRIMMING HEDGES p200

◁ **LAVANDULA ANGUSTIFOLIA** *Lavender makes a firm and fragrant edging. For unity, choose plants of a single cultivar.*

Taxus baccata ♔
Yew
☼ ☀ ✳ ✳ ✳ ● **H** 1.2–3.7m/4–12ft **S** 60–90cm/2–3ft

Among the classiest of hedges, yew is sometimes by-passed in favour of faster-growing conifers. It cannot keep pace with the cypresses but grows very quickly when well cared for. There are golden forms as well as dark green. Set plants 45cm (18in) apart in spring or autumn. Trim twice, in summer and autumn. Yew will re-generate from old wood if severe pruning proves necessary.

Thuja plicata
Western red cedar
☼ ✳ ✳ ✳ ● **H** 1.5–3m/5–10ft **S** 75–90cm/30–36in

The scale-like leaves of this conifer are glossy on the surface but greyish beneath, offering attractive contrast in a formal hedge. Its growth rate is faster than yew, but slower than cypress. Dark green *T.p.* 'Atrovirens' ♔ is a good choice for hedging. Choose a sheltered location to plant 50cm (20in) apart in spring or autumn. Trim during late summer.

Lavandula angustifolia 'Hidcote' ♔
Lavender
☼ ✳ ✳ ✳ ● **H** 45–60cm/18–24in **S** 30cm/12in

For a low, informal hedge, covered in purple flowers in summer, choose aromatic lavender. The flowers attract bees and this hedge makes an ideal edging for a herb garden or potager. An alternative to buying lots of small plants is to sow seed of a low-growing mixture, though the resulting plants will vary. Space 23–30cm/9–12in apart. Clip lightly after flowering and in spring.

Prunus laurocerasus ♔
Cherry laurel
☼ ☀ ✳ ✳ ✳ ● **H** 1.8–3m/6–10ft **S** 90cm/3ft

Choose laurel with its large, glossy leaves for a handsome formal or informal evergreen hedge. Racemes of white spring flowers are followed by red, cherry-like fruits if clipping has not been too severe. A good hedge to plant under trees. *P.l.* 'Rotundifolia' and *P. lusitanica* ♔ (Portuguese laurel) are worthy options. Set young plants 75–90cm/2ft 6in–3ft apart in autumn or spring. Trim with secateurs in spring or summer.

Rosa 'The Fairy' ♔
☼ ✳ ✳ ✳ ✿ ● **H/S** 60–90cm/2–3ft

Although low and spreading in habit, this useful Dwarf Polyantha rose, with small, neat foliage, can be used to create an attractive informal hedge around a pond, or to divide one part of the garden from another. Clusters of small, soft pink but scentless flowers open from summer to autumn. Its low, arching growth knits together well to provide a strong garden feature, which becomes completely smothered in blooms. Plant 75cm (30in) apart between autumn and spring. Prune to tidy in early spring.

Buxus sempervirens   *Fagus sylvatica*   *Prunus laurocerasus*

KEY: ♔ *Award of Merit* ☼ *sun* ☀ *semi-shade* ✿ *shade* ✳ *half-hardy* ✳✳ *frost-hardy* ✳✳✳ *fully hardy* ✿ *deciduous* ● *evergreen* ✿ *semi-evergreen* **H** *height* **S** *spread*

Shrubs for small gardens

There is a limit to the number of shrubs that can be squeezed into a small garden. Although one or two larger shrubs may be used for impact, those with a compact shape coupled with a long season of interest and usefulness as ground cover are more important. Repetition works well visually and most shrubs are easy to propagate by summer cuttings.

Caryopteris x *clandonensis* 'Heavenly Blue'

98

Brachyglottis 'Drysdale'

☼ ❄❄❄ ● **H** 90cm /3ft **S** 1.2m /4ft

An invaluable evergreen shrub bearing closely felted, grey-green leaves with white undersides and scalloped margins; the bright yellow, daisy-like flowers appear from midsummer through to early autumn. Both this and B. 'Sunshine' look great in association with purple flowers. To retain the compact shape of these shrubs, prune annually after flowering, cutting back the flowered stems to strong new shoots lower down and prune out any frost-damaged growths in spring. Thrives in any well-drained soil.

Caryopteris x clandonensis 'Heavenly Blue' ♀

☼ ❄❄❄ ○ **H** 90cm /3ft **S** 90–120cm /3–4ft

The dark blue flowers of this shrub make a lovely contrast with its grey-green, aromatic leaves. The fluffy flowers are produced from late summer to early autumn, when most other shrubs have retired from centre-stage, making it doubly welcome. Plant in well-drained, light soil and prune annually in early spring, cutting down all the previous year's flowered stems to within short spurs of the woody framework.

Ceratostigma willmottianum ♀ Hardy plumbago

☼ ❄❄❄ ○ **H** 90cm /3ft **S** 90–150cm /3–5ft

Resembling a plumbago, this valuable shrub blooms from late summer to early autumn and continues with an autumn display of red-tinted foliage. Once established, it is reliably hardy although the new shoots are prone to frost-damage. For the best results, cut back the previous year's flower stems to strong, lower growths in early spring.

Daphne odora 'Aureomarginata'

☼ ☼ ❄❄ ● **H** 1.2m /4ft **S** 90–150cm /3–5ft

When its clusters of pink and white flowers open between midwinter and early spring, this daphne is one of my favourite small shrubs. The leaves are edged with gold and the perfume from

---

BUYING SHRUBS

❖

- Check the label to make sure the plant's dimensions will fit into a small garden and earn its keep.

- Do not be seduced by flowers on a shrub; look for a well-shaped plant with plenty of healthy shoots.

- Examine both pot and compost. The plant should be well established, neither isolated in a mass of compost, nor pot-bound, with many roots growing from the bottom of the pot.

- Expect the foliage to look healthy. Signs of wilting and damaged leaves could indicate root problems caused by drying out or clumsy watering, so do not buy.

Ceratostigma willmottianum

Exochorda x *macrantha* 'The Bride'

• *see also:* EVERGREEN SHRUBS FOR YEAR-ROUND INTEREST p100; PLANTING AND MOVING SHRUBS p204; PROPAGATING BY CUTTINGS p232

△ DAPHNE ODORA 'AUREOMARGINATA' *The pale pink flowers of this evergreen daphne emit a sweet fragrance which carries far on a warm, still day.*

99

the flowers, particularly on sunny days, is thrown out and carried on the air. To keep plants strong and healthy, mulch annually with well-rotted organic matter and protect from frost.

Exochorda × macrantha 'The Bride' ♀
Pearl bush

☼ ❄ ❄ ❄ ♡ **H/S** 1.2–1.8m/4–6ft

There are few small, white-flowered shrubs to rival this one. In late spring it is laden with masses of large flowers on arching branches and blends well with other plants in mixed borders. Prune annually by removing about a fifth of the oldest branches immediately after flowering, cutting out those stems which have just flowered back to strong, lower-growing shoots.

Lavandula stoechas subsp. pedunculata ♀
French lavender

☼ ❄ ❄ ❄ ● **H/S** 45–60cm/18–24in

The grey-green leaves of this plant are the perfect foil for a late spring to midsummer display of dark purple flower spikes topped by bright purple

bracts that look just like rabbits' ears. Its fragrance is unlike the familiar smell of more traditional lavenders. The hardiness of these plants depends on being planted in well-drained soil. Cut back spent flower stems after flowering.

Pittosporum tenuifolium 'Tom Thumb' ♀

☼ ❄ ❄ ❄ ● **H/S** 90cm/3ft

One of the hardiest of all the pittosporums, this outstanding dwarf evergreen bears bronze-flushed foliage during spring and summer, which turns a shiny purple-red in winter; small sprigs are useful for flower arranging. The dense, rounded shape can be used, like box, in a structural role. Plant in a sheltered spot. Pruning is not usually necessary.

Ribes sanguineum 'Brocklebankii' ♀
Flowering currant

☼ ❄ ❄ ❄ ♡✿ **H/S** 90–120cm/3–4ft

This fine shrub will light up a summer border with its acid yellow-green foliage. Some find its bright pink spring flowers a little brash, but they make only a fleeting appearance.

It thrives on most soils. Prune after flowering by cutting straggly stems back to strong, low shoots.

Skimmia japonica 'Rubella' ♀

☼ ☼ ❄ ❄ ❄ ● **H/S** 1.2m/4ft

This neat plant features dark red buds, borne all winter, which burst into fragrant, pink-tinged white flowers in spring. Being a male skimmia, this clone will not produce berries, but it can act as a pollinator for female plants. Avoid yellowing, chlorotic leaves by enriching a well-drained soil with well-rotted organic matter and keeping plants out of full sun.

Viburnum tinus 'Eve Price' ♀
Laurustinus

☼ ☼ ❄ ❄ ❄ ● **H/S** 1.5–2.2m/5–7ft

Valuable for its shade tolerance, this compact, floriferous evergreen produces heads of pink buds opening to white flowers from late winter into spring. At other times of year its dark green foliage creates a good backdrop for other plants. Place in a sheltered spot away from wind.

Evergreen shrubs for year-round interest

We use our gardens less during winter yet we still need to preserve an interesting outlook. To do this effectively, half to two-thirds of your shrubs should be evergreen. Include shrubs with a variety of different leaf colours and textures as well as good flowering shrubs and the effect will never be gloomy.

Drimys lanceolata

100

Aucuba japonica
Himalayan laurel, Spotted laurel

☼ ☀ ☀ ✿ ❄ ❄ ❄ ● **H/S** 1.8–2.5m/6–8ft

The best spotted form of the tough aucubas is *A.j.* 'Crotonifolia' ♀, a female form liberally speckled with yellow on bright green. However, to brighten a gloomy corner, opt for *A.j.* 'Picturata', a male whose leaves boast a central splash of gold. Though it has a tendency to revert, it does not take much effort to cut away green shoots as they appear.

Choisya ternata Sundance ♀
Golden Mexican orange blossom

☼ ☀ ❄ ❄ ❄ ●

H 1.5m/5ft **S** 1.2–1.5m/4–5ft

This popular shrub deserves inclusion for its marvellous shining yellow foliage,

Aucuba japonica 'Picturata'

guaranteed to draw the eye. Despite this, I still prefer the plain-leaved *Choisya ternata*, for the contrast between its rich green leaves and its white, scented blossom in spring and late summer. Flowers are scarce on the golden form. Both will thrive in alkaline soil.

Cupressus macrocarpa
'Golden Pillar'
Golden Monterey cypress

☼ ❄ ❄ ❄ ❄ ● **H** 3–4.5m/10–15ft **S** 1.8–3m/6–10ft

I usually avoid the Monterey cypress on account of its thug-like tendency to grow fast and tall, but this cultivar is different. Its bright, golden-yellow foliage is stunning all year round and becomes a great asset to any border. It looks good planted next to green-, blue- and grey-leaved plants.

VARIEGATED YEAR-ROUND EVERGREENS

❖

Elaeagnus x ebbingei 'Gilt Edge' ♀
Euonymus japonicus
'Ovatus Aureus' ♀
Ilex aquifolium 'Ferox Argentea' (holly)♀
Myrtus communis 'Variegata' (myrtle)
Pittosporum tenuifolium
'Irene Paterson' ♀

Drimys lanceolata
Mountain pepper

☼ ❄ ❄ ❄ ● **H** 2.5m/8ft **S** 1.8m/6ft

One of my favourite evergreens, this shrub seems to perform better in a cool, sheltered, lightly shaded spot than in full light. My plant has made a compact, loosely conical shape, 1.5m (5ft) tall, over a period of seven years. Dark red stems bear slender, sweetly aromatic, bright green young foliage and darker old leaves with pale undersides. They are joined by clusters of creamy-white flowers in late spring. Mulch with well-rotted leafmould in late winter. Hardy to -12°C (10°F).

Elaeagnus pungens 'Maculata' ♀

☼ ❄ ❄ ❄ ❄ ● **H/S** 2.5–3.7m/8–12ft

The winter garden would not be complete without a specimen of this tried and tested evergreen. Its leaves are gilded by an irregular central splash of golden yellow, leaving two tones of green around the outside. The undersides are pale and silvery, while the stems and midribs are metallic bronze-gold. Snip out any plain green shoots as and when they occur. Elaeagnus is a particularly useful shrub for seaside gardens as it will tolerate coastal winds.

• *see also:* SHRUBS FOR SMALL GARDENS p98; SHRUBS FOR SPRING/SUMMER/AUTUMN/WINTER COLOUR pp102–109; PLANTING AND MOVING SHRUBS p204

◁ **CUPRESSUS MACROCARPA** *'GOLDEN PILLAR' has been enlivened for summer by training a climbing Ipomoea lobata through it.*

that spray out attractively. Cut out older stems of large shrubs after flowering.

Nandina domestica ♈
Heavenly bamboo
☼ ☀ ❋ ❋ ❋ ❦

H 1.2–1.8m/4–6ft   **S** 90–150cm/3–5ft

The elegant shape and foliage of this neat, bamboo-like shrub are joined by panicles of white flowers in midsummer. Young leaves are a glowing red and the older foliage takes on a bright reddish-purple hue in winter. Red fruits form, which turn black: for the best fruit, choose *N.d.* 'Richmond'. This shrub needs shelter from cold winds and a well-drained soil to preserve its hardiness.

Photinia x fraseri 'Red Robin' ♈
☼ ☀ ❋ ❋ ❦   **H/S** 3–4.5m/10–15ft

Choose this handsome shrub for its pliable stems of long, leathery leaves, which start off a brilliant bronze-red when young. It makes a good alternative to pieris where the soil is not acid

Photinia × fraseri 'Red Robin'

SMALL OR LARGE?
❖

Whether you are planting the entire garden from scratch or trying to establish the shrubby backbone of a border, it is tempting to buy time by buying big. One disadvantage is that prices rise in direct proportion to the length of time it took the nursery to grow the plant on. And shrubs that have become used to container-growing usually establish less well than smaller plants whose young roots develop more naturally in open soil. Buying young is more economical too.

enough. Suits most soils, but site well away from frost pockets as new shoots can be damaged by late frosts. Responds well to pruning if size needs restricting.

Rhamnus alaternus 'Argenteovariegata' ♈
Variegated Italian buckthorn
☼ ☀ ❋ ❋ ❋ ❦

H 1.8–4.5m/6–15ft   **S** 1.8–3m/6–10ft

Some evergreens can be overbearing but the small, silvery leaves of this rhamnus ensure a delicate effect to brighten up sheltered corners. Dark stems of grey-green leaves have silvery-white margins and can be trained up sunny walls or clipped into rounded shapes.

Rhamnus alaternus 'Argenteovariegata'

101

Lonicera nitida 'Baggesen's Gold' ♈
☼ ☀ ❋ ❋ ❋ ❦   **H/S** 1.5m/5ft

This common shrub provides a welcome splash of gold all year and is easy to grow in most gardens. Long shoots bearing neat, oval leaves arch over each other like a golden waterfall. The small leaves create a texture that is usefully juxtaposed against large-leaved shrubs; the foliage can become bleached in full sun. May be grown as a low hedge.

Mahonia x media 'Charity' ♈
☼ ☀ ❋ ❋ ❋ ❦   **H/S** 2.2–3.7m/7–12ft

Any tall, evergreen, architectural shrub that flowers in winter is worth its weight in gold. The leaves of mahonia are about 60cm (2ft) long, comprising many dark green, spiny leaflets. From late autumn to late winter it bears erect racemes of slightly scented, deep yellow flowers

Shrubs for spring colour

Spring is such an eagerly awaited season that it makes sense to plant for an early show, to create as long and as lively a season of colour and perfume as possible. Place shrubs for spring interest at intervals around your garden, underplanted with groups of bulbs and spring-flowering herbaceous perennials.

102

Berberis × lologensis 'Apricot Queen'

Berberis × lologensis 'Apricot Queen' ♀
☼ ☼ ❋ ❋ ❋ ❧ **H/S** 2.5–3m /8–10ft

In late spring, the arching stems of this colourful shrub are packed with beautiful, clear apricot-orange flowers; it often produces a secondary flush of bloom in summer. The small, dark, glossy leaves are armed with spines, making it an ideal deterrent. Prune, if necessary, after flowering.

Ceanothus 'Puget Blue' ♀
Californian lilac
☼ ❋ ❋ ❋ ❧ **H/S** 2.5–3m /8–10ft

The small, dark green leaves alone make this an attractive plant. By late spring and early summer, when it is smothered with masses of small, deep blue flowers, it becomes spectacular. Plant in the shelter of a warm wall or fence to give protection from the worst of the winter weather. Suits most soils; trim after flowering if needed.

Euphorbia characias ♀
☼ ❋ ❋ ❋ ❧ **H** 1.2m /4ft **S** 90–120cm /3–4ft

Stems resembling dense tails and furnished with long leaves are decorated from early spring to early summer by cylindrical heads of lime-green 'flowers', consisting mainly of bracts. I like the dark centres of this species, although the acid-yellow colouring of *E.c.* ssp. *wulfenii* ♀ is exceptionally fine. After flowering, it pays to cut the spent flower stems to within 15cm (6in) of the ground. This retains vigour and keeps the foliage fresh. Bear in mind that the milky sap of this plant can cause skin irritation.

× *Ledodendron* 'Arctic Tern' ♀
☼ ❋ ❋ ❋ ❧ **H/S** 60cm /24in

Take a close look at this cross between a rhododendron and a ledum, to appreciate its sinuous branches covered with smooth, pale brown bark. Neat foliage is present year-round, but the

Ceanothus 'Puget Blue'

small shrub comes alive with a mass of pure white blooms in spring. Provide an acid, humus-rich soil and find time to dead-head after flowering.

Magnolia stellata 'Waterlily' ♀
Star magnolia
☼ ❋ ❋ ❋ ❋ ○ **H** 2.5m /8ft **S** 3m /10ft

Opening before the foliage, the white flowers of this cultivar are up to 13cm (5in) wide and packed with as many as 32 petals. Guaranteed to turn heads, this shrub will form the main attraction of a spring border. Young plants begin bushy but expand with age, so make provision for this when planting. Tolerates most soils, including alkaline, but appreciates moisture and organic matter.

Rhododendron luteum ♀
Common yellow azalea
☼ ❋ ❋ ❋ ❋ ○ **H/S** 2–3m /6–10ft

Choose this azalea for its cheerful, sweetly perfumed yellow flowers, which herald warm weather by blooming in late spring and early summer. There is another display in autumn when the leaves turn crimson, purple and orange before falling. With its informal habit, this shrub lends itself to a wilder corner of the garden, where it could perhaps be underplanted with bluebells. It must have an acid soil.

• **see also:** SHRUBS FOR SMALL GARDENS p98; EVERGREEN SHRUBS FOR YEAR-ROUND INTEREST p100; PLANTING AND MOVING SHRUBS p204; PROPAGATING BY CUTTINGS p232

△ **BOLD CLUMPS OF** Euphorbia characias *subsp.* wulfenii *'John Tomlinson' bear acid-yellow flowerheads that show up well against the darker foliage.*

SCENTED SPRING-FLOWERING SHRUBS

❖

Corylopsis pauciflora ♀ ♂

Cytisus × praecox 'Warminster' ♀ ♂

Daphne × burkwoodii 'Somerset' ❧

Daphne laureola ♠

Erica arborea var. *alpina* ♀ ♠

Fothergilla gardenii ♂

Magnolia liliiflora 'Nigra' ♀ ♂

Osmanthus × burkwoodii ♀ ♠

Rhododendron mucronatum ❧

103

Rhododendron yunnanense
☼ ◐ ❄ ❄ ❄ ❧♂ **H** 4.5m/15ft **S** 3m/10ft

Although this delightful rhododendron is hardly compact, I would choose it if my soil were acid enough. I have seen its variable white, pale pink or dark pink flowers with pretty, spotted throats laugh at late frosts that have devastated every other rhododendron in the same garden. Select a plant in bloom to be sure of picking a specific colour and plan a pretty, wild corner around it. Like most of its tribe, it prefers an area of cool atmosphere and high rainfall and must have an acid soil.

Stachyurus praecox ♀
☼ ◐ ❄ ❄ ❄ ♂ **H/S** 1.5–2.5m/5–8ft

This Japanese native makes a strong feature in late winter and early spring, when its reddish-brown branches are strung with hanging racemes of small, greenish-yellow, bell-shaped flowers, like exotic catkins. These form during autumn and wait all winter on the plant. Prefers an acid, humus-rich soil, yet tolerates

lime in the soil; dig in plenty of leafmould or well-rotted compost before planting.

Syringa vulgaris 'Congo'
Lilac
☼ ❄ ❄ ❄ ♂ **H** 4.5m/15ft **S** 4m/12ft

Wandering around a late-spring garden during dusk would not be the same without the scent of lilac. There are many cultivars with single and double flowers, in light or dark colours, from which to choose. This form dates from 1896 and makes a compact plant with deep purple buds opening to large

heads of single, intensely lilac-purple flowers. Restrict the size by shortening older stems after flowering.

Viburnum carlesii 'Diana'
☼ ◐ ❄ ❄ ❄ ♂ **H/S** 1.8m/6ft

With fresh, newly opened spring foliage as a foil, the pink flowerheads open from red buds, then fade to white. The sweet fragrance lingers in the air and is guaranteed to turn heads. The leaves, bronze-tinged when young, spend the summer as a green backdrop for other plants, then can show some reddish tints during autumn.

Magnolia liliiflora 'Nigra'   *Rhododendron cv.*   *Stachyurus praecox*

KEY: ♀ *Award of Merit* ☼ *sun* ◐ *semi-shade* ● *shade* ❄ *half-hardy* ❄❄ *frost-hardy* ❄❄❄ *fully hardy* ♂ *deciduous* ♠ *evergreen* ❧ *semi-evergreen* **H** *height* **S** *spread*

Shrubs for summer colour

With good planning, there can be a succession of colourful and interesting flowering shrubs performing from early summer to autumn. Once established, they are largely able to look after themselves, though most will benefit from an annual pruning. This improves flower quality, helps to control shape and size and can prolong the lives of otherwise short-lived shrubs.

Phygelius capensis

104

Buddleja × *weyeriana*

☼ ❄ ❄ ❄ ⟳ **H** 1.8–3.7m / 6–12ft **S** 1.5–3m / 5–10ft

Buddlejas are reliable summer flowerers and this one can be guaranteed to light up a fading border. Both the arching shoots and new leaves are felted with greyish hairs when young. The honey-scented yellow flowers are held in clusters towards the ends of shoots. *B.*x. 'Sungold' ♀ bears bright golden-yellow flowers. Control the plant's height by pruning hard every spring.

PRUNING BUDDLEJA
❖

Buddlejas like *B.* × *weyeriana* and *B. davidii* are usually cut back hard in early spring as the buds swell. Leave them taller for the backs of borders. An autumn pruning is an option in milder areas.

Deutzia × *rosea*

☼ ❄ ❄ ❄ ⟳ **H/S** 1.2m / 4ft

This rounded, compact shrub flowers beautifully in early summer, when the arching branches become covered with soft pink, star-shaped flowers that blend well with stronger pinks and purples. It is best placed towards the front of a shrub border. Prune immediately after flowering by cutting up to one fifth of the oldest branches down to ground level and cut flowered shoots back to lower buds.

Fabiana imbricata f. *violacea* ♀

☼ ❄ ❄ ❄ ◨ **H/S** 1.5–2.2m / 5–7ft

Although this unusual shrub resembles a giant heather, it belongs to the same family as potatoes, tomatoes and petunias. Its scale-like foliage is joined by a profusion of pale mauve, tubular

---

GOOD-VALUE
SUMMER COLOUR
❖

Ceanothus × *delileanus* 'Gloire de Versailles' ♀ ⟳

Cistus × *hybridus* ♀ ◨

Perovskia 'Blue Spire' ♀ ⟳

Potentilla fruticosa 'Elizabeth' ♀ ⟳

Weigela florida 'Foliis Purpureis' ♀ ⟳

---

flowers from early to midsummer. Provide shelter from wind and a well-drained soil. Leggy plants can be pruned back in spring, but cutting into old wood can be a gamble.

Fuchsia magellanica 'Versicolor' ♀

☼ ☼ ❄ ❄ ❄ ◨ **H/S** 90cm–1.2m / 3–4ft

Hardy fuchsias are easy to grow and bring useful colour to gardens during late summer. The superb foliage of this plant begins grey-green and white (or yellow), liberally flushed with purple-pink, and matures to a slatey green, irregularly edged with creamy white. The slim, tubular flowers are red and purple. Prune back frost-damaged stems in spring and remove any straggly branches. Will grow much larger in milder and coastal areas.

Hibiscus syriacus 'Red Heart' ♀

☼ ❄ ❄ ❄ ⟳ **H** 1.8–3m / 6–10ft **S** 1.2–1.8m / 4–6ft

Although slow-growing, a mature, hardy hibiscus in full bloom is a wonderful sight. Hibiscus are among the last shrubs to burst into growth in spring and they wait until late summer before producing their large, trumpet-shaped blooms. This cultivar bears dramatic white flowers, 6cm (2½in) across, with dark maroon centres. Good for chalky soils. Pruning is not usually needed.

• *see also:* SHRUBS FOR SMALL GARDENS p98; SHRUBS FOR SPRING/AUTUMN/WINTER COLOUR pp102–109; PLANTING AND MOVING SHRUBS p204

△ **FOR LASTING COLOUR** *choose shrubby mallows such as* Lavatera *'Rosea', which produces masses of flowers all summer long. It is seen here in a border with lavender and* Alchemilla mollis.

For best results, provide well-drained soil and shelter from cold winds. An annual hard pruning in early spring, to remove old growth, will rejuvenate a plant and help it to live longer.

Philadelphus 'Virginal' ♚
Mock orange
☼ ◐ ✳ ✳ ✳ ✿
H 2.5–3.7m /8–12ft **S** 1.8–2.5m /6–8ft

The deliciously sweet perfume of mock orange fills the early to midsummer air with fragrance. This form is vigorous and upright, bearing double flowers of purest white. Prune after flowering by removing a fifth of the oldest growths down to ground level. Cut flowered stems back to new, strong shoots lower down the stems.

Hydrangea serrata 'Bluebird' ♚
Blue lacecap hydrangea
☼ ◐ ✳ ✳ ✳ ✿ **H/S** 1.2m /4ft

Hydrangeas provide welcome late-summer colour and perform best when given a cool, moist root run and light shade. In classic lacecap fashion, a dome of blue fertile flowers forms a hazy centre surrounded by an abstract pattern of ray florets, which will vary in colour according to soil. On chalk, expect a reddish-purple tinge, while on acid soils they will be violet-blue. Prune by thinning or cutting back hard in spring.

Kolkwitzia amabilis
Beauty bush
☼ ✳ ✳ ✳ ✳ ✿
H 1.8–3m /6–10ft **S** 1.8–2.5m /6–8ft

Deep pink, tubular flowers with patterned, yellow throats smother the arching branches of this delightful shrub in early summer; look out for *K.a.* 'Pink Cloud' ♚, for its deep pink blooms. For the rest of the year it creates a leafy background. Easy to

please, the beauty bush tolerates a wide range of soils. Prune after flowering by shortening or removing up to a third of the flowered stems.

Lavatera 'Rosea' ♚
Tree mallow
☼ ✳ ✳ ✳ ✳ ✿ **H/S** 1.5–1.8m /5–6ft

For sheer long-standing, mid- to late summer flower power, this shrub is unbeatable; it is also easy to grow. Deep rosy-pink flowers 10cm (4in) across open profusely over grey-green leaves.

Phygelius x *rectus* 'Winchester Fanfare'
Cape figwort
☼ ✳ ✳ ✳ ✳ ✿ **H/S** 75cm–1.2m /30in–4ft

In common with other Cape figworts, this cultivar provides great summer colour and, given a well-drained soil, is easy to grow. The tubular flowers, an unusual shade of orange-pink, hang from the stems like inverted trumpets. The foliage will die back during severe winters, but re-grows in spring.

Hibiscus syriacus 'Red Heart'   *Hydrangea serrata* 'Bluebird'   *Kolkwitzia amabilis*

KEY: ♚ *Award of Merit* ☼ *sun* ◐ *semi-shade* ● *shade* ✳ *half-hardy* ✳✳ *frost-hardy* ✳✳✳ *fully hardy* ✿ *deciduous* ● *evergreen* ✿ *semi-evergreen* **H** *height* **S** *spread*

Shrubs for autumn colour

Autumn is a precious season, when the lowering rays of the sun seem especially designed to illuminate glorious autumn tints and voluptuous fruits. I like to savour the last warm days before the onset of winter and always plan for some seasonal surprises. Many shrubs perform during autumn as well as scoring high with spring or summer flowers.

Clerodendrum trichotomum

106

Calluna vulgaris 'Spook'
Ling, Scots heather

☼ ❋ ❋ ❋ ◗ **H** 45cm / 18in **S** 45–60cm / 18–24in

With its downy grey foliage, this ling has an ethereal quality enhanced by tall spikes of mauve flowers borne from late summer to early winter. The faded flowers remain of great value throughout winter, adding to its ghostly appearance, especially when shimmering with hoar frost. Shear off the dead flower stems in spring. Must have an acid soil.

Clerodendrum trichotomum var. *fargesii* ♀

☼ ❋ ❋ ❋ ♡ **H/S** 3.7–6m / 12–20ft

This is one of my favourite shrubs. After a slow start in spring, large, dark green leaves make a bold show. Sprays of scented, starry white flowers appear from pink-flushed sepals during late summer and autumn, developing into jewel-like, turquoise berries sitting on calyces that resemble shocking pink cushions. Plant in a sheltered spot. Pruning is not usually required.

Calluna vulgaris 'Spook'

Cotinus 'Flame' ♀
Smoke bush

☼ ◑ ❋ ❋ ❋ ♡

H 3.7–6m / 12–20ft **S** 3–4.5m / 10–15ft

The delights of this large shrub include the summer display of long, pink-tinged flower plumes, which seem to hover above the foliage like smoke. There are pyrotechnics from the foliage in autumn, as it turns from light green to brilliant red and orange. Plant in moist, well-drained soil which, for the best tints, should not be too fertile. Prune out unwanted branches after flowering.

Euonymus alatus ♀
Winged spindle

☼ ◑ ❋ ❋ ❋ ♡ **H/S** 1.8–2.5m / 6–8ft

This medium-sized shrub produces reliable autumn colour, even on alkaline soils, when the dark green leaves turn crimson-pink. Insignificant late spring flowers develop into round, reddish-purple fruit, some opening to reveal orange seeds. The leaves and fruits eventually fall to reveal stems with four cork-like wings running their length.

Fothergilla major ♀

☼ ◑ ❋ ❋ ❋ ♡

H 1.8–2.5m / 6–8ft **S** 1.2–1.8m / 4–6ft

Before the new leaves arrive in spring, this rounded shrub starts producing sweetly fragrant, white flower spikes that are largely composed of stamen-like little white bottlebrushes. During autumn the bold leaves, 10cm (4in) long, pass through a kaleidoscope of orange, yellow and red colours before they fall. Provide a moist, woodland-type acid soil, enriched with organic matter. Gentle pruning after flowering will keep the size down.

Fothergilla major

Hamamelis vernalis 'Sandra' ♀
Ozark witch hazel

☼ ◑ ❋ ❋ ❋ ♡ **H/S** 2.2m / 7ft

Small yellow flowers appear from late winter to early spring, but the main delights of this shrub lie in its magnificent foliage. The leaves are flushed with purple on emerging, but mature to green with purple undersides until the autumn, when they turn incredible colours of rich red, orange and yellow. It grows best in a neutral to acid soil but tolerates chalky soils better than most witch hazels. These plants are propagated commercially by grafting, which tends to make them expensive shrubs to buy.

• *see also:* SHRUBS FOR SMALL GARDENS p98; SHRUBS FOR SPRING/SUMMER/WINTER COLOUR pp102–109; PLANTING AND MOVING SHRUBS p204

Hydrangea paniculata 'Pink Diamond'

☼ ☀ ❄❄❄ ◯

H 1.8–3m / 6–10ft   **S** 1.5–2.2m / 5–7ft

The 30cm (12in) long, pink-flushed flower panicles blend well with other colours of the season and last from late summer right through autumn. For quality flowerheads, a drastic pruning in early spring is recommended, reducing last year's stems to within two or three buds of the previous season's wood; I prefer to thin out older stems every two to three years. Choose a sheltered spot on moist but well-drained soil, enriched with organic matter.

Rosa 'Geranium' (moyesii hybrid) ♔

☼ ❄❄❄ ◯ **H** 1.8–2.5m / 6–8ft **S** 1.5–2.2m / 5–7ft

In early summer, on arching branches, this shrubby rose produces bright red single flowers, 5cm (2in) across, with a boss of creamy yellow stamens in the middle. By autumn, these have matured into a lasting crop of elegant, flask-shaped, crimson-orange hips. For a good

Viburnum opulus

set of hips, plant in a moist soil that has been enriched with organic matter and mulch in late winter.

Staphylea pinnata **Bladdernut**

☼ ☀ ❄❄❄ ◯

H 3–4.5m / 10–15ft   **S** 1.8–2.7m / 6–9ft

This underrated shrub has a long season of interest, beginning in late spring with hanging clusters of scented white flowers tinged with pink. These develop into curious, green, bladder-like pods that hang like cocoons from the branches and turn a lovely silvery colour by

autumn. For a good set of pods, keep moist in summer. Untidy plants can be renovated by hard pruning in winter.

Viburnum opulus **Guelder rose**

☼ ☀ ❄❄❄ ◯

H 3.7–4.5m / 12–15ft   **S** 2.7–3.7m / 9–12ft

Heads of white lacecap-like flowers appear from late spring to early summer, followed by an autumnal display of opulent, shiny red fruits. At the same time, the maple-like leaves turn from dark green to their orange and red autumn colours. *V.o.* 'Compactum' ♔ suits smaller gardens; for yellow fruits, choose *V.o.* 'Xanthocarpum'. For best results, plant in a moist soil.

◁ **AUTUMN SURPRISES** *Shrubs like* Cotinus coggygria (left) *and* Rhus typhina *'Dissecta' (centre)* *ensure the garden ends its season with an explosion of colour instead of just fading out.*

PRUNING HEATHERS
❖

Having enjoyed the dried flowers of *Calluna vulgaris* 'Spook' throughout winter, it is time to shear back in spring. Clip over to remove all of the old flower spikes and help keep the plant compact.

107

Erica × *darleyensis* 'Silberschmelze'

Shrubs for winter colour

To be able to enjoy flowering shrubs and dazzling stem colours in the depths of winter is a triumph of good planting. Winter blooms tend to be smaller and paler than their summer rivals but they are often sweetly scented. Even when the weather is cold and unwelcoming, sprigs of flowers, and eventually whole sprays, from mature shrubs can be picked to enjoy indoors.

108

Abeliophyllum distichum
White forsythia
☼ ❅ ❅ ❅ ⚘ **H/S** 1.5m /5ft

This shrub is worth cosseting for its precious display of delicate, fragrant, slightly off-white flowers. Each bears four dainty petals that show up against the stark, leafless stems during late winter and early spring. Site in a sheltered position to protect the blooms from frost, preferably against a warm wall or fence to ripen the wood for flowering.

Acer pensylvanicum 'Erythrocladum' ♛
Moosewood, Striped maple
☼ ☼ ❅ ❅ ❅ ⚘ **H/S** 3–4.5m /10–15ft

This shrub is slow to mature but the wait is worthwhile. After the leaves have yellowed and fallen, young shrimp-pink shoots are revealed in all their splendour, maturing to orange-red with typical snakebark white stripes. Plant in a moist, fertile soil, apply controlled-release shrub fertilizer every spring and mulch annually.

Chimonanthus praecox
Wintersweet
☼ ❅ ❅ ❅ ⚘ **H** 2.5–3m /8–10ft **S** 1.8–2.5m /6–8ft

This desirable shrub demands patience, as it frequently takes around five years

to establish itself and start flowering. After that, each winter, the reward will be a display of deep yellow, pendent flowers, marked with maroon inside. The sweet, spicy fragrance wafts on the air. Plant where low rays of winter sun can illuminate the blooms.

Cornus sanguinea 'Midwinter Fire'
Dogwood
☼ ❅ ❅ ❅ ⚘ **H** 90–120cm /3–4ft **S** 90cm /3ft

This dogwood creeps into the limelight

STOOLING A CORNUS

Dogwoods like *Cornus sanguinea* 'Midwinter Fire', grown for its winter stems, need to be cut back in early spring. Remove the previous year's growth to within a short stump of older wood. The stems will then re-grow for next winter.

---

during autumn, when its leaves turn a delicate yellow flushed with pinkish-orange before falling quite late to reveal superb stem colours. Glowing orange-yellow stem bases become suffused with reddish-pink towards the tips. Prune all the stems right down to within a bud or two of the older wood at the base every spring.

Erica × *darleyensis* 'Silberschmelze'
Darley Dale heath
☼ ❅ ❅ ❅ ❧

H 30–38cm /12–15in **S** 45–60cm /18–24in

Winter-flowering heaths and heathers provide first-class flowering ground cover during the colder months. This one opens its white flowers in late autumn and blooms until spring. Both *E.* × *darleyensis*, *E. carnea* and their cultivars will tolerate virtually any soil, including alkaline, provided it is well-drained. Shear off spent flowers in early spring to encourage compact growth.

Hamamelis × *intermedia* 'Diane' ♛
Witch hazel
☼ ☼ ❅ ❅ ❅ ⚘ **H/S** 3–3.7m /10–12ft

With their spidery and fragrant yellow, orange or red flowers, witch hazels brighten up the garden during late winter. *H.* × *intermedia* 'Pallida' ♛ is

• *see also:* SHRUBS FOR SMALL GARDENS p98; SHRUBS FOR SPRING/SUMMER/AUTUMN COLOUR pp102–107; PLANTING AND MOVING SHRUBS p204

possibly the classiest and most sweetly fragrant, but 'Diane' bears interesting red flowers and the bonus of bright red and orange autumn tints. Plant in a moist, well-drained, neutral to acid soil.

Lonicera × purpusii 'Winter Beauty' ♔

☼ ☼ ✻ ✻ ✻ ◖◗ **H** 2m /6ft **S** 2.5m /8ft

It is possible to have a love/hate relationship with the winter-flowering honeysuckles. On one hand the pale, sweetly fragrant flowers borne in winter and early spring are delightful on the bushes and useful for vases. On the other hand, these climbers are ungainly and space-consuming in summer. They thrive well in most soils and, at most, need only an occasional thinning after flowering.

Rhododendron 'Olive' ♔

☼ ✻ ✻ ✻ ●

H 90–120cm /3–4ft **S** 75–90cm /30–36in

This early-flowering rhododendron opens its trusses of purple-pink flowers,

---

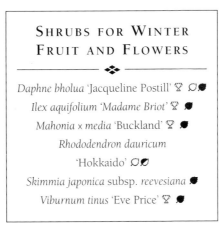

SHRUBS FOR WINTER FRUIT AND FLOWERS

❖

Daphne bholua 'Jacqueline Postill' ♔ ◖ ●
Ilex aquifolium 'Madame Briot' ♔ ●
Mahonia × *media* 'Buckland' ♔ ●
Rhododendron dauricum 'Hokkaido' ◖◗
Skimmia japonica subsp. *reevesiana* ●
Viburnum tinus 'Eve Price' ♔ ●

4cm (1½in) long and wide, in late winter against neat, shiny, dark green leaves. Plant shallowly in moist, well-drained acid soil, away from cold winds and early morning sun. Protect blooms against frost and dead-head straight after flowering. Mulch with leafmould.

Sarcococca hookeriana var. digyna ♔
Christmas box

☼ ☼ ✻ ✻ ✻ ● **H** 1.2m /4ft **S** 1.5m /5ft

The thickets of stems bear elegantly

Viburnum × *bodnantense* 'Dawn'

tapering leaves which, though they tend to blend into the background during most months of the year, come alive with clusters of small, fragrant white flowers in winter. The sweet scent that is carried on the air seems strangely at odds with such an unassuming, though useful, ground cover shrub. Plant near doorways or along well-used paths to enjoy the benefit of its fragrance. Propagate by taking summer cuttings or removing suckers in winter.

Viburnum × bodnantense 'Dawn' ♔

☼ ☼ ✻ ✻ ✻ ◖

H 2.5–3m /8–10ft **S** 1.8–2.2m /6–7ft

Even if severe frost damages the open flowers, my favourite winter-flowering shrub has plenty more waiting for the next mild spell. The clusters of pink buds, opening to sweetly scented, paler pink tubular flowers, are produced almost continuously from early winter to early spring. Prevent shrubs becoming tall and woody by occasionally thinning out the older stems after flowering.

◁ **ALL WITCH HAZELS BEAR** *fragrant, spidery flowers. Those of* Hamamelis × *intermedia* 'Diane' *are dark red, followed in autumn by bright leaf colours.*

KEY: ♔ *Award of Merit* ☼ *sun* ☼ *semi-shade* ✿ *shade* ✻ *half-hardy* ✻✻ *frost-hardy* ✻✻✻ *fully hardy* ◖ *deciduous* ● *evergreen* ◖◗ *semi-evergreen* **H** *height* **S** *spread*

Plants to cover sunny walls

Plants for walls fall into two categories: climbers and wall shrubs. Being specially adapted to cling or twine, climbers are an obvious solution for a vertical surface. Many wall shrubs lend themselves to being trained upwards and tender wall shrubs, as well as climbers, benefit from the shelter offered by a wall that faces the sun most of the day. Its warmth is absorbed by the wall during daytime and given off at night.

Solanum crispum

110

Abutilon vitifolium

☼ ✽✽✽ ✺ **H** 3–4.5m/10–15ft **S** 2.5–3m/8–10ft

Choose this hardy abutilon if a wall needs covering quickly. Although not a climber, it requires no support and from late spring to early summer will be covered with saucer-shaped, purplish-blue flowers 8cm (3in) across. The hairy leaves are shaped like those of a maple. Plant in well-drained soil and, if necessary, prune after flowering to curb size. Remove frost-damaged stems in spring.

Actinidia kolomikta ♔

☼ ✽✽✽ ✺ **H/S** 3.7–5m/12–16ft

Related to the kiwi fruit, this twining climber is grown for its large, heart-shaped leaves, which take on bizarre colours when young. Their tips become coloured with white and pink as if paint had been splashed on them. Small white flowers are borne during early

Actinidia kolomikta

summer, but they are inconspicuous. Prune back to restrict size if necessary after the colours have faded; new shoots are prone to frost damage.

Buddleja crispa

☼ ✽✽✽ ✺ **H/S** 2.5–3m/8–10ft

The stems and leaves, covered by dense white felt, are easily to train against a wall. They provide an ideal silvery backdrop to the panicles of scented, orange-throated lilac flowers that open during mid-to late summer. Plant in well-drained soil and provide shelter. Prune in spring by reducing the length of side shoots that flowered the previous year.

Cytisus battandieri ♔
Pineapple broom/Moroccan broom

☼ ✽✽✽ ✺ **H/S** 3.7–4.5m/12–15ft

This delightful shrub is easy to train against a high wall or fence. Tie in the long stems that bear handsome, silvery trifoliate leaves, pruning out any that are unwanted after flowering. Within a year or two, young plants should produce

▷ **FOR A FAST-GROWING SHRUB**
in a warm, sunny position, choose Cytisus battandieri.

showy, upright candles of yellow, pea-like, pineapple-scented flowers from early to midsummer. Plant in poor, well-drained soil and avoid disturbance.

Piptanthus nepalensis
Evergreen laburnum

☼ ☼ ✽✽✽ ✺ **H** 2.5m/8ft **S** 1.8m/6ft

This striking shrub thrives against a sheltered wall if planted in well-drained soil; stems can be trained in when young. Laburnum-like leaflets are dark bluish-green above and blue-white beneath, an effect that contrasts well with the dark green stems. Yellow, pea-like flowers appear during late spring and early summer. Thin by removing the older and weaker stems of mature specimens every year or two after flowering. Propagate by seed sown in spring or basal cuttings in summer.

• *see also:* PLANTS TO COVER FENCES p114; CLIMBING PLANTS FOR ARCHES AND PERGOLAS p116; USING CLIMBERS p206; GROWING CLIMBERS p208

WALL PLANTING

❖

Thoroughly improve the soil and soak the area prior to digging the planting hole, which should be at least 30cm (12in) away from the wall. Soak the rootball of the new plant and tease out congested roots before planting. Make sure young plants receive adequate water while establishing. Soil at the foot of a wall is often in a rain shadow, remaining dry even when the rest of the garden is moist.

UNUSUAL PLANTS FOR SUNNY WALLS

❖

Acacia dealbata ♀ ♠
Ceanothus impressus ♀ ♠
Eriobotrya japonica ♀ ♠
Fremontodendron 'California Glory' ♀ ♠
Jasminum officinale ♀ ♡♠
Mutisia oligodon ♠
Rhamnus alaternus
'Argenteovariegata' ♀ ♠
Ribes speciosum ♀ ♠

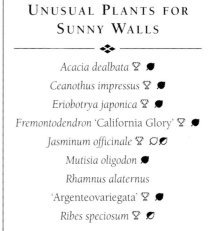

Robinia hispida ♀
Rose acacia

☀ ❊❊❊ ♡ **H** 2.5–3.7m /8–12ft **S** 2.5m /8ft

A showy wall shrub, this one starts flowering at a younger stage than most wisterias, producing bunches of showy, pink, pea-like flowers in early summer. The foliage produces a delightful effect with its light green, oval leaflets, whose midribs extend just beyond the blade. Mature shoots are covered with bristles and are rather brittle. Thrives on poor soils but needs shelter from cold winds.

Rosa banksiae var. *banksiae* 'Lutea' ♀
Yellow Banksian rose

☀ ❊❊❊ ♠ **H** 6m /20ft **S** 3.7m /12ft

This classic, slightly tender rose is ideal for training up a sheltered house wall. Although slow to establish, the wait is rewarded by a distinguished display of

delicately fragrant, soft yellow, double flowers in late spring. Held in sprays, the small individual blooms are profuse, so they almost cover the plant. Prune flowered shoots back to within a few buds of the framework after flowering.

Rosa 'Madame Grégoire Staechelin' ♀

☀ ❊❊❊ ♠ **H** 3.7–6m /12–20ft **S** 2.5–3.7m /8–12ft

Choose this superb rose for a high, sunny wall. Its handsome, dark green, glossy foliage is joined by a display of sumptuous, fully double, rounded pink flowers, which hang down slightly. Although there is no repeat flowering, there will be a display of rounded red hips. Prune back to within small spurs of the framework in autumn or spring.

Solanum crispum 'Glasnevin' ♀
Chilean potato vine

☀ ❊❊❊ ♠ **H** 2.5–4.5m /8–15ft **S** 2.5m /8ft

This vigorous shrub is ideal for covering a wall, to which it can be loosely trained. Try it with *Abutilon* x *suntense*, so they provide a mass of purple together, though the solanum opens its starry, yellow-centred blooms all summer,

continuing long after the abutilon has finished. Plant in well-drained soil and prune after flowering if necessary.

Wisteria sinensis ♀
Chinese wisteria

☀ ❊ ❊❊❊ ♡ **H** 2.5–6m /8–20ft **S** 2.5–4.5m /8–15ft

Probably the most desirable of climbers, wisterias can be wall-trained by tying in a framework of growths laterally, espalier fashion. Shorten the main shoots by half in winter while establishing, then prune laterals to 25cm (10in) each summer and to two or three buds in winter. Enjoy the rather fleeting late-spring display of fragrant, lilac-blue racemes of flowers.

Piptanthus nepalensis   *Wisteria sinensis*

Plants for shady walls

Some plants not only tolerate a shady position, but thrive better in one. In a garden that receives a lot of sun elsewhere, a stretch of cold wall or fence can be a positive boon, offering plants shade and a cool root run. The following climbers and wall shrubs can then be used as a backdrop for other ornamental shrubs that prefer cool shade in summer, like rhododendron and hydrangea.

112

FIXING TO WALLS

❖

Some climbers and most wall shrubs need tying or training to their supporting wall or fence as they grow. Parallel, horizontal wires stretched tight between two eyes about 60cm (2ft) apart work well, while trellis is both attractive and effective. A simple solution is to tap masonry nails into the mortar between bricks where needed and tie stems individually to these.

Azara microphylla ♛
☼ ☼ ❄ ❄ ❄ ❦ **H** 3m/10ft **S** 2.2m/7ft

Although it is the hardiest of its tribe, this shrub or small tree from Chile and Argentina will still thrive best when given the shelter of a wall. Small, shiny, neatly arranged dark green leaves are joined in late winter and spring by small, vanilla-scented yellow flowers, composed mainly of stamens. Plant in well-drained soil, enriched with organic matter.

Camellia japonica 'Alba Plena'
☼ ❄ ❄ ❄ ❦ **H** 3m/10ft **S** 1.8m/6ft

Cultivars of *Camellia japonica* can reach greater dimensions than predicted, but are easily controlled by pruning. The small, formal, double white flowers of this cultivar open in early spring and should be protected from frosts. Prune back unwanted and outward-facing shoots after flowering. Keep moist during summer, when the flower buds set. Scale insects can be a problem if unchecked, causing sooty mould. Plant in acid soil, enriched with organic matter.

Hedera helix
'Oro di Bogliasco'

Chaenomeles speciosa 'Moerloosii' ♛
Japanese quince, Japonica
☼ ☼ ❄ ❄ ❄ ○ **H/S** 2.5m/8ft

Train the stems of this spreading shrub into a fan shape against a wall or fence. With clusters of flowers the colour of apple blossom, it is guaranteed to brighten a gloomy wall during early and mid-spring. After flowering, prune back unwanted, outward-facing shoots to within three buds of the older framework.

Hedera helix
'Oro di Bogliasco' Ivy
☼ ❄ ❄ ❄ ❦ **H** 6m/20ft **S** 3.7m/12ft

Although slow to establish, a young plant of this excellent ivy will begin to climb in earnest some three years after being planted. Clinging with stem roots, it never looks back, producing masses of bright green leaves, each marked with a central gold splash. Eventually, the growth will need curbing annually, usually in late winter. Bryobia mites can cause speckling.

• *see also:* PLANTS TO COVER FENCES p114; CLIMBING PLANTS FOR ARCHES AND PERGOLAS p116; USING CLIMBERS p206; GROWING CLIMBERS p208

◁ **VIRGINIA CREEPER** (Parthenocissus quinquefolia) *can be relied on to light up a wall or fence with its brilliant autumn colour.*

Jasminum nudiflorum ♀
Winter jasmine

☼ ☼ ❊ ❊ ❊ ◯ **H/S** 3m /10ft

Deserving of its popularity, winter jasmine is a reliable performer and easy to grow. Plant at least one for a profusion of cheerful yellow flowers borne during the depths of winter against bright green stems. Train in new stems after flowering, then prune out the old and unwanted stems as well as shortening laterals to three or four buds.

Parthenocissus quinquefolia ♀
Virginia creeper

☼ ☼ ❊ ❊ ❊ ◯ **H/S** 15m /50ft

The hanging stems of this climber are furnished with leaves composed of five leaflets 10cm (4in) long. The stems drape down from the established framework, which anchors itself by means of tendrils armed with disc-like suckers. The autumn finale is a display of brilliant red and purple tints before leaf-fall. Insignificant summer flowers turn into attractive blue-black fruits that birds love. Prune back in winter and train in the framework stems where needed.

Pileostegia viburnoides ♀

☼ ☼ ❊ ❊ ❊ ● **H** 6m /20ft **S** 3.7m /12ft

There are few self-clinging evergreen climbers for shady walls, which makes this plant especially desirable. The disadvantage is that it takes a few years to establish and flower well. But the panicles of small, creamy-white flowers eventually make a good late-summer show against the long, leathery leaves. Mature plants layer themselves freely.

Prunus cerasus 'Morello' ♀
Morello cherry

☼ ❊ ❊ ❊ ❊ ◯ **H/S** 2.2m /7ft

A fan-trained morello is attractive, edible, self-fertile and easy to protect from frost and birds. It takes about four years to train two lower side shoots to form the fan. Thereafter, thin out new growths in spring, leaving one behind each fruiting lateral. After harvesting in late summer, cut back the fruited laterals, leaving the newer shoots to bear next year's crop.

Pyracantha 'Mohave'
Firethorn

☼ ☼ ❊ ❊ ❊ ● **H** 4m /12ft **S** 5m /15ft

Neat-growing firethorns may be trained formally or informally against walls. They can make trim moustaches under windows or form parallel tiers up house walls. Look forward to their white, early-summer blossom, followed by a crop of bright red berries lasting into winter. Shorten laterals after flowering, leaving the developing berries in place. Tidy in spring by removing old fruit trusses.

Pileostegia viburnoides

Hydrangea anomala

Hydrangea anomala subsp. *petiolaris* ♀
Climbing hydrangea

☼ ☼ ❊ ❊ ❊ ◯ **H/S** 7.5m /25ft

A classic choice for a shady wall, this climber needs space. Its attractive foliage makes a good foil for the airy white flowerheads produced in summer. These consist of central female flowers, with a constellation of larger sterile flowers around the perimeter. The stems, which cling to a wall with aerial roots, can be cut back to restrict size immediately after flowering.

113

KEY: ♀ *Award of Merit* ☼ *sun* ❂ *semi-shade* ✽ *shade* ❊ *half-hardy* ❊❊ *frost-hardy* ❊❊❊ *fully hardy* ◯ *deciduous* ● *evergreen* ◐ *semi-evergreen* **H** *height* **S** *spread*

Plants to cover fences

Fences make good instant boundaries for a garden but they can look rather stark. The answer is to smother them with climbers or wall shrubs, bearing in mind they may need to be pulled away from the fence periodically for maintenance purposes. Many of the climbers described on the preceding pages are also suitable for growing against fences. Do not overlook annuals such as canary creeper and sweet peas.

Passiflora caerulea

114

Ampelopsis glandulosa var. *brevipedunculata* 'Elegans'
☼ ☼ ❀ ❀ ⟳ **H/S** 1.2m / 4ft

This dainty vine, grown for its mottled foliage of pink and cream over green, clings to its support by means of twining tendrils. The flowers are insignificant but can be followed by a crop of berries that turn from pinkish-purple to blue. Trim back in spring if necessary and, for fence maintenance, cut back hard. Plant in well-drained soil.

Cotoneaster horizontalis ♔
Herringbone cotoneaster
☼ ☼ ❀ ❀ ❀ ⟳ **H** 1.2m / 4ft **S** 1.5m / 5ft

By nature a ground-covering plant, this shrub also grows upwards to decorate a fence with stems of neat, deep-green leaves arranged fishtail-fashion. Small,

pink-tinged white flowers open in spring, followed by a profusion of red fruits that persist even after the leaves have turned red and, by midwinter, have fallen. Plant with winter jasmine for a stunning effect. Prop away from the fence for maintenance purposes. Tolerates a dry spot.

Euonymus fortunei 'Silver Queen' ♔
☼ ☼ ❀ ❀ ❀ ● **H** 3m / 10ft **S** 1.2m / 4ft

When offered the support of a fence or other structure, this handsome, evergreen shrub takes on a climbing habit. Its leathery, oval leaves bear irregular margins of creamy white, which show up well against a dark background and take on a pinkish tinge in cold weather. Prop growth away from the fence to carry out maintenance.

Geranium 'Ann Folkard'
☼ ☼ ❀ ❀ ❀ ⟳ **H** 60cm / 2ft **S** 1m / 3ft

I find this scrambling, herbaceous geranium extremely useful to plug gaps between existing fence plants and tie them together with its growth. It not only sends its wispy stems of yellow-green leaves in all directions but brightens the area with a long season of saucer-shaped magenta flowers, from midsummer to mid-autumn. Cuttings root easily in water or compost.

Lathyrus latifolius ♔
Everlasting pea
☼ ☼ ❀ ❀ ❀ ⟳ **H** 1.8m / 6ft **S** 1.5m / 5ft

With pink or purple flowers packed closely like clusters of sea-shells, this perennial relative of the sweet pea is such a good climber. Plants romp up trellis in spring and early autumn, after which they die back for winter. *L. l.* 'White Pearl' ♔ bears superb white flowers. Plants tolerate poor soil and some dryness at the roots better than sweet peas do but, sadly, they are unscented.

Lonicera japonica 'Halliana' ♔
Japanese honeysuckle
☼ ☼ ❀ ❀ ❀ ● ⟳ **H** 4.5m / 15ft **S** 3m / 10ft

A fence will completely disappear under the abundance of Japanese honeysuckle.

Cotoneaster horizontalis

Lathyrus latifolius

Lonicera japonica 'Halliana'

• *see also:* PLANTS TO COVER WALLS p110–113; CLIMBING PLANTS FOR ARCHES AND PERGOLAS p116; USING CLIMBERS p206; GROWING CLIMBERS p208

△ ROSA 'CLIMBING ICEBERG' *will decorate a fence with its clusters of double white flowers.*

Twining stems with paired oval leaves need initial support, then cling to themselves. White flowers, which age to butter-yellow, appear from spring to late summer, scenting the air for some distance. For maintenance, cut the plant back or replant with a rooted layer.

Passiflora caerulea ♈
Blue passion flower
☼ ☀ ✳ ✳ ✿ **H/S** 4.5m /15ft

There are few more exotic climbers than this tough passion flower, which opens its flowers during summer. The coronas are blue and white, like colourful sea anemones. The orange fruits are decorative but, though edible, are dry and unpalatable. Plant in poor, well-drained soil and offer initial support for the tendril-clad stems. Prune to tidy in spring and cut back for fence maintenance.

Rosa 'Climbing Iceberg' ♈
☼ ✳ ✳ ✳ ✿✿ **H/S** 3m /10ft

The pleasant, light green foliage of this rose is complemented by clusters of double white flowers from summer to autumn. Prune during autumn in milder regions, which tidies the rose for winter, otherwise prune in early spring. Tie strong stems to the fence to create a framework, then shorten lateral growths to short spurs. Loosen ties and lay the rose down from the fence for the purposes of maintenance.

Rosa 'Paul's Scarlet Climber'
☼ ✳ ✳ ✳ ✳ ✿✿ **H** 3m /10ft **S** 2.5m /8ft

This rose blooms only once in summer but becomes smothered by semi-double scarlet flowers held in clusters; it makes an ideal fence partner for 'Climbing Iceberg'. Neither has much fragrance, but visual impact is more important at

the back of a border, against a fence. A tough rose, it will tolerate poor soils. Prune as for 'Climbing Iceberg' (*above*).

Rubus cockburnianus Golden Vale
Whitewashed bramble
☼ ✳ ✳ ✳ ✳ ✿ **H/S** 1.2–1.8m /4–6ft

This easy shrub performs well all year. From spring to autumn, the prickly stems are clothed in golden-yellow, fern-like leaves. These drop in autumn to reveal ghostly white stems that make an outstanding feature all winter. Prune in early spring, either by cutting all stems close to the ground or, to retain height, by thinning out only weak and unwanted stems. Prop away from the fence for maintenance.

KEY: ♈ *Award of Merit* ☼ *sun* ☀ *semi-shade* ✳ *shade* ✳ *half-hardy* ✳ ✳ *frost-hardy* ✳ ✳ ✳ *fully hardy* ✿ *deciduous* ✿ *evergreen* ✿ *semi-evergreen* **H** *height* **S** *spread*

Alpine and rock garden plants

A collection of alpines can be a joy, especially for those with small gardens, as it enables many different sorts of plant to be grown in a restricted space. For those, like me, who garden on a poor but well-drained, sandy soil, they are an ideal solution, enjoying the conditions of a wide, shingle bed, where they flourish and spread into large clumps or tufts.

Iberis sempervirens

Arabis alpina subsp. *caucasica* 'Variegata'
Rock cress

☼ ❋ ❋ ❋ ● **H** 8–15cm/3–6in **S** 45cm/18in

This tough little perennial is still thriving in my garden after seven years of almost complete neglect. Rosettes of stiff, softly hairy leaves with irregularly toothed margins are edged with cream, and lightly fragrant white flowers open in late spring. Plant in well-drained soil; drought and poor soils are tolerated well. Take individual rosettes as offsets in summer.

THE ANSWER LIES IN THE SOIL

❖

Most alpines require well-drained soil in order to thrive. Though hardy, many find it difficult to survive cold winters if their feet are damp and waterlogged. Gardeners on sandy, well-drained soils need only add well-rotted compost to improve fertility (never add rotted manure, as this is too strong). On heavy, waterlogged soils you need both to break up solid subsoil and to add plenty of grit and organic matter to the topsoil. Where soils are totally unsuitable, consider using raised beds or sinks for alpines.

Geranium dalmaticum ♀
Cranesbill

☼ ❋ ❋ ❋ ⌀ **H** 8–15cm/3–6in **S** 50cm/20in

Stems of deeply divided leaves forming five to seven segments make a substantial mound all year round. Pretty, sugar-pink flowers, just over 2.5cm (1in) across with orange pollen, open in summer, leaving seedheads which are characteristically cranesbill-shaped. Plant in well-drained soil enriched with organic matter. Sow ripe seed into pots in a cold frame or lift, divide and replant in spring.

Iberis sempervirens ♀
Candytuft

☼ ❋ ❋ ❋ ● **H** 30cm/12in **S** 38cm/15in

This sub-shrub makes a good mass of dark green, paddle-shaped leaves, which in late spring and early summer are joined by rounded heads of densely

Pulsatilla vulgaris

packed white flowers. Trim back after flowering. For blooms opening in late winter and early spring, seek out *I.* 'Dick Self'. Plant in well-drained neutral or alkaline soil. Cuttings root easily in summer.

Phlox subulata 'Amazing Grace'
Moss phlox

☼ ❋ ❋ ❋ ● **H** 10cm/4in **S** 20cm/8in

Cushion-like mounds of soft, narrow leaves on lax stems are present year-round. From late spring to early summer, attractive, rounded flowers of palest pink with deep pink eyes open from dainty buds. Plant along the edges of paths, or in shingle beds, rock gardens and containers where the soil is well-drained but fertile. Take cuttings of non-flowering shoots in spring.

Pulsatilla vulgaris ♀
Pasque flower

☼ ❋ ❋ ❋ ⌀ **H** 38cm/15in **S** 30cm/12in

These are among my favourite flowers. The perennial plants die right down for winter, pushing up a new crop of finely divided, silky leaves and silky-haired buds in spring. The divine purple, bell-shaped flowers each bear a central boss of golden stamens and are followed by decorative seedheads typical of the

• *see also:* GROWING AND CARING FOR ALPINES p216; RAISING PLANTS FROM SEED p230; OTHER MEANS OF PROPAGATION p234

◁ **GROWING ALPINES** *in a raised sink lets us appreciate their exquisite detail close to. The bed includes alpine beauties such as phlox, saxifrage and tanacetum.*

Sedum spathulifolium 'Cape Blanco' ♀
Stonecrop

☼ ❋ ❋ ❋ ● **H** 5–10cm /2–4in **S** 60cm /24in

Silvery-white, succulent leaves crowd into rosettes at the tops of pink-tinged stems, forming a mat. The innermost leaves are covered with a white bloom. In summer, stems of starry yellow flowers rise above the foliage. To propagate, nip off rosettes of leaves on short stems and root in pots of gritty compost.

Sisyrinchium 'E.K. Balls'

☼ ❋ ❋ ❋ ◐ **H** 25cm /10in **S** 15cm /6in

Among the many mound-forming, spreading rock garden plants it is nice to grow a species with fans of grassy, sword-shaped leaves. There are several sisyrinchiums with blue or purple summer flowers and they are all good; this one bears a succession of starry mauve blooms with yellow centres.

ROCK PLANTS FOR
SINK GARDENS
❖

Asperula gussonii ●
Armeria maritima ●
Dianthus erinaceus ●
Erinus alpinus ♀ ●
Erodium reichardii ◐
Papaver miyabeanum ◐
Salix serpyllifolia ◯
Saxifraga burseriana 'Gloria' ♀ ●
Sempervivum tectorum ♀ ●
Thymus serpyllum 'Minimus' ●

---

buttercup family. Plant in fertile, well-drained soil. Sow seed when fresh or take root cuttings in winter.

Rhodanthemum hosmariense ♀
☼ ❋ ❋ ❋ ● **H** 15–30cm /6–12in **S** 38cm /15in
This sub-shrub offers amazing garden value, since the mound of deeply lobed, filigree silvery foliage is joined by white, daisy-like flowers 5cm (2in) across from spring to autumn. Plant in well-drained soil alongside a path or in a gravel bed or rock garden; it hates winter wet. Propagate by spring-sown seed or by short cuttings rooted in early summer.

Scutellaria orientalis
Helmet flower, Skullcap
☼ ❋ ❋ ❋ ● **H** 20–25cm /8–10in **S** 60cm /2ft
I love this evergreen perennial for its clusters of typical skullcap flowers; they have long yellow tubes with brighter yellow hoods and pouting, often red-marked underlips. The foliage is constant and the flowers open all through summer. Plant in gritty neutral to alkaline soil. Propagate from spring-sown seed or summer cuttings.

Plant in well-drained neutral to alkaline soil. Divide clumps in spring.

Thymus richardii subsp. *nitidus*
Thyme
☼ ❋ ❋ ❋ ● **H/S** 15cm /6in
While many thymes are spreading, this sub-shrub forms an upright bush. The narrow, oval, greyish-green leaves are aromatic and make a soft backdrop to rounded clusters of pale purple flowers. Those of the cultivar 'Peter Davis' are a good, strong pink. Plant in well-drained, gritty soil. Take cuttings in mid- to late summer for replacements since the plants are usually short-lived.

Rhodanthemum hosmariense

Sedum spathulifolium 'Cape Blanco'

KEY: ♀ *Award of Merit* ☼ *sun* ❋ *semi-shade* ❋ *shade* ❋ *half-hardy* ❋❋ *frost-hardy* ❋❋❋ *fully hardy* ◯ *deciduous* ● *evergreen* ◐ *semi-evergreen* **H** *height* **S** *spread*

Cottage garden plants

The cottage garden style has been popular ever since the idea of gardens evolved. Our modern-day equivalent may well be a romanticized version of the subsistence plots of old, but it relies on a fulsome planting of flowering annuals and perennials, rich with colour and variety. At its best at the height of summer, with its jumble of flowers and bright colours, the cottage style has seductive charm.

Iris 'Jane Phillips'

122

Achillea filipendulina 'Gold Plate' ♈
Yarrow

☼ ❄ ❄ ❄ ◼ **H** 1.2m /4ft **S** 75cm /30in

Slightly domed heads, packed full of small, golden-yellow flowers, seem to hover over the leaves of this tall perennial from summer to early autumn. Choose a roomy site and rig up some support early in the season, otherwise the stems, though strong, can collapse. Combines well with silver, blue and purple flowers. Lift, divide and replant old clumps in early spring.

Alcea rosea Chater's Double Group
Hollyhock

☼ ❄ ❄ ❄ ✿ **H** 2–2.5m /6–8ft **S** 60cm /2ft

Although perennial, hollyhocks are usually treated as biennials. Seed is sown in spring, to plant in autumn for flowers the following summer. Widely grown in the mid-1800s, hollyhocks were almost wiped out by rust disease. There are single and double-flowered cultivars from which to choose.

Alcea rosea
(semi-double)

SUPPORTING PLANTS

A very natural way of supporting lax-stemmed plants like ox-eye daisies is to save twiggy prunings. Pushed into the soil and angled towards the stems, they are unobtrusive and flexible.

This peony-flowered seed strain is a remnant from the old Saffron Walden seed firm of Chater and includes reds, yellows and maroons. Plant in fertile soil for the best results. Strong plants usually survive despite rust.

Delphinium 'Faust' ♈

☼ ❄ ❄ ❄ ✿ **H** 1.8m /6ft **S** 60cm /2ft

To grow the best delphiniums, first select good named varieties. These distinguish themselves by producing spires of closely arranged summer flowers, with the topmost buds opening

CREATING THE COTTAGE GARDEN STYLE

• Set strong shapes in the bones of the garden, then use informal plants to create billowing borders. Arches and bowers create a romantic scene.

• Colonize the soil beneath roses with thyme, viola, stachys and gypsophila.

• Include some plants with spires of flowers, like foxglove, lupin, hollyhock and delphinium.

• Edge paths with catmint or lavender; do not be afraid to use repetition.

• Introduce self-seeders such as aquilegia, sweet rocket, *Lychnis coronaria* and Shirley poppies.

before the lowest flowers start to age. 'Faust' bears semi-double blue, purple-shaded flowers with dark eyes. Thin the developing shoots to three or four in spring, taking the remainder as cuttings. Protect from slugs all year round and support the flower spikes. Plant in well-conditioned soil and keep moist.

Gypsophila paniculata
Baby's breath

☼ ❄ ❄ ❄ ✿

H 75cm–1.2m /30–48in **S** 90–120cm /3–4ft

This pretty, airy perennial associates well

• *see also:* RAISING PLANTS FROM SEED p230

◁ **THE RIGHT INGREDIENTS,** *like spire-forming verbascum, centaurea, calendula, leucanthemum, phlox and* Lychnis chalcedonica, *produce a romantic cottage garden profusion.*

123

with most plants, including roses. Blooms rising through the froth of tiny white flowers transform the combination into an instant bouquet. Linear leaves build up quietly during spring, before the flowers burst forth in summer. Plant in light, preferably alkaline, well-drained soil as they can be killed by winter waterlogging.

Iris 'Jane Phillips' ♀
Bearded iris
☼ ◐ ✳ ✳ ✳ ○ **H/S** 90cm /3ft

Popular and widely available, this lovely, tall iris bears clear, sky-blue flowers. Sniff into the blooms for their sweet scent, which is reminiscent of cheap sweets or old-fashioned soap. Their structural, sword-shaped leaves bring form to riotous borders. When the clumps become congested, lift, cut off the healthy outer growths, shorten the leaves and replant into well-drained soil after flowering or in early autumn.

Lychnis coronaria
Dusty miller, Rose campion
☼ ◐ ✳ ✳ ✳ ● **H** 60–80cm /24–32in **S** 45cm /18in

The dusty miller can withstand drought and malnutrition, but not dampness in the air or at the roots. Under the right conditions, it will form colonies of silver-felted basal leaves and stems of shocking pink summer flowers. I prefer the more refined white-flowered form, *L.c.* Alba Group ♀ with a soft pink eye. Both seed themselves with abandon or you can divide and replant in spring.

Nepeta 'Six Hills Giant'
Catmint
☼ ✳ ✳ ✳ ✳ ○ **H/S** 90cm /3ft

Billowing clumps of aromatic catmint are very reminiscent of cottage gardens. Tiny, lavender-blue flowers open against narrow, toothed, grey-green leaves and attract both bees and cats. If you cut back after the first exuberant flush, fresh growth will result. Plant in well-drained soil. Take summer cuttings and look out for natural layers.

Papaver rhoeas Shirley Series
Shirley poppy
☼ ✳ ✳ ✳ ○ **H** 60–90cm /2–3ft **S** 45cm /18in

Bred from the common annual cornfield poppy in a process of selection by the Reverend W. Wilks in Shirley, Croydon, these lovely poppies date from 1880. Their silky flowers are single with a white base, yellow or white stamens and no black markings. Once sown, the strain can be maintained by allowing only the best to seed. They fit ideally into an informal, cottage garden style.

Rosa 'Cornelia' ♀
☼ ◐ ✳ ✳ ✳ ✳ ○ **H/S** 1.5m /5ft

Although a modern shrub rose, this one is in keeping with a cottage garden philosophy. Flowering reliably over a long period, it bears sprays of highly fragrant, soft pink flowers, suffused with warm apricot. Buds are more intensely coloured than open blooms, giving a range of shades. Prune lightly in early spring.

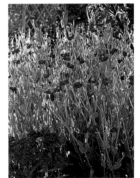

Lychnis coronaria   *Nepeta* 'Six Hills Giant'

Salvia x *sylvestris* 'Mainacht' ♀
☼ ✳ ✳ ✳ ○

H 70cm /28in **S** 45cm /18in

Erect spikes of deep indigo-blue flowers rise up on this clump-forming perennial during early and midsummer, contrasting well with silver, pink and yellow colours in the border. The mid-green leaves are attractively scalloped and covered in soft hairs. Plant in good, moist, but well-drained soil. Lift, divide and replant older clumps in autumn or spring.

Wildflowers

The natural beauty of wildflowers has great appeal and gardeners may find colonies of violets, heartsease pansies, bluebells, foxgloves, hedge mustard, and more, already established in their plots. Evolved to suit local conditions, these plants often thrive where cultivated plants fail, so learn to enjoy them as assets, not weeds. The best way to introduce wildflowers deliberately is by seed, though plants can also be found for sale.

Viola odorata

124

Agrostemma githago
Corncockle

☼ ✳ ✳ ✳ **H** 60–90cm /2–3ft **S** 30cm /12in

Now rather uncommon in the wild, this cornfield annual was once considered a weed. Slender, downy stems with narrow, grey-green leaves are joined in summer by pinkish-purple flowers with white centres. In the garden, treat it as a hardy annual, sowing straight into the ground during spring. Thin the seedlings and push twiggy prunings into the soil as support. Collect seed for the following year.

Anemone nemorosa ♥
Wood anemone

☼ ☼ ✳ ✳ ✳ ○ **H** 8–15cm /3–6in **S** 30cm /12in

I remember these spring flowers from childhood walks through an old wood of chestnut, oak and birch in Kent. They carpeted the ground with their starry white blooms against bright green foliage, completing their flowering before the leaves unfurled above. Plant where soil is moist and enriched with leafmould, though dryness is tolerated in summer when they are dormant. Divide rhizomes in spring.

Crambe maritima
Seakale

☼ ✳ ✳ ✳ ○ **H** 30–75cm /12–30in **S** 60cm /2ft

This native perennial of the sea shore bears glaucous blue-green, cabbage-like leaves and heads of white flowers in early summer. Use it to colonize a shingle garden mixed with other seaside plants like viper's bugloss (*Echium vulgare*) and bladder campion (*Silene uniflora*). Young shoots can be forced for eating. Plants often seed themselves naturally. Divide in early spring or take root cuttings in winter.

Cymbalaria muralis
Ivy-leaved toadflax

☼ ☼ ✳ ✳ ✳ ○ **H** 15cm /6in **S** 60cm /2ft

This pretty perennial creeper is often seen colonizing dry stone walls, banks and steps. Its fleshy leaves are almost kidney-shaped and it produces mauve and yellow summer flowers, typical of the toadflax family. Its seedheads bend away from the light and are thus more likely to shed their seeds back into the wall or bank they inhabit. Propagate by seed or division.

Echium vulgare
Viper's bugloss

☼ ✳ ✳ ✳ ● **H** 60–90cm /2–3ft **S** 30cm /12in

I have seen this plant growing wild on the sea shore and in rough, open grassland. It also makes a good patch of colour in the garden. A biennial with bristly leaves and stems, it needs to be sown during spring, to plant in autumn and bloom the following early summer. Spikes of purple-pink buds open to violet-blue flowers.

Anemone nemorosa

Echium vulgare

Fritillaria meleagris

• **see also:** CHOOSING A LAWN p190; RAISING PLANTS FROM SEED p230; OTHER MEANS OF PROPAGATION p234

◁ **CREATING A WILDFLOWER** *meadow from scratch is not easy and takes patience. The results are worthwhile when native plants like ragged robin and buttercups start to thrive.*

CREATING A COLOURFUL MEADOW

❖

The secret behind establishing a wildflower meadow is to start with poor soil. Where land has been artificially fertilized and conditioned, grasses and undesirable weeds flourish at the expense of desirable wildflowers and the area may take several years to settle down. In agricultural situations, the sward of grasses and flowers is cut for hay from mid- to late summer after the species have had a chance to flower and seed. To create a haven for insects, cut at varying times to leave different heights of grass.

Fritillaria meleagris ♀
Snake's head fritillary

☼ ☼ ❄ ❄ ❄ ♢ **H** 30cm/12in **S** 8cm/3in

Possibly not a true native, this intriguing plant has suffered from habitat loss. Yet several colonies have been preserved in their ancient, damp meadowland. The chequered pinkish-purple, sometimes white, flowers make an incredible sight in spring, nodding on their slender stalks. Cultivated plants are easily purchased and seem to establish better than dry bulbs. Plant in well-drained soil. The growth always dies back in summer.

Lychnis flos-cuculi
Ragged robin

☼ ☼ ❄ ❄ ❄ **H** 60–75cm/24–30in **S** 75cm/30in

The wet soils of marshland and damp woodland are the haunts of this lovely perennial, which is becoming a favourite garden wildflower. Its distinctive, ragged pink flowers, with much divided petals, appear in late spring and early summer. For the garden, raise plants from seed sown when ripe or in spring. Once established, divide in spring.

Lythrum salicaria
Purple loosestrife

☼ ☼ ❄ ❄ ❄ ♢ **H** 90–120cm/3–4ft **S** 45cm/18in

Spires of purple-pink loosestrife are a familiar sight along rivers and waterways from midsummer to autumn. This decorative perennial also has a place beside garden ponds and in bog gardens. Plant in moist soil and provide support if lacking strong reeds. Sow seed in spring; thereafter lift and divide clumps in spring or take basal cuttings.

Verbascum thapsus
Aaron's rod, Great mullein

☼ ❄ ❄ ❄ ● **H** 1.2–1.8m/4–6ft **S** 45cm/18in

This biennial spends its first year as a large rosette of soft, silvery-white leaves, rising up to a felty spike of close-packed yellow flowers in the second summer. It grows in waste areas and roadsides, often seeding itself into gardens. Try including its foliage in a winter bedding scheme. Sow seed in late spring or early summer.

Viola odorata
Sweet violet

☼ ☼ ❄ ❄ ❄ ✿ **H** 20cm/8in **S** 30cm/12in

This delicately scented violet grows in hedgerows and, with its heart-shaped leaves and jewel-like blue, sometimes white, early spring flowers, makes a lovely plant at the base of a garden hedge or in semi-wild areas between trees. Plant in moist, well-drained soil. Propagate by seed or division after flowering.

Lythrum salicaria

Easy-care plants

Maintaining a beautiful garden can take anything from the occasional half hour to full-time care, depending on the style of garden and type of plants in it. Those short of time should steer clear of vegetables, bedding plants, containers and old-style herbaceous borders. Concentrate instead on a mixture of shrubs and perennials requiring the minimum of fuss.

△ **THE BROOM** Cytisus x praecox *'Allgold'*
celebrates spring with a mass of yellow pea flowers.

128 *Abies procera* 'Glauca Prostrata'
☼ ✹ ✹ ✹ ◗ **H** 75cm / 30in **S** 1.8m / 6ft

The low-growing branches of this conifer eventually shade out competing weeds. Growth is slow and little formative pruning is required other than removing maverick shoots that travel upwards rather than outwards. Stems bear glaucous, silvery-blue needles when young, which mature to grey-green. Plant in well-drained neutral to slightly acid soil.

Abies procera
'Glauca Prostrata'

Berberis x *ottawensis* 'Superba' ♔
☼ ☼ ✹ ✹ ✹ ○
H / S 2.5m / 8ft

Attractive, reddish-purple leaves turn crimson before falling in autumn, making this a good shrub for fleshing out the back of a border. Clusters of small, red-flushed yellow flowers open in spring, followed by red fruits. Suits any soil including shallow chalk. Prune out a quarter of the stems annually after flowering to keep plants fresh.

Buddleja globosa ♔
Orange ball tree
☼ ☼ ✹ ✹ ✹ ○◗ **H / S** 3–4.5m / 10–15ft

This shrub bears small orange flowers packed tightly into round heads 2.5cm (1in) across in early summer. They are scented but, though attractive to bees and butterflies, are not particularly sweet. I find the silvery stems and long, dark green leaves of this shrub very attractive. Tough and reliable, it will grow in most soils and needs little, if any, pruning.

Buxus sempervirens ♔
Box
☼ ☼ ✹ ✹ ✹ ◗ **H / S** 1.2–1.5m / 4–5ft

With neat, dense, evergreen foliage, box lends itself perfectly to being clipped

---

EASY-TO-GROW FLOWERS
❖

Abelia x *grandiflora* ♔ ○
Buddleja davidii 'Dartmoor' ♔ ○
Coreopsis verticillata 'Zagreb' ○
Erigeron 'Rosa Juwel' ○
Forsythia x *intermedia* 'Spectabilis' ○
Osmanthus delavayi ♔ ◗
Pulmonaria saccharata 'Mrs Moon' ○
Rosa 'Flower Carpet' ♔ ○

---

into tight shapes such as pyramids and spirals as well as low hedges. Ready-grown topiary shapes tend to be expensive, because the growth is slow and nursery skill is involved, but they are a worthwhile way to obtain a living sculpture. Maintenance consists of two clips each growing season and a spring application of slow-release fertilizer.

Cytisus x *praecox*
Broom
☼ ✹ ✹ ✹ ○ **H / S** 1.2m / 4ft

Nothing could be easier than caring for a broom. The arching shoots are covered with masses of pale yellow flowers in mid- and late spring, after which silky-haired leaves grow. As soon as flowering has finished, cut all stems hard back but without cutting into old wood. Plant this shrub into any well-drained soil, including chalk.

• *see also:* PLANTING AND MOVING SHRUBS p204; PROPAGATING BY CUTTINGS p232

Euonymus fortunei
Emerald 'n' Gold ♀

☼ ☼ ☼ ✽ ✽ ✽ ✿

H 60cm /2ft **S** 90cm /3ft

This versatile shrub makes good ground cover and is a bold gap-filler in borders as well as a useful ingredient for a winter container. The gold-edged, evergreen leaves make bright splashes in otherwise gloomy shrubberies. Search under mature shrubs for branches which have layered themselves. Cuttings root easily in summer.

Geranium wallichianum
'Buxton's Variety' ♀

☼ ☼ ✽ ✽ ✽ ♡ **H** 30cm /12in **S** 90cm /3ft

Hardy border geraniums are a reliable group, creating easy, effective, perennial ground cover. This cultivar makes a spreading mound decorated by rounded blue flowers with veined white centres from summer to autumn. It tolerates most soils. Divide in spring or take basal cuttings.

Leycesteria formosa
Himalayan honeysuckle

☼ ☼ ✽ ✽ ✽ ♡ **H/S** 1.8m /6ft

Handsome foliage and strings of maroon-pink bracts and small white flowers from summer to autumn seem handsome refinements for such an

Mahonia aquifolium

enduring shrub. Even better, the flowers develop into red-purple berries and the leaves drop in autumn to reveal bright green stems. Suits any well-drained soil. Pruning is optional: either do not prune, thin lightly after flowering or cut almost to the base in early spring.

Mahonia aquifolium
Oregon grape

☼ ☼ ✽ ✽ ✽ ✿ **H** 90cm /3ft **S** 1.5m /5ft

An Oregon grape seeded itself in our rose hedge, grew to flowering size, recovered from an accidental felling and grew to bloom again. Attractive as well as resilient, leaves of spiny-toothed leaflets turn red in winter and clusters of scented yellow flowers open in spring, followed by blue-black berries. Good for dry shade. Sow seed when ripe or take cuttings in late summer.

Silene schafta ♀

☼ ☼ ✽ ✽ ✽ ✿ **H** 25cm /10in **S** 30cm /12in

Clumps of slender stems bearing narrow leaves rise up to produce masses of pink flowers from midsummer to autumn. These have long, striped tubes and flare out to five-notched petals. Raise this perennial from autumn-sown seed or root basal cuttings in spring. Suits well-drained neutral to alkaline soils.

Euonymus fortunei **Emerald 'n' Gold**

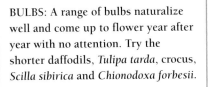

PLANTS THAT LOOK AFTER THEMSELVES

❖

BULBS: A range of bulbs naturalize well and come up to flower year after year with no attention. Try the shorter daffodils, *Tulipa tarda*, crocus, *Scilla sibirica* and *Chionodoxa forbesii*.

PERENNIALS: Avoid those needing support and regular division. Try *Aquilegia vulgaris*, *Rudbeckia fulgida* 'Goldsturm' and *Sedum spectabile*.

SHRUBS: Choose types that need little or no pruning, including *Potentilla fruticosa* and its cultivars, *Lonicera nitida* 'Bagessen's Gold' and hollies.

129

CLIPPING TOPIARY

❖

A box spiral provides year-round structure. Because its growth is slow compared to privet, one or two clips a growing season will suffice. Keep slopes parallel, like a living helter-skelter.

Scented plants

Scent is a powerful addiction and, once attuned, a gardener will find delicious fragrances at every turn. It took me years to realize that most bearded iris were scented and that Magnolia soulangiana *was worth a sniff. Leaves are often aromatic too, but they may need to be brushed or rubbed to release their scent. Dried leaves and petals can be used to make pot-pourri.*

Mentha × piperita f. citrata

130

Cercidiphyllum japonicum ♥
Katsura

☼ ☼ ❋ ❋ ❋ ○ **H** 15m/50ft **S** 10m/33ft

The dying yellow, orange and red leaves of this dainty woodland tree produce the scent of caramel as they fall in autumn. If you rub one, the unexpected aroma of burnt sugar is released. Plant in soil enriched with organic matter, in a sheltered spot because the coppery young leaves are prone to spring frost-damage. Usually grows multi-stemmed unless trained to a single trunk.

Convallaria majalis ♥
Lily-of-the-valley

☼ ☼ ❋ ❋ ❋ ○ **H** 23cm/9in **S** 17cm/7in

Their show might be short-lived, but I really look forward to the arching stems of sweetly scented, white, bell-shaped flowers set against paired leaves. Most gardens have a moist, shaded spot for these perennials to colonize. Within a few years, one or two small plants will have spread to a sizeable mass. Divide and replant rhizomes in autumn.

Dianthus 'Doris' ♥
Modern pink

☼ ❋ ❋ ❋ ● **H** 25–45cm/10–18in **S** 40cm/16in

Pinks are excellent for clothing the edges of paths and they like a well-nourished, well-drained, neutral to alkaline soil. 'Doris' is pretty, with scented, double, sugar-pink flowers marked towards the centre with darker pink. The main flush is in early summer, but rigorous dead-heading and a midsummer feed will encourage more blooms. Propagate by summer cuttings.

Lathyrus odoratus ♥
Sweet pea

☼ ❋ ❋ ❋ ❋ **H** 1.8m/6ft **S** 90cm/3ft

Among modern-day sweet pea cultivars and mixtures are many sold for their scent. But for something more unusual, with guaranteed perfume, seek out their ancestor for the beauty of its strongly fragrant magenta and purple flowers. Their charm makes up for the lack of long stems and frilly petals. Sow seed of this annual into pots in autumn or spring, planting out later into well-nourished soil, near a support for the stems to climb. Dead-head rigorously to prolong blooms.

Lilium regale ♥
Regal lily

☼ ☼ ❋ ❋ ❋ ○ **H** 60–180cm/2–6ft **S** 30cm/1ft

One of the easiest and least fussy lilies to grow, one bulb quickly builds up into a clump on most soils. As many as 30 white, trumpet-shaped blooms with yellow throats and purple-pink outsides open in summer. Their strong, heady perfume wafts out on the air, particularly during evening. Plant 15cm (6in) deep in spring or, preferably, in autumn.

Convallaria majalis   *Lathyrus odoratus cv*   *Magnolia grandiflora 'Exmouth'*

• *see also:* PLANTING AND CARING FOR HERBACEOUS BORDERS p210; SOWING AND USING HARDY ANNUALS p212; OTHER MEANS OF PROPAGATION p234

◁ **AMONG THE MOST SUCCESSFUL** *of garden lilies,* Lilium regale *scents the air for some distance. Bulbs settle down quickly, multiplying to form a colony.*

Myrtus communis

> ## BEST FOR FRAGRANCE
> ❖
>
> *Akebia quinata* 🌿
> *Aquilegia fragrans* ✿
> *Chimonanthus praecox* ✿
> *Choisya ternata* ♀ 🌿
> *Clematis heracleifolia* var. *davidiana* 'Wyevale' ♀ ✿
> *Cytisus battandieri* ♀ 🌿
> *Daphne bholua* 'Jacqueline Postill' ♀ 🌿
> *Elaeagnus* × *ebbingei* 🌿
> *Erysimum cheiri* cvs. 🌿
> *Gladiolus callianthus* ♀ ✿
> *Hamamelis* × *intermedia* 'Pallida' ♀ ✿
> *Heliotropium arborescens* 🌿
> *Hosta plantaginea* ✿
> *Lavandula angustifolia* 'Twickel Purple' ♀ 🌿
> *Lonicera japonica* 'Halliana' ♀ 🌿
> *L. periclymenum* 'Serotina' ♀ ✿
> *L.* × *purpusii* ✿
> *Mentha* × *piperita* f *citrata* ✿
> *Philadelphus* 'Sybille' ♀ ✿
> *Rosmarinus officinalis* 🌿
> *Viburnum* × *burkwoodii* 'Anne Russell' ♀ 🌿

Magnolia grandiflora

☼ ❄❄ 🌿 **H** 6–18m/20–60ft **S** 4.5–15m/15–50ft

Worth growing for its 20cm- (8in-) long glossy leaves alone, this evergreen shrub or tree is usually trained against a warm, sunny wall. Large, creamy-white flowers up to 25cm (10in) across have an exotic, citrus perfume and are even more desirable for being sparsely produced from summer to autumn. Choose *M.g.* 'Exmouth' ♀ for its hardiness or *M.g.* 'Goliath' ♀ for its broad leaves and massive blooms. Tolerates alkaline soils.

Myrtus communis ♀
Myrtle

☼ ❄❄ 🌿 **H/S** 2–3m/6–10ft

During late summer and early autumn, pink, fist-like buds open to small, creamy-white flowers with prominent stamens. These have a sweet, spicy fragrance that combines well with the bright green, aromatic leaves. A Mediterranean shrub, myrtle enjoys a well-drained soil and will flourish against a sunny, sheltered wall. Strike semi-ripe cuttings in late summer.

Nicotiana alata
Tobacco plant

☼ ◐ ❄ ✿ **H** 90–120cm/3–4ft **S** 60cm/2ft

Greenish-yellow flowers remain closed during the daytime but flare open in the evening, revealing white mouths and filling the air with a powerful, almost too-sweet perfume. Treat as a half-hardy annual, sowing under glass in spring to flower during summer. Leave the plants in and they may reveal their perennial nature by growing back the following spring.

Pelargonium crispum 'Variegatum' ♀
Lemon-scented pelargonium

☼ ❄ 🌿 **H** 45cm/18in **S** 30cm/24in

One of a number of scented-leaved pelargoniums, this, for me, has the nicest lemon perfume. Rub one of the neat, cream-edged leaves gently and a mild, mouthwatering fragrance is released. Pale mauve flowers appear throughout summer. This upright, tender plant needs protection from frost during winter. Propagate from summer cuttings.

Rosa Alec's Red

☼ ❄❄❄ ✿ **H** 90–120cm/3–4ft **S** 90cm/3ft

Sinking one's nose into the satiny, warm red petals of this rose on a hot summer's day is a memorable experience. A reliable modern hybrid tea, it produces a succession of large flowers in a voluptuous shade of dark cherry-red. Its rich fragrance is powerful but pleasant. Plant this rose into well-nourished soil. Prune, then feed and mulch the roots annually in early spring.

Plants with variegated leaves

Used with restraint, variegated plants have a lightening and an enhancing effect: let them contrast without clashing by setting them against plain green or gold leaves. Variegation is the result of irregular leaf pigments and, because there is less chlorophyll, variegated species often grow more slowly than their all-green counterparts and may need more light. Too much light, however, can scorch or bleach white or cream markings.

132 *Aralia elata* 'Aureovariegata'
Japanese angelica tree
☼ ☼ ❋ ❋ ❋ ⟳ **H/S** 2.5–4.5m/8–15ft
The leaves of this structural shrub, which can reach 1.2m (4ft) long, are broken into two sets of leaflets. Each is irregularly margined with yellow, fading to silvery-white with maturity. This and the equally lovely *A.e.* 'Variegata' ♈ are propagated by grafting and are therefore costly to buy. They can also look gaunt when leafless in winter. Plant in good soil and shelter from cold winds.

Astrantia major
'Sunningdale Variegated' ♈
Masterwort
☼ ❋ ❋ ❋ ⟳ **H** 30–90cm/1–3ft **S** 45cm/18in
Choose this exciting perennial to brighten shady areas. Its deeply lobed leaves, patterned with three shades of green, are roughly margined with creamy white. In early to midsummer, the leaves are joined by long stems of pale pink flowerheads, which are much favoured by flower-arrangers. The blooms are tiny, but held in umbels surrounded by a ruff of bracts. Plant in moist, well-drained soil. Lift, divide and replant in autumn or spring.

Cornus alternifolia 'Argentea' ♈
☼ ☼ ❋ ❋ ❋ ⟳ **H** 3–4m/10–13ft **S** 2.5–3m/8–10ft
Pagoda dogwood
This small tree has branches of silver-variegated foliage arranged in horizontal tiers like the roofs of a pagoda or the layers of a wedding cake. Dainty, white-margined leaves give the tree a light, festive air; insignificant white flowers appear in early summer. Plant this dogwood in a sheltered spot. Propagation is carried out commercially by grafting.

Euphorbia marginata
Snow-on-the-mountain
☼ ☼ **H** 30–90cm/1–3ft **S** 30cm/1ft
This unusual annual is grown for its variegated foliage and white flowerheads with petal-like bracts. Young plants begin green, but the uppermost leaves are striped and margined with white, with those at the top almost completely white. Useful for flower arranging. Sow seed in spring, either into modules or straight into the ground outside. The sap can be an irritant.

Cornus alternifolia 'Argentea'

> ### WOODY PLANTS WITH VARIEGATED LEAVES
> ❖
>
> *Buddleja davidii* 'Harlequin' ⟳
> *Cornus alba* 'Elegantissima' ♈ ⟳
> *Euonymus fortunei* Emerald Gaiety ♈ ❧
> *Hedera colchica* 'Dentata Variegata' ♈ ❧
> *Hydrangea macrophylla* 'Tricolor' ♈ ⟳
> *Jasminum officinale*
> 'Argenteovariegatum' ♈ ⟳
> *Myrtus communis* 'Variegata' ❧
> *Osmanthus heterophyllus* 'Goshiki' ❧
> *Philadelphus coronarius* 'Variegatus' ♈ ⟳
> *Salvia officinalis* 'Icterina' ♈ ❧
> *Thuja plicata* 'Zebrina' ❧
> *Viburnum tinus* 'Variegatum' ❧

• *see also:* RAISING PLANTS FROM SEED p230; OTHER MEANS OF PROPAGATION p234

◁ **LIGHT UP A CORNER** *of the garden by planting* Aralia elata *'Aureovariegata'. Branches of pale-edged leaflets have a layered, structural effect and stand out against other plants.*

scented, cool-blue flowers of early summer are a bonus. Borne 2–6 per stem, each is marked with a fuzzy yellow beard. Plant in fertile, well-drained soil. Lift old clumps after flowering or in early autumn, remove the fresh ends of the rhizomes, cut the foliage down by half and replant.

Mentha suaveolens 'Variegata'
Pineapple mint

☼ ❋ ❋ ❋ ⟳ **H** 60–90cm/2–3ft **S** 90cm/3ft

Less rampant than some mints, the pineapple mint can be restricted to its allotted space by chopping away excess roots at virtually any time of the year. Hairy, toothed, somewhat wrinkled leaves have irregular creamy margins and, when crushed, yield a fruity aroma. Flowers are rarely produced.

Polemonium caeruleum Brise d'Anjou
Jacob's ladder

☼ ☀ ❋ ❋ ❋ ⟳ **H/S** 60cm/2ft

The distinct yellow edges to the leaflets of this perennial reinforce the common

name by appearing even more ladder-like than those of the species. Mounds of twinned foliage are topped by stems of violet-blue flowers in summer. Plant in moist but well-drained soil. Divide clumps in spring.

Polygonatum x *hybridum* 'Striatum'
Solomon's seal

☼ ☀ ❋ ❋ ❋ ⟳ **H** 60–90cm/2–3ft **S** 25cm/10in

Slightly arching stems bear fresh green leaves striped with white, particularly at the margins and tips. In late spring, 2–6 tubular, creamy-white flowers hang from each leaf axil, producing a distinctive effect of the leaves arching upwards from the stems and the flowers hanging down. Divide rhizomes in spring.

Weigela 'Florida Variegata'

☼ ☀ ❋ ❋ ❋ ⟳

H 1.8–2.5m/6–8ft **S** 1.2–1.8m/4–6ft

For a small garden, the plain-leaved weigelas are something of a luxury, as their pink flowers last for only a short period in early summer. If you choose this form of the shrub you will add attractive, white-margined foliage for the rest of the season. Thin immediately after flowering by removing older stems without compromising its natural shape.

133

REVERSION

❖

Some variegated plants, particularly shrubs, are unstable and have a tendency to revert to green. The plain green shoots that appear generally grow strongly and can take over the plant if not checked. Watch out for the appearance of these and cut them out.

Hosta fortunei var. *albopicta* ♈
☼ ❋ ❋ ❋ ⟳

H 30–45cm/12–18in **S** 60–75cm/24–30in

There are many lovely variegated hostas, useful for lightening up shady corners, planting in containers and for flower-arranging. This one is outstanding for its pale lime-green leaves, edged with two-tone green markings. Plant in moist soil and protect against slugs and snails. Lift, divide and replant in early autumn or spring.

Iris pallida 'Argentea Variegata'
Bearded iris

☼ ❋ ❋ ❋ ⟳ **H** 90cm/3ft **S** 75cm/30in

The sword-like leaves of pale green, striped with silver-white, are most attractive, in addition to which the

Iris pallida
'Argentea Variegata'

Polemonium caeruleum
Brise d'Anjou

Weigela
'Florida Variegata'

Decorative seedheads

Growth, development, flowering, fading and seeding are all fascinating stages in a plant's life cycle. Choosing plants that die gracefully and produce long-lasting seedheads adds yet another dimension to the garden. As well as encouraging drifts of pods and seedheads to decorate the garden in autumn, try cutting some seedheads just before the seeds mature, for use in dried-flower arrangements.

Physalis alkekengi

Acanthus spinosus ♈
Bear's breeches

☼ ☼ ❄ ❄ ❄ ◖ **H** 1.2m /4ft **S** 60–90cm /2–3ft

Tall spires of tubular white flowers, peeping from beneath shiny purple bracts, rise up from the clumps of large, deeply cut leaves of this perennial from late spring to midsummer. These dry to papery husks bearing large seeds; leave them on the plant as they look wonderful covered in hoar frost. Sow seed or divide clumps in spring and take root cuttings in winter.

Allium cristophii ♈
Ornamental onion, Star of Persia

☼ ❄ ❄ ❄ ◯ **H** 30–60cm /1–2ft **S** 20cm /7in

A narrow growth habit means that bulbs can be slotted between and among other plants in the garden during autumn, setting them 15–20cm (6–8in) deep.

In early summer, round heads 20cm (8in) across, on tall stems, are packed with starry purple flowers. The flowers fade to leave green, then parchment-coloured seedheads, which persist into winter and which dry well.

Astilboides tabularis
(formerly *Rodgersia tabularis*)

☼ ❄ ❄ ❄ ◯ **H/S** 90–120cm /3–4ft

Treated to rich, moist soil, the rounded, lobed and softly hairy leaves of this perennial grow tall and lush, joined by panicles of small, creamy-white flowers in early and midsummer. Plant where the slanting rays of late winter sun will catch the fluffy, rounded seedheads and bring them to life. Especially useful for bog or waterside plantings. Lift, divide and replant in spring.

Eryngium giganteum ♈
Miss Willmott's ghost

☼ ❄ ❄ ❄ ❄ ◯ **H** 90–120cm /3–4ft **S** 30–60cm /1–2ft

Toothed, silvery bracts make a ghostly and elaborate collar around each domed umbel of tiny blue flowers. The stems can be cut and dried just before the flowers open in summer. Although a short-lived perennial, this prickly customer is usually treated as a biennial; it self-seeds with abandon. Plant in well-drained soil.

Nigella damascena
Love-in-a-mist

☼ ❄ ❄ ❄ **H** 60–75cm /2–3ft **S** 45cm /18in

Some hardy annuals can be used to provide a unifying theme for garden beds and borders. Simply sow nigella seed into the ground, thin out the seedlings and wait for the blue flowers of varying intensity, each sitting in a ruff of finely divided leaves. These fade to leave inflated capsules with prominent styles. Choose *N.d.* 'Miss Jekyll' for sky-blue flowers on plants 45cm (18in) tall.

Lagurus ovatus
Hare's tail

☼ ❄ ❄ ❄ **H** 50cm /20in **S** 30cm /12in

To give a soft, natural feel to the garden, sow patches of this annual, Mediterranean grass straight into the soil in spring. Narrow, grassy foliage is

Eryngium giganteum

Lagurus ovatus

Papaver somniferum

134

• *see also:* RAISING PLANTS FROM SEED p230; PROPAGATING BY CUTTINGS p232; OTHER MEANS OF PROPAGATION p234

△ **THE STARRY FLOWERS** *of* Allium cristophii *burst open during early summer, forming magnificent rounded heads.* Nigella damascena *grown from spring sowings are setting their decorative pods.*

COLLECTING SEED

❖

Saving seed from the garden is an economical and excellent method of building up numbers of species to create drifts. Seed from highly bred plants will not come true and should be viewed as experimental only. When collecting from variable annuals and biennials, like some types of poppy, be prepared to rogue out undesirable plants before their pollen influences the rest. Collect pods and capsules into paper bags labelled with the plant name and date. Keep dry until there is time to clean the seed from its husks and pods. Store in paper envelopes in a cool, dry place until you are ready to sow them.

joined by a long succession of soft, oval spikelets throughout summer. Green at first, then tinged purple with maturity, they finally bleach to buff as they age. Pick just before maturity for drying.

Papaver orientale
Oriental poppy
☼ ✳ ✳ ✳ ✿ **H** 60–120cm / 2–4ft **S** 30cm / 12in

The silky petals fall from the blowsy, short-lived flowers of oriental poppies to reveal a seed capsule of great beauty. The top is covered by a cap composed of velvety maroon spokes over a smooth, pale green pod housing the maturing seeds. Plant in fertile, well-drained soil; lift and divide in spring or take root cuttings at virtually any time.

Physalis alkekengi ♀
Chinese lantern
☼ ◑ ✳ ✳ ✳ ✿ **H** 60cm / 2ft **S** 60–90cm / 2–3ft

Surreal, bright orange, lantern-like calyces develop during late summer from creamy-white flowers. Papery in

---

SILKY SEEDHEADS AND
STUNNING PODS

❖

Clematis tangutica ✿
Papaver somniferum (annual)
Omphalodes linifolia ♀ ✿
Pulsatilla vulgaris ♀ ✿
Staphylea pinnata ✿

---

texture, they can be dried for decorative use or left to turn into winter skeletons, revealing the orange-red berries inside. A spreading, rhizomatous perennial, it will creep into empty border spaces but is rarely a pest. Divide in early spring.

Ricinus communis 'Carmencita' ♀
Castor oil plant
☼ ✳ ◐ **H** 1.2–1.5m / 4–5ft **S** 90–150cm / 3–5ft

Although a shrub in warmer countries, the true castor oil plant is usually grown as an annual in colder climates. Raise from spring-sown seed and plant out in

early summer to enjoy the exotic, lobed, bronze-red leaves. Insignificant flowers are followed by clusters of red, spiny seed capsules. All parts are poisonous.

Scabiosa stellata 'Paper Moon'
☼ ✳ ✳ ✳ **H** 45cm / 18in **S** 23cm / 9in

This hardy annual bears exquisite seedheads, valued for drying. The spherical flowerheads are an insipid mauve-pink with larger outer florets developing into a ball of pale, stiff, papery cells. Sow into modules or straight into the soil in spring.

The spring flower garden

Everyone looks eagerly for the first spring flowers, many of which flourish naturally in woodland shade. For beauties like dog's-tooth violet (Erythronium) and trilliums, it is worth creating special beds enriched with leafmould, but others can be sprinkled through beds and borders. Enjoy their dainty display before the more flamboyant flowers of summer appear.

Helleborus orientalis 'Sirius'

136

Aquilegia vulgaris
Columbine, granny's bonnet

☼ ☀ ❄ ❄ ❄ ○ **H** 75cm /30in **S** 45cm /18in

These herbaceous perennials, easily raised from spring-sown seed, will begin flowering during their second year, in late spring. Their spurred flowers, usually in shades of pink and purple, resemble an old-fashioned bonnet. Consult seed catalogues for double forms and those with bright yellow foliage. Once established, they will seed around and, in my garden, have proved tolerant of poor, dry soil.

Dicentra 'Stuart Boothman' ♀
Bleeding heart

☼ ❄ ❄ ❄ ○ **H/S** 30cm /12in

Delicate, blue-grey, ferny foliage appears in early spring from perennial rhizomes; good for masking the foliage of snowdrops as they die down. Two-tone pink flowers, shaped like Dutchman's trousers, provide a show from mid-spring into summer. One plant can be divided in early spring to form a carpet.

Doronicum 'Miss Mason' ♀
Leopard's bane

☼ ❄ ❄ ❄ ○ **H/S** 45cm /18in

Give this herbaceous perennial a well-drained soil, or it has a tendency to rot away during winter. I like this variety because its 8cm (3in) wide, yellow daisy flowers are held well above the foliage from mid-spring to early summer. It combines well with leucojum and can be used as spring bedding. Divide large plants in spring or early autumn.

SMALL SPRING BULBS TO PLANT UNDER SHRUBS

❖

Anemone blanda (wood anemone) ♀

Leucojum vernum (spring snowflake)

Chionodoxa forbesii and *C.f.* 'Pink Giant' (glory-of-the-snow)

Erythronium dens-canis (dog's-tooth violet) ♀

Puschkinia scilloides

Scilla mischtschenkoana

Scilla siberica ♀

Erysimum 'Bowles' Mauve' ♀

☼ ❄ ❄ ❄ ◗ **H/S** 75cm /30in

This evergreen, perennial wallflower earns its place in the garden by bearing its purple flowers from spring into summer. In common with most wallflowers, it appreciates well-drained, slightly alkaline soil. A trim after flowering will delay the time when an older plant needs replacing by a successor raised from cuttings struck the previous spring.

Fritillaria imperialis
Crown imperial

☼ ❄ ❄ ❄ ○ **H** 90–120cm /3–4ft **S** 30cm /12in

Plant the large, foxy-smelling bulbs

Aquilegia vulgaris var. *stellata*   *Dicentra* 'Stuart Boothman'

• *see also:* PLANTING AND CARING FOR HERBACEOUS BORDERS p210; PLANTING BULBS p214; RAISING PLANTS FROM SEED p230; OTHER MEANS OF PROPAGATION p234

Lunaria annua variegata

◁ **THE TALL BACKDROP**
of Fritillaria imperialis
*makes a striking foil for a
clump of the nodding-flowered*
Leucojum aestivum.

20cm (8in) deep in well-drained soil
during autumn. Early spring should
see fresh buds nosing their way up
through the soil; by late spring, they
have risen to produce a display of
bell-shaped, orange or yellow flowers,
crowned by a tuft of leafy bracts.

Helleborus orientalis
Lenten rose

☼ ❄ ❄ ❄ ● **H/S** 45cm /18in

These choice evergreen, herbaceous
perennials produce their saucer-shaped
flowers from late winter to mid-spring.
Promiscuous, they hybridize readily and
most plants seen in gardens are hybrids.
Flower colours can be white, cream,
green, pink and deep maroon-red,
sometimes attractively marked with
darker spots or flecks.

Leucojum aestivum 'Gravetye Giant' ♈
Snowflake

☼ ◐ ❄ ❄ ❄ ◖ **H** 60cm /2ft **S** 23cm /9in

Plant bulbs 10cm (4in) deep in autumn
in moist, well-conditioned soil to bloom
the following spring. White, nodding,
green-tipped flowers are suspended
from the main stem by slender stalks.

Lunaria annua variegata
Variegated honesty

☼ ◐ ❄ ❄ ❄ ● **H** 90cm /3ft **S** 60cm /2ft

Sow this biennial in the early summer of
one year to flower during the late spring
of the next. The first year's rosette of
leaves is plain green, the cream-edged
leaves being produced as the plant
rises up to produce its pink flowers.
Disc-shaped green pods turn whitish-
silver in autumn and persist all winter.

NARCISSUS AND TULIPS FOR INFORMAL PLANTING
❖

Narcissus 'Ice Wings'

Narcissus 'Jack Snipe'

Narcissus poeticus

Tulipa greigii

T. praestans 'Van Tubergen's Variety'

Tulipa 'Spring Green' ♈

Tulipa tarda ♈

Omphalodes linifolia ♈
Venus' navelwort

☼ ❄ ❄ ❄ ● **H/S** 30cm /12in

Sow this pretty biennial into well-
drained soil one summer to produce
airy white flowers the following spring.
Thereafter, a rash of blue-green
seedlings will appear every autumn and
can be thinned and transplanted where
needed. So-called because the seedpods
resemble tummy buttons!

Pulmonaria saccharata
Lungwort

☼ ◐ ❄ ❄ ❄ ◖ **H** 30cm /12in **S** 45cm /18in

Among these eminently collectable
herbaceous perennials, this species is
one of my favourites. The rosette of
silver-spotted leaves persists all winter,
with stems of furry buds rising to reveal
pink flowers from early to late spring.
Remove old leaves after flowering.

Pulmonaria saccharata

KEY: ♈ *Award of Merit* ☼ *sun* ◐ *semi-shade* ● *shade* ❄ *half-hardy* ❄❄ *frost-hardy* ❄❄❄ *fully hardy* ◖ *deciduous* ● *evergreen* ◖ *semi-evergreen* **H** *height* **S** *spread*

The summer flower garden

There are so many colourful summer-flowering perennials, annuals and bulbs that creating stunning summer borders is easy. Nevertheless, planning is needed to make sure the display continues from early to late summer, when there can be a lull in the garden. Reserve a few pots of annuals like Rudbeckia 'Marmalade' to fill gaps after a midsummer overhaul.

138

Anthemis tinctoria 'E.C. Buxton'

☼ ✳ ✳ ✳ ◼ **H** 60–90cm/2–3ft **S** 75cm/30in

Once established, anthemis prove to be drought-tolerant border plants giving a long show of bright, daisy-like flowers. The blooms of this cultivar are palest lemon yellow with deep yellow centres. As you cut down the fading flowers, more develop; the filigree foliage persists throughout winter. May require support. Divide during autumn on sandy soils but in spring on clay.

Campanula lactiflora 'Prichard's Variety' ♔
Milky bellflower

☼ ◐ ✳ ✳ ✳ ◯ **H** 1.2–1.5m/4–5ft **S** 60cm/2ft

Provide support for this tall campanula by pushing sticks into position from late spring, or planting it among the stems of dogwood. Panicles of dark, violet-blue flowers are borne in summer and early autumn. Plant in fertile, neutral to alkaline soil, keep moist and trim back after flowering for a second flush. Divide in spring or autumn.

Cleome hassleriana 'Colour Fountain'
Spider flower

☼ ✳ ✳ **H** 90–150cm/3–5ft **S** 60cm/2ft

Tall annuals like cleome and tithonia never fail to impress me. That they can produce such height and flower-power in one season from seed is truly a marvel. Allow space in the border for the hairy stems of palmate leaves, topped by elegant racemes of scented pink, white or purple flowers with long, prominent stamens. Sow under glass in spring to plant out when all danger of frost has passed. Plant in fertile soil and keep moist.

▷ **CREATE DEEP BORDERS** *to accommodate a good mix of perennials that will provide colour and shape all summer. Plug any gaps with plants such as Nicotiana sylvestris (top left) and colourful larkspurs, both raised annually from seed.*

Coreopsis verticillata 'Zagreb'
Tickseed

☼ ✳ ✳ ✳ ◯

H 60–75cm/24–30in **S** 30–45cm/12–18in

An ability to tolerate poor, dry, sandy soils certainly recommends this perennial to me. Another North American daisy, it is equally happy on clay. Masses of fine, fern-like, bright green leaves are joined by a profusion of dainty, golden-yellow flowerheads in early to midsummer. The pointed petals have a simple beauty. Lift, divide and replant in spring.

Echinacea purpurea 'Magnus'
Purple coneflower

☼ ✳ ✳ ✳ ◯ **H** 60–120cm/2–4ft **S** 50cm/20in

The impressive hallmarks of this North American perennial are their large pink daisies, with superb, domed orange centres opening from late summer to autumn on sturdy stems. It tolerates poor, dry soils, but the plants will be shorter. To establish several groups cheaply, raise plants from spring-sown seed. Lift, divide and replant in spring or autumn.

PLANTING HALF-HARDY ANNUALS

❖

Fill gaps in a border with colourful bedding plants like pelargoniums and *Gypsophila muralis*. Planted in early summer, they will bloom till autumn, outlasting the perennial daisies.

• **see also:** PLANTING AND CARING FOR HERBACEOUS BORDERS p210; SOWING AND USING HARDY ANNUALS p212; OTHER MEANS OF PROPAGATION p234

Inula hookeri

Eremurus robustus
Foxtail lily
☼ ❋ ❋ ❋ ◐ **H** 1.8–2.5m / 6–8ft **S** 90cm / 3ft

Buy foxtail lilies as succulent roots to plant in the autumn in well-drained but nourishing soil. Plant them with their crowns just under the surface. In late spring, a rosette of basal leaves appears, followed by the flower spike, which can be prone to late frosts. This rises to a great height and is studded with masses of pointed buds held out on thin stalks, opening to small, sugar-pink flowers with yellow pollen. The leaves die back as the flowers fade.

Inula hookeri
☼ ◑ ❋ ❋ ❋ ◐ **H** 60–75cm / 24–30in **S** 60cm / 2ft

Soft, hairy buds open to reveal daisy-like yellow flowers with slightly darker centres and dainty, narrow petals. Both the leaves and stems of this perennial are softly hairy. Happy plants quickly form large clumps that seem to do better in light shade and benefit from some support. Plant in moist but well-drained soil. Divide in spring or autumn.

Knautia macedonica
☼ ❋ ❋ ❋ ● **H** 60–75cm / 24–30in **S** 60cm / 2ft

Deep wine-red, scabious-like flowers about 2.5cm (1in) across are held on hairy, branching stems well above the basal foliage all summer. Plants are easy to raise from spring-sown seed, which enables several clumps to be grown, or you can take basal cuttings in spring. Plant in well-drained, alkaline to neutral soil.

Monarda 'Cambridge Scarlet' ♔
Bergamot, Bee balm
☼ ◑ ❋ ❋ ❋ ◐ **H** 90cm / 3ft **S** 60cm / 2ft

I wish I could grow these beautiful perennials, but despite their origins in dry North American scrub and woodland they dislike my poor, sandy soil. To succeed, they need moist, well-drained soil or regular watering during droughts; waterlogging is not tolerated either. In bloom, the tall stems of aromatic leaves are topped by mop-like heads of scarlet petals from midsummer to early autumn. Lift and divide the rather shallow rhizomes in spring.

Paeonia lactiflora 'Bowl of Beauty' ♔
Peony
☼ ◑ ❋ ❋ ❋ ◐ **H/S** 75–90cm / 30–36in

Peonies are the prima ballerinas of the early herbaceous border, giving a short-lived but voluptuous display. When choosing, be aware that flowers can be single, semi-double, double or, as here, anemone-form. Rich pink petals surround and contrast with a central mass of creamy stamens. Plant in soil enriched with organic matter from autumn to spring, when conditions are right, shallowly planting the crown no more than 2.5cm (1in) deep.

Monarda 'Cambridge Scarlet'

Paeonia lactiflora 'Bowl of Beauty'

The autumn flower garden

With the onset of cooler temperatures and moist soil, the garden often takes on a new lease of life after the heat and dryness of high summer. With careful planning, a range of fresh flowers can open during late summer and continue into the autumn. Their spry beauty makes an appropriate accompaniment to fruits, seeds and autumn tints.

Kniphofia rooperi

140

Anemone × hybrida 'Honorine Jobert' ♛
Japanese anemone

☼ ☼ ❄ ❄ ❄ ○ **H** 1.2m/4ft **S** 75cm/30in

Large white flowers, each with a central boss of gold stamens, open from rounded buds from late summer well into autumn. These are held on branching stems, which have risen from basal leaves during the summer. Plant during autumn in moist soil enriched with organic matter and allow plants to establish into fine clumps, as their deep, woody tap roots resent disturbance.

Aster amellus 'King George' ♛
Italian starwort

☼ ❄ ❄ ❄ ○ **H** 60cm/2ft **S** 45cm/18in

Although related to Michaelmas daisies, the Italian starworts sprout out from a

Aster amellus 'King George'

woody base rather than from creeping rhizomes. This makes them more fragile to grow, but they have the distinct advantage of mildew resistance. 'King George' bears large, violet-blue flowerheads with contrasting, golden-yellow centres. These perennials must have well-drained soil. Root basal cuttings in spring.

Dahlia 'Alltami Corsair' ♛
☼ ❄ ○ **H** 1.4m/4ft 6in **S** 75cm/30in

The simplest approach with the tall, showy dahlias is to buy tubers and plant them 10–15cm (4–6in) deep in mid-spring. Support with canes or stakes, feed well and pinch out the growing tip at 45cm (18in) to encourage branching. This semi-cactus type bears deep crimson blooms. Feed well and they can reach 15–20cm (6–8in) across. Wait until the leaves are frosted before lifting and drying tubers. Store frost-free, covered with dryish compost. For cuttings, make tubers sprout under glass in early spring and strike the young shoots.

Gladiolus callianthus ♛
☼ ❄ ❄ ○ **H** 75–100cm/30–40in **S** 15cm/6in

Plant corms 10–16cm (4–6in) deep in groups between existing plants for a lovely surprise in autumn. Long stems bearing short-lived flowers over a long

period rise up above the surrounding plants. Each fragrant white bloom is delicately shaped, with beautiful dark maroon markings inside. In cold areas lift, dry and store corms in a frost-free place during winter. On my light, sandy soil they usually survive average winters.

Kniphofia rooperi
Red hot poker

☼ ☼ ❄ ❄ ❄ ● **H** 1.2m/4ft **S** 90cm/3ft

The orange-red flowers turn to yellow as they fade, making the conical flowerheads of this perennial two-tone. These are produced throughout autumn, rising on stems above the tufts of long green leaves, and certainly earn their space in the garden. Plant this South African native in soil enriched with organic matter and divide established clumps in spring.

Nerine bowdenii ♛
☼ ❄ ❄ ○ **H** 45cm/18in **S** 30cm/12in

Plant bulbs into well-drained soil during spring with their necks just protruding. In exposed gardens, site along the base of a sunny wall for protection. Stems push through the soil in autumn, each bearing a beautiful, fresh pink flower. These are ideal for flower-arranging and

• *see also:* PLANTING AND CARING FOR HERBACEOUS BORDERS p210; SOWING AND USING HARDY ANNUALS p212; OTHER MEANS OF PROPAGATION p234

AUTUMN
SCENE-STEALERS
❖

Amaryllis belladonna ♫

Aster cordifolius 'Photograph' ♀ ♫

Cimicifuga simplex 'White Pearl' ♫

Clematis heracleifolia 'Wyevale' ♀ ♫

Chrysanthemum 'Mary Stoker' ♫

Chrysanthemum 'Nantyderry
Sunshine' ♫

Helianthemum helianthoides ♫

Helianthus salicifolius ♫

Schizostylis coccinea 'Sunrise' ♀ ✿

141

△ **FLOWERING FROM** *late summer to autumn,* Anemone × hybrida *is a classic of the late border.*

some gardeners set their spare bulbs in a row in the vegetable garden for this purpose. Strappy leaves appear with the flowers. Divide after flowering.

Physostegia virginiana
Obedient plant

☼ ◐ ❋ ❋ ❋ ♫ **H** 45–60cm /18–24in **S** 45cm /18in

Flower stems rise up in late summer and autumn, bearing tubular, pinkish-purple flowers one on top of the other, usually facing in just two directions. These are hinged and, if you push one, it will stay put, hence the common name of this perennial. They enjoy moist, fertile soil but tolerate poorer ones. Sow seed in autumn or spring; divide while dormant.

Rudbeckia fulgida var. sullivantii 'Goldsturm' ♀
Coneflower

☼ ◐ ❋ ❋ ❋ ♫ **H** 60cm /2ft **S** 45cm /18in

Golden-yellow, slightly pleated outer petals contrast beautifully with the inner cone of disk florets, which are a deep chocolate-brown, glowing purple in sunlight. Of North American origin, this compact perennial will tolerate poor, dry

soils well, but grows larger and faster in fertile soils with more body. Divide rhizomatous clumps in autumn or spring.

Sedum spectabile ♀
Ice plant

☼ ❋ ❋ ❋ ❋ ♫ **H/S** 45cm /18in

Mounds of succulent, grey-green leaves and flat heads of green buds add structure in summer. Star-shaped pink flowers, loved by bees and butterflies, open in late summer and autumn. It is worth leaving the old flowerheads on until midwinter. Ice plants make a good, solid edging to a border and thrive even

Physostegia virginiana 'Vivid'

on poor, drought-prone soils; too much fertility causes flopping. Lift, divide and replant in spring or autumn.

Tricyrtis formosana ♀
Toad lily

☼ ◐ ❋ ❋ ❋ ♫ **H** 75cm /30in **S** 45cm /18in

This woodland plant from Taiwan makes good clumps in the dappled shade between trees, opening clusters of exotic, star-shaped white or palest pink flowers that are spotted, toad-like, with purple-red. Plant in fertile soil conditioned with leafmould. Lift, divide and replant the rhizomes in early spring.

Sedum spectabile

KEY: ♀ *Award of Merit* ☼ *sun* ◐ *semi-shade* ● *shade* ❋ *half-hardy* ❋❋ *frost-hardy* ❋❋❋ *fully hardy* ♫ *deciduous* ✿ *evergreen* ✿ *semi-evergreen* **H** *height* **S** *spread*

The winter flower garden

Many of the plants featured here are bulbs that bloom in late winter. Used in conjunction with flowering shrubs, they can give the illusion of an early spring. Particularly precious are plants like Christmas rose, winter iris and pansies, capable of flowering in the depths of winter. All make welcome additions to winter posies collected for the house.

Helleborus argutifolius

142

Crocus tommasinianus ♛

☼ ❄ ❄ ❄ ♡ **H** 8–10cm / 3–4in **S** 8cm / 3in

In late winter a sunny border can be transformed into a rich carpet of pale lilac or rich purple, depending on which form of this excellent crocus is grown. Naturalizing well, they increase by seed and offsets, spreading themselves liberally through beds and lawn. All trace of the plants will have disappeared by the time serious spring and summer flowers begin their show. Plant corms 8–10cm (3–4in) deep in well-drained soil during autumn.

Cyclamen coum ♛

☼ ❄ ❄ ❄ ♡ **H/S** 5–8cm / 2–3in

Delicate buds open to fresh white, pink or red flowers above new foliage in late winter. Rounded leaves vary from plain deep green through those with silvery patterning to some, like the Pewter

Group ♛, which are almost entirely silver. Plant so that tubers sit just below the surface in rich, well-drained soil. Left undisturbed, they usually self-seed.

Eranthis hyemalis ♛
Winter aconite

☼ ☼ ❄ ❄ ❄ ♡ **H/S** 5–10cm / 2–4in

With leaves like bright green collars and their pretty, yellow, buttercup-like flowers, eranthis are a promise of spring in late winter. Position them so they can push through gaps in borders or to naturalize in grass. Plant tubers 5cm (2in) deep in autumn or, better still, plant when in growth. Choose good soil enriched with organic matter.

Galanthus nivalis ♛
Common snowdrop

☼ ❄ ❄ ❄ ♡ **H/S** 8–15cm / 3–6in

Although there are many more exotic

snowdrops from which to choose, the charm of the common sort, with its single, nodding flowers, is hard to resist. Plant the bulbs 10cm (4in) deep in groups, ideally when in growth or when dormant during early autumn. Given rich soil that stays moist during their growth and light shade for summer, they quickly naturalize, forming attractive groups.

Helleborus argutifolius ♛
Corsican hellebore

☼ ☼ ❄ ❄ ❄ ♣ **H** 60–120cm / 2–4ft **S** 90cm / 3ft

A good plant for problem areas, this hellebore is tough and capable of surviving on poor, dry soils, though it would prefer a moist, humus-rich root run. Leaves composed of three spiny-toothed leaflets are deep green above and pale below. Pendent green flowers open in late winter. Remove the old flowers and leaves to make way for new ones in late spring. The seed germinates easily when ripe.

Helleborus niger 'Potter's Wheel'
Christmas rose

☼ ❄ ❄ ❄ ♡ **H** 30cm / 12in **S** 45cm / 18in

Rigorous selection produced this fine form of the Christmas rose, which is

Cyclamen coum

Galanthus nivalis

• *see also:* PLANTING BULBS p214

Iris reticulata   *Scilla mischtschenkoana*

143

△ **CHEERFUL WINTER ACONITES**, *one of the earliest bulbs to flower, lifts the spirits in winter.*

propagated by seed commercially. Superior plants produce huge, rounded, long-lasting blooms 10cm (4in) across in late winter. Glistening white sepals with green bases surround a central cluster of golden stamens, shown off to perfection by tall stems and an outward-looking habit. Plant in good soil enriched with organic matter. Divide large clumps after flowering.

Iris reticulata ♥

☼ ❄ ❄ ❄ ◘ **H** 15cm/6in **S** 8cm/3in

Fragrant, jewel-like flowers open in late winter as the pointed leaves break through the soil. These vary in colour from pale to deep purple or blue with bright yellow markings on each outward petal. Plant groups of bulbs into well-drained soil, 8–10cm (3–4in) deep, during autumn. Apply a high-potash liquid fertilizer every two weeks while in growth and these iris will naturalize into good clumps.

Iris unguicularis ♥
Winter iris

☼ ❄ ❄ ❄ ◗ **H** 45–60cm/18–24in **S** 60–90cm/2–3ft

For the best show of pale lavender-blue flowers in the depths of winter, plant this iris in poor, well-drained, neutral to alkaline soil. Mine flourish in an impoverished gap between the house wall and a tarmac drive. The grass-like foliage becomes untidy, so remove dead leaves twice a year. Divide rhizomatous clumps after flowering or in autumn.

Scilla mischtschenkoana

☼ ☼ ❄ ❄ ❄ ◘ **H** 10–15cm/4–6in **S** 8cm/3in

Plant the small bulbs 8–10cm (3–4in) deep during early autumn to bloom in late winter. The pretty, pale blue flowers do not require direct light to open and therefore make good underplanting for shrubs like camellia and fothergilla. They enjoy moisture while growing, but prefer dry soil in summer.

Viola x *wittrockiana*
Universal Series ♥
Winter-flowering pansy

☼ ❄ ❄ ❄ ◗ **H** 15–23cm/6–9in **S** 23–30cm/9–12in

Brightly coloured winter pansies are hard to resist when they fill garden centres during the autumn. Their blooms open during mild midwinter spells and continue to give a grand finale in spring. Use to fill gaps in borders, as bedding displays and for containers. Plants are raised from seed sown in late spring or early summer.

WINTER FOLIAGE
❖

To provide a foliage accompaniment to these winter-flowering beauties, try *Arum italicum* subsp. *italicum* 'Marmoratum' ♥. Reaching a height of 23-60cm (9-24in), the beautifully marbled, arrow-shaped leaves appear to wither during hard frosts, then bounce back when it thaws. Produced in autumn, the foliage persists through winter and spring, then dies back in summer. Pale green cuckoo-pint type flowers appear in early summer followed by stems of bright red berries, which are poisonous.

KEY: ♥ *Award of Merit* ☼ *sun* ☼ *semi-shade* ❁ *shade* ❄ *half-hardy* ❄❄ *frost-hardy* ❄❄❄ *fully hardy* ◘ *deciduous* ◗ *evergreen* ◗ *semi-evergreen* **H** *height* **S** *spread*

Annuals to grow from seed

One of the easiest and cheapest ways to fill areas with colour for the summer is to sow annuals straight into the soil in spring. Once conditions are warm enough for weeds to start germinating, they can be sown. Some make excellent cut flowers, so reserve a few rows in the vegetable plot too – they will attract beneficial insects like hoverflies and bees. Fully hardy annuals can also be sown in autumn, to give earlier flowering the following year.

Convolvulus tricolor
'Royal Ensign'

144

Amaranthus caudatus
Love-lies-bleeding, Tassel flower

☼ ❋ **H** 90–150cm /3–5ft **S** 45–75cm /18–30in

These impressive plants make tassel-like panicles 45–60cm (18–24in) long of tiny, crimson-purple flowers from summer to autumn. Resembling long strands of red millet, they show up well against the large, bright green leaves. Some selections yield plants with red, green or yellow flower tassels. For the best results, keep moist and support with twiggy sticks. Collect seed in autumn.

Amaranthus caudatus

Centaurea cyanus 'Blue Diadem'
Cornflower

☼ ❋ ❋ ❋ **H** 75cm /30in **S** 15cm /6in

A classic cornfield annual, the double, deep blue flowers measure up to 7cm (2½in) across. Cornflowers cut well for vases and some seed selections cater specifically for this, with long stems and blending shades of blue, pink and white blooms. Suitable also for bedding, there are dwarf seed strains at a diminutive 20–30cm (8–12in) high.

Chrysanthemum carinatum 'Tricolor Mixed'
Painted daisy

☼ ❋ **H** 30–45cm /12–18in **S** 30cm /12in

Bred from a Moroccan native, these showy annuals bear single, daisy-like flowers up to 8cm (3in) across of white, yellow, orange or pink flowerheads banded with deeper colours. These appear above deeply divided, almost succulent, grey-green leaves. Another good strain is 'Court Jesters' ♛ with its brilliant flowers. Support with short, twiggy sticks.

Clarkia Royal Bouquet Series
Godetia

☼ ☀ ❋ ❋ ❋ **H** 60–90cm /2–3ft **S** 30cm /12in

Satiny, frilly-petalled double flowers in shades of pink, red, mauve or white are the rewards for sowing seed straight into the soil in autumn or spring. Godetias are ideal for cutting. Choose good soil of medium fertility and, even though stems are fairly sturdy, provide twiggy sticks early on.

Eschscholzia californica

Convolvulus tricolor 'Royal Ensign'

☼ ☀ ❋ ❋ ❋ **H** 30–40cm /12–16in **S** 30cm /12in

Growth begins upright but the stems then sprawl, making them ideal for the front of a border. Deep blue, trumpet-shaped flowers have white centres and yellow throats; up to 5cm (2in) wide, they are extremely decorative. Although related to bindweed, this annual does not have pernicious roots.

Eschscholzia Thai Silk Series
Californian poppy

☼ ❋ ❋ ❋ **H** 20–25cm /8–10in **S** 30–38cm /12–15in

Lovers of the plain and simple swear by the species E. *californica* ♛, with its shiny, bright orange petals. It is extremely fine, but so are the exotic-looking cultivars of the Thai Silk Series. Double or semi-double flowers open in a range of shimmering colours including red, pink and orange suffused with bronze. Sown into poor, well-drained soil, they will self-seed.

• *see also:* SOWING AND USING HARDY ANNUALS p212

145

Limnanthes douglasii

Iberis amara

Iberis amara 'Giant Hyacinth Flowered Mixed'
Hyacinth-flowered candytuft

☀ ❋ ❋ ❋ **H** 30cm/12in **S** 15cm/6in

Flowerheads rise into a spike of lightly scented, white, pink or red four-petalled flowers which cut well or can be used to create drifts towards the front of borders. The more petite candytuft, a favourite of children, is the shorter, flat-headed *I. umbellata*. Sow in spring or autumn.

Limnanthes douglasii ♀
Poached egg plant

☀ ❋ ❋ ❋ **H**/15cm/6in **S** 23cm/9in

Despite self-seeding with abandon, this easy plant remains within the confines of its group and, if handled with care, will not spread all over the garden. The fresh, finely divided leaves are soon studded with masses of bright, yolk-like yellow flowers, each petal edged white. Mine flower well without thinning.

Linaria maroccana 'Fairy Bouquet'
Toadflax

☀ ❋ ❋ ❋ **H** 23cm/9in **S** 15cm/6in

There are some delightful, dainty annuals among the toadflaxes. Small snapdragon blooms of jewel-like white, yellow, pink, salmon, orange, carmine or lavender, often in combination, adorn the stems of this variety while neat, linear leaves take up little space. Sown into light, well-drained soil, they self-seed freely.

Papaver commutatum ♀
Ladybird poppy

☀ ❋ ❋ ❋ **H** 45cm/18in **S** 15cm/6in

Children love to grow this easy annual because the bright red flowers, up to 8cm (3in) across, bear a black blotch at the base of each glistening petal. These rise up from low-growing rosettes of divided leaves. Poor, dry soils are tolerated well but flowers will be larger in better nourished soil and if watered.

Selecting clematis

There are few plants more versatile than clematis and every garden has room for at least some. In addition to being grown against walls and fences, clematis are effective either clothing trellis or, in combination with other plants, growing over an arch as well as weaving through shrubs in a border. Most clematis are easy to grow.

C. 'Vyvyan Pennell'

146

C. alpina 'Frances Rivis' ♈
Alpine clematis
☼ ☼ ❄ ❄ ❄ **H** 2.5m/8ft **S** 1.5m/5ft

Buds appear in spring, opening to reveal blue flowers followed by fluffy seedheads. Good for clothing the bases of climbing roses on a pergola, this clematis need only be pruned (after flowering) if it outgrows its space.

C. armandii
☼ ❄ ❄ **H** 5m/15ft **S** 3m/10ft

This vigorous evergreen needs a sheltered wall. Attention to siting will be rewarded by masses of vanilla-scented white flowers in early spring, set against long, shiny leaves. Plants are best left unpruned, but overgrown specimens can be cut hard after flowering.

C. 'Comtesse de Bouchaud' ♈
☼ ☼ ❄ ❄ ❄ **H** 2.4m/8ft **S** 1.8m/6ft

Large, rose-pink flowers are borne from mid- to late summer regardless of aspect, making this a useful clematis for a north-facing wall or fence. Prune hard in late winter, but never into old wood.

C. x durandii ♈
☼ ❄ ❄ ❄ **H/S** 90cm/3ft

More of a scrambler than a climber, this indigo-flowered clematis needs a shrub for support; it is excellent for pegging down between winter-flowering heathers. Flowers are produced in midsummer and plants can be pruned back hard in autumn.

C. 'Elsa Späth' ♈
☼ ❄ ❄ ❄ **H** 2.4m/8ft **S** 1.2m/4ft

A straightforward plant for a beginner, this hybrid produces large, deep blue flowers readily all summer. Established plants need little pruning, but if growth becomes tangled, tackle this at the end of winter.

C. 'Etoile Rose'
☼ ❄ ❄ ❄ ❄ **H** 1.8m/6ft **S** 90cm/3ft

Like others in the *C. texensis* group, the deep pink flowers of this dainty plant are characteristically tulip-shaped, appearing from mid- to late summer. Prune off dead growth in late winter.

C. 'Henryi' ♈
☼ ❄ ❄ ❄ **H** 3m/10ft **S** 90cm/3ft

I love white-flowered clematis and this is one of the best. Huge blooms open during midsummer, with a show of smaller flowers in late summer and autumn. No regular pruning is needed.

C. 'Lasurstern' ♈
☼ ❄ ❄ ❄ ❄ **H** 2.4m/8ft **S** 90cm/3ft

This stalwart plant opens its massive blue flowers, each blessed with a boss of creamy anthers, during midsummer and often again in late summer. No regular pruning is needed.

C. macropetala 'Markham's Pink' ♈
☼ ☼ ❄ ❄ ❄ **H** 3m/10ft **S** 1.5m/5ft

The freely produced sugar-pink flowers have a splendid delicacy. Opening in late spring and early summer, they appear semi-double with their skirt of petal-like stamens. If pruning is necessary, carry out after flowering.

Clematis armandii

C. 'Comtesse de Bouchaud'

C. 'Lasurstern'

• *see also:* FEEDING PLANTS p186; SPECIAL PRUNING NEEDS p240

CLEMATIS THROUGH THE SEASONS

❖

SPRING:

C. alpina

C. macropetala

EARLY SUMMER:

C. montana, C. 'Nelly Moser' ♀

C. 'Mrs Cholmondeley' ♀

LATE SUMMER:

C. 'Kardynal Wyszyński'

C. 'Marie Boisselot' ♀

AUTUMN:

C. flammula

WINTER:

C. tangutica (seedheads)

LATE WINTER:

C. cirrhosa var. *balearica* ♀

△ **CLOTHING A MELLOW BRICK WALL** *are Clematis 'Snow Queen' (right) and C. 'Elsa Späth'.*

C. montana
Mountain clematis

☼ ☼ ❊ ❊ ❊ **H** 9.5m/30ft **S** 3m/10ft

This easy, rampant clematis is excellent for covering old garden buildings and scrambling into trees. White or pink blooms open in late spring. For reliable perfume, opt for named varieties like white 'Alexander' or pink 'Elizabeth'. Prune after flowering if needed.

C. 'Niobe' ♀

☼ ☼ ❊ ❊ ❊ **H** 1.8–3m/6–10ft **S** 90cm/3ft

Deep maroon-coloured mid- to late summer flowers make this a most desirable plant, which blends well with silver, purple and pink. Pruning is not vital, but stems can be cut to the topmost pair of fat buds in late winter.

C. 'Pink Fantasy'

☼ ☼ ❊ ❊ ❊ **H** 1.8m/6ft **S** 90cm/3ft

Large pink flowers open from mid- to late summer and change hue from an intense pink on opening, to pink-flushed white when mature. Said to show resistance to wilt, this clematis should be pruned hard in late winter.

C. 'Bill MacKenzie' ♀

☼ ☼ ❊ ❊ ❊ **H** 6m/20ft **S** 3m/10ft

Blooming from midsummer to autumn, silken seedheads persist well into winter. The nodding, yellow, lantern-shaped flowers are blessed with colourful red anthers. Use to scramble over pergolas and up into trees. Prune hard in late winter.

C. 'Ville de Lyon'

☼ ❊ ❊ ❊ **H** 3m/10ft **S** 1.2m/4ft

Rounded red flowers open from late summer into autumn, each graced with a central boss of golden stamens. Prune hard in late winter for the longest season of flowers.

C. 'Vyvyan Pennell' ♀

☼ ❊ ❊ ❊ ❊ **H** 2.4m/8ft **S** 90cm/3ft

One of the best doubles, the early summer blooms are an exotic mixture of violet-blue with warm flushes of carmine and yellow anthers. In common with other double-flowered clematis, pruning is unnecessary.

C. 'Niobe'

Choosing and using roses

This marvellous group of plants offers so many different attributes: there are efficient ground coverers, pretty patio roses for containers and small beds, shrubs for mixed borders and climbers to clothe vertical surfaces, not to mention bush roses for colour and cut flowers. When choosing roses, consider length of flowering time, quality of perfume and disease resistance.

R. 'Korresia'

GROUND COVER ROSES

148

R. 'Suffolk'

☼ ❁ ❁ ❁ ❁ ✿ **H** 45cm /18in **S** 90cm /3ft

Some ground cover roses are large, so for smaller gardens it is useful to know this small, neat plant. Expect a show of single scarlet flowers, each decorated by golden stamens, to be produced all summer, followed by orange-red hips. Pruning is not compulsory, but I reduce mine by half in late winter.

R. 'Flower Carpet' ♔

☼ ❁ ❁ ❁ ❁ ✿

H 75cm /30in **S** 1.2m /4ft

Vigorous, disease-resistant rose introduced in 1992, with clusters of double, shocking pink flowers. 'Flower Carpet White' is easier to assimilate with other plantings.

R. 'Flower Carpet'

PATIO ROSES

R. 'Marie Pavie'

☼ ☼ ❁ ❁ ❁ ❁ ✿ **H/S** 45cm /18in

Although the idea of patio roses seems modern, this pretty dwarf polyantha type dates from 1888. Making a good, bushy shape, the clusters of fragrant white flowers, with a faint blush of pink

continue to open over a long period. A strong rose: prune out dead wood in winter.

R. 'Queen Mother' ♔

☼ ❁ ❁ ❁ ❁ ✿ **H** 40cm /16in **S** 60cm /2ft

A healthy, modern dwarf cluster-flowered rose, bred in 1991. The foliage is glossy and joined by a succession of rounded, double, pink flowers from summer to autumn. Slightly fragrant, they open fully to reveal yellow stamens. Prune in late winter by reducing the size by up to half.

R. 'Sweet Dream' ♔

☼ ❁ ❁ ❁ ❁ ✿ **H/S** 45cm /18in

What this rose lacks in perfume, it makes up for by producing masses of double, apricot-shaded flowers. Introduced 1988.

BUSH ROSES

R. 'Korresia'

☼ ❁ ❁ ❁ ❁ ✿ **H** 75m /30in **S** 60cm /2ft

I tend not to choose yellow roses, but this cheerful, cluster-flowered (floribunda) rose, bred in 1974 is one of the most popular. Light green leaves are joined by sprays of double, fragrant blooms, full of wavy petals, from summer to autumn. Prune by cutting growth back by half or more in late winter.

R. 'Margaret Merril' ♔

☼ ❁ ❁ ❁ ❁ ✿ **H** 75cm /30in **S** 60cm /24in

Since its introduction in 1978, this cluster-flowered (floribunda) rose has become popular for its deep fragrance and superbly shaped, high-centred, white blooms. Flushed faintly with pink, they contrast well with the dark green foliage and reach 10cm (4in) across. Cut back by half or so in early spring.

R. 'Mevrouw Nathalie Nypels' ♔

☼ ❁ ❁ ❁ ❁ ✿ **H** 75cm /30in **S** 60cm /2ft

This sweetly fragrant, cluster-flowered polyantha dates from 1919. Dark glossy leaves and rose-pink, semi-double flowers appear from summer to autumn.

R. 'Reconciliation'

☼ ❁ ❁ ❁ ❁ ✿ **H** 90cm /3ft **S** 60cm /2ft

I adore the peachy-blush tones of this large-flowered (hybrid tea) rose, bred in 1995. The well-formed blooms are highly fragrant and as decorative in a vase as in the garden. Prune by cutting growth to desired height in late winter.

R. 'Savoy Hotel' ♔

☼ ❁ ❁ ❁ ❁ ✿ **H** 80cm /32in **S** 60cm /2ft

This large-flowered (hybrid tea) type dates from 1989. The petals of its tall, slightly scented, double blooms are light pink on top but darker on the reverse.

• *see also:* PLANTS TO COVER SUNNY WALLS p110; PLANTS TO COVER FENCES p114; CLIMBING PLANTS FOR ARCHES AND PERGOLAS p116; SPECIAL PRUNING NEEDS p240

SHRUB ROSES

R. 'Graham Thomas' ℣

☼ ❋ ❋ ❋ ❂ **H/S** 1.2m /4ft

The best known of David Austin's English Roses, a modern group obtained by crossing selected old roses with modern hybrid teas and floribundas to enjoy the best aspects of both. Cupped, rich yellow, double blooms emit a strong tea rose fragrance. Glorious to look at, they are slightly quartered and packed full of petals. Prune stems by half to one third in early spring. Introduced in 1983.

R. x centifolia 'Muscosa' ℣
Old pink moss

☼ ❋ ❋ ❋ ❂ **H/S** 1.2m /4ft

This rose (1700) produces rich pink blooms from mossy, aromatic buds.

R. 'Königin von Dänemark' ℣

☼ ❋ ❋ ❋ ❂ **H** 1.5m /5ft **S** 1.2m /4ft

This is an alba dating from 1826. Though it flowers only once in summer, it is worth growing for its fragrant, rose-pink, quartered blooms, 9cm (3½in) across.

◁ **A PERGOLA** *makes an ideal climbing frame for rambler 'Bobbie James', pruned and trained.*

R. 'Prosperity' ℣

☼ ❋ ❋ ❋ ❂ **H** 1.5m /5ft **S** 1.2m /4ft

This hybrid musk (1919) bears dark leaves and clusters of scented, double, pink-flushed, creamy-white flowers.

CLIMBING AND RAMBLING ROSES

R. 'Bobbie James' ℣

☼ ❋ ❋ ❋ ❂ **H** 10m /30ft **S** 6m /20ft

Plant with caution, as the long stems reach high into trees and up into any support offered. Large clusters of small but very fragrant creamy-white, semi-double flowers open in summer, each one lit up by central golden-yellow stamens. Introduced in 1961. Prune, if necessary, by taking out older stems in late summer.

R. 'Guinée'

☼ ❋ ❋ ❋ ❂ **H** 4.5m /15ft **S** 2.2m /7ft

Having grown this climber, I can confirm its reputation as a weak grower, as it has taken some time to settle in. But patience and good cultivation are more than amply rewarded by its deep red blooms a little over 10cm (4in) across with a perfume of exquisite intensity and quality. Introduced in 1938. Train in as many shoots as possible and cut back unwanted side shoots to short spurs in early spring.

R. 'François Juranville' ℣

☼ ❋ ❋ ❋ ❂ **H** 6m /20ft **S** 4.5m /15ft

Coral pink, slightly quilled petals have a touch of yellow at the base and open to flattish, double blooms of fruity fragrance. Choose this rambler, introduced in 1906, for pergolas and to climb up into small trees. Should pruning be necessary, cut out older stems immediately after flowering and tie in new replacement growths.

R. 'Golden Showers' ℣

☼ ❋ ❋ ❋ ❂ **H** 3m /10ft **S** 1.8m /6ft

This reliable, yellow-flowered climber dates from 1956. Large blooms are produced in succession, even on a north-facing wall.

R. 'Sympathie'

☼ ❋ ❋ ❋ ❂ **H** 3m /10ft **S** 2.5m /8ft

A vigorous climber dating from 1964, bearing clusters of cupped, double, deep red flowers from summer to autumn.

R. 'Zéphirine Drouhin' ℣

☼ ❋ ❋ ❂ **H** 3m /10ft **S** 1.8m /6ft

This extremely popular thornless climber is a bourbon, introduced in 1868. Among its attributes are deep pink, scented flowers borne over a long period. It tends to suffer from mildew, but is less prone when grown on a north-facing wall.

R. 'Margaret Merril'   R. 'Reconciliation'   R. 'Graham Thomas'

KEY: ℣ *Award of Merit* ☼ *sun* ❋ *semi-shade* ❀ *shade* ❋ *half-hardy* ❋❋ *frost-hardy* ❋❋❋ *fully hardy* ○ *deciduous* ● *evergreen* ❂ *semi-evergreen* **H** *height* **S** *spread*

Ornamental grasses and bamboos

Hakonechloa macra
'Alboaurea'

Enjoying a surge of popularity, grasses are very much part of a new, relaxed style of planting. They are grown not only for their foliage but also for their decorative flowerheads, which often persist into autumn and early winter. Bamboos are chosen for their beautiful stems and oriental appearance. They rarely flower, but some species bloom simultaneously all over the country.

150

Deschampsia cespitosa 'Goldtau'
Tufted hair grass, Tussock grass
☼ ☼ ✳ ✳ ✳ 🍃

H 60–90cm / 2–3ft **S** 60–75cm / 24–30in
The main flowering period is from summer to autumn, when tall spikes of golden-bronze flowers emerge from tufted, rich green foliage and persist until early winter. Plant in groups for an impressive display. Keep soil slightly moist and cut down faded flowers in early spring. Divide in early spring.

Elymus hispidus
Hairy couch grass
☼ ✳ ✳ ✳ 🍃

H 45–75cm / 18–30in **S** 30–45cm / 12–18in
Even a single specimen of this plant is effective, its steely blue foliage at its best from spring to autumn. An occasional de-thatch will keep it pristine, but carry out a severe haircut in early spring before new growth starts. A good plant for dry, sandy soils, it is easily propagated by seed or by division in spring.

Hakonechloa macra 'Aureola' ♀
☼ ☼ ✳ ✳ ✳ ⟳

H 30–38cm / 12–15in **S** 30–45cm / 12–18in
Set in a group of five or more, the arching mounds of this grass will amaze anyone with an eye for form and colour. Grown in a container, the flexible, bright

yellow leaves, marked down their length with fine green lines, will cover its sides. *H.m.* 'Alboaurea' is similar, with green, white and yellow leaves. Pale green flowers open in panicles, late summer to mid-autumn. Divide in spring.

Milium effusum 'Aureum'
Bowles' golden grass
☼ ✳ ✳ ✳ 🍃

H 30–45cm / 12–18in **S** 23–30cm / 9–12in
This grass seeds itself around in partially shaded areas, creating informal drifts of bright, lime-green leaves, at their best from spring to late summer. Small, golden, flower-bearing spikes are borne in nodding panicles from late spring to midsummer. For best results, plant in rich, moist but well-drained soil. Divide in early spring.

Milium effusum 'Aureum'

Miscanthus sinensis 'Kleine Fontäne'
☼ ✳ ✳ ✳ ✳ ⟳ **H** 90–120cm / 3–4ft **S** 60–90cm / 2–3ft
The erect, then gently arching leaves of this grass are joined by silky flower spikes in autumn. But for lasting foliage effect, choose *M.s.* 'Morning Light', whose tall green leaves have narrow creamy margins. The latter is of architectural interest all winter, with foliage turning orange-yellow. In spring, cut down to make way for new growth and divide.

Pennisetum alopecuroides 'Woodside'
Fountain grass
☼ ✳ ✳ ✳ ⟳

H 60–120cm / 2–4ft **S** 45–90cm / 18–36in
In summer, yellow-brown flowerheads resembling bottle brushes appear on this decorative grass. These persist into autumn and associate well with the

Pleioblastus auricomus

• *see also:* OTHER MEANS OF PROPAGATION p234

△ **ONE OF THE MOST CLASSIC** *and striking of bamboos is* Phyllostachys nigra, *whose canes mature to black. Here is it seen in an extremely ornamental role, beside water.*

REVEALING THE STEMS

Bamboos like this *Phyllostachys aureosulcata* 'Spectabilis' give year-round value for little maintenance. To smarten them up, remove lower side branches and weed out weak canes, which clutter up a structured clump.

foliage as it turns golden. Grow as specimens or in groups. Plant in fertile, well-drained soil. Divide in late spring.

Phyllostachys aureosulcata 'Spectabilis'
Yellow-groove bamboo

☼ ☼ ✳ ✳ ✳ ✳ 🍃

H 3–6m /10–20ft **S** 1.2–4m /4–13ft

Plenty of water and an annual spring mulch will get this beautiful bamboo off to a roaring start. The culms (canes) are custard-yellow with green grooves and the foliage is elegant and complementary. Cut out weak canes on a regular basis (*see below left*), leaving the most vigorous to mature. Remove lower side branches to expose the straight stems. Divide in early spring.

Phyllostachys nigra ♥
Black bamboo

☼ ✳ ✳ ✳ 🍃 **H** 3–5m /10–15ft **S** 1.8–3m /6–10ft

Although tolerant of partial shade, the sun will show off the shiny black canes to advantage. These begin olive-green, mottled with black, and reach perfection when three years old. It makes a wonderful specimen for a large pot. Feed and water well from spring to early summer and thin out weaker shoots regularly. Divide in early spring.

Pleioblastus auricomus ♥

☼ ✳ ✳ ✳ 🍃 **H** 1.2–1.5m /4–5ft **S** 90–150cm /3–5ft

This splendid bamboo will brighten up the dullest border with the light effect of its bright green and golden-yellow striped foliage. Plant away from cold, drying winds and cut down to the

CHOICE BAMBOOS AND GRASSES

❖

Arrhenatherum elatius ssp. *bulbosum* 'Variegatum' ⟳

Chionochloa rubra 🍃

Chusquea culeou ♥ 🍃

Fargesia nitida ♥ 🍃

Festuca glauca 'Elijah Blue'

Festuca glauca 'Golden Toupée' 🍃

Luzula nivea 🍃

Melica ciliata ⟳

Stipa gigantea ♥ 🍃

151

Miscanthus sinensis 'Kleine Fontäne'

ground annually in autumn for the best results. Use in small gardens where year-round colour is required. Divide rhizomes in spring.

Stipa tenuissima

☼ ✳ ✳ ✳ ⟳ **H** 45–60cm /18–24in **S** 30cm /12in

The upright, bright green leaves of this grass are topped by silver-white flowers all summer. These are borne in fluffy, feathery, waving panicles which waft readily in the breeze. Plant in drifts of three or five in light, well-drained soil and cut down to the basal clump in early winter. Split clumps in mid-spring.

Plants for summer containers

Pots, tubs, baskets and window boxes filled with plants are an ideal way of adding seasonal colour and providing focal points. Being mobile, containers can be moved around the garden as required. Although they demand regular watering and feeding, their care involves no back-breaking digging or weeding. For a summer display, plant up during late spring or early summer.

152

Argyranthemum gracile 'Chelsea Girl' ♀
Marguerite, Paris daisy
☼ ❄ 🍂 **H/S** 60cm/24in

A succession of small, white, yellow-centred daisies are borne on slender stems above finely divided, fern-like foliage all summer. Use this tender perennial for a pot or as the centrepiece for a large hanging basket. Pot up in autumn and overwinter in a frost-free greenhouse. Take cuttings in summer or in spring. Be vigilant against aphids.

Begonia Illumination Series ♀
☼ ❄ ❄ ⟳ **H** 60cm/24in **S** 30cm/12in

This trailing, tuberous begonia is the ideal solution for a hanging basket hung against a shady wall. Plant out in early summer and watch its trailing stems colonize the basket, producing masses of double, brightly coloured blooms 8cm (3in) in diameter. The tubers can be dried off to store in a frost-free place during winter. Start into growth in warmth the following early spring.

Brachyscome iberidifolia
Swan river daisy
☼ ❄ ⟳ **H** 45cm/18in **S** 35cm/14in

A spreading nature makes this annual ideal for hanging baskets and window boxes. Dissected, fern-like leaves are a backdrop to masses of blue, sometimes violet or white, daisy-like flowers, each with a contrasting yellow centre, which combine well with other container plants in full sun. Sow seed under glass in spring.

Fuchsia 'Annabel' ♀
☼ ❄ ⟳ **H/S** 30–60cm/12–24in

There are many fuchsias, suiting all tastes and different containers. These tender perennials fare better out of full sun and are good for shady plantings. 'Annabel' is a bushy sort with double white blooms touched with a faint flush of pink. Take cuttings during summer and overwinter in a frost-free greenhouse. Prune plants back in early spring.

Helichrysum petiolare 'Roundabout'
☼ ❄ 🍂 **H** 15cm/6in **S** 30cm/12in

Strong foliage plants are an important ingredient of successful container plantings. Felty, silvery-leaved *Helichrysum petiolare* ♀ and its cultivars are ideal to offset stronger coloured flowers. With small leaves and low, spreading growth, 'Roundabout' will not swamp a hanging basket; its grey-green leaves have cream edges. Summer cuttings will rot if kept too humid.

Argyranthemum gracile

Begonia 'Illumination Apricot'

Brachyscome iberidifolia

• *see also*: GROWING IN CONTAINERS p224; GROWING IN HANGING BASKETS p228; PROPAGATING BY CUTTINGS p232

◁ **TRAILING PETUNIAS** *such as Surfinia Blue Vein are hard to beat for impact with their vigorous growth and abundance of large flowers. Use them in window boxes, hanging baskets and to smother the front of large tubs.*

Verbena 'Silver Anne' ♛
☼ ❋ ❋ ● **H** 30cm/12in **S** 60cm/24in

There are several perennial verbenas with a trailing habit, ideal for containers. 'Silver Anne' is robust enough to hold its own in a basket packed with fuchsias and pelargoniums, opening scented flowerheads of pink fading to silvery pink. Take cuttings in summer and overwinter in a frost-free greenhouse. Prune ungainly plants in spring.

153

Mimulus × *hybridus* Magic Series
Monkey musk

☼ ☼ ❋ **H** 20cm/8in **S** 30cm/12in

These bushy, spreading, tender perennials hail from my favourite plant family, Scrophulariaceae, and are related to foxgloves and toadflax. Treat as annuals by sowing seed under glass in spring. The colour range is luscious, including rich reds, yellows and oranges as well as pastel shades, most with spotted throats. Ideal for shady hanging baskets and window boxes.

Pelargonium 'L'Elégante' ♛
Ivy-leaved geranium

☼ ❋ ● **H** 20–25cm/8–10in **S** 20cm/8in

The foliage of this neat, trailing, tender perennial is extremely decorative. Ivy-shaped leaves bear irregular cream edges that turn pink in good light and clusters of single white flowers are borne throughout summer. Propagate from summer cuttings and overwinter in frost-free conditions. Prune gangly, mature plants in early spring.

Pelargonium 'L'Elégante'

Petunia Surfinia Series
☼ ❋ **H** 30cm/12in **S** 60–90cm/2–3ft

Trailing petunias are hugely popular for window boxes and hanging baskets, as they make long stems packed full of large, trumpet-shaped flowers. Most are scented and the range includes Blue, Purple, White, Hot Pink, Blue Vein and Pink Vein. They can be propagated by cuttings but, since they are virus-prone, it is advisable to buy healthy young plants each spring.

Portulaca grandiflora
Sundance Hybrids
Sun plant

☼ ❋ **H/S** 15cm/6in

Drought tolerance is a useful asset for plants that are grown in containers. The attractive red stems and fleshy, cylindrical, needle-like foliage of this succulent South American annual blend well with aeonium, agave and pelargoniums. Sundance Hybrids have a bushy, trailing habit and bear double flowers in a range of colours that includes bright pinks, reds, orange, white and yellow. Sow seed under glass in spring.

PLANTING AND CARE
❖

- Make sure all containers have drainage holes; use pot feet or tiles to raise them off the ground.

- Always use good potting compost; try an equal mixture by volume of a soilless variety and John Innes No. 2.

- Do not stand pots outside until all danger of frost has past.

- At planting time, incorporate slow-release fertilizer and moisture-retaining granules into the compost.

- Apply general-purpose liquid feed at least weekly for most plants.

Winter and spring containers

Autumn is the time to remove fading summer flowers from your troughs and pots and replant them for winter and spring. Use tough evergreen shrubs and perennials to give bulk and shape, with trailing ivies and smaller pansies, bellis and primulas for colour and infill. Push dwarf-growing, spring-flowering bulbs around the roots of other plants for a seasonal surprise.

Tanacetum parthenium 'Aureum'

154

Ajuga reptans 'Braunherz' ♛
Bugle

☼ ❋ ❋ ❋ ◗ **H** 15cm /6in **S** 60cm /24in

The low rosettes of shiny, dark maroon leaves on this perennial ground cover can plug gaps in winter and spring arrangements. They even flourish in the sides of hanging baskets. Spikes of blue flowers, 15cm (6in) tall, appear in late spring and early summer. On dismantling the container, plant a bugle in the ground and it will quickly multiply, ready to supply future plantings.

Bellis perennis Pomponette Series ♛
Daisy

☼ ☼ ❋ ❋ ❋ ◗ **H/S** 10–15cm /4–6in

Sow seed in early summer to yield plants that will bloom in the autumn and spring. Neat, domed, red, pink or white double flowerheads up to 4cm (1½in) across are packed full of quilled petals. Although treated as biennials, they are perennial and the clumps can be divided after flowering. Watch out for aphids.

Brassica oleracea Osaka Series
Ornamental cabbage

☼ ❋ ❋ ❋ ◗ **H** 30cm /12in **S** 45cm /18in

Although these colourful, annual cabbages can be raised for an autumn planting from spring-sown seed, they are usually the result of impulse buying. As temperatures fall, the wavy-edged leaves towards the hearts intensify in colour to bright pink, red or creamy white. Plants remain decorative until midwinter, after which they begin to fade and to elongate.

EVERGREENS FOR WINTER AND SPRING CONTAINERS

❖

Bergenia 'Wintermärchen'
Blechnum penna-marina
Erica carnea 'Springwood White' ♛
Euonymus fortunei Emerald 'n' Gold ♛
Euonymus fortunei 'Silver Queen' ♛
Hedera helix 'Königers Auslese'
Helleborus niger ♛
Santolina chamaecyparissus ♛
Solanum capsicastrum
Thymus x *citriodorus* 'Aureus' ♛
Viola x *wittrockiana* Universal Series ♛

Carex hachijoensis 'Evergold' ♛
Golden sedge

☼ ☼ ❋ ❋ ❋ ◗ **H** 23cm /9in **S** 45cm /18in

This perennial grass has tufts of mop-like foliage that are of great decorative value to window boxes; the narrow leaves are marked along their length with an irregular, creamy-yellow stripe. Propagate by division in spring. The plants do not object to being lifted for use in the autumn and replaced in spring, as long as they are well watered.

Bellis perennis 'Prolifera'

Ornamental cabbages

• *see also:* GROWING IN CONTAINERS p224; YEAR-ROUND CONTAINERS p226; GROWING IN HANGING BASKETS p228

Chamaecyparis lawsoniana 'Ellwood's Gold' ♈

☼ ☀ ❋ ❋ ❋ ● H 3m/10ft S 1.5m/5ft

Dense, yellow-green foliage, tipped with gold, makes this slow-growing conifer a year-round feature. Its height will be restricted by container growing. Use as a centrepiece to a large pot, or set two or more smaller specimens along the length of a window box for structure. Keep the roots moist, or the foliage will turn brown.

Gaultheria procumbens ♈
Checkerberry

☼ ☀ ❋ ❋ ❋ ● H 15cm/6in S 60–90cm/2–3ft

Attractive, aromatic, evergreen leaves are joined by little, pale pink, bell-shaped flowers in summer. By the autumn, these flowers are being followed by scarlet fruit and the leaves often turn red too, as temperatures drop. Plant this shrub in any container, using ericaceous compost as gaultherias are acid-loving. It also makes good ground cover for shade. Remove rooted suckers in spring.

Gaultheria procumbens

Ophiopogon planiscapus 'Nigrescens' ♈

☼ ☀ ❋ ❋ ❋ ● H 20cm/8in S 30cm/12in

With its shiny, almost black, strappy leaves, this hardy, evergreen perennial resembles a dark spider plant. Plant it near pale colours in order to show off its striking foliage. Ideal for hanging baskets, it is also usefully drought-tolerant. Rhizomatous roots quickly spread and send up new plants, forming a clump. Divide in spring.

Primula Wanda Series
Hybrid primrose

☼ ☀ ❋ ❋ ❋ ● H 10cm/4in S 15cm/6in

These brightly coloured primroses come in shades of yellow, blue, pink, red, burgundy, orange or white, usually with a yellow eye. In late spring, plant them into a shady corner of the garden, from where they can be lifted, divided and used again the following autumn.

Tanacetum parthenium 'Aureum'
Golden feverfew

☼ ❋ ❋ ❋ ● H 45cm/18in S 30cm/12in

Where you have used a lot of plain-green-leaved plants, find space in your container for a few young plants of this gold-leaved perennial. Its compact, basal growth consists of slightly divided, ferny, aromatic leaves that sit well in baskets and troughs. Plant out in the garden for summer and the leaves will rise up to open small, white, daisy-like flowers. Raise from seed in spring.

Vinca minor
Lesser periwinkle

☼ ☀ ❋ ❋ ❋ ●

H 10–20cm/4–8in

S 60–120cm/2–4ft

Plants of this evergreen shrub make trailing alternatives to the ubiquitous ivies. Neat, evergreen leaves are held opposite each other on long stems and are joined, mainly in spring, by pretty blue flowers. Other cultivars bear white or plum-purple blooms. There are doubles as well as plants with variegated foliage. Propagation is by division or summer cuttings.

CONTAINER GROWING TIPS
❖

- Try cultivating a stock of useful evergreens that can be lifted out of the garden in the autumn and replaced in spring.

- Check containers regularly for watering, even throughout winter. Baskets and boxes in the rain-shadow of walls are particularly susceptible to drying out.

- Hanging baskets can be vulnerable to freeze-drying for long periods when chill winds are blowing. Stand them on solid pots in a sheltered spot until milder weather returns.

- Inspect the shoots and buds of bellis, pansies and polyanthus regularly for aphids.

155

▽ **ALTHOUGH PRIMULAS** *can be raised from seed, these cheerful perennials are more often bought in bloom to select favourite colours.*

Unusual container plants

There is often a need for permanently planted containers, for prominent places in the garden or to embellish hard surfaces. Architectural plants make eye-catching subjects for permanent positions and some small trees, as well as many shrubs and perennials, are suitable. Restricting the roots in pots reduces their ultimate height and slows down their rate of growth. Some of these unusual plants are tender and need winter protection.

Acer palmatum var. dissectum

156

Acer palmatum var. *dissectum* ♚
Japanese maple

☼ ☼ ❄ ❄ ❄ ✿ **H** 1.8m /6ft **S** 3m /10ft

Japanese maples make elegant trees for permanent containers; my own mature maple has been growing happily in the same wooden half-barrel for the last ten years. The bright green, young spring foliage matures into finely dissected, lobed leaves that turn orange and red in autumn, and tiny, purple-red flowers mature into glistening, winged fruits. Even the winter tracery of its domed, spreading branches is appealing. Shelter from winds and late frosts.

Agapanthus campanulatus
African blue lily

☼ ❄ ❄ ❄ ✿

H 60–120cm /2–4ft **S** 45cm /18in

Although these showy, rather variable perennials are hardy, containerizing means they can be moved to a sheltered position for the winter. The rounded blooms, 10–20cm (4–8in) across, are borne on tall stems rising above strap-shaped leaves. The heads are usually composed of

Agapanthus campanulatus

bright blue flowers, though they can be pale or darker blue or even white. Apply liquid fertilizer every two to three weeks from spring to flowering in summer.

Cordyline australis 'Torbay Dazzler'
Cabbage palm

☼ ❄ ❄ ❄ ◗ **H** 2.5–3m /8–10ft **S** 90–250cm /3–8ft

Extraordinarily showy plants, cabbage palms provide an architectural feast with their eruption of long, spiky leaves. Those of 'Torbay Dazzler' are striped and margined with creamy yellow, with pink flushes towards the base. Move under the protection of glass or to a sheltered spot for the winter, as their leaves are prone to damage from cold winds.

Corylus avellana 'Contorta' ♚
Corkscrew hazel, Twisted nut

☼ ☼ ❄ ❄ ❄ ✿

H/S 4.5m /15ft

For an unusual winter feature, choose this shrub whose stems twist and spiral as they grow. The leaves drop in autumn to reveal sculptural stems, further decorated by the usual 5cm- (2in-) long

pale yellow hazel catkins in late winter. Underplant with early-flowering bulbs and marble-leaved arums. Remove suckers and any unwanted stems during the winter.

Melianthus major ♚
Honey bush

☼ ❄ ❄ ❄ ✿ **H** 1.2–1.8m /4–6ft **S** 90–180cm /3–6ft

Valued for its silvery blue-green, tooth-edged leaflets, this tall, imposing shrub behaves more like a herbaceous perennial if left outside during cold winters. In anything but a sheltered position, it would die off, but plants in pots can be brought under glass for winter. Grow melianthus as a lone specimen or as a bold ingredient for a large mixed container planting.

Polystichum polyblepharum
Japanese tassel fern

☼ ❄ ❄ ❄ ❄ ◗ **H** 60–75cm /24–30in **S** 90cm /3ft

I love this hardy fern and enjoy the promise held in its upright coils of new fronds in spring. At first, they are covered in golden hairs, which persist around the margins of older fronds like sparse eyelashes. For the best results, move into a greenhouse for the winter. The spores are freely produced and often germinate in the pots of other plants.

• *see also:* GROWING IN CONTAINERS p224; YEAR-ROUND CONTAINERS p226

Rhododendron yakushimanum
'Heinje's Select'

◁ THE LARGE, BLUE-GREEN *leaflets of the honey bush* (Melianthus major) *make a striking silhouette.*

PERMANENT CONTAINER PLANTS

Buxus sempervirens ♀ ♠

Eucomis bicolor ♡

Hakonechloa macra 'Alboaurea' ♡

Hosta sieboldiana var. *elegans* ♀ ♡

Mirabilis jalapa ♡

Phormium 'Sundowner' ♀ ♠

Phyllostachys nigra ♀ ♠

Pinus sylvestris 'Beuvronensis' ♀ ♠

Pleioblastus auricomus ♀ ♠

GROWING TIPS FOR PERMANENT SUBJECTS

- Unless otherwise stated, use a mixture of equal parts John Innes No. 2 potting compost and a soilless potting mix for containers.

- Do not plant small specimens straight into large containers, as their roots will be surrounded by too much wet compost and may rot. Start them off in small pots and pot them on gradually, when necessary, in spring.

- A spring application of an appropriate slow-release fertilizer will ensure healthy growth. Some subjects will also benefit from a dose of well-balanced liquid fertilizer every two to four weeks from spring to midsummer.

- If the soil at the top of the container becomes eroded, topdress with a layer of fresh compost.

Prunus incisa 'Kojo-no-mai'
Fuji cherry

☼ ❋ ❋ ❋ ♡ **H/S** 2.5m / 8ft

A small tree with much sculptural beauty, this diminutive, ornamental cherry excels as a potted specimen and, as such, grows slowly, remaining in the same pot for many years. Enjoy its tracery of branches in winter, its mass of delicate, single, pale pink spring blossoms opening from red buds and the foliage, which turns red in autumn.

Rhododendron yakushimanum

☼ ❋ ❋ ❋ ♠ **H/S** 90–180cm / 3–6ft

Olive-green leaves are coated with silvery hairs when young and felted beneath with the softest pale brown. Water and feed regularly in summer to ensure a good set of buds, which show pink in spring, opening to white flower clusters. Plant in ericaceous compost and use a liquid feed balanced for acid-lovers.

Sciadopitys verticillata ♀
Japanese umbrella pine

☼ ☼ ❋ ❋ ❋ ♠

H 10–20m / 30–70ft **S** 6–8m / 20–25ft

Umbrella pines are impressive specimen plants, especially when young, with whorls of glossy, linear leaves like the spokes of an umbrella. Mine has reached a neat, conical shape 2.7m (9ft) high and 90cm (3ft) wide in 11 years and is still growing in a large Versailles tub. Keep moist; give a well-balanced liquid feed fortnightly from spring to midsummer.

Vaccinium corymbosum ♀
Highbush blueberry

☼ ☼ ❋ ❋ ❋ ♡ **H/S** 1.5m / 5ft

Few gardeners will have a sufficiently acid soil to grow blueberries well, but anyone can plant them into ericaceous compost in a container. The shrub's arching shoots bear oval leaves and pale,

bell-shaped flowers in late spring, followed by decorative, edible berries. The foliage turns red in autumn. For the best fruit, choose two different cultivars, such as 'Bluecrop' and 'Herbert'.

KEY: ♀ *Award of Merit* ☼ *sun* ☼ *semi-shade* ● *shade* ❋ *half-hardy* ❋❋ *frost-hardy* ❋❋❋ *fully hardy* ♡ *deciduous* ♠ *evergreen* ♠ *semi-evergreen* **H** *height* **S** *spread*

Plants for pools

Aquatic plants not only add to the beauty of a pond, they are also essential for its well-being. Submerged, oxygenating plants revitalize the water and the floating leaves of sun-lovers like water lilies shade part of the surface and discourage the rapid build-up of algae. The roots of aquatic plants are also great for removing minerals on which the algae feed.

158

Aponogeton distachyos
Water hawthorn

☼ ◐ ✱ ✱ ✿ **S** 1.2m /4ft

The long, oval, floating leaves of water hawthorn make a change from the rounded pads of lilies. White, fragrant, hawthorn-like flowers with purple-brown anthers open in spring and autumn and are held just above the water on forked branches. Divide the rhizomes of mature plants when dormant and repot into aquatic baskets. Roots must be 30–90cm (1–3ft) deep.

Ceratophyllum demersum
Hornwort

☼ ◐ ● ✱ ✱ ✱ ○ **S** indefinite

The slender stems of this useful oxygenator are clothed with whorls

Aponogeton distachyos

▷ **PYGMY WATER LILIES** *like Nymphaea 'Pygmaea Helvola' are ideal where space is restricted, or to build up a collection in a moderately sized pond.*

of fine, forked leaves, giving an overall feathery appearance. Few roots are produced, though the stems sometimes root into the mud at the bottom of the pond. Stem tips form into resting buds and sink for winter, drifting back up in spring. Propagate simply by pulling away some stem and floating it in water. Grows in water 60–90cm (2–3ft) deep.

Eichhornia crassipes
Water hyacinth

☼ ✱ ● **H/S** 45cm /18in

It is hard to think that such an exotic aquatic has become a weed of tropical waterways worldwide. The inflated leaf stalks allow the water hyacinth to float, while dark, purplish roots hang down into the water. In hot summers, stalks of pale blue flowers marked with yellow and purple are produced. Lift and overwinter on trays of moist, soilless compost at a minimum temperature of 13°C (55°F).

Hottonia palustris
Water violet

☼ ✱ ✱ ✱ ○ **H** 30–90cm /1–3ft **S** indefinite

As the water warms up in early spring, growth rises to the pond surface. Long stems bear deeply divided foliage above and below water. Stems of pale pinkish-lilac flowers are borne in spring. Plant in the muddy bottom of still, preferably slightly acid, shallow water, to 45cm (18in) deep. Propagate by stem cuttings in spring and summer.

Hydrocharis morsus-ranae
Frogbit

☼ ✱ ✱ ✱ ○ **S** indefinite

Running stems produce new plantlets, so frogbit soon spreads to cover an area of water with its floating leaves like tiny, kidney-shaped lily pads. Small, papery,

• *see also:* POND CARE p222

white flowers with yellow centres
appear in summer. The plants are
mostly free-floating, but will root into
shallow mud, sinking to overwinter as
buds. To propagate, cut plantlets away
from the parents. Needs a water depth
up to 30cm (12in).

Myriophyllum aquaticum
Parrot's feather, Diamond milfoil
☼ ❋❋ ◯ **H** 30cm/12in above water **S** indefinite

Submerged or marginal, parrot's feather
pokes its stems of feathery foliage above
water and will climb happily up the
pond's banks. Submerged leaves are
longer than emergent ones; the summer
flowers are so tiny that nobody really
notices them. Propagate by cuttings.
Grow in baskets of loamy soil in water
15–90cm (6–36in) deep.

Nymphaea 'Froebelii'
Water lily
☼ ❋❋❋ ◯ **S** 90cm/3ft

Although ideal for smaller ponds,
including barrel ponds, the 10–13cm
(4–5in) diameter flowers are still a good
size. These are deep pinkish-red with
central stamens of orange-red. Its leaves
are an attractive bronze as they unfurl
in spring. Plant in a water depth of
15–30cm (6–12in). Propagate by
division of rhizomes in spring.
Separate offsets or remove plantlets.

Nymphaea 'Pygmaea Helvola' ♀
Pygmy water lily
☼ ❋❋ ◯ **S** 25–40cm/10–16in

For restricted areas, or moderate ponds
where more than one lily is to be
grown, this is ideal. Leaves, heavily
mottled with purple, are attractive and
not overpowering. They are joined by
semi-double, clear yellow flowers

Eichhornia crassipes

Nymphaea 'Froebelii'

159

USING AQUATIC BASKETS
❖

Containers for aquatics are usually
made of plastic and resemble baskets
with wide mesh sides. Line first with
hessian, before setting the plants in
good loam. Do not use fertilized
compost, as this will enrich the
water and encourage algae. Finish off
with a good layer of pebbles to settle
the loam before carefully lowering
into the pond. Containers can be
raised to the correct planting depth
by standing on a ledge or blocks.
Fertilizers specially formulated for
use in ponds can be bought in sachet
or tablet form for
hungry feeders
like water lilies.

5–8cm (2–3in) across in summer.
Plant in depths of 15–23cm (6–9in).
Propagate by lifting, dividing and
replanting into baskets for aquatics.

Nymphoides peltata
Fringed water lily
☼ ❋❋❋ ◯ **S** indefinite

Suitable for a wildlife pool, the leaves
resemble small lily pads and grow from
long runners, quickly colonizing the
water surface. Bright yellow flowers
2cm (¾in) with fringed petals are
held above the water by stout stalks
in summer. Water depth 15–60cm
(6–24in). Propagate by division in
spring or separate runners in summer.

Stratiotes aloides
Water soldier
☼ ❋❋❋ ◯ **H** 15cm/6in above water **S** indefinite

A curious free-floating plant, the rosette
of spiky leaves hangs half in and half
out of the water. As the temperature
drops in autumn, rosettes sink to the
warmer depths of the pond, rising again
the following spring. White flowers are
sometimes borne in summer. New
plants form from spreading stems and
can be separated in spring. Water depth
30–90cm (1–3ft).

KEY: ♀ *Award of Merit* ☼ *sun* ☼ *semi-shade* ☀ *shade* ❋ *half-hardy* ❋❋ *frost-hardy* ❋❋❋ *fully hardy* ◯ *deciduous* ● *evergreen* ◐ *semi-evergreen* **H** *height* **S** *spread*

Marginals and bog garden plants

Marginals are plants that like to grow in the shallow water at the edges of ponds and streams. They are an important group for pond wildlife. Bog garden plants prefer to grow in moist soil, but do not usually like standing in water for any length of time; in fact they usually dislike waterlogging and need surprisingly good drainage.

Butomus umbellatus

160

Butomus umbellatus ♀
Flowering rush
☼ ❈ ❈ ❈ ♡ **H** 90–150cm / 3–5ft **S** 45cm / 18in

Tall, rush-like foliage is joined by showy umbels, 10cm (4in) across, of fragrant, dark-centred, pink flowers in late summer. The water depth can vary between 5–25cm (2–10in), with plants either flourishing in the mud at the edges of wildlife pools, or growing from baskets standing in deeper water. Divide rhizomes in early spring, just before growth starts.

Caltha palustris ♀
Marsh marigold, Kingcup
☼ ❈ ❈ ❈ ♡ **H/S** 45cm / 18in

One of the easiest and most satisfying marginals to grow, marsh marigolds are relatively well behaved and, although they spread into good clumps, are not invasive. Toothed, kidney-shaped leaves make a deep green background for bright yellow, waxy flowers borne in spring. Plant in boggy ground, or very shallow water to 15cm (6in) deep. Divide in early spring or late summer.

Iris pseudacorus 'Variegata'
Yellow flag
☼ ❈ ❈ ❈ ♡ **H** 90–150cm / 3–5ft **S** 90cm / 3ft

The young spears of this iris, rising sword-like and half green, half creamy-yellow, make an exciting contrast with other foliage in spring. They are joined by yellow flowers in mid- to late summer. An extremely vigorous iris, this is only suitable for medium to large-sized ponds and needs supervision. Lift, divide and replant immediately after flowering.

Menyanthes trifoliata
Bogbean
☼ ❈ ❈ ❈ ♡ **H** 20–30cm / 8–12in **S** indefinite

With dark pinkish-maroon spreading rhizomes and trifoliate leaves that stick upwards from the water surface, bogbean is a handsome plant even before its stems of small summer flowers appear. These open white from pink buds and each of the five petal lobes is fringed. Water depth should be 15–23cm (6–9in). Cut rhizomes into sections and peg into wet earth.

Caltha palustris 'Flore Pleno'

Myosotis scorpioides

CREATING A BOG GARDEN
❖

- Unless the soil is naturally moist, create a bog garden by laying an inexpensive or old flexible pond-liner over a flat-bottomed hole about 60cm (2ft) deep.

- Pierce the liner here and there across the bottom with a garden fork to allow drainage.

- Shovel in a 5cm (2in) layer of pea shingle over the liner to keep the drainage holes clear.

- The most efficient way to water is below soil level, so place a seep hose, or an old hosepipe perforated with holes, onto the shingle with the inside end sealed and the other end clear of the hole.

- Fill the hole with good soil enriched with organic matter; tread to firm.

- Bog gardens can be made adjacent to a pond by extending the same liner, but this can be unwise, as the bog garden may draw water from the pond, causing the level to drop.

- To conserve moisture, apply a 5cm (2in) mulch of well-rotted compost, composted bark, mushroom compost (though not where acid-loving plants will grow) or pebbles while the soil is damp.

- Water an existing bog garden using a seep hose at the surface.

• *see also:* POND CARE p222

Myosotis scorpioides
Water forget-me-not

☼ ☼ ❄ ❄ ❄ ○ **H** 15–30cm /6–12in **S** 30cm /12in

This makes a really good waterside plant, with branching, rhizomatous stems growing first outwards, then upwards. Familiar, pale-eyed, blue flowers are borne in early summer. Grow in wet soil or plant into an aquatic basket stood in shallow water, with the surface no deeper than 10cm (4in). Propagate by sowing seed on to wet compost, or planting ready-rooted sections of rhizome.

Osmunda regalis ♈
Royal fern

☼ ❄ ❄ ❄ ○ **H** 1.2–1.8m /4–6ft **S** 1.2–3.7m /4–12ft

The stately fronds are fresh green, unfurling themselves in spring from massive rhizomes. Spores are produced on fertile fronds, which bear clusters of rust-brown sporangia towards their tips. In autumn its colour turns orange and russet. Plant in moist, preferably acid soil, enriched with organic matter.

◁ IRIS PSEUDACORUS 'VARIEGATA' *establishes easily and quickly in a pond. The foliage provides bright colour and strong vertical shapes.*

Although individuals spread into large colonies, they can be controlled. Divide in early spring or autumn.

Primula pulverulenta ♈
Candelabra primula

☼ ❄ ❄ ❄ ○

H 60–90cm /2–3ft **S** 30cm /12in

This striking primula overwinters as a small rosette, which grows and sends up stout flower stems covered by white, mealy 'farina' in late spring. Deep pink flowers with darker eyes are arranged in several whorls up the stem. Plant into wet, boggy neutral to acid soil, enriched with organic matter. Sow seed as soon as it is ripe, or divide the plant while dormant.

Schoenoplectus lacustris subsp. *tabernaemontani* 'Zebrinus'
Striped rush

☼ ❄ ❄ ❄ ●

H 90cm /3ft **S** 60cm /2ft

Virtually leafless, grey-green stems are patterned as if by a strobe light, with creamy-white bands. Sometimes the stems revert to green and these must be cut out before they take over. This versatile rush can be planted in boggy poolside soil or submerged by up to 30cm (12in) of water. Propagate by rooting sections of rhizome in spring or summer.

Scrophularia auriculata 'Variegata'
Water figwort

☼ ❄ ❄ ❄ ○ **H/S** 90cm /3ft

In spring there is a ground covering of attractive foliage, the leaves having creamy, irregular margins and markings. Having enjoyed this display, watch the rosettes of leaves elongate into tall stems bearing typical figwort flowers of greenish-maroon throughout summer. Plant into wet, boggy soil for the best results. Divide clumps or root basal cuttings in spring.

161

Trollius × cultorum 'Lemon Queen'
Globeflower

☼ ☼ ❄ ❄ ❄ ○ **H** 60cm /2ft **S** 45cm /18in

I have always loved globeflowers and in particular these hybrids, with their characteristic bowl-shaped flowers. In this case they are pale, shimmering lemon, but can be yellow, orange or gold; they appear from spring to midsummer. Plant into moist soil enriched with organic matter. Lift, divide and replant as growth begins or after flowering.

Primula pulverulenta   *Osmunda regalis*

Plants for damp, shady sites

Never view damp, shady areas of the garden as a problem, because they give an opportunity for growing a wide range of plants that would never thrive in thin, parched soils in full sun. Shade can be turned into a positive asset and in fully lit gardens often has to be specially created for the comfort of people and plants alike.

162

Aruncus dioicus ♛
Goatsbeard

☼ ☀ ❋ ❋ ❋ ⟳ **H** 1.2–1.8m / 4–6ft **S** 1.2m / 4ft

For goatsbeard to reach its full potential it needs moisture at the roots; this will enable it to tolerate full sun or shade. Tiny cream flowers are packed into feathery panicles in early and midsummer. The fern-like foliage is susceptible to attack by slugs and snails. This is a good perennial for a relaxed, wild-looking area. Divide in autumn or in early spring.

SHADY CHARACTERS

❖

TREES AND SHRUBS

Hydrangea macrophylla cvs ⟳
Leycesteria formosa ⟳
Prunus padus ⟳

UNDERPLANTINGS

Asplenium scolopendrium ♛ ❧
Astilbe 'Straussenfeder' ♛ ⟳
Athyrium filix-femina ♛ ⟳
Blechnum spicant ♛ ❧
Cimicifuga racemosa ♛ ⟳
Dryopteris filix-mas ♛ ⟳
Filipendula rubra 'Venusta' ♛ ⟳
Hosta 'Wide Brim' ♛ ⟳
Impatiens walleriana cvs
Polygonatum odoratum ⟳
Uvularia grandiflora ♛ ⟳

Blechnum penna-marina

☼ ☀ ❋ ❋ ❋ ❧ **H** 15–20cm / 6–8in **S** indefinite

This fern is a useful evergreen to plant between taller specimens in a dark, damp corner of the garden where the soil has been enriched with leafmould. Here, the rhizomes will spread and form a mat, sending up divided fronds that start bronze-tinted and turn deep green. It is also good for shady winter containers. Divide at any time.

Camellia x *williamsii* 'Donation' ♛
☼ ❋ ❋ ❋ ❧ **H** 2.2–4.5m / 7–15ft **S** 1.5–2.5m / 5–8ft

One asset of this popular camellia is that once the large, pink, semi-double flowers are finished, they shatter quickly, the petals falling in a pink pool beneath the plant. Plant into well-conditioned, moist but well-drained, slightly acid soil. Make sure it remains moist in summer, when flower buds are setting. Cuttings, taken in late summer, are a challenge to root.

Camellia x *williamsii* 'Donation'

Darmera peltata ♛
☼ ☀ ❋ ❋ ❋ ⟳

H 90cm–180cm / 3–6ft **S** 90cm / 3ft

A good performer, this perennial thrives along the banks of streams and in the moist soil of a bog garden. The umbrella-like leaves grow tall and lush, turning from green to red in autumn. Stout stems bearing heads of small pink flowers appear in late spring. Divide in autumn or early spring.

Epipactis gigantea
Giant helleborine

☼ ☀ ❋ ❋ ❋ ⟳

H 30–40cm / 12–16in **S** 60–150cm / 2–5ft

To my mind, this North American native is among the easiest of hardy orchids. Plant in a cool, shady place where the soil can be enriched by leafmould and stays moist but does not get waterlogged. Spreading by rhizomes, a wide colony soon forms. Greenish-yellow flowers marked with maroon appear in late spring and early summer. Divide in early spring.

Hydrangea quercifolia ♛
Oak-leaved hydrangea

☼ ☀ ❋ ❋ ❋ ⟳ **H** 1.8m / 6ft **S** 2.5m / 8ft

As the botanical name suggests, this shrub bears large leaves shaped like those of an oak tree. Conical panicles of white flowers open from midsummer to autumn, becoming pink-tinged with age.

• *see also:* RAISING PLANTS FROM SEED p230; PROPAGATING BY CUTTINGS p232; OTHER MEANS OF PROPAGATION p234

△ **IN MOIST SOIL** *beneath trees, candelabra primula, hosta and ligularia thrive along stream margins.*

At this point they contrast with the foliage as it turns bronze-purple before falling. Plant in moist soil enriched with organic matter. Pruning is generally unnecessary.

Kirengeshoma palmata ♔
☼ ❄ ❄ ❄ ↻ **H** 60–120cm / 2–4ft **S** 75cm / 30in

Stems of slightly lobed, bright green leaves end in delicate showers of nodding, bell-like, pale yellow flowers. Plant in moist, slightly alkaline soil enriched by leafmould and it will spread by rhizomes. This perennial from Japan looks great in a shaded woodland garden. Divide in autumn or as growth begins in spring.

Matteuccia struthiopteris ♔
Ostrich fern, Shuttlecock fern
☼ ❄ ❄ ❄ ↻ **H** 1.2m / 4ft **S** 90cm / 3ft

Spring is the best time to appreciate the beauty of the shuttlecock fern, when the erect new 'shuttlecock' fronds burst out from each crown, maturing to fine structures with opposite ranks of narrow pinnae (frondlets). Shorter, spore-bearing fronds with inrolled margins appear in late summer and autumn. The creeping rhizomes produce separate ferns a sensible distance from the parent. Propagate either by lifting these or by sowing spores when ripe.

Smilacina racemosa ♔
False Solomon's seal
☼ ☼ ❄ ❄ ❄ ↻ **H** 75–90cm / 30–36in **S** 60cm / 2ft

Candles of small, creamy-white flowers are produced during mid- to late spring at the tips of stems bearing attractive foliage. Use as bold clumps in moist, rich soil around shrubs as well as in conjunction with spring bulbs. They also combine beautifully with hostas, astilbes and ferns. Divide this rhizomatous perennial in autumn or early spring.

Trillium cuneatum
Wake robin
☼ ☼ ❄ ❄ ❄ ↻ **H** 30–60cm / 1–2ft **S** 30cm / 12in

Ever since I first saw a large clump of this stunning North American perennial, I coveted this plant for my garden. Patience is required, as growth from tiny rhizomes is slow. Each reddish stem holds a collar of three large, mottled leaves, from the centre of which a deep maroon flower with upright petals opens in spring. Plant in moist soil enriched with organic matter and divide clumps after flowering.

Hydrangea quercifolia

Smilacina racemosa

KEY: ♔ *Award of Merit* ☼ *sun* ☼ *semi-shade* ✿ *shade* ❄ *half-hardy* ❄ ❄ *frost-hardy* ❄ ❄ ❄ *fully hardy* ↻ *deciduous* ● *evergreen* ◐ *semi-evergreen* **H** *height* **S** *spread*

Plants for dry shade

Most gardens have a patch of dry shade, perhaps under a tree or alongside a hedge. These impoverished areas are usually inhospitable, all the goodness and moisture being sucked out of the soil by greedy tree roots. Plants that can tolerate dry shade are invaluable but you should always condition your soil by digging in plenty of organic matter and add a mulch after planting.

Symphoricarpos x *doorenbosii*
'Mother of Pearl'

164

Aucuba japonica 'Rozannie'
Spotted laurel, Japanese laurel

☼ ☼ ☼ ❄ ❄ ❄ ❦ **H/S** 90cm/3ft

Despite the common name, this aucuba is not spotted but bears glossy, mid-green, slightly toothed leaves. It is bisexual and the spring show of small maroon flowers should set a reliable crop of red fruit; the assistance of hand pollination may be required. Root semi-ripe cuttings in summer.

Cyclamen hederifolium ♛

☼ ❄ ❄ ❄ ♡ **H** 10–13cm/4–5in **S** 15cm/6in

Jewel-like flowers in shades of pink with darker bases unfurl from pointed buds in late summer and autumn, preceding the beautifully patterned leaves. The flower stalks coil, bringing the developing seedpods to ground level. Leave the surrounding soil undisturbed and these plants will self-seed. Plant under trees, in soil enriched with organic matter, where the ground will be dry during summer dormancy. Choose young potted plants rather than dried tubers.

Epimedium x *versicolor* 'Sulphureum' ♛
Barrenwort, Bishop's mitre

☼ ❄ ❄ ❄ ❦ **H** 30cm/12in **S** 90cm/3ft

Grown chiefly for their pointed, heart-shaped foliage, the epimediums are closely related to shrubby berberis, in whose family they belong. They are all lovely, making first-class ground cover with impenetrable root systems. This one bears coppery-tinged spring foliage and yellow flowers in spring. Clip back the old leaves in late winter, before the new growth appears. Divide in autumn.

Euphorbia amygdaloides var *robbiae* ♛
Mrs Robb's bonnet

☼ ☼ ☼ ❄ ❄ ❄ ❦

H 30–60cm/1–2ft **S** 30cm/12in

An unassuming perennial, this euphorbia knits into a good, ground-covering colony able to thrive in poor, dry soils. Plants are brightened, from spring to summer, by greenish-yellow flower structures that peep like eyes from above glossy foliage. Its sap is an irritant however. Spreads by rhizomes and portions can easily be separated to make new plants.

Geranium phaeum
Dusky cranesbill, Mourning widow

☼ ☼ ☼ ❄ ❄ ❄ ♡ **H** 75cm/30in **S** 45cm/18in

A tall cranesbill grown for its small but unusual deep maroon flowers, which complement the maroon, marked, lobed leaves. Flowers can also be violet-blue, pale mauve or white and are borne in late spring and early summer. Suitable for planting under shrubs and trees, it brings an element of lush coolness to dry areas. Divide in autumn.

Liriope muscari ♛
Lilyturf

☼ ☼ ❄ ❄ ❄ ❦ **H** 30cm/12in **S** 45cm/18in

Clump-forming, tuberous perennials produce tufts of long leaves, joined in autumn by spikes of bobbly purple flowers. Most effective grown as a group, lilyturf associates well with autumn crocus and colchicum. Pick over periodically to remove brown leaves. For a lighter effect, track down *L.m.* 'Gold Banded' with gold-, then cream-edged leaves. Lift, divide and replant in spring.

Epimedium x *versicolor* 'Sulphureum'

Polystichum setiferum

• *see also:* DIGGING AND IMPROVING YOUR SOIL p180; RAISING PLANTS FROM SEED p230; PROPAGATING BY CUTTINGS p232; OTHER MEANS OF PROPAGATION p234

△ **WOOD SPURGE** (Euphorbia amygdaloides) *flourishes and spreads in the dry shade beneath trees in a woodland setting. Acid, yellow-green flower structures combine well with blue scillas.*

> ## GROUND COVER FOR DRY SHADE
> ❖
> *Bergenia* 'Bressingham Ruby' 🍂
> *Danae racemosa* ♀ 🍂
> *Daphne laureola* 🍂
> *Euonymus fortunei*
> Emerald 'n' Gold ♀ 🍂
> *Geranium macrorrhizum* 'Album' ♀ 🍃
> *Lunaria annua* 🍂
> *Lamium maculatum* 'Pink Pewter' 🍂
> *Mahonia aquifolium* 'Apollo' ♀ 🍂
> *Meconopsis cambrica* ♡
> *Omphalodes cappadocica* ♀ 🍂
> *Pachysandra terminalis* ♀ 🍂
> *Phlomis russeliana* ♀ 🍂
> *Skimmia japonica* subsp. *reevesiana* 🍂
> *Vancouveria hexandra* ♡
> *Viburnum davidii* ♀ 🍂

165

Luzula nivea
Snowy woodrush
☼ ☼ ❄❄❄ 🍂 **H** 30–60cm /1–2ft **S** 45cm /18in

In my garden I chose this perennial to grow under the canopy of a Judas tree and the plants have thrived. Easily raised from autumn- or spring-sown seed, each makes a tuft of leaves edged with fine white hairs. In summer, stems bearing clusters of pure white flowers appear. Clumps can be divided in spring.

Osmanthus heterophyllus
'Purpureus'
☼ ☼ ❄❄❄ 🍂 **H/S** 1.8–2.5m /6–8ft

These holly-like, slow-growing evergreen shrubs are useful for small gardens. Although they tolerate dry shade, be warned that in poor soil their growth will be extremely slow. Nevertheless, this purple-leaved form is attractive when, in spring, the new growths are a shiny blackish-purple, later turning dark green. Propagate by summer cuttings.

Polystichum setiferum ♀
Soft shield fern
☼ ☼ ❄❄❄ 🍂 **H/S** 90cm /3ft

Although ferns are associated with damp, shady places, the soft shield fern can cope with dry conditions. Its new fronds look like octopus tentacles and mature to soft, much divided, mossy green pinnae. Older fronds bear plantlets that can be detached and inserted into small pots of compost. Or lay an entire frond plus plantlets on the surface of moist compost. Divide multi-crowned clumps in spring.

Symphoricarpos × doorenbosii
'Mother of Pearl'
Snowberry
☼ ☼ ❄❄❄ ♡ **H/S** 1.8m /6ft

Because of its indestructible nature, the snowberry is often dismissed as a garden plant, but it is a good gap-filler for shady corners. Thickets of arching stems with neat, rounded leaves produce small, bell-shaped, greenish-white flowers in summer, followed by large crops of white fruit. Because of their suckering habit, propagation is easy. Dig out unwanted plants to control their spread.

> ## DIVIDING A FERN
> ❖
> To split this large, soft shield fern I lift the whole plant, then drive two forks back to back between two crowns of growth, finally teasing the roots apart by hand.
>
>

Plants for dry sunny sites

There is a wealth of plants which enjoy dry, sunny conditions and are naturally drought-tolerant. Many have hairy or silvery foliage and their leaves tend to be small and narrow, to prevent excessive moisture loss. In general, these plants dislike having wet feet in winter and a well-drained soil is essential for their survival.

Rosmarinus officinalis 'Majorca Pink'

166

Aster turbinellus ♥

☼ ❄ ❄ ❄ ♡ **H** 1.2m /4ft **S** 60cm /2ft

Wiry stems bearing small, narrow leaves will need support, but are happy to lean against nearby shrubs. From early to late autumn, masses of pale violet flowers with yellow centres open, resembling small Michaelmas daisies. Tolerant of poor soils, this perennial from the USA comes back year after year. Lift, divide and replant in spring or autumn.

Catananche caerulea 'Bicolor'
Cupid's dart

☼ ❄ ❄ ❄ ♡ **H** 60–75cm /24–30in **S** 30cm /12in

Easily raised from spring-sown seed, catananche will bloom in its first summer and can be dotted in groups throughout a border. This short-lived perennial is slender, producing tufts of long, narrow grey-green leaves and, from midsummer to autumn, solitary, papery flowerheads, each perched on a long slender stalk. The flowers of the species are blue, but in this variety they are white with purple centres.

Aster turbinellus

Cercis siliquastrum ♥
Judas tree

☼ ◐ ❄ ❄ ❄ ♡ **H/S** 2.5–10m /8–30ft

Sun and good drainage are the prerequisites of this Mediterranean tree, which can grow on a single main stem or, multi-stemmed, as a shrub. The pink flowers are pea-like and the kidney-shaped leaves glaucous blue-green. Plant out when young, then avoid disturbance. Choose a sheltered spot because the flower buds (arising directly from both old and young branches) and young leaves are vulnerable to late spring frosts. Propagate by autumn-sown seed.

Geranium palmatum ♥

☼ ◐ ❄ ❄ ● **H** 60–90cm /2–3ft **S** 90cm /3ft

This stately geranium has proved hardy in my garden. Although perennial, treat as a biennial. It can be sown, or will seed itself freely to germinate in spring and build up rosettes of large, intricately lobed leaves, providing valuable winter foliage. Branching stems of generous purple-pink flowers with deeper centres appear the following summer.

Linaria triornithophora
Three-birds-flying toadflax

☼ ❄ ❄ ❄ ♡ **H** 90cm /3ft **S** 60cm /2ft

A perennial which flowers all summer long and spreads itself about, weaving its thin stems between other plants, should be more widespread, yet the three-birds toadflax is relatively uncommon. The whorled flowers resemble pale pink-purple snapdragons, each having a long spur, purple-striped throats and yellow on the lower lip. They are easily propagated by seed or division.

Lotus hirsutus
Hairy Canary clover

☼ ❄ ❄ ❄ ● **H/S** 75cm /30in

Given good drainage, this small, silvery Mediterranean shrub is easy to grow and will seed itself into undisturbed soil. Expect pink-tinged stems clothed with small, softly hairy grey-green pinnate leaves. Pea-like white flowers flushed with pink are borne in summer, followed by purplish seedpods. Stems may die back in winter, so prune to tidy up in early spring. Take cuttings in summer.

PLANTS FOR A SHINGLE GARDEN

❖

Allium sphaerocephalon ♡
Helichrysum italicum ●
Iris chrysographes ♡
Penstemon 'Pink Dragon' ●
Phygelius × rectus 'Moonraker' ●
Pinus sylvestris 'Beuvronensis' ♥ ●
Rosmarinus officinalis 'Majorca Pink' ●
Sedum 'Herbstfreude' ♥ ♡
Teucrium fruticans 'Azureum' ♥ ●

• ***see also:*** RAISING PLANTS FROM SEED p230; PROPAGATING FROM CUTTINGS p232; OTHER MEANS OF PROPAGATION p234

△ **COMBAT DROUGHT** *with a shingle-mulched bed. Moisture is conserved and weeds suppressed so that cypress, yucca, helianthemum and gazanias can thrive in the well-drained soil.*

OREGANO HAIRCUT
❖

Not only does *Origanum laevigatum* 'Herrenhausen' flower for a long period, attracting butterflies and bees, but if you cut it back after blooming it will make a mat of evergreen foliage for the winter.

Olearia 'Waikariensis'
Daisy bush

☼ ❄ ❄ ❄ ◗ **H/S** 1.8m /6ft

With shared origins in New Zealand, this shrub is similar to the more common *O.* x *haastii*, but bears longer leaves. Olive-green leaves are silvery-white beneath and stems are pale too. White daisy-like flowers are produced from early to midsummer, followed by many seeds with hairy parasols. Plant in well-drained soil. Take semi-ripe cuttings in late summer.

Origanum laevigatum
'Herrenhausen' ♀
Oregano

☼ ❄ ❄ ❄ ◗ **H** 60cm /2ft **S** 45cm /18in

Neat, aromatic leaves, a plentiful summer-long display of small, closely packed purple-pink flowers and a neat basal rosette of evergreen foliage are valuable attributes. This sun-lover also attracts many butterflies and bees. Provide support if stems are not to sprawl and prune down to the basal rosette after flowering. Plant in well-drained soil. Propagate by division.

Salvia sclarea var. turkestanica
Clary sage, Sweaty Betty

☼ ❄ ❄ ❄ ◗

H 75–120cm /30–48in **S** 60–90cm /2–3ft

This biennial or short-lived perennial has a strong scent which, though pleasant at first, lingers like stale sweat. Basal growth of large leaves builds up during the first year, then persists throughout winter. In summer, spikes of white and purple flowers with persistent, papery bracts rise up. Raise from spring-sown seed; the plants will self-seed thereafter.

Salvia sclarea var. *turkestanica*

Verbena bonariensis

☼ ❄ ❄ ✺ **H** 1.5m–1.8/5–6ft **S** 60cm /2ft

Strong stems bearing long, narrow, toothed dark green leaves rise narrowly, making this a useful perennial for slotting in between other plants. Heads packed full of dark buds persist at the ends of branches, opening to small purple flowers from summer into autumn. Plant in well-drained soil. Sow seed in spring.

Verbena bonariensis

KEY: ♀ *Award of Merit* ☼ *sun* ✦ *semi-shade* ◗ *shade* ❄ *half-hardy* ❄ ❄ *frost-hardy* ❄ ❄ ❄ *fully hardy* ✺ *deciduous* ◗ *evergreen* ◖ *semi-evergreen* **H** *height* **S** *spread*

Exposed and windy sites

The key to success when growing plants in an exposed site is to create a windbreak to protect vulnerable species from cold, drying winds. Once this is established, ordinary plants should thrive on the calm side of the barrier. A mixture of tough trees and shrubs will filter the wind more effectively than solid barriers, which can create currents and draughts.

Chamaecyparis nootkatensis 'Pendula' ♔
Nootka cypress

168

☼ ❄ ❄ ❄ ✿ **H** 15m/50ft **S** 6m/20ft

Use tall, tough conifers among the ingredients of an informal windbreak some distance from the house. The Nootka cypress has interesting bark that sheds in plates. The branches of this pendulous cultivar sweep in an elegant, horizontal fashion, bearing sprays of sharp but scale-like, strong-smelling foliage joined by greenish cones.

Crataegus monogyna 'Stricta'
Hawthorn

☼ ☼ ❄ ❄ ❄ ✿

H 6–9m/20–30ft **S** 3–3.7m/10–12ft

All hawthorns can tolerate exposure to cold and wind, but this narrow, columnar form with erect branches is probably the toughest of all. It will suit a wild, countryside garden and bears masses of fragrant white blossom in late spring, followed by red fruits much-loved by birds. Propagation by budding or grafting is usually left to the nursery.

Laburnum x *watereri* 'Vossii' ♔
Golden rain

☼ ❄ ❄ ❄ ✿ **H/S** 7.5m/25ft

The biggest deterrent to planting these useful small trees is that all parts of the plants are highly poisonous if eaten. With good reason, the parents of young children worry about the temptation of seedpods when they fall. This cultivar produces a reduced crop of seed and bears exceptionally long racemes of yellow, pea-like flowers, up to 60cm (2ft) in length, from late spring.

Philadelphus 'Beauclerk' ♔
Mock orange

☼ ☼ ❄ ❄ ❄ ✿ **H/S** 2.5m/8ft

One of the tall philadelphus would make a good, floriferous addition to an informal windbreak. This cultivar is grown for its profusion of highly scented, single white flowers, 5cm (2in) across, borne in late spring and early summer. Prune by thinning out older stems immediately after flowering. Propagate by summer cuttings, or hardwood cuttings in winter.

Populus x *candicans* 'Aurora'
Balm of Gilead

☼ ❄ ❄ ❄ ✿ **H** 15m/50ft **S** 6m/20ft

The ultimate size of this tree may sound offputting, but young specimens can be cut down or 'stooled' every year in late winter, so that plants grow as multi-stemmed shrubs to about 2.5–3m (8–10ft) high. This results in even larger heart-shaped leaves marked with white, cream and pink. Keep poplars well away from buildings, as their roots can be invasive.

Prunus spinosa
Blackthorn, Sloe

☼ ❄ ❄ ❄ ✿ **H** 5m/15ft **S** 3.5m/12ft

The common blackthorn is a pretty, small tree or large shrub, often appearing from seed in a garden. Early

Philadelphus 'Beauclerk'

TOUGH CHOICES FOR EXPOSED PLACES

❖

Cotinus coggygria ♔ ✿ (smoke bush)
Cornus alba 'Spaethii' ♔ ✿ (dogwood)
Fagus sylvatica ♔ ✿ (beech)
Mahonia aquifolium ✿
Quercus robur ♔ ✿ (common oak)
Salix caprea ✿ (willow)
Sorbus aucuparia ✿ (rowan)
Taxus baccata ♔ ✿ (yew)

• *see also:* PLANTS FOR COASTAL GARDENS p174

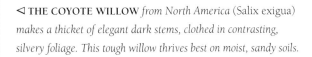

◁ **THE COYOTE WILLOW** *from North America* (Salix exigua) *makes a thicket of elegant dark stems, clothed in contrasting, silvery foliage. This tough willow thrives best on moist, sandy soils.*

169

Spiraea × vanhouttei

Viburnum opulus 'Xanthocarpum'

to blossom in spring, the tiny white flowers shine out against the dark wood. They are followed by round black fruit, or sloes, which are sour, but good for making sloe gin. Prune to thin and shape trees or shrubs during winter.

Salix exigua
Coyote willow

☼ ❊ ❊ ❊ ○ **H** 3.7m/12ft **S** 5m/15ft

One of the loveliest of willows, this species shows at its best when the wind sways the thickets of dark stems and whispers through their long, narrow, silvery foliage. Yellow catkins appear in spring at the same time as young, silky leaves. Thrives in moist, sandy soils but can tolerate some dryness. Propagate by hardwood cuttings in winter.

Sorbus aria 'Lutescens' ♆
Whitebeam

☼ ❊ ❊ ❊ ❊ ○ **H** 10m/30ft **S** 8m/25ft

Choose this whitebeam to add a delightful small tree to a boundary windbreak. Generously sized, tooth-edged leaves are silvery above and below, though their surfaces turn grey-green with age. This gives the tree a shimmering effect, augmented in spring by bunches of white flowers, which turn into dark red berries. Thrives on chalky or acid soil.

Spiraea × vanhouttei ♆

☼ ❊ ❊ ❊ ○ **H** 2m/6ft **S** 1.5m/5ft

Most of the spiraeas make good infills to plug holes in a windbreak. This one is a superb sight in early summer when the arching stems are smothered with clusters of small white flowers, so the

whole shrub resembles a cascading white waterfall. Prune established spiraea bushes after flowering by thinning out the older stems. Propagate by summer cuttings.

Viburnum opulus 'Xanthocarpum' ♆
Guelder rose

☼ ❊ ❊ ❊ ❊ ○

H 3–3.7m/10–12ft **S** 2.5–3m/8–10ft

The yellow-fruited guelder rose makes an attractive addition to a natural looking windbreak. Maple-like leaves are joined, in late spring and early summer, by heads bearing small, central fertile flowers, surrounded lacecap-style by sterile florets. These turn to showy bunches of yellow fruit then, as a finale, the leaves turn red before falling. It tolerates chalk. Propagate by semi-ripe cuttings taken in summer.

Plants for acid soils

Gardeners who find themselves gardening on acid, or lime-free, soil will be able to grow plants largely forbidden to those whose soil is alkaline or even neutral. Most acid-loving plants appreciate coolness and moisture, so light shade and a soil enriched with organic matter are an advantage. The best known acid-lovers are heathers and rhododendrons, which I have omitted in favour of more unusual plants.

Meconopsis grandis

170

Andromeda polifolia
Bog rosemary
☼ ☼ ❋ ❋ ❋ ● **H** 40cm/16in **S** 60cm/2ft

A low-growing shrub native to peat bogs, andromeda is best grown towards the front of a raised bed, or in a rock garden to avoid soil splashes and being swamped by other plants. Its needle-like foliage is reminiscent of rosemary and pink, bell-shaped flowers appear from spring to early summer. Mulch to retain moisture. Propagate by summer cuttings or layering.

Cassiope lycopodioides ♔
☼ ☼ ❋ ❋ ❋ ● **H** 8cm/3in **S** 25cm/10in

Plant in a similar situation to andromeda, so that its mat-like growth can be appreciated on a bank or raised area. Scale-like leaves strung tightly around long stems lends a mossy appearance, belied by the white, bell-shaped flowers in late spring. Plant in a position sheltered from late frosts. Propagate by summer cuttings or layering.

Celmisia spectabilis subsp. magnifica
☼ ☼ ❋ ❋ ❋ ● **H/S** 30cm/12in

The splendid New Zealand celmisias prefer a cool, moist climate but it is possible to grow them in hotter, drier areas as long as the soil is enriched with organic matter and never waterlogged. Perennial rosettes of long silvery leaves are joined by sturdy stems bearing large, white, daisy-like blooms with yellow centres, mainly during early summer. Divide rosettes in spring.

Enkianthus campanulatus ♔
☼ ☼ ❋ ❋ ❋ ● **H** 2.5–3m/8–10ft

Being able to provide this shrub with cool, moist roots is as important as acid soil. Then it will thrive, making clusters of leaves under which hang a prolific display of delicate looking, bell-shaped flowers in spring and early summer. Pink-veined over cream, they have a shell-like appearance. Take cuttings in summer.

CREATING AN ACID BED

It is possible to grow acid-loving plants even in gardens with unsuitable soils and sites, if a special bed is created.

Choose a lightly shaded site, perhaps against a north-facing wall, and make a raised bed, about three bricks deep. Excavate to a depth of 30cm (12in) on neutral soils; on chalky soils, take out more and line the base with a sheet of polythene, with holes pierced for drainage. Put lime-free stones or rubble in the base to improve drainage and refill with neutral topsoil containing plenty of added leafmould, pine-needle mould and well-rotted garden compost. Leave to settle and add more organic matter before planting.

Gaultheria mucronata ♔
☼ ☼ ❋ ❋ ❋ ● **H/S** 90–120cm/3–4ft

These compact, bushy shrubs look somewhat surreal when covered in the round white, pink or purple-red berries for which they are grown. These follow small, white or pink-flushed, urn-shaped early summer flowers. Male and female varieties are needed to set fruit, usually with one male to a group of females. The glossy foliage is also pleasant. Propagate by summer cuttings.

Enkianthus campanulatus

Gaultheria mucronata 'Stag River'

• *see also:* DIGGING AND IMPROVING YOUR SOIL p180; RAISING PLANTS FROM SEED p230; PROPAGATING BY CUTTINGS p232; OTHER MEANS OF PROPAGATION p234

◁ **THE GIANT DAISY HEADS** *of* Celmisia
spectabilis *are long-lasting and attract attention.*
A raised bed can be enriched with leafmould to
create a moist, slightly acidic root run.

closest to the Himalayan habitat of this
perennial. In these conditions, plants
will grow tall and healthy but in a hot,
dry climate they are usually stunted and
short-lived. Huge rosettes of hairy leaves
build up and stunning blue flowers with
orange anthers open in early summer.
Raise from fresh seed.

171

Gentiana sino-ornata ♀
☼ ❋ ❋ ❋ ✿ **H** 5–7cm / 2–3in **S** 15–30cm / 6–12in
Cultivate gentians in large carpets and
they will provide a superb sight in full
bloom. This one bears linear, grass-like
foliage, against which the blue flowers
glisten in autumn. Unless the garden
conditions are naturally cool and moist,
site in light shade and ensure that the
soil is moist and enriched with organic
matter. Propagate by division or by
rooting offsets in spring.

Grevillea rosmarinifolia ♀
☼ ❋ ❋ ❋ ● **H/S** 2.2m / 7ft
Choose a sheltered position for this
drought-tolerant, exotic-looking
Australian shrub and it will prove hardy
on well-drained soils. Mine begins
flowering in early spring, continuing well
into summer. New buds then start to set.
The flowers are pinkish-red, with curved
styles that protrude like antennae. Site
away from paths as the needle-like
foliage is prickly. Take summer cuttings.
Thin to reduce size after flowering.

Kalmia latifolia ♀
Calico bush
☼ ❋ ❋ ❋ ❋ ● **H/S** / 1.8–3m / 6–10ft
Consistent with most other acid-lovers,
this shrub prefers a cool, moist

environment if it is to grow healthily
to its full height. From late spring to
summer, the flower buds look like
piped sugar icing and open to clusters
of bowl-shaped pink flowers patterned
by paler stamens and dark pollen. This
is a good woodland plant that resents
being container-grown. Propagate by
summer cuttings or layering.

Meconopsis grandis ♀
Himalayan blue poppy
☼ ❋ ❋ ❋ ❋ ◐ **H** 60–120cm / 2–4ft **S** 60cm / 2ft
A cool, moist environment where
the soil is rich yet well-drained comes

Kalmia latifolia 'Clementine Churchill'

Pieris 'Forest Flame' ♀
☼ ☼ ❋ ❋ ❋ ❋ **H** 2.2–3.5m / 7–12ft **S** 1.8m / 6ft
The brilliant red new growths of this
shrub are vulnerable to spring frosts,
so site with care. The leaves turn to
pink, cream and finally green as
they mature. The white flowers are
arranged in drooping panicles in
mid- and late spring. Plant pieris
in well-drained soil nourished by
plenty of organic matter and sheltered
from wind. Summer cuttings are a
challenge to strike.

ACID-LOVING SHRUBS
❖

Camellia japonica 'Doctor Tinsley' ♀ ●

Crinodendron hookerianum ♀ ●

Corylopsis pauciflora ◐

Cornus florida ◐ (dogwood)

Disanthus cercidifolius ♀ ◐

Embothrium coccineum ●

Fothergilla major ♀ ◐

Hamamelis vernalis 'Sandra' ◐

Illicium anisatum ●

Rhododendron 'Sappho' ♀ ●

Styrax wilsonii ◐

Vaccinium corymbosum ♀ ●

Plants for chalky soil

Chalk is often seen as a disadvantage, but there are many wonderful plants that flourish even on thin soils over chalk. Add plenty of organic matter to chalky soils in order to help plants establish quickly as well as to conserve moisture. For a gardener new to chalky soil it is vital to check the tolerance of each plant before buying or trying to grow it.

Cistus × purpureus

172

Clematis 'Huldine'

☼ ◐ ❄ ❄ ❄ ♡ **H** 3–4.5m / 10–15ft **S** 1.8m / 6ft

Like the rest of the clematis tribe, 'Huldine' thrives on chalk. Small but plentiful white flowers with mauve reverses are borne in summer. Plant deeply in autumn and feed plants well during late spring and early summer. Prune to within short spurs of older wood in late winter.

Cistus × purpureus ♀
Rock rose

☼ ❄ ❄ ❄ ♥ **H/S** 90cm / 3ft

On well-drained soil, cistus should prove to be hardy, if short-lived, shrubs. Their sticky shoots are aromatic in the sunshine and studded with deep pink, tissue-like flowers throughout summer. Each petal is marked at the base with a dark maroon

Cornus mas

spot. Propagate by summer cuttings. Untidy shrubs can be pruned in early spring, but do not cut into old wood.

Cornus mas ♀
Cornelian cherry

☼ ◐ ❄ ❄ ❄ ♡ **H/S** 4.5m / 15ft

Grown as a large shrub or small tree, the cornelian cherry varies in height according to the depth and fertility of soil. The leaves, 10cm (4in) long, turn red and purple in autumn before falling. The branches light up in late winter when clusters of small, fragrant yellow flowers open. These are followed by red, edible fruit in summer. Propagate by seed or summer cuttings.

Erysimum cheiri 'Blood Red'
Wallflowers

☼ ❄ ❄ ❄ ♥ **H/S** 45cm / 18in

Wallflowers are short-lived perennials treated as biennials. Sow directly into soil in late spring, plant out in autumn and enjoy their richly scented flowers the following spring. Alternatively, buy

△ **SITED INSIDE** *the protective canopy of other trees here,* Magnolia × loebneri *'Leonard Messel' looks magnificent when wreathed with its starry blooms in spring.*

• *see also:* DIGGING AND IMPROVING YOUR SOIL p180; RAISING PLANTS FROM SEED p230; PROPAGATING BY CUTTINGS p232; OTHER MEANS OF PROPAGATION p234

Paeonia mlokosewitschii

Papaver orientale 'Beauty of Livermere'

bare-rooted plants in autumn. This cultivar bears deep red blooms and blends well with pansies, tulips and daffodils in beds or containers.

Hypericum 'Rowallane' ♈
St. John's wort
☼ ☀ ✳ ✳ ✳ ✿ **H** 1.8m /6ft **S** 90cm /3ft

Choose a sheltered site for this shrub, which will reward your consideration by producing a fine display of bright golden-yellow flowers, 5–8cm (2–3in) across, from late summer to autumn. These are cup-shaped and decorated by prominent stamens. Thin out older stems in spring. Propagate by summer cuttings.

Magnolia x *loebneri* 'Leonard Messel' ♈
☼ ☀ ✳ ✳ ✳ ○ **H** 8m /25ft **S** 6m /20ft

One look at the starry, pale lilac-pink flowers of this magnolia in spring reveals that there is *M. stellata* in its parentage. Plant in moist soil for this small tree or large, rounded shrub to achieve its potential. Pruning is not a good idea with magnolias, so take its eventual size into account when siting.

Paeonia mlokosewitschii ♈
Caucasian peony
☼ ☀ ✳ ✳ ✳ ○ **H/S** 90cm /3ft

This elegant, herbaceous perennial sends up stems of attractively divided, blue-green foliage and its distinctive, bowl-shaped, soft yellow flowers open in late spring and early summer. As with all peonies, make sure the crowns are buried by no more than 2.5cm (1in), or they may not flower well. Propagate by division in autumn, taking care not to damage the roots.

Papaver orientale 'Beauty of Livermere' ♈
Oriental poppy
☼ ✳ ✳ ✳ ○ **H** 90–120cm /3–4ft **S** 90cm /3ft

The many cultivars of these early-summer flowering herbaceous perennials are drought-tolerant and suitable for chalky soils. This bears blooms 10–15cm (4–6in) across, composed of huge, silky-red petals with a black blotch at the base of each. Provide with some twiggy support. Propagate by division in spring or autumn, or root cuttings in late autumn.

Romneya coulteri ♈
Tree poppy
☼ ✳ ✳ ✳ ○ **H/S** 1–1.8m /3–6ft

Romneyas are perennials that either thrive and colonize or quietly die. One is advised to plant in the shelter of warm, sunny walls in well-drained soil, yet there are apocryphal stories of colonies invading buildings and pushing through the floors. Stems of glaucous, grey-green leaves bear white summer blooms with golden stamens. Propagate by 8–10cm (3–4in) root cuttings in spring.

Scabiosa caucasica 'Clive Greaves' ♈
Scabious, Pincushion flower
☼ ✳ ✳ ✳ ✿ **H/S** 60cm /2ft

Attractive to bees and butterflies as well as making excellent cut flowers, the large lavender-coloured blooms are most desirable. Borne in mid- and late summer, the flowerheads are 8cm (3in) across with pale centres. Young plants can be difficult to establish, so make sure they are not overgrown by neighbouring plants in the border. Divide established plants or take basal cuttings in spring.

KEY: ♈ *Award of Merit* ☼ *sun* ☀ *semi-shade* ✿ *shade* ✳ *half-hardy* ✳✳ *frost-hardy* ✳✳✳ *fully hardy* ○ *deciduous* ● *evergreen* ✿ *semi-evergreen* **H** *height* **S** *spread*

Hip

GARDENING
IN PRACTICE

❖

SOME PEOPLE CONSIDER gardening to be an art, others see it as a science. I personally think of it essentially as a practical craft, with overtones of both other disciplines. After all, no matter how artistic or scientific you may be, the manual skills of practical gardening are essential if you wish plants to grow well for you.

Plant propagation, lawn care, greenhouse management and soil preparation, as well as the planting and aftercare of trees, shrubs, hedges, perennials and annuals, are the real backbone of gardening and the subjects of this chapter. 'Book learning,' as my mentor, the aptly named school gardener Mr Lavender, always said, is a good way to get a superficial understanding of a subject – but, in the case of gardening, there is no substitute for getting your hands dirty to really begin to know plants and get the best out of them.

He was right, of course. But since I first learnt the art of plant care under his guidance, much in gardening has changed. There is no longer any need, for example, to spend your winters double digging or scrubbing out clay flower pots. New, simplified techniques, plus modern equipment and innovative garden products, now make it possible for gardeners with limited time and facilities to get good results from their plants – and to have much enjoyment and satisfaction from gardening along the way.

Sue Phillips

SUE PHILLIPS

Knowing your soil

Soil is the raw ingredient of gardening, but soils vary greatly in both type and fertility. If the soil is of good quality – deep and fertile – plants virtually grow themselves, but if it is out of condition you will have to improve its structure and its fertility before growing anything in it. So look for a few basic clues to your soil type and its state of health before embarking on planting.

SOIL TEXTURE

There are three main soil types – sandy, clay and loam – and it is important to know which type you have. Assessing the texture of your soil will give the best clues. Since the soil's texture depends on the kind of rock from which its particles were originally formed, you will never be able to change the basic type but there are ways in which you can improve and condition it. Most garden soils are in fact a mixture of several types, and the soil can vary quite considerably, even within the same garden.

Sandy soil feels gritty when rubbed between your hands and the particles do not stick together. Water runs away quickly after rain: you will see that any puddles vanish fast. Sandy soil is light, easily dug and warms up quickly after winter. It drains well but its composition also means that valuable nutrients leach out quickly. It therefore needs the frequent addition of huge amounts of organic matter in some form, such as well-rotted garden compost, which decomposes very quickly in this sort of soil.

◁ CLAY SOILS *are heavy to work but can be rough-dug in winter to allow frost to break them down.*

Clay soil is sticky when wet, and puddles last a long time after rain. When dry, clay soil becomes very hard and often cracks badly. Because it compacts into a dense, airless soil, it is heavy to dig but it holds water and therefore nutrients well, although it is prone to waterlogging. Clay soils need the addition of well-rotted organic matter too, but they should also have gritty sand or fine bark chippings dug in to improve their drainage and help aerate them, which makes them easier to work. Because clay has a naturally small particle size, the soil texture needs 'opening up' so that roots can penetrate and plants thrive in it. Heavy blue or yellow clay subsoils should not be dug, to avoid mixing the infertile lower layer with better soil above – simply pile on deep mulches to improve the soil.

Loam is easily recognizable as good garden soil; when cultivated and raked it breaks down to a crumb-like finish. It is rich, retains water without getting waterlogged and plants grow well in it.

Especially if it is dark in colour, loam may need very little improvement, although it is good practice to add organic matter to help maintain its fertility.

SOIL FERTILITY

The gardener's aim is to have a well-balanced, fertile soil but it often takes time and effort to achieve this, especially if you inherit a new plot in which the soil is compacted and full of builder's rubble. But all soils benefit from mixing in some form of organic material, such as compost, which improves both the soil's texture and its fertility.

THE SOIL'S pH VALUE

❖

4.5 or less: Very acid. Rhododendrons, heather and other ericaceous plants grow best.

4.5–5.5: Acid. Ericaceous plants will grow here but liming makes the ground suitable for a wider range of plants.

5.5–6.5: Slightly acid to nearly neutral; a majority of garden plants will thrive.

7.00: Neutral (the pH of pure water).

8.00: Chalk or limestone soil; only lime-lovers are happy here.

• *see also:* PLANTS FOR ACID SOILS p170; PLANTS FOR CHALKY SOIL p172; DIGGING AND IMPROVING YOUR SOIL p180; MAKING COMPOST p182

◁ **SOIL THAT IS** *kept in good heart by correct cultivation will produce heavy crops of fruit, flowers and vegetables year after year.*

▷ **RHODODENDRONS** *are happiest in acid soil, so check your soil's pH level before growing them to ensure they will thrive.*

Humus is decomposed plant material, broken down by the action of bacteria and other soil organisms like earthworms. It is a natural soil improver and source of nutrients. Worms play an important role in improving soil by making burrows which help aeration and drainage, and by digesting organic matter to make humus and release trace elements. The best way to encourage worms is to add plenty of organic matter to the soil.

The colour of soil will give you clues as to its condition and fertility. A dark colour is an indication that soil has previously been well cultivated and contains plenty of humus. Very light coloured soil often suggests a large proportion of sand or chalk, both of which make a soil dry out fast. Yellow or blue lumps or layers, found below the soil surface, are a sign of badly drained, infertile, heavy clay subsoil.

SOIL ACIDITY

Soil can also vary in its degree of acidity or alkalinity, often referred to as its pH.

It is possible to get a rough idea of whether your soil is very acid or alkaline by observing the plants that grow happily in it. If, for example, rhododendrons or other acid-lovers like camellias, skimmias, heathers or pieris, grow well in neighbouring gardens, it is reasonable to guess that the local soil is acid. Chalky rocks at the side of the road or chalk-loving plants such as pinks, potentillas and cistus growing wild suggests chalky soil. Since the soil's pH determines which plants will grow well in it, it is always worth doing a pH test to check your soil's acidity. Small, inexpensive kits are available in garden centres to do this. Extremely acid soil can be neutralized by using lime, if necessary, while limy soil can be neutralized with sulphur chips and plenty of organic matter, which is usually slightly acidic in reaction. However, the best solution is always to choose appropriate plants for an acid or a chalky soil.

USING A SOIL TEST KIT

Take several soil samples from all round the garden, using a trowel to remove a 'core' of soil. Take only soil from below the top 5cm (2in) for the test and avoid areas that have been used for bonfires or mixing cement. Mix all the samples together well or, if the soil is obviously different in some areas, make several separate tests. Follow the manufacturer's instructions on the kit. The usual procedure is to fill the tube with soil from the sample up to a given mark, then add distilled water to the level of the next mark. A chemical is then added, the sample shaken well and the pH determined by comparing the colour of the mix to those on the test card.

Digging and improving your soil

Organic matter is the lifeline of the garden and you should add it at every opportunity for good soil structure and fertility. Dig it in deeply by double digging when you first prepare a new bed, fork more in when getting annual beds ready for planting, and spread it over the ground as a mulch in permanent shrub, rose, perennial and mixed borders.

ORGANIC MATTER

Bulky organic matter can take several forms, all of which improve soil structure by creating air spaces between the fine mineral particles that make up the soil. More air spaces mean better drainage and aeration, which in turn improve growing conditions for plants by making it easier for their roots to penetrate. It also encourages worms, whose activities condition the soil.

Organic matter is primarily a soil conditioner; it supplies only a small amount of nutrients, the most important of which are the trace elements needed in only minute amounts and rarely provided by chemical (or inorganic) fertilizer. For this reason you should add

180

△ SOW GREEN MANURE *crops as a carpet under tall plants like sweetcorn. Once the main crop is harvested, dig in the green manure.*

both organic matter and fertilizer to bring the soil to the state of fertility needed for the intensive cultivation required from gardening.

COMPOST AND MANURES

Since you will need organic matter in large amounts, it makes sense to use whatever is available locally, most conveniently and cheaply. Choose from manure, spent hops or old mushroom compost, all of which can be bought in bags from a garden centre if you do not have a local source. You can also recycle used growing bags, or make your own garden compost by recycling garden and household waste via a compost bin: anything organic will serve the purpose

so long as it is well rotted before use. During the stages of its decomposition, plant material is attacked by soil bacteria and nitrogen is consumed in the process; therefore, if 'fresh' materials are dug into the garden, this will result in a nitrogen shortage.

GREEN MANURES

Green manure crops are deliberately sown in order to be dug in; their role is to improve the soil by providing both nutrients and organic matter. Green manure crops, which include clover, buckwheat and grazing rye, are sown like a carpet covering the ground and normally dug in before they flower. Different crops can be used for long- or short-term cover, and for summer or winter use. Long-term green manure crops are a good way of occupying vacant land so that improvement is

△ TO IMPROVE *the texture and drainage of heavy clay soils, dig in coarse, sharp sand or fine grit at 1–2 bucketfuls or more per sq m.*

SOIL CARE TOOL KIT

The basic soil care tools are a spade and a digging fork. It is often easier to dig heavy soil with a fork; a fork is also best for spreading compost or manure when improving the soil. But it is better to use a spade on light soil, which would trickle through the tines of a fork. Long-handled spades make the job of digging less of a strain, particularly for people liable to backache.

• *see also:* KNOWING YOUR SOIL p178; MAKING COMPOST p182

△ **ADDING LIME** *to acid soil prevents minerals being chemically 'locked up' in the soil.*

taking place in 'down' time. Short-term crops are a way of storing nutrients in the soil during winter, when they may otherwise be leached out by rain, and of returning them to the ground when dug in. Dig green manure crops into the soil six weeks before sowing or planting.

ORGANIC MULCHES

Another way of adding organic matter to the soil is by spreading a layer on top as a mulch. After the initial soil preparation has been done and the beds planted with shrubs or perennials, this is in fact the only way of adding organic material to the soil. A mulch is a layer of material, organic or otherwise, covering the soil. It works by keeping germinated weed seeds and seedlings in the dark, preventing them from growing; it has little effect on established perennial weeds. Suitable mulching materials include well-rotted garden compost or manure, spent mushroom compost, cocoa shell or bark chippings. These are spread annually in a layer 2.5cm (1in) or 5cm (2in) thick over the soil between plants when the soil is moist and weed-free. The mulch is slowly drawn into the soil by the action of worms and will need to be 'topped up' annually. Spring is the usual time but on light soil it is best to apply a mulch in both spring and autumn.

DEEP BEDS AND RAISED BEDS

Deep beds are narrow, deeply prepared beds used for the intensive cultivation of vegetables. After digging and incorporating quantities of organic matter, the beds are never walked on so the soil does not get compacted. These enriched beds are worked on from paths alongside them and crops planted closer than usual to produce higher yields. Extra organic matter is spread on top or lightly forked in. Raised beds, used in low-maintenance gardens or to provide better drainage for alpine plants, works in the same way, using a 'no dig' technique after initial deep preparation and improving the soil by spreading organic mulches on top.

DIGGING THE SOIL

❖

1 *Divide your plot in half lengthwise and dig a trench the depth and width of your spade, running halfway across one end. Remove soil and pile it up outside the plot.*

2 *Spread a 5cm (2in) layer of organic matter in the bottom of the trench. Working backwards, dig along the edge of the trench, turning the soil over into it as you work. This fills the first trench with soil, creating a second trench alongside it.*

3 *Continue to dig and add organic matter, creating successive trenches. When you reach the end of the plot, work your way back up the other side. Fill in the last trench with soil removed from the first.*

181

4 *For double digging, make the trench the width of two spades. Dig organic matter into the base using a fork, breaking up the soil to the full depth of its prongs. Continue digging down the plot, turning the soil into successive double-width trenches. Use soil removed from the last trench to fill the first.*

Making compost

Home-made garden compost is easy to make using a variety of waste materials from the kitchen and garden. By recycling your garden waste you can cheaply create a useful form of organic matter to improve soils and mulch borders. Composting also reduces the amount of material being thrown away and pointlessly taking up room in landfill sites.

△ **A COMPOST BIN**
is the ideal domestic recycler, turning kitchen peelings, garden weeds, lawn clippings and other soft, natural waste into free soil-improver.

182

▷ **NEW MATERIAL**
should be added in layers 15cm (6in) deep, each capped with fresh soil or fresh manure to make it work properly; top the finished heap with a layer of soil.

MAKING LEAFMOULD

Autumn leaves, especially oak, take longer to break down than normal compost ingredients – usually a year or more. Small quantities of leaves can be added to a compost heap, mixed in with plenty of soft materials, but large amounts are best composted separately in a leafmould cage, made by tacking wire netting round four corner posts. Each time leaves are gathered up, tip them into the cage, spread them out, dampen and cover with soil. When well-rotted, leafmould is valuable for creating special beds for choice woodland plants, topdressing woodland borders or using as a mulch.

THE SECRETS OF SUCCESS

All manner of soft waste can be used to make compost, including fruit and vegetable peelings from the kitchen. Suitable material from the garden includes weeds, old bedding plants and the leafy debris removed when clearing flower beds; in addition soft hedge clippings and lawn mowings can be composted. For best results, use a mixture of materials – too much of one ingredient can make the heap slimy, especially if very soft, green materials like grass clippings are used.

To speed up the rotting process, add compost ingredients in 15cm (6in) layers, dampening the material if dry, before capping with a bucketful of garden soil or animal manure (fresh, unrotted manure makes a good compost 'starter'), which provides vital bacteria to encourage the heap to rot. Alternatively, sprinkle with a handful of sulphate of ammonia (to provide nitrogen) or a compost activator product.

Continue adding to the heap in this way until the container is full, then finish with a layer of soil. Once a heap is

completed, do not add any further material as this will simply delay the rotting process. Start a second heap instead, if you have space. Two or more compost heaps are needed for peak efficiency, so that one is rotting down while another is being filled.

COMPOST BINS

For small quantities of waste, a compost bin is the answer. Various models are available in garden centres: they resemble plastic dustbins without bases and, by containing the compost, encourage it to

• *see also:* DIGGING AND IMPROVING YOUR SOIL p180

△ A WELL-MADE, FREESTANDING COMPOST HEAP *should take 6–12 months to rot down
sufficiently that the compost is ready to use; it will need turning sides-to-middle halfway through.*

heat up quickly and evenly. Since they
have solid sides and a lid, material is
composted evenly through the bin, so
that material round the edges breaks
down properly too – there should be no
need to 'turn' the heap halfway through
the composting time.

COMPOST HEAPS

With bigger gardens that generate large
quantities of compostible waste, an
open compost heap is the most
economical method. Make a container
of loose wooden slats, or of wire mesh

supported by four corner posts, or even
a loose heap of material. In order to
work, this will need to be big: at least
a 1m (3ft) cube. Being open-sided, the
heat will be concentrated in the middle,
so turn the heap after three months in
order that material from the sides takes
a turn in the centre, where it can be
composted. Ideally, you should cover
a compost heap with plastic sheeting in
winter or rainy weather to keep the heat
in and excess water out.

WORM BINS

Worm-worked compost is pure
wormcast and very rich. It is made
using special bins like dustbins with a
tap in the base. A breeding colony of
tiger worms or brandling worms
(available from organic gardening
supply firms or from fishing tackle and

◁ A MULCH OF *well-rotted compost, 2.5–5cm
(1–2in) thick, covers the soil around plants to
retain moisture and smother weeds.*

<table><tr><td>

COMPOST MATERIAL
TO AVOID

❖

• Never put perennial weeds or
diseased plant material onto a
compost heap, as the heat generated
inside it may not be enough to kill
the organisms, and you risk
spreading them when the compost
is later used round the garden.

• Avoid woody material like prunings
or the stems of herbaceous plants –
these will compost down in time but
they take longer than other compost
ingredients, thus occupying the
heap for longer. If woody materials
cannot be disposed of by other
means, chop them into short lengths
or put them through a mechanical
shredder, which will shorten the
rotting time, and if possible
compost them separately.

• Lawn mowings from grass treated
with chemical weedkillers should
be kept apart from other compost
ingredients for up to six mowings
after treatment, and composted
separately for at least six months.
Use for non-edible plants.

</td></tr></table>

pet shops in summer) is introduced to
a layer of pre-rotted material in the base
of the bin. Small amounts of finely
chopped, soft material like household
peelings and similar scraps are then
added every few days, to keep the
worms 'fed'. Fluid that accumulates in
the bin is drained off regularly via the
tap, and diluted to use as a plant food.
When full of soil-like material, the
worms are sieved out to start a new bin.
Worm bins need care in setting up and
they are tricky to manage until you get
used to them, so follow the maker's
instructions with your bin.

Watering your garden

△ **A WATERING CAN**
is a vital accessory.

Plants are made up of over 90 per cent water, which is taken in through their roots and lost through their leaves by transpiration. When short of water, the plant's natural processes cannot take place properly and their growth suffers; plants may wilt or even die. But nowadays water meters, dry summers and hosepipe bans mean that we must use water wisely and deliver it precisely where it is needed, without using wasteful sprinklers.

THE ESSENTIALS

An outdoor tap is a necessity for any serious gardener. It should be lagged to protect it from freezing in winter and should have a device fitted to it that prevents water flowing back into the mains. In addition, a hosepipe approximately one and a half times the length of the garden will enable you to reach every corner, allowing for detours round beds. If there are a lot of intensively cultivated beds, containers and a greenhouse, it will save time to install a simple watering system consisting of perforated pipes through which water can seep slowly, or of individual nozzles set alongside plants. This can be linked to a timing device such as a 'water computer' fixed to the tap, which automatically switches the water on and off at preset intervals – ideal for busy people or for holidays.

HOW AND WHEN TO WATER

The worst way to water is little and often. It is much better to give plants a good soaking, whether they are in containers or the open ground. Then let them drain so they are not left standing in water, and do not water again until they start to dry out. You cannot rely on

△ **SPECIAL GADGETS** *are available to divert water from downpipes into water butts to use on the garden. Several butts can be linked together.*

watering at regular intervals, since conditions change and plants' water needs vary. Check whether container-grown plants need watering by sticking a finger into their pots; outdoors, dig a 10cm (4in) hole with a trowel: while the surface soil may be dry, the soil further down can be moist enough. During cold weather, plants are best watered in the morning so that their foliage is dry again

△ **TOMATOES ARE** *thirsty plants needing plenty of water. Insert empty pots into a growing bag so that water seeps in slowly and evenly.*

before nightfall – this helps to prevent the spread of fungal disease. In hot weather, however, it is far better to water in the evening, so the plants have all night to take up the moisture before the sun comes out and evaporates it. Do not forget about watering in winter. Containers planted with winter bedding, rock plants or evergreens need watering occasionally – check them weekly.

• *see also:* FEEDING PLANTS p186

184

TIPS FOR EFFICIENT WATERING

○ Use water where it is most needed: shallow-rooted plants such as vegetables, annuals and any newly planted shrubs have top priority for watering, along with those in containers and under glass.

○ Do not waste water on lawns: a sprinkler uses up to 250 gallons (1,000 litres) of water an hour, which is about as much as a family of four uses in the house in two days. The grass may turn brown but it grows back when autumn rains arrive. Do not feed lawns that are suffering stress as a result of water shortage; this often causes scorching.

○ Mature trees and shrubs can fend for themselves; watering only encourages their roots to come to the surface, which in turn makes the plants less able to cope in dry conditions.

○ Use water-retaining gel crystals in tubs and hanging baskets, and also fork them into the soil of dry flower beds, especially if they contain annual bedding plants.

○ Make intensively cultivated deep beds for growing vegetables, salads and soft fruit, instead of growing them on a large scale, and only grow as much as you actually need – this saves both work and water.

○ When watering new shrubs, deliver water directly to their roots by making funnels from old plastic soft drinks bottles with the base cut off, instead of splashing it over the soil surface where it evaporates quickly.

○ Hoe regularly; weeds compete with cultivated plants for water, and hoeing creates a 'dust mulch' that helps to prevent evaporation from the moist soil deeper down.

185

△ GIVEN ADEQUATE MOISTURE, *healthy, well-fed plants put on a superb show in summer. A perforated pipe round the edge of this border enables shallow-rooted plants to be watered easily.*

DEALING WITH DROUGHT

❖

• Cut down on the need for watering in dry summers by deep preparation of the soil when making a new bed. Double dig, adding plenty of well-rotted organic matter to hold water.

• Make your own compost and fork as much organic matter as possible into the soil during the winter digging. Mulch beds with up to 5cm (2in) of compost or bark in autumn or early spring, while the soil is moist; do not mulch dry soil as this simply makes it harder for rain to penetrate. Use grit to mulch rock gardens.

• Install rainwater diverters to the downpipes of the house to fill up water butts or plastic barrels. This will enable you to take advantage of any showers.

• If drought is a regular occurrence in your region, consider modifying the design of your garden in order to have more paved areas instead of a thirsty lawn. You might include gravel features planted with drought-resistant shrubs and Mediterranean-style plants instead of placing the emphasis on bedding plants.

Feeding plants

In the wild, plants can live in unimproved, even poor, soil using only the recycled nutrients from dead animals and plants that decompose naturally in the earth around them. Centuries of adaptation have ensured the survival of the fittest species. But in gardens, where we grow artificially bred plants in intensively cultivated beds or in containers, plants need extra nutrients.

Bonemeal

Pellets of poultry manure

Growmore

FERTILIZERS

186

General fertilizers supply the three main nutrients – nitrogen, potassium and phosphorus – in the ideal balance. Organic products also supply minor ones, such as iron and magnesium, and trace elements. The function of each is shown in the table opposite. There are many products on sale, but you will need only a few to cover all your requirements.

△ **SOLID FERTILIZERS** *come in a variety of types and grades. Read the packet to see the exact nutrients each provides.*

▷ **PERENNIALS** *planted closely together in a flower border will benefit from being fed during the growing season if you want them to flower for as long as possible.*

△ **SPRINKLE A HANDFUL** *of general fertilizer around shrubs at the start of the growing season, following the manufacturer's instructions. Hoe well in and water if necessary.*

SOLID FERTILIZERS

Granular or powder fertilizers are designed to feed plants growing in garden beds and borders; they are mainly used when preparing the ground ready for planting but are sometimes sprinkled on and watered in for additional feeds during the growing season. Plants take up this type of feed through their roots. General fertilizers are the best for all-round use, providing a balance of all the main plant nutrients and can be used both for initial soil preparation and applied during the growing season. 'Straight', single-nutrient fertilizers are for occasional use if a particular nutrient is needed in

larger amounts than the others – such as sulphate of potash to encourage flowering and fruiting of heavy-yielding crops like fruit trees and bushes.

LIQUID FEEDS

Liquid or soluble feeds have to be diluted in water. They are the best choice for plants growing in pots and other containers. Since the nutrients are already dissolved there is no risk of concentrated fertilizer touching roots and scorching them.

SLOW-RELEASE FEEDS

Slow-release feeds and fertilizer sticks or tablets are an alternative to soluble

• *see also:* MAKING COMPOST p182; WATERING YOUR GARDEN p184

PLANT NUTRIENTS AND THEIR BENEFITS

MAJOR NUTRIENTS

Nitrogen (N): used by plants in growing healthy leaves and stems.

Potassium, potash (K): for the production of healthy flowers and fruit.

Phosphorus, phosphate (P): healthy roots.

MINOR NUTRIENTS

Iron and magnesium are ingredients of chlorophyll. Calcium builds cell walls.

Iron deficiency causes yellowing (chlorosis) of leaves; seen when acid-lovers such as rhododendrons are not grown in acid soil.

Magnesium deficiency causes yellow leaves with green veins (seen in tomato plants and roses).

Calcium deficiency causes blossom end rot in tomatoes and bitter pit in apples; often linked to an irregular water supply.

Trace elements A huge range of other minerals are needed in minute quantities.

▽ **FOLIAR FEEDS** *are usually sprayed on to plant leaves; use them to give your plants a boost.*

feeds for containers; one application is usually enough to keep plants fed for a whole growing season.

FOLIAR FEEDS

Foliar feeds are liquid fertilizers sprayed on to leaves at low concentrations; they are a useful way to get nutrients into plants whose roots are damaged or which are in need of a tonic. Some root feeds can also be used for foliar feeding when further diluted, but check instructions.

SPECIAL-PURPOSE FEEDS

Special blends of liquid or solid feeds are sold to suit the needs of particular plants, for instance rose feeds, lawn feeds and tomato feeds. These are sometimes combined with chemical treatments – such as weedkiller in lawn feed – in which case they must be used for their intended purpose. Some have a wider use, such as high-potash liquid tomato feed, which can be used for all flowering plants as well as tomatoes. Use it for plants such as fuchsias, grown in pots and containers.

FERTILIZER DO'S AND DONT'S

187

✔ Always follow manufacturer's instructions precisely.

✘ Never exceed the recommended rate of use: excess fertilizer can scorch plant roots. If a product is over-applied by mistake, drench the soil or compost with plenty of water to wash out the excess.

✔ Apply at the start of the growing season, when the weather is good and new growth has started. Top up nutrients regularly during the growing season but tail off towards the end of it, as feeding then stimulates soft growth that may be damaged by frost.

✘ Don't apply feeds when plants are under stress due to water shortage or attack from pest or disease, nor in dormant seasons.

✔ Use solid fertilizers on moist ground, then hoe them in. If the soil surface is dry, water well in.

✘ Don't leave fertilizer granules lodged in foliage – they will scorch. Wash them off with clean water.

Lawn tools

If you have a lawn a mower is vital, but a small collection of other tools will also prove useful for its maintenance. Choose all lawn tools with care, taking into account the size of your lawn and the quality you want. Many specialist tools are used only once or twice a year and can always be hired, which will save on storage space as well as money and enable you to use a powered rather than a manual version.

188

LAWN EDGING

For making a sharp lawn edge, the traditional tool is a half-moon edger, which has a semi-circular blade. This can also be used for cutting turf when removing pieces, for instance to repair a bald patch. However, it is perfectly possible to use any sharp and straight-edged spade for both jobs.

Long-handled shears

▷ **THE MOST CONVENIENT**
way of neatening the edges of a lawn after mowing is to use these manual shears. Their long handles enable you to do the job without bending.

Long-handled shears come in two types. The best known are the edging shears shown below. Others have blades turned through 90° and are used to trim off tufts missed by the mower. Electrically powered lawn edgers can be pushed round the edge of the grass, making the job easy and involving no bending. Some rotary line trimmers can be used for lawn edging – look for lightweight models.

RAKING A LAWN

For raking up lawn mowings or dead leaves, or for removing moss, a springbok lawn rake is a useful tool. This has long wire 'fingers' instead of the short, stiff teeth of a conventional garden rake. Electrically powered lawn rakers are also available; these have collection boxes on the front and look like small mowers with rotating wire 'teeth' instead of cutting blades. The height can be adjusted according to the job in hand. Many of the above can be hired.

SPIKING A LAWN

To tackle compaction, turf needs regular spiking in autumn; a spiker is also useful for helping a lawn to take up water at the end of a dry spell. You can use a garden fork but, unless the lawn is very small, this is very tiring and takes a long time – you need to push the tines in 7–10cm (3–4in) deep every 15cm (6in) in each direction across the lawn. Mechanical spikers, which look like spiked rotating drums with handles for pushing, do a good job and hollow-tine spikers – something like multiple pogo sticks –

Rotary lawn spiker

• *see also:* ROUTINE LAWN CARE p194

◁ A TOP-QUALITY LAWN *is the result of good soil preparation followed by regular feeding, weed control and mowing. For a bowling-green finish, set the mower blades to cut 1.2cm (¹/₂in) high.*

are best on heavy clay soils. An alternative to spiking is to use a mechanical device with a slashing action – often used on sports turf – to alleviate compaction. Some rotary mowers have slashing attachments that fit on to the blades.

CHOOSING A MOWER

❖

ROTARY PETROL-DRIVEN MOWERS are rugged machines that can be used on long or rough grass, and cut even when grass is damp. Due to their wheels, they do not cut right up to the lawn edge and leave a rough edge that needs to be tidied afterwards.

Electric cylinder mower

CYLINDER MOWERS give the best finish, producing a quality cut and the traditional striped effect. Petrol models are expensive and best for large lawns; cheaper electric cylinder mowers are also available and old-fashioned manual mowers are still useful for tiny lawns. The grass must be dry to get a good cut with a cylinder mower. They will run up to the edge of a lawn, so only light trimming is needed afterwards.

HOVER MOWERS glide over lawn edges and round awkward curves, so are useful where there are several island beds and in small, congested gardens. Models without a grass collection box should be used often, before the grass gets too long, otherwise the clippings will need to be raked up afterwards. The more powerful models usually have grass boxes.

ELECTRIC MOWERS are the cheapest to buy and need little maintenance, but are only for small gardens. Use in conjunction with an RCD for safety due to the risk of cutting cables – never connect more than two extension cables together. They are easily stored by hanging up in a shed or garage.

PETROL MOWERS are a good choice for larger lawns but they are more expensive, noisy in use and need annual servicing. But a large model should last a long time if well-maintained. They need plenty of storage space.

Electric rotary mower

SAFETY TIPS

✔ Always plug electrical equipment into a circuit breaker or RCD (residual current device), which instantly cuts off the power if a cable is damaged, preventing electric shocks.

✘ Never use an electric mower or other piece of equipment when it is raining or the grass is wet.

✘ If a cable gets cut, do not repair it with tape – either replace the cable or, if practical, shorten it to remove the damaged part then reconnect the plug to the new end.

✔ Always employ a qualified electrician to do electrical repairs.

✘ Never attempt to unblock or adjust the blades of an electric mower without first unplugging it from the electric supply or disconnecting the spark plug of petrol mowers to ensure the blades cannot accidentally be engaged.

✔ Wear strong boots to protect your feet when mowing – never soft shoes or open sandals. If using a rotary mower, wear goggles to protect your eyes from the stones, grit and dirt that are sometimes thrown up.

✔ The new generation of cordless electric mowers makes the perfect solution for small gardens. There are no cables so they are safe as well as being quiet and easy to use.

189

Choosing a lawn

Grass is the traditional choice for a lawn. But where summer water shortages make it difficult to keep grass in good condition, alternative lawns with built-in drought tolerance may be a better solution. In tiny town gardens in permanent shade or on poor clay soil, the best option may be to lay gravel or paving instead.

△ **WILDFLOWER LAWNS** *are cut in spring and in autumn, once all the flowers have shed their seed.*

190

▽ **GENEROUS CURVES** *in a lawn will enable you to manoeuvre the lawn mower effectively round them.*

GRASS LAWNS

Think carefully about your lawn from a practical as well as a visual point of view, particularly for ease of mowing. Choose a geometric shape – circle, square, hexagon or rectangle – for a formal garden or a formal feature within a different style of garden. For a country garden or an informal style of garden, choose a lawn with broad curves and possibly inset island beds. Choose meandering grass paths running through naturalistic borders in a cottage or wild-style garden. A hard path or paved edging to a lawn makes mowing easy as the mower glides over the edge of the grass; it will also prevent overhanging plants in adjacent borders from smothering the grass and causing bare or yellow patches.

WILDFLOWER LAWNS

Ideal for wildlife gardens and for more unkempt areas away from the house, a wildflower lawn is created by sowing a mixture of grass and wildflower seed, or by planting pot-grown plants into established turf and allowing them to spread naturally. Scattering packets of seed over turf does not work. Wildflower lawns are not, however, flowering versions of normal lawns – they look more like old-fashioned hay meadows. Left long, they are cut once or twice a year, in early spring and in autumn, so that the flowers can complete their life cycle and shed seed. You can achieve a wildflower effect in a domestic lawn by allowing 'weeds' such as daisies and speedwell to remain, and by refraining from using weedkillers or fertilizers. This keeps the grass growth weak but encourages wildflower species.

△ **CLOVER LAWNS** *are drought-tolerant and need little mowing as they are naturally compact.*

CLOVER LAWNS

In response to more regular hot, dry summers, clover lawns are becoming increasingly popular. Specially compact strains of white clover are sown alone or mixed with grass. The resulting 'lawn' stays green during periods of drought and makes its own nitrogen using the nitrogen-fixing nodules on the clover roots, which feed the grass growing with it. In summer, clover lawns attract bees, so take care if walking barefoot.

• *see also:* MAKING THE MOST OF GRASS p32; LAWN TOOLS p188, ROUTINE LAWN CARE p194

△ **CHAMOMILE AND THYME** *lawns make an aromatic 'carpet' but will not withstand wear.*

TURF OR SEED?

Turf is most people's first choice as it gives an instant lawn, but it is expensive and needs to be laid with care. Always choose specially cultivated turf grown from seed. Meadow turf is a cheaper option but is often full of weeds and inferior grasses. Turf can be laid on well-prepared, firmed and levelled sites from autumn through winter until late spring, as long as the soil is neither muddy nor frozen.

Seed is cheaper and usually gives better results than turf in the long run, but it takes several months to turn from a seedbed into usable lawn. The periods when grass seed can be successfully sown are limited, as it germinates best in early autumn and late spring. Various seed mixtures are available: choose hard-wearing grass for use in a family back garden, fine grass for a more ornamental lawn, and shade- or drought-tolerant mixtures for 'problem' areas.

CARING FOR NON-GRASS LAWNS

✔ Raise from plants, not seed.
✘ Do not mow: clip with shears when needed or use a hover mower to 'top' the plants lightly.
✘ Never use lawn weedkillers as they kill clovers and herbs. Hand-weed if required, though dense planting minimizes the need.
✔ Plant through a weed-barrier fabric topped with gravel to prevent weeds.
✘ Do not walk on these lawns much: they are not hard-wearing.

HERB LAWNS

Chamomile and thyme are the most popular choices. For chamomile lawns, choose the non-flowering variety 'Treneague', while any variety of creeping thyme, in gold, silver or green, will provide good ground cover. Both need a very well-drained, sunny site to thrive but neither will tolerate much wear. Inset 'stepping stones' of paving slabs if you need to cross the area often. Or you could make a chequerboard pattern of adjacent paving slabs and herb-planted squares for an unusual effect. When preparing the soil for a herb lawn, incorporate plenty of grit or gravel and, unless the soil is naturally fast-draining, raise the area with a 5cm (2in) layer of gravel and plant through it.

ALPINE LAWNS

A range of low, carpeting and mound-shaped rock plants are grown with clumps of dwarf bulbs to form a very decorative 'lawn'. The effect is of a Persian carpet, with colours changing throughout the seasons. But this is not a lawn for walking on – use paved or gravel paths or 'stepping stones' through it. Prepare the ground as for a herb lawn.

HEATHER CARPET

Use prostrate varieties and clumps of compact, bushy species of heather to create an undulating effect. Though it withstands some light wear, a heather carpet is safest with paths or paving running through it. It needs a sunny, well-drained soil, rich in organic matter.

Starting a new lawn

Whether you are replacing a neglected old lawn that is beyond restoration, or starting a new lawn on a bare plot, good initial site preparation is vital to its success. Thorough preparation prevents problems later on and makes the lawn easy to look after. Once grass covers the ground, it is more difficult to deal with problems like perennial weeds, poor soil or uneven ground.

192

CLEARING THE SITE

It is best to begin site clearance several months before you lay the lawn, to allow time for treating perennial weeds. This also enables you to tackle the heavy work in easy stages. Start by removing any builders' rubble and similar debris. Then kill the existing grass or perennial weeds by watering the area with a translocated weedkiller that acts on roots and foliage yet leaves the soil safe to sow or plant once the weeds are dead; allow six to eight weeks for this to work. Once the weeds are dead, dig or rotovate deeply, removing the roots of any perennial weeds. Leave the soil alone for a few weeks and if any weeds regrow, re-treat them as before. If annual weeds appear, simply hoe to prevent them setting seed.

IMPROVING THE GROUND

To condition the soil, spread organic matter or gritty sand (for clay soil) over the area and dig it in. Take the opportunity to level minor depressions as you work: if the site is seriously uneven, strip off the topsoil, level the

▷ **SOME GARDEN DESIGNS** *alternate areas of lawn with hard surfaces like gravel or paving, so part of the garden is usable after wet weather.*

• *see also:* DIGGING AND IMPROVING YOUR SOIL p180

subsoil, then replace the topsoil without mixing the two.

A week before sowing or turfing, sprinkle on a general fertilizer, such as blood, fish and bone or a special pre-lawn fertilizer, and rake well in. As you rake, continue levelling the soil and remove stones and debris. Then tread the area well to consolidate the soil and rake again, leaving the surface level, evenly firm with no soft spots that will sink later, and with a crumb-like surface. It may need raking several times to achieve this finish.

SOWING SEED

Timing is crucial: sow in late-spring or in early autumn. Autumn sowing is best if your summers are hot and dry, as the new grass has longer to get established before drought occurs. Choose an appropriate seed for the site and the way you intend to use the lawn: fine lawn mixtures need a high standard of regular maintenance while modern rye grasses are hard-wearing and reliable for family use. Special seed mixtures are available for shade and other difficult situations, while some have wildflower seeds added to create a wildflower lawn. Scatter the seed evenly at 25g (1oz) per square metre (practise first on a sheet of paper on the garage floor); marking the area into metre squares with canes or string makes for greater accuracy. Rake the seed into the soil surface, then water if rain does not fall within 24 hours.

LAYING TURF

This can be done any time during the winter from mid-autumn until late-spring, except when the soil is very wet and muddy or during cold, frosty weather. Cultivated turf is expensive but

LAYING TURF

1 *After digging the ground deeply, sprinkle the fertilizer dressing evenly over the soil and rake well in, levelling the ground and removing stones and roots as you go.*

2 *Firm the whole area over, using your feet and allowing the weight to sink through your heels. A roller will only flatten down the peaks and leave the hollows loose.*

3 *To avoid footmarks pitting the surface of the prepared soil, work from a long plank. Start at one edge and work forwards across the area. Unroll the turves and lay them out in a row, with their edges butting tightly together.*

4 *Firm down the first row with the back of a rake. Move the plank on a little and lay the second row of turf like bricks in a wall, so the joints between adjacent turves do not run continuously. Water regularly until established.*

193

will be weed-free and of superb quality; meadow turf can be patchy and might contain weeds. The box above shows the main steps involved in laying turf.

AFTERCARE

Water thoroughly if the weather is dry, and keep off new lawns either until the turf has rooted into the soil (test by trying to lift a corner after about six weeks) or until a seed-raised lawn has had its first couple of cuts. Mow new turf as soon as it needs it. Give a seed lawn its first cut when its longest tufts are 5cm (2in) long using hand shears, as mowers can pull new grass out. Make the next two cuts with a lightweight (that is, hover) mower with the blades set fairly high.

Do not worry about weeds in a new lawn, especially a seed-raised one; upright weeds will soon die out once regular mowing starts. Rosette weeds can be tackled later, using spot weedkiller. Avoid using weedkiller or fertilizer on new lawns for the first six months.

Routine lawn care

Grass is not difficult to keep in good condition and establishing a routine of basic care, mainly involving regular mowing and feeding, will help you to maintain a green, dense and problem-free lawn. A well cared-for lawn will also withstand drought and wear better than a lawn that is left to struggle.

MOWING

Mow once a week or more in summer, and once a month in winter. Not only does this keep a lawn tidy, it also helps to thicken the grass up and deters weeds; regular topping should control all upright weeds without the use of weedkillers. For normal lawns, 2–2.5cm (¾–1in) is the shortest you need mow them, cutting a little shorter on fine-quality lawns. Alter the height of cut by adjusting the mower blades to leave grass 1.2cm (½in) longer in winter and during dry spells in summer, reducing the height again when growing conditions improve.

Always trim round lawn edges after mowing to keep the grass looking neat, using either edging shears, an electric lawn edger or a suitable rotating line trimmer. Properly made lawn edges allow easier trimming and prevent grass 'creeping' into the surrounding borders. To maintain clean edges, go round the lawn with a spade or half-moon edger every spring, pulling away the soil to leave a firm vertical edge to the turf, 5–7.5cm (2–3in) deep.

FEEDING

Feeding grass keeps it green and thick. Thinning and patchy grass encourages the growth of weeds as seed can germinate more easily in bare soil; seedlings get smothered in dense grass, which acts like a living mulch. Use a high-nitrogen lawn feed in late spring, substituting a combined feed-and-weed or moss treatment product (if either are a problem bear in mind that small patches of weed or moss can be individually spot-treated). The late spring feed is the most important one. If lawns receive heavy wear, for instance small family lawns or those used for games or sports in additional to normal use, it is advisable to repeat regular lawn feeds

△ **HOLD LONG-HANDLED SHEARS** *vertically, pressing the blade close to the lawn to get a clean cut. Keep the lower blade horizontal, holding its handle still; use the upper blade to cut.*

◁ **TO GIVE A LAWN** *the traditional striped effect, use a cylinder mower and turn it at the end of each strip, working back in the opposite direction.*

• *see also:* LAWN TOOLS p188

△ **IF THE SOIL IS DRY,** *apply liquid lawn feed, using a hand-held dilutor that fits on to the end of a hosepipe. Liquid feed also gives lawns a boost.*

ROTARY TRIMMERS
❖

These are handy machines for trimming long grass where a lawn butts up against a fence or wall, or where a mower will not reach. Do not use round trees or hedges as the spinning line can cut into the bark and damage it. Most trimmers are electric but petrol versions are available. Follow the usual safety precautions.

every six weeks until midsummer. In autumn, treat lawns to a programme of care designed to help them through winter and prepare them for next year. Start by raking well, either by hand or

△ **HOLLOW-TINE SPIKERS** *remove entire cores of soil each time they are pressed down into the soil. Sweep up the deposited soil, then brush grit into the holes left in the lawn, to improve both aeration and drainage.*

with a mechanical raker, to remove moss and thatch-like debris that accumulates round the base of grass stems. The material gathered can be composted. Regular treading down of a lawn compacts it, which closes air spaces in the soil, causing poor drainage and an unhealthy lawn, so spike in autumn to relieve any compaction (*see left*). Finish by applying a specially formulated autumn lawn fertilizer containing very little nitrogen, encouraging good root action rather than lush, leafy growth. On heavy clay soils, a light top-dressing of fine grit helps to leave a firm surface that does not get muddy in wet weather and assists surface drainage. Other lawns can be improved by top-dressing with sifted compost or rich soil. Apply a bucketful per square metre, and work it in with the back of a rake or a besom broom, so as not to smother the grass.

DO'S AND DON'TS FOR THE BEST RESULTS

✔ Use a spreader to ensure even application of granular products, which are not easy to apply by hand. Measure out liquid products carefully and dilute at the correct rate. Mark the lawn out into metre squares using string, to ensure accurate application.

✔ Do water in granular feed and lawn treatments if it does not rain within 48 hours after applying them. Or use a liquid formulation that does not need watering in.

✗ Do not use lawn weedkillers just before it rains. The product, taken in through weed leaves, needs 12 hours or more in which to work – it is de-activated in the soil.

✔ Do use an autumn formulation lawn fertilizer in spring and summer instead of the usual feed if you want to thicken up the grass without encouraging lush green growth that will need more mowing.

✔ Do buy a separate watering can to use only for applying liquid lawn weedkillers; however well you wash out a can, the tiny traces that remain are enough to harm sensitive plants.

✗ Do not use lawn feeds, even liquid products, on a lawn that has turned brown due to drought. They will not help and may make things worse by scorching the grass. Wait until after prolonged rain when the grass has started to grow again naturally, then rake out the worst of the dead grass and apply half-strength lawn feed.

195

Dealing with lawn problems

A perfect lawn sets off the whole garden; conversely, one that is obviously suffering can make even the best-kept garden look somewhat neglected. If you treat lawn problems correctly and as soon as they are spotted, most of them will be quickly and easily cured.

△ **SLICES OF LOG**
make good natural 'stepping stones' across a lawn.

196

ERADICATING WEEDS

Weeds are generally a problem where grass is thin or has bare patches; regular feeding thickens grass so weeds cannot get a foothold. Upright weeds are rarely a problem in lawns as frequent mowing weakens and kills them. The commonest lawn weeds are low-growing rosettes and mat-forming kinds like daisies, dandelion, creeping buttercup, clover, speedwell and trefoil that pass safely under the blades of a mower. Tackle broad-leaved weeds individually, using spot lawn weedkiller. If a large area needs treating, use liquid weedkiller or granular feed-and-weed treatments. Clover, speedwell and trefoil are harder to kill; use a liquid product specially for small-leaved lawn weeds, or dig them out singly with a trowel or daisy grubber. Mat-forming weeds like trefoil come out easily if you find the centre of the plant and twist until the roots come out.

▽ **VISUALLY**, *a lawn is the outdoor equivalent of carpet in the living room. It too needs regular care to keep it hardwearing and looking its best.*

• *see also:* ROUTINE LAWN CARE p194

▷ GRASS PATHS *are susceptible to excess wear. Firm the surface by sprinkling gritty sand to stop it going muddy in wet weather.*

DEALING WITH MOSS

Moss tends to be a problem in shade, damp areas, badly compacted soil, or where the grass is scalped by a mower cutting too close over bumps in the lawn. Firstly, you need to improve the lawn's drainage and relieve any compaction in order to deter the invasion of moss. Moss can, however, occur in any lawn after a wet winter. Treat it using a liquid mosskiller or combined granular feed-and-mosskiller product for lawns in mid-spring. Moss turns black when dead and should then be raked out. Live moss is harder to remove, and small fragments will remain and regrow.

ALGAE AND LIVERWORT

These are mostly a problem on heavy clay soils during wet weather, when the lawn can become dangerously slippery. Rake or scrape off the worst, then hollow-tine spike the lawn or slash the area and brush gritty sand into the holes to improve surface drainage. Some brands of liquid lawn mosskillers also kill algae and liverwort: check the information on the packet.

FAIRY RINGS

True fairy rings are persistent circles of small toadstools that are present all year, shrivelling up in summer but rehydrating after rain. The circles slowly get bigger, leaving weak yellow grass inside and a ring of lush, bright green grass just outside that of the fungi. There is no easy cure; you will need to dig out soil from the ring to a depth of 45cm (18in), treat

with a phenol-based soil sterilant if available, fill the hole with new topsoil and re-turf. Occasional toadstools in autumn are nothing to worry about and they vanish at the first frost.

DAMAGE CAUSED BY WEAR

Regular use in one direction will wear a bare 'path' across a lawn and you would do best to lay a hard path or stepping stones over your route to the shed, garage or compost heap. If you need to push heavy barrows over the lawn in wet weather, avoid making ruts by unrolling a temporary 'path' of heavy-grade plastic netting where and when it is needed.

REPAIRING BROKEN EDGES

Replace collapsed or torn lawn edges by cutting out a square of turf that includes the broken area. Turn it round and fit it back into the gap, so the 'hole' is now inside the lawn, leaving a firm outer edge to the lawn. Fill hole with seed compost or fine garden soil, sprinkle grass seed over, rake it into the surface and water.

DEALING WITH DROUGHT

During prolonged drought grass turns first yellow, then brown. It is rarely actually dead and will soon recover once autumn rains start. Do not feed a lawn during drought to try and turn it green

– it simply makes things worse by scorching it. Once the rain comes, spike the lawn thoroughly to assist water penetration (rain is slow to sink into bone-dry lawns and often just lays on the top and evaporates). Do not feed until after the grass has greened up naturally.

YELLOW PATCHES

These have various causes. If you see a bitch use the lawn, dilute the urine with a bucket of water. Avoid petrol spills from the mower by refuelling it on a hard surface, not on the grass, and fill fertilizer spreaders on the path too, as spills scorch the grass.

OVERALL NEGLECT

It is usually cheaper and easier to restore a neglected lawn than to replace it. Follow a routine of regular cutting, feeding with lawn feed at six-weekly intervals from mid-spring to midsummer and treating in spring to eradicate moss or weeds, followed by the full autumn care programme outlined earlier.

197

SEEDING WORN PATCHES

❖

Balding patches spoil the appearance of a lawn, allow weeds to colonize and make it muddier in wet weather. The solution is to reseed thin or patchy areas in spring or autumn. Rake off dead grass and loosen soil with the points of a fork. Sprinkle on grass seed and scuffle in, then water well and cover with netting.

Planting a hedge

A hedge is the traditional garden surround. A living boundary, it is more permanent than fencing but needs more space and greater upkeep. Depending on the type of hedge and the plant chosen, a hedge can provide a year-round backdrop for other plants, a dense, evergreen barrier, an informal flowering boundary or a neat dwarf edging to beds or paths.

△ **HEDGES DO NOT** *have to be straight; this curved hedge of* Berberis thunbergii *makes an architectural feature leading to the flight of steps.*

SOIL AND SITUATION

Always choose hedging plants that like the conditions in your garden. On a chalky soil and an exposed site, beech is the best choice; otherwise, *Lonicera nitida* is good for most exposed situations. Conifer hedges need a soil that is well-drained but never dries out badly, as this can cause browning of the foliage. In shade, choose box, which needs only a few hours of direct sunlight each day. Beech and hornbeam which, though not evergreen, retain their brown leaves in winter, are the favourites for a traditional garden. Evergreen hedges such as yew or box make an ideal backing for a herbaceous border and are also suitable for dividing a large garden into 'rooms'. Yew can be clipped to as little as 30cm (12in) wide and, being slow-growing, clipping need be done only once a year, in late summer. Good seaside hedges include escallonia and *Griselinia littoralis*; in mild regions, hardy fuchsias make colourful boundaries.

THE HEIGHT

Select plants that are appropriate for the height of hedge required. No hedge will stop at a certain height but some, such as thuja, make an easily maintained, low to medium hedge, while Leylands cypress needs regular, severe pruning to keep it to a reasonable height; yew, beech, hornbeam and privet are also suitable for tall hedges. Informal, flowering hedges should be chosen with regard to the natural size of the plants used as they are pruned only lightly to permit flowering, and cannot be cut hard to keep them shorter. For a low or medium hedge of around 1m (3ft), choose box, berberis, thuja or *Prunus cistena*. For an informal, low edging to beds or paths, choose naturally compact, slow-growing plants such as santolina or lavender.

BUYING PLANTS

Popular hedging plants such as beech and hornbeam can often be bought inexpensively between late autumn and spring as bare-rooted plants; they must be planted during the dormant season. First soak the roots in tepid water for eight hours to rehydrate the plants and 'heel' them into a patch of ground if they cannot be planted straight away. Suitable shrubs for hedging, including berberis, shrub roses and conifers like thuja, are normally only sold as

---

WHICH HEDGE PLANT?

FORMAL EVERGREEN
yew, holly, thuja, box, privet,
Lonicera nitida
FORMAL DECIDUOUS
beech, hornbeam, Prunus cistena
'Crimson Dwarf'
INFORMAL FLOWERING
Rosa rugosa, *forsythia, spiraea,*
berberis, escallonia, hebe
PRICKLY
(LIVESTOCK- AND INTRUDER-PROOF)
hawthorn, holly, pyracantha,
berberis, species roses
DWARF
dwarf box (Buxus sempervirens
'Suffruticosa'), *lavender, rosemary,*
cotton lavender (Santolina)
MIXED WILDLIFE
hawthorn, hazel, elder, dog rose,
blackthorn

198

• *see also:* HEDGES AS BOUNDARIES AND FEATURES p30; FLOWERING AND FRUITING HEDGES p94; PLANTING AND MOVING SHRUBS p204

plants represent the best value as they establish faster than large plants and grow rapidly to catch up with them.

container-grown plants, making a hedge quite expensive. However, they can be planted at most times of year, except when the ground is frosty, muddy or during drought, when plants are difficult to establish. Spring and autumn are ideal planting times. Small

PLANTING

Plant formal hedges of beech, hornbeam, hawthorn and privet in double rows 38–45cm (15–18in) apart, with plants the same distance apart in the row but staggered, to produce a dense, solid hedge quickly. Plant conifers and bushy shrubs in a single line 38–45cm (15–18in) apart. Before planting, dig a trench 1m (3ft) wide and fork as much well-rotted organic matter or tree planting compost as possible into the bottom. Add general fertilizer and bonemeal at the manufacturer's recommended rate and mix thoroughly into the soil before replacing it in the trench. Plant hedging plants in the same way as for normal garden shrubs.

AFTERCARE

To avoid having a hedge that is bare at the base, cut plants back hard after planting. Prune bare-rooted plants to 15cm (6in) above ground and container-grown plants by one-third. This encourages vigorous branching from the base, which produces a dense, strong, well-shaped hedge with leaves down to the ground. Feed in spring by scattering general fertilizer or rose food along each side of the hedge, if possible, and watering it well in. Remove weeds and ivy from the base of the hedge regularly and mulch in spring, especially while the hedge is young.

199

◁ **PLANT A PRIVET HEDGE** *into well-prepared soil: once in place, a hedge can last many decades and this is the only chance you will have to improve growing conditions. Cut hard back after planting to create a hedge that will be fully clothed with foliage right down to the ground.*

Trimming hedges

From the time it is planted, a hedge needs trimming correctly to encourage it to form a good shape and to keep the plants leafy to ground level. Depending on the type of hedge, it will subsequently need regular clipping or pruning to keep it neat, shapely and within bounds. The right technique and good-quality tools make the job easy and efficient.

CREATING A NEW HEDGE

After planting and cutting hard back, clip little and often, perhaps four to six times in the second year after planting, depending on the plant's speed of growth; aim to remove the tips of the new growth to encourage plenty of side shoots to develop. As the hedge grows taller, shape it so that it is slightly wider at the base than the top – a top-heavy hedge can splay open after rain or snow and, if the base is shaded by the overhanging top, the bottom of the main stems soon become bare. Use a line held up by poles as a cutting guide to ensure the height of the hedge is level.

ESTABLISHED FORMAL HEDGES

Once the hedge reaches the required height, it will need less frequent clipping. Slow-growing hedges like beech, box and yew usually need cutting only twice, in early summer and late summer. Fast-growing hedges like *Lonicera nitida* and privet require regular clipping between late spring and late summer, every time the hedge starts to look shaggy, usually about every six weeks. Start clipping from the base of the hedge and work your way up, as this makes it easier to shape the sides correctly. Prune large-leaved hedges such as laurel with secateurs rather than clipping them with shears or a hedge trimmer, so that leaves are not cut in half.

INFORMAL HEDGES

After planting, informal flowering hedges should be hard pruned to a third of their

△ **LAUREL IS** *a popular hedging plant but has large leaves which, when cut in half by hedge trimmers, turn brown and unsightly. Instead use secateurs and remove straggly shoots by hand.*

height, to encourage them to thicken up at the base. Thereafter they are not clipped to give straight edges like a formal hedge, but instead are pruned to retain the natural shape of the plant. As a general rule, prune hedges that flower before early summer, such as forsythia or ribes, immediately after flowering, and later-flowering hedges, such as roses, in mid-spring. Country-style hedges are also usually pruned to keep them tidy; for a more natural look, a hedge of hawthorn could be formally clipped, but leaving occasional plants to grow up through the hedge to develop into trees.

HEDGE-TRIMMING TOOLS

❖

SHEARS: hand shears are good for small formal hedges but tiring to use over large areas; use sheep shears for dwarf flowering hedges.

SECATEURS: use for informal flowering hedges and large-leaved plants such as laurel.

POWER HEDGE-TRIMMERS: these are the most practical option for large areas of hedging. Cordless types need recharging often but are ideal for small areas, while electric models with cables are the most popular.

PETROL-DRIVEN HEDGE-TRIMMERS: these are expensive and heavy to use but useful for large hedges a long way from a power point. Consider hiring someone to cut your hedges as an alternative to buying expensive specialist equipment.

200

• *see also:* PRUNING TOOLS p236; WHY PRUNE? p238

CLIPPING FOR TOPIARY

Box and yew are the favourite subjects for topiary. Since both are slow-growing, once their shape is established they can usually be maintained with two clips a year, in early and late summer; clip more often if this is necessary to maintain a clear outline. When creating new topiary, use an internal framework of poles or wire netting to support large or complicated shapes; small- to medium-sized simple shapes with a wide base and a domed outline can remain unsupported. While training a new shape, clip 4–6 times a year using hand shears, removing the tips of new shoots to encourage side shoots to thicken it out. If you are training into a complicated shape, use secateurs to prune fiddly features.

△ **YEW TOPIARY** is trained into formal geometric cubes, with mophead hollies emerging from them.

DWARF HEDGES

Clip formal dwarf box in early and late summer using sheep shears to keep it tidy. Flowering dwarf hedges, such as lavender and santolina, should be lightly clipped with sheep shears immediately after flowering to remove dead flowerheads and re-shape the plants, but without cutting back into old wood, which can kill them. Rosemary may be either pruned or clipped after flowering, depending on the growth habit of the variety used: dense, bushy forms are best clipped with shears, while upright or open types should be pruned using secateurs to prevent spoiling the natural shape of the shrub or leaving leaves cut in half, which will then turn brown.

◁ **PETROL-DRIVEN** powered hedge clippers are convenient for a large garden too far from a power point to use electric models, but they are heavy to use and expensive to buy. You could hire the equipment or let a contractor cut hedges for you. Wear gloves and goggles to use safely.

SAFETY TIPS

LADDERS: when clipping tall hedges, place two pairs of stepladders securely on level ground with a plank between them and make sure it is stable before starting work; ask someone to hold ladders stable. Purpose-made pruning platforms are also available.

ELECTRIC CABLE: make sure electric cable is secured over your shoulder and well out of the way of blades when using powered hedge-trimmers; plug into a RCD so the current switches off instantly in case of accidents.

Planting and caring for trees

Trees add impact and height to a garden, cast desirable shade or provide a feature on a boundary or in the middle of a lawn. Choose a tree with care to ensure that it does not outgrow its space, deprive nearby plants of nutrients or cause any structural damage. Fortunately, there are plenty of attractive, small to medium-sized ornamental trees that are easy to maintain.

202

CHOOSING A TREE

Forest and parkland trees are unsuitable for most gardens, as they grow far too big, create dense shade beneath which nothing grows, and remove large volumes of water daily from the soil when they are in leaf. It is better to choose a decorative garden tree with a compact habit and small root system. Check nursery labels or reference books to find a tree's ultimate height and spread, to see whether it is a suitable size for your garden. Avoid large willow species near drains as their roots seek water and can cause obstructions.

When buying, select a tree with a symmetrical shape, with five or more strong branches evenly spaced round the trunk. A tree with a lopsided head or a bent trunk can be improved once it is planted but it takes several years to rectify serious defects; better to have a tree that earns its keep in the garden from the start. (In wild or cottage-style gardens, craggy, asymmetrically shaped trees add character, so in this case you might choose a misshapen tree deliberately and prune it to exaggerate the effect.) Check that the foliage is healthy and the trunk undamaged, with sound bark from top to bottom.

PLANTING A TREE

Dig a hole at least twice the size of the tree's rootball, fork plenty of organic matter into the bottom and mix in some general fertilizer or, in autumn or winter, bonemeal. If the soil is prone to waterlogging, dig over the whole area to improve a wide root-run, adding grit or bark chippings for aeration.

Water the tree well before removing it from its pot. If it is pot-bound, with roots wound tightly round the inside of the pot, gently tease a few large roots out from the mass.

Stand the tree in the hole, and check that the top of the rootball is level with the surrounding soil. Hammer in a short tree stake alongside the rootball. Fill round the roots with a mix of good topsoil and organic matter.

Firm gently, water well and, when any sinkage has taken place, use tree ties

---

BEST TREES FOR SMALL SPACES

❖

Good trees for small gardens include birch, *Crataegus* 'Paul's Scarlet', snowy mespilus (*Amelanchier lamarckii*), crab apples (*Malus*), mulberry (*Morus nigra*) and Cheal's weeping cherry (*Prunus* 'Kidu-shidare-zakura'). For something more unusual try *Gleditsia triacanthos* 'Sunburst', with golden, cut-leaf foliage and 'Ruby Lace', whose red foliage turns bronze-green, or *Caragana arborescens* with yellow pea flowers which reaches 3.5m (12ft) and is ideal for windy or coastal sites.

• *see also:* TREES FOR SMALL GARDENS p88; COLUMNAR TREES p90; TREES WITH FRUIT AND BERRIES p92

◁ **THE GOLDEN ROBINIA** (R. pseudoacacia *'Frisia') makes an outstanding medium-sized tree for a sunny situation. It thrives in dry soil so is ideal for areas prone to summer drought.*

them, especially the area overhung by the edge of the canopy of branches since this is where the 'feeding' roots are. Mulch round trees with a 2.5–5cm (1–2in) layer of any well-rotted organic material or bark chippings. Grass competes with young trees for water and nutrients so leave established trees grown in grass with a ring of soil round the trunk at least 90cm (3ft) across. Keep new trees well watered in summer but leave established ones to take care of themselves. A late-summer feed high in potash and phosphates (such as liquid tomato feed) will help to ripen the current year's growth and encourage spring-flowering trees to produce buds. Prune trees only if it is necessary to remove damaged, diseased or overcrowded growth.

TREES IN SMALL SPACES

Where space is short, consider cutting back suitable trees to rejuvenate them when they get too big. Done every 2–3 years, this even makes them grow as shrubs. *Acer negundo* 'Flamingo', with pretty pink, cream and green variegated leaves, can be cut back almost to ground level in spring when it gets too big. The same can be done with eucalyptus and the Judas tree (*Cercis siliquastrum*) to keep them bushy instead of letting them turn into a tree. Or use large shrubs such as the strawberry tree (*Arbutus unedo*), *Garrya elliptica* or *Clerodendrum trichotomum* 'Fargesii' and remove their lower branches to turn them into small standard trees.

203

to hold the trunk against the stake. Check that the buffer is between trunk and stake to prevent the bark chafing. Finally, mulch with a 2.5–5cm (1–2in) layer of bark chippings or garden compost to retain moisture.

TREE CARE
In mid-spring, at the start of the growing season, when the soil is moist, feed and mulch both newly planted and established trees. Sprinkle general fertilizer or rose food evenly around

△ **USE A PRUNING SAW** *to reshape a lopsided or overgrown tree: remove an entire branch at its junction with the trunk or a larger branch.*

△ **LEAVE A GRASS-FREE** *circle around trees in lawns to prevent competition for water and nutrients. Mulch in spring to retain moisture.*

Planting and moving shrubs

Shrubs flesh out the framework of the garden. Depending on type, they can fill large areas quickly, or supply seasonal flowers for mixed borders – particularly useful in early summer – as well as fruit, berries or foliage tints in late summer. Evergreen shrubs are invaluable for providing all-year round effects.

204

• *see also:* SHRUBS FOR SMALL GARDENS p98; EVERGREEN SHRUBS FOR YEAR-ROUND INTEREST p100

PLANTING A CONTAINER-GROWN SHRUB

• Prepare the planting site by digging in plenty of well-rotted organic matter such as garden compost or manure if making a new bed; in previously well-cultivated soil, dig a hole at least twice the size of the pot the plant is growing in and fork well-rotted compost into the bottom of it.

• Water the shrub well before knocking it out of its pot, and if the rootball appears to be a solid mass of roots, gently tease out a few large roots, otherwise they will not be able to break loose after planting and the shrub will remain in virtually suspended animation.

• Turn the shrub so that its best side faces the front and place in the hole, with the top of the rootball roughly flush with the soil surface.

• Fill in round the roots with a mixture of good topsoil and well-rotted organic matter, firm gently and water well to settle the soil round the roots. Keep watered in dry spells.

CHOOSING HEALTHY SHRUBS

Look for symmetrically shaped plants with plenty of evenly spaced branches and healthy green leaves; avoid leggy or lopsided specimens as it takes time and heavy pruning to rectify defects. If the surface of the container is covered with moss, liverwort or weeds, this may indicate that the plant has been on sale for some time. If the

◁ **JAPANESE MAPLES** (Acer palmatum *and cultivars) such as 'Garnet' make spectacular small specimen trees. They thrive in well-drained but moisture-retentive soil and light shade.*

leaves also look pale or stunted, or dead twigs or leaves are present, then suspect generally poor care and wait until you can find a better specimen.

WHEN TO PLANT

Autumn is generally the best time to plant, since this allows new shrubs to get established while the soil is naturally warm and moist; container-grown shrubs can, however, be planted at any time of year except when the soil is very muddy, frosty or suffering from drought. Late spring and early autumn are the best times for planting evergreens; if they experience water shortage after planting they lose their leaves and take a long time to recover; conifers often go brown round the base and may never replace the damage with new foliage.

MOVING SHRUBS

Sometimes it becomes necessary to move a shrub that has been planted in the garden for a long time, perhaps due to overcrowding. Certain shrubs, such as magnolia, resent disturbance and should never be moved but most can be moved with care. The ideal time to move deciduous shrubs is in early spring, just before the start of the growing season, though they can be moved at any time between leaf fall in autumn and bud burst in spring. Small, shallow-rooted or recently planted shrubs can simply be dug up with a large ball of roots and moved to a new, well-prepared site, in one go. Keep them well watered after the move.

Large or well-established shrubs

In the case of large or long-established plants, it is best to start preparing for a move a year or more in advance. The previous autumn or spring, dig a narrow trench 60cm (2ft) deep round the plant, about as far from the trunk as the outermost branches extend. Cut through any large roots you find, and cut under the plant to sever any thick tap roots at that depth. Then fill the trench with a mixture of good topsoil and planting compost or well-rotted organic matter to encourage fibrous roots to form. A year or more later, the shrub will have grown the sort of root system that allows it to be moved safely. Lift with as much fibrous root as possible, have the new site well prepared and sit the shrub in place straight away. Keep well watered.

Evergreen shrubs and conifers

Early autumn is the best time of year to move evergreens and conifers; water thoroughly a few days before moving them. Dig them up with plenty of roots and transfer immediately to the new, well-prepared planting hole. Use temporary stakes to prevent wind-rock

▷ **EVEN LARGE RHODODENDRONS** *move surprisingly well since they have a shallow root system. If you have time, prepare the plant a year in advance to encourage it to grow lots of new, fibrous roots into a compost-rich trench.*

205

until well established and protect with a surrounding windbreak for their first winter. In an exposed situation, spray plants with anti-transpirant spray to reduce moisture loss through their leaves (often sold in autumn to prevent Christmas trees shedding their needles).

MOVING A SMALL SHRUB

1 *Dig the shrub up carefully with a large rootball and lift it on to a polythene sheet (use this for surplus soil too, to protect a lawn).*

2 *Drag the plant on the plastic sheet to its new home. Have the planting hole ready-prepared and lift in place, then replace the soil.*

Using climbers

Growing climbing plants is a wonderful way to cover bare walls and fences or to mask unsightly outbuildings. Climbers can also be trained over arches and pergolas, or against a framework of poles or pillars to give height to the back of a border. And you can grow climbers up through unproductive old fruit trees – and through each other – to make the most of every vertical space.

▷ CLEMATIS, ROSES *and honeysuckle grown together in the same space create a varied tapestry effect.*

206

▽ OBELISKS *make an attractive support for decorative climbers grown in a border.*

CLIMBERS TO CLOTHE VERTICAL FEATURES

Climbing roses, honeysuckle or clematis are the traditional choice for arches, arbours and pergolas and scent is an important factor to take into account. But consider unusual alternatives too, such as *Trachelospermum asiaticum*, a slightly tender, evergreen climber with fragrant white flowers in summer, and summer jasmine (*Jasminum officinale*), a cottage-style climber with heavily scented white flowers. The purple grape, *Vitis vinifera* 'Purpurea', and the pink-, cream- and green-variegated *Ampelopsis glandulosa* var. *brevipedunculata* 'Elegans' add foliage contrast. Grow two or three climbers together for a generous effect – most kinds team well with climbing roses.

For pillars, choose smaller-growing climbing or rambler roses, and wind the stems round so they 'concertina' all round the pillar instead of growing straight up. This allows more of the stem to grow horizontally, and it is on this growth that most flowers are produced, so the pillar will bloom all the way up, instead of only at the top.

Choose large, vigorous climbers to ramble up through trees and make an impact quickly. Suitable choices for large trees include species clematis, strong rambler or climbing roses such as 'Rambling Rector', the vine, *Vitis coignetiae* and *Celastrus scandens* (bittersweet). Clematis are ideal for colonizing old fruit trees, and not-too-vigorous kinds look effective twining their way among the 'arms' of espaliers or interwoven through fruit tunnels.

• *see also:* PLANTS TO COVER WALLS p110–113; PLANTS TO COVER FENCES p114; CLIMBING PLANTS FOR ARCHES AND PERGOLAS p116; GROWING CLIMBERS p208

GROWING AGAINST WALLS

Where climbers would be too vigorous or tend to get out of control, wall shrubs often make a good substitute. Shrubs such as glossy, small-leaved pyracantha or ornamental quince (*Chaenomeles*) can be trained as a narrow fan, espalier or bush shape more or less flat against a wall, where they make a pleasing outline. It is also a good idea to grow lax shrubs, such as *Abeliophyllum distichum* (which has almond-scented flowers in spring) and winter jasmine (*Jasminum nudiflorum*), against a wall, as they flop untidily otherwise. Where there is plenty of room, large wall shrubs like the evergreen *Magnolia grandiflora* and the pineapple broom (*Cytisus battandieri*) make a dramatic feature.

CLIMBERS IN CONTAINERS

❖

Many climbers need more root-room than containers permit but clematis make excellent subjects for tubs and large (45cm/18in) pots; check the label and choose those, such as *C. florida* 'Sieboldii', that do not grow too big. Plant in loam-based compost and push trellis or an obelisk into the pot for the plant to grow up. Keep well fed with liquid tomato feed during the growing season and place where their roots will be in cool shade, perhaps surrounded by other planted containers or with pebbles on the top of the compost.

Shady walls

A few climbing roses are happy on a shady wall: choose red 'Danse du Feu', maroon 'Souvenir du Dr Jamain' or yellow 'Mermaid'. Climbing hydrangea (*H. petiolaris*) and its relative *Schizophragma* will thrive on a cool wall, as do wall-trained *Garrya elliptica* and winter jasmine. Team the latter with large-leaved, variegated ivies for good effect. In deeper shade, use varieties of euonymus, which climbs modestly when grown against a wall.

◁ WHEN GROWING *climbers against a wall or fence that is likely to need maintenance, fix trellis to the wall and train the climber to it.*

CREATING A SCREEN

❖

The fastest way to create a living screen is not to plant a hedge, but to grow climbers up a fence or trellis support. In this way you can achieve the desired height instantly, with a reasonable degree of plant cover within the first growing season, yet the screen never grows too tall and any trimming can be done quite conveniently. Choose a mixture of climbers such as winter jasmine and ivy for a country-garden look or all of the same kind for a more hedge-like effect, for example *Clematis armandii*. Vigorous, fast-growing climbers such as Virginia creeper or wisteria are quite suitable for large screens but lose their leaves in winter. Include some evergreen climbers, such as ivies or euonymus, for all-year-round cover. A slightly slower alternative is to grow wall shrubs in the same way and trim them closely for a dense, more formal appearance: pyracantha is stunning grown in this way.

Sunny walls

Save this very desirable habitat for slightly tender plants in need of protection and a warm, sunny spot: these include climbers such as passion flower (*Passiflora caerulea*), campsis, Chilean potato vine (*Solanum*), parrot-bill (*Clianthus puniceus*) or *Rosa banksiae*, and wall-trained shrubs *Fremontodendron californica*, myrtle or ceanothus. Look out too for more unusual candidates such as *Billadiera longiflora*, which has large, decorative, blue berries. If a severe cold spell threatens, it is quite easy to secure frost-protection fleece to the wall and drop it down over the plants.

Growing climbers

The growing conditions where climbers are usually planted are not naturally good. At the base of walls, for example, the soil is often full of rubble while under trees, spreading tree roots create dry, impoverished conditions. And both walls and trees tend to deflect rain from the soil. Since climbers will live in the same spot for many years, it is worth taking trouble over soil preparation before planting them.

PLANTING AGAINST A WALL

When planting a climber at the foot of a wall, you need to do more than just prepare a planting hole; you must improve the entire bed to give the climber a good root-run. Remove as much rubble as possible and deeply dig in plenty of well-rotted organic matter; if the soil is really poor or full of builder's debris, replace it with good-quality topsoil. Put up supports before planting, since it is much harder to do so afterwards. Dig a deep hole and plant so that the main stem is 45cm (18in) away from the wall; insert a stake and lean it against the wall for the plant to grow along. Be prepared to water in dry spells while plants are young, as the base of a wall, especially a south-facing one, is always a dry site.

PLANTING UNDER A TREE

When planting a climber to grow up through a tree, choose a spot on the north side of the tree if possible, as the climber will grow towards the light; if it is planted on the bright side of the tree, it may refuse to climb. Prepare a very large planting hole, as you will need to allow room to work round the tree roots, and

▷ **VIRGINIA CREEPER** *looks wonderful framing the windows and doors of old stone houses, especially in its autumn colours.*

mix in plenty of organic matter with the soil. Plant at least 60cm (2ft) from the trunk of a small tree. If the tree is large, plant just under the outermost extent of its canopy of branches, at the 'drip line', where there is more light and water. Incline a stake from the base of the

---

PLANTING A CLIMBER

❖

1 *Dig a planting hole about twice the size of the plant's rootball and add well-rotted organic matter mixed with general fertilizer.*

2 *Check the depth of the hole: clematis should be planted so that the rootball is about 15cm (6in) below the soil surface.*

3 *Tease out a few of the thickest roots if the plant is slightly pot-bound. Put in place and fill with topsoil mixed with rotted organic matter.*

208

• *see also:* USING CLIMBERS p206

climber to the trunk or up into the lower branches, fix firmly in place and use this to 'lead' the plant up on to its support.

TRAINING CLIMBERS

New plants can be shy to start climbing. To encourage self-clinging species,

4 *Untie the plant stems from the cane and spread them out in a wide fan, with the bottom stems almost horizontal; tie in place.*

FORMS OF SUPPORT

❖

Some climbers, like ivy and Virginia creeper, support themselves using aerial roots that cling to bare walls; avoid growing these on crumbly surfaces as the aerial roots can make them worse. Other plants, such as honeysuckle and clematis, will twine or cling to supports with their leaf-stems without needing to be tied; trellis or rigid netting fixed to the wall or fence is ideal for these. Climbers such as roses, as well as fan-trained trees and wall shrubs with stiff stems, need tying in place: horizontal wires stretched at 30cm (12in) intervals up the wall, or wall nails outlining the shape of the plant's framework, are the best methods of support.

dampen the wall with water, especially on hot days. Twiners and clingers often need a little persuasion too; after planting, tie the stems up to their support with soft string and from then on they should manage without help. When growing up brick pillars or the uprights of a pergola, fix netting in place to give them something to grip on to.

Stiff-stemmed climbers like roses need to be tied in regularly during the growing season to stop them drooping down the wall and becoming untidy. Tie in their stems every 45cm (18in) or so, and check that the ties are not cutting into the stems as they thicken. Train roses and wall shrubs so their main stems are evenly spaced over the area of wall to be covered and use this as the framework to which they are pruned every year.

TRAINING TIPS

○ Do not allow wisteria to grow round drainpipes or gutters: its woody stems expand as they grow and can force pipes off the wall.

○ Wooden fences need occasional maintenance in the form of timber treatment and garden walls need repainting, so it is a good idea to grow climbers on trellis; this can be detached and laid flat on the ground, complete with climber, for access to the fence or wall.

○ Space trellis or support wires 10cm (4in) from a wall to allow air circulation between the plant and the wall. This stops the plant from overheating and prevents problems associated with damp. Use vine eyes to carry the wires or fix cotton reels between wall and trellis to maintain the necessary distance.

○ Keep climbing roses and honeysuckle well watered in dry spells to prevent mildew on their foliage; this can be a symptom of dryness at the roots.

○ If climbers become bare at the base, use their bare stems as a support for fast-growing decorative annual climbers such as asarina or canary creeper (*Tropaeolum peregrinum*).

○ Container-grown climbers sold in flower at garden centres may not bloom again for several years after planting as a result of the plant being given a larger root-run. This is not a cause for concern since it will generally start flowering again as soon as it is well established. It is not uncommon for a wisteria to take seven years before it begins flowering.

209

Planting and caring for herbaceous borders

Herbaceous plants are those that die down every autumn, spend the winter as dormant roots underground, then send up new shoots in spring. Traditionally, they were always grown in herbaceous borders – large, formal beds backed by a hedge or fence. But in small gardens, informal-shaped island beds surrounded by lawn are a popular and more practical way of growing them, or individual plants may be grown in containers.

PLANTING HERBACEOUS PERENNIALS

210

Herbaceous plants bought container-grown at the garden centre can theoretically be put in at most times of year, but the best season to plant is in spring, when the first shoots are visible but before there is much leafy growth. This way you can be certain that the pot contains a live plant (it is not always easy to tell in autumn or winter when the foliage has died down), and the plant has some time in which to get established before starting to flower. If you plant it when in flower, you can expect a fairly short flowering season. All herbaceous plants will, however, perform far better the second year after planting, once they have rooted well in and started to spread.

△ **FOR A TRADITIONAL FINISH,** *edge herbaceous borders with a strip of timber or with terracotta or Victorian-style rope twist tiles.*

Preparing the soil

Good soil preparation is vital before planting perennials. Once in place, these plants cover the soil all summer and it is difficult to improve the ground or tackle perennial weeds such as bindweed without damaging the border plants. Begin by completely eradicating any perennial weeds; some people like to leave the bed fallow for a season to allow this to be done thoroughly. Use a glyphosate-based weedkiller and repeat as often as necessary until no regrowth occurs. Then dig in as much well-rotted organic matter as possible. Double digging is well worth the effort, as it increases the depth of good soil available to plant roots and improves the moisture-holding capacity of the soil – this will be a great advantage in dry summers. Improve the texture of clay

◁ **HERBACEOUS BORDERS** *look their best in summer, when flowering plants like helenium, heuchera and achillea make a blaze of colour.*

• *see also:* MAKING COMPOST p182, WATERING YOUR GARDEN p184; WEEDS AND WEEDING p248; FEEDING PLANTS p186

△ IN LATE SUMMER *or autumn, when plants die back naturally, cut the old foliage and flower stems close to ground level to tidy the border.*

soil by digging in grit at the same time. Finally, rake in a dressing of general fertilizer immediately before planting.

FORMAL OR INFORMAL?

Traditional formal borders backed by hedges look impressive but are labour-intensive; the hedge can harbour pests such as slugs as well as weeds and it shades plants from one side, causing slightly leggy growth that requires more staking. Since you will need access for cutting the hedge, try to leave a path 60cm (2ft) wide between it and the back of the border from which to work – or place a few slabs along the back to use as 'stepping stones', to avoid treading on plants. Herbaceous borders generally need to be at least 90cm (3ft) wide so the plants look in scale with their surroundings. Island beds are more informal in appearance. Their advantage is that the plants are exposed to light from all sides and consequently grow tough and compact, so that only the tallest, like delphiniums, need support.

Group herbaceous plants in threes or fives of a kind so they make large clumps quickly and have more effect in a large border. In small beds a single specimen may be enough, especially of the more vigorous species. Place tall plants to the back and in the centre of a border, with the shortest at the front, creating a tiered effect that allows all the flowers to be seen properly. In informal gardens, the effect of flowers spilling over the lawn is charming, but in more formal surroundings a 'mowing strip' is an advantage. This is a row of bricks or other small paving units forming a narrow divider along the front of the border onto which the front row of plants can fall forward. This prevents them getting under the blades of a mower and also saves the grass from developing bare and yellow patches which become evident in autumn, when the plants are cut back. A mowing strip also provides a dry path from which to weed in wet weather.

△ AFTER FLOWERING *in early and mid-summer, cut* Alchemilla mollis *back close to ground level to encourage fresh, new foliage.*

CARING FOR HERBACEOUS PERENNIALS

○ Mulch flower borders in early spring when the soil is moist and weed-free, using a 2.5–5cm (1–2in) layer of well-rotted organic matter. If a dry spring is likely in your area, mulch in autumn instead.

○ Feed plants in mid-spring when some growth is above ground; prevent fertilizer lodging in the crowns of plants as it may scorch them (if this happens, flush it out with plenty of water). For peak performance, top up the nutrients every 6–8 weeks by sprinkling fertilizer between plants and hoeing it in or, if the soil is dry, by liquid feeding.

○ Support tall or floppy perennials using bushy pea-sticks, proprietary support frames or bamboo canes, according to the type of plant. Put supports in place in mid- to late spring, before the plants grow tall enough to start flopping.

○ Deadhead flowers as soon as they are over to encourage a further flush; some plants, such as lupins, pulmonaria and astrantia, are best cut down almost to ground level after flowering as this encourages a second flush of growth and possibly more flowers.

○ Tidy up dead stems and leaves in autumn, cutting them off almost to ground level and putting the plant material on the compost heap.

○ Divide large clumps of perennials every 3–5 years, discarding the woody centre of the plant and replanting the younger outer portions of it.

211

Sowing and using hardy annuals

Hardy annuals are the easiest plants to raise from seed. They need no special facilities and can be sown straight into the garden in spring, as they withstand colder conditions than bedding plants. Hardy annuals include many old-fashioned flowers, like nasturtium, calendula, cornflower, larkspur, clarkia, godetia and sweet peas, all of which characterize cottage-style gardens.

212

SOWING IN SITU

Sowing where plants are to flower is a practical option only where the soil is free from weed seeds as a result of many years' good cultivation. Otherwise, make a 'stale seedbed' by preparing the site and leaving it fallow the previous year, hoeing weekly to kill germinating weed seeds; do not turn the soil over before sowing as this would expose a new crop of weed seeds to the light, which then germinate. To achieve a traditional cottagey, Persian-carpet style annual bed, rake the soil lightly then mark out a pattern of informal shapes with the point of a stick or by trickling an outline of sand. Sow one variety in each of the shapes created, putting the tallest to the back, then rake lightly to cover the seed. Thin only if the seedlings come up too thickly.

SOWING IN ROWS FOR TRANSPLANTING

Where the soil is likely to contain weed seeds, it is safest to sow hardy annual seed in rows, so that the emerging seedlings are easy to distinguish from those of weeds. Any spare

◁ **WHERE SOIL** *is well-cultivated and free from weeds, annuals sown in situ make a quick and easy carpet of colour; it needs little work as the closely planted annuals smother weeds.*

piece of well-cultivated ground can be used, but a vacant corner of the vegetable garden is usually most convenient. Prepare the soil as for sowing vegetables and sprinkle the seed thinly along a shallow drill. Cover thinly – on heavy clay soil or silty ground likely to cap (form a hard crust on the surface), cover the seed with compost or vermiculite, as this gives better germination. When seedlings emerge, thin to leave them about 5cm (2in) apart, and when big enough to handle easily, transplant them to their flowering

• *see also:* DECORATIVE SEEDHEADS p134; ANNUALS TO GROW FROM SEED p144; RAISING PLANTS FROM SEED p230

◁ **A MIXTURE OF PLANT TYPES**, *here including the feathery foliage of cosmos, makes up the traditional cottage garden border. Hardy annuals such as calendula marigolds and sunflowers will seed themselves gently around, without needing to be replanted each year.*

positions. Hardy annuals are most effective planted in groups among shrubs, or they can be massed together in flower beds.

SOWING IN TRAYS

Sometimes, perhaps due to lack of space, it is more convenient to sow hardy annuals in trays. Prepare the trays and sow in the same way as for half-hardy annual bedding plants, in early to mid-spring. But since hardy annuals need no heat, the trays can be placed in an unheated greenhouse, sunroom, enclosed porch or cold frame, or can even be stood outdoors, covered by cloches or a sheet of glass. They will germinate as soon as weather conditions are warm enough.

When the seedlings are big enough to handle, either prick them out as for bedding plants and grow them on in a cold frame, or simply thin the seedlings out to leave the remainder 5cm (2in) apart in the same tray. Plant them out when they are big enough. This method is a useful way of raising a few plants to put into containers or to fill gaps in small beds.

AUTUMN SOWING

Hardy annuals can be given an early start by sowing them in mid-autumn under cold glass. Sow several seeds per 13cm (5in) pot and allow all the seedlings to grow; this will produce a bushy plant fast. Compact varieties of nasturtium and calendula, make bright spring-flowering pot plants for a cold greenhouse. Taller varieties of annuals can be put out into the garden once the worst of the weather is over – they will provide welcome splashes of colour in the lull between the last of the spring bulbs and bedding and the first flowers of the summer bedding.

△ **SWEET PEAS** *are an old favourite hardy annual. Seeds are often sown under cold glass in autumn to give early blooms for cut flowers but spring-sown plants flower later into the summer.*

MAKING THE MOST OF HARDY ANNUALS

○ Some hardy annuals self-seed, especially nigella, alyssum, nasturtium and calendula. They rarely become a nuisance and their seedlings can create a charming, country-garden effect by appearing randomly among shrubs in borders or cracks in paving.

○ Saving your own seed is a practical proposition with hardy annuals; look out for ripening seedpods and capsules in summer and gather before the seed falls naturally. Allow the seedhead to dry thoroughly, then extract the seed and store in paper envelopes to sow in autumn or spring.

○ If sown early enough, hardy annuals will begin flowering slightly ahead of summer bedding plants. Regular feeding, watering and dead-heading help keep them flowering over the longest possible period. However, they come to an end earlier, so you should anticipate many kinds being over by midsummer. If you want some late-flowering colour, make a late sowing at the end of spring or in early summer.

○ Being rather tougher than summer bedding plants, hardy annuals are useful flowers to plant in cold locations or in containers and hanging baskets in an exposed situation. Both the canary creeper (*Tropaeolum peregrinum*) and trailing nasturtiums are especially good for hanging baskets.

213

Growing and caring for alpines

The term alpine includes dwarf bulbs, rosette plants such as sempervivums, low ground-hugging species, compact mound-shaped plants and miniature shrubs, all of which need well-drained conditions. Alpines are rarely grown, as they used to be, in rockeries, since it is undesirable to remove limestone and other rock from their natural habitats, but attractive, alternative ways of growing them include raised beds and sink gardens.

RAISED BEDS

On heavy soils, or where drainage is not very good, building a raised bed makes it easy to create conditions where surplus water can run away quickly. The walls may be made of brick, stone or walling blocks to suit the particular garden; dry stone walling gives a natural, rural look while walling blocks make a more formal effect. The bed is filled with a mixture of grit, weed-free topsoil and peat substitutes such as coir or leafmould in roughly equal proportions; this mixture gives good drainage yet retains enough moisture for alpine plants. The top of

216

▷ **IN THIS ENTHUSIAST'S PLOT,** *a heavily planted raised rock feature forms a complete garden. The decorative mulch of stone chippings creates well-drained conditions for alpine plants.*

a raised alpine bed is often decorated with pieces of rock and, after planting, topped with a dressing of stone chippings.

SCREE BEDS

A scree bed can be made on level ground or on a slight slope, where the soil is naturally free-draining, or it can be created in a raised bed. A garden scree bed is intended to duplicate the conditions that are found in natural scree at the foot of a mountain, where small pieces of rock debris build up. In a garden, a scree bed contains a mixture of equal parts of gravel and soil, which provides very good drainage, topped with a layer of pebbles or rock chippings, which furnish a natural-looking background for alpine plants. The sharper drainage means that choicer alpines can be grown than would survive in a normal garden bed. This type of bed can be decorated with pieces of rock too.

▷ **IN SPRING,** *weed carefully between clumps of alpine plants in a raised bed and top up the layer of stone chippings or gravel. This improves surface drainage and acts as a mulch, to retain moisture and smother weeds.*

• *see also:* MAKING COMPOST p182, WATERING YOUR GARDEN p184

MAKING A FAKE STONE SINK

❖

Real stone sinks are very expensive but ceramic sinks can be coated with a substance called hypertufa to make them resemble stone.

1 *First spread outdoor adhesive over the outside of the sink to make a rough surface on to which the mixture can grip.*

2 *When the adhesive is dry, mix equal volumes of coarse sand, cement and coarse coir or peat to a slightly sticky paste with water. Slap it roughly over the outside of the sink by hand, wearing rubber gloves, to leave a craggy finish. Use a wire brush to contour the surface as it dries.*

3 *Allow several weeks for the coating to set before planting up the sink.*

PLANTING UP A SINK GARDEN

❖

Sink gardens are like mini-screes or raised beds in a container. They are the perfect way to house a small collection of choice, compact alpines and make a very attractive feature for a patio. If they are raised up, they bring the plants to eye level, where their intricate beauty can be appreciated in detail.

1 *Fill the sink with a mixture of one part John Innes potting compost No. 3, one part coir or leafmould and one part coarse, gritty sand.*

2 *Plant the sink with a varied selection of mound-shaped, rosette and creeping plants, choosing plenty of evergreens for year-round interest.*

3 *Decorate the surface with a 'mulch' of stone chippings and perhaps one or two small chunks of rock.*

4 *Despite their reputation for drought-tolerance, alpines grown in a sink garden will need to be watered during dry spells due to the restricted volume of soil in the container, which may easily dry out all too quickly.*

YEAR-ROUND ALPINES

Given good growing conditions, alpines are very little trouble and will provide interest in the garden throughout the year.

SPRING CARE

In early spring, weed thoroughly and take precautions against slugs. The majority of alpines are spring-flowering, so rock features should look their best now. This is also a good time to add new plants to the display. After flowering, take cuttings using the soft, young shoots of the new growth. Root in pots of seed compost in a cool, shady spot protected from the weather – a well-ventilated cold frame in shade is perfect. Many alpines are best propagated regularly so that old or exhausted plants can be replaced; it is sometimes possible to detach portions of spreading species with some root to make new plants. Give a light feed during this season.

SUMMER CARE

In dry weather, even alpines may need watering, but it is best to give a thorough soaking then leave them alone – light waterings just bring roots to the surface and make plants less able to manage on their own.

AUTUMN CARE

In autumn, remove dead foliage from the plants and clear fallen leaves. Top up surface chippings, tucking them under rosette plants to help deter slugs and improve drainage round the neck of the plants – this helps to prevent rotting in winter.

WINTER CARE

Protect delicate plants from excess wet by covering them with an inclined sheet of glass to deflect rain; do not use cloches as it is essential for alpines to have plenty of fresh air.

Choosing a greenhouse

A greenhouse is the ultimate garden accessory. It allows you to raise your own plants from seeds and cuttings and to grow food crops such as tomatoes and cucumbers that do best under cover. In a heated greenhouse you can overwinter half-hardy perennials, grow and display greenhouse pot plants like cineraria, and cultivate specialist collections such as fuchsias or cacti.

TYPES OF GREENHOUSE

Greenhouses are made of metal or wood. Cedar greenhouses look best in the garden but they need regular timber treatment and are more expensive; those made of aluminium are maintenance-free. The most popular greenhouse size is 2.5m by 1.8m (8ft by 6ft) and economy models are available at DIY superstores. But you will have to go to a specialist manufacturer to supply larger sizes, unusual shapes, stronger models suitable for windy areas and greenhouses with superior glazing systems (best if you plan to heat). Round greenhouses take up least room but offer a large growing area for plants; lean-to greenhouses make use of a house wall and trap heat better than freestanding models.

△ **A VICTORIAN-STYLE** *greenhouse makes a feature in the garden. This model has ventilators running the length of the ridge, which helps to keep temperatures down in summer.*

218

◁ **ALTHOUGH WOODEN** *greenhouses need regular timber treatment, their advantage is that you can easily fasten bubble wrap or shading fabric onto them using nothing more than drawing pins.*

• *see also*: GARDEN BUILDINGS p54; USING A GREENHOUSE p220

OPTIONAL EXTRAS

❖

- An electric propagating case is the most economical way to maintain a high temperature in a small area: use for propagating plants in spring or autumn, and for overwintering small, delicate plants that need a higher temperature than the rest of the greenhouse.

- An automatic watering system is a great time-saver: main feeder tubes run along staging or the border, from which micro-tubes drip water on to individual plants. The system may be supplied from a container of water in the greenhouse or the mains tap. A 'computer' can be added to time waterings automatically.

EQUIPPING THE GREENHOUSE

Fit automatic ventilator openers to prevent the greenhouse overheating if you are away from home during the day; extra ventilators or a louvred vent in the back wall of the house are also useful. You can install blinds to help keep the temperature down, though this can also be achieved by painting the outside of the glass with liquid shading in summer. You will need staging to grow pot plants or to care for seedlings in trays; two-tier staging doubles the available growing space. Most owners have staging down one side of the house and

▷ IN SPRING, *greenhouse space is at a premium when seed sowing and plant potting are under way. Staging makes the best use of heated space.*

leave a soil border on the other; crops like tomatoes are best grown in the ground. A paved floor provides a firm base for staging and makes it easy to keep the greenhouse clean.

HEATING

Heating allows the greenhouse to be used to the full all year round. Electricity is the best means, provided the greenhouse is within comfortable distance of the house, as it can be accurately controlled by thermostat to avoid wastage, and there is nothing to refill. Employ a contractor to lay on the supply, using armoured cable buried deep underground, and have an RCD (residual current device) built in to cut off the power in the event of accident. Alternatively, use a modern bottled gas heater with a thermostat. Aim to give just enough heat to keep the greenhouse frost-free, setting the thermostats to 5°C (40°F), to reduce electricity bills while keeping plants happy.

SPRING MAINTENANCE
- Water plants and seedlings lightly at first, increasing the frequency as the season progresses.
- Begin liquid feeding once the plants start to grow at a faster rate.
- Ventilate when the weather is warm.
- Clean the propagator and place clean silver sand in the base of it; begin seed sowing.
- In late spring, prick out seedlings and pot up rooted cuttings, re-potting any plants that need it.

SUMMER MAINTENANCE
- Water daily; stand plants on damp capillary matting spread over the tops of staging to help keep compost moist. Liquid-feed the pots regularly.
- Put up shading to help keep temperatures down.
- Take precautions against pests such as aphids and whitefly.

AUTUMN MAINTENANCE
- Reduce watering as plant growth slows down; remove capillary matting from staging and hand-water pots individually. Water in the morning so plants are not left wet overnight – damp, cool air encourages the spread of fungal diseases.
- Remove shading and, on a fine day, take everything out of the greenhouse and wash down the inside with warm water and greenhouse disinfectant, cleaning the glass and staging thoroughly.
- Put up insulation such as bubble plastic over the inner roof and walls. Return plants inside and bring tender plants under cover too.
- Turn greenhouse heating on.

WINTER MAINTENANCE
- Keep watering to a minimum; ventilate when the weather permits.
- Check that an adequate temperature is being maintained by using a max-min thermometer.

219

Using a greenhouse

Given careful management, it is possible to grow many different kinds of plants together, including food crops and ornamental pot plants, as well as raising plants from seeds and cuttings. Never be tempted to overfill the greenhouse, however; pests and diseases spread fast and are hard to tackle in overcrowded conditions, and the plants tend to grow tall and leggy.

GROWING FOOD CROPS

Vegetables that enjoy warm conditions, such as tomatoes, peppers, aubergines and cucumbers, can be grown in borders in the greenhouse during the summer months. They should be harvested and cleared away by early autumn to make room for plants needing frost protection being brought in from outside. Use the border soil in winter to grow spring onions and lettuce for out-of-season salads.

220

GROWING ORNAMENTALS

Tiered staging is an ideal way to display mixed summer collections of coleus, tuberous begonia, browallia, abutilon, clivia, heliotrope, gerbera and large-flowered fuchsia or petunia which would be spoiled by weather outdoors. For flowering displays in winter use indoor azalea, cyclamen, cineraria, *Primula obconica* and *P. malacoides*. Train tender climbers such as bougainvillea, plumbago, passion flower or hoya up the walls.

OVERWINTERING

Half-hardy perennials used for outdoor displays in summer, such as fuchsia, pelargonium, felicia and scaveola, can be overwintered in a frost-free greenhouse. Take cuttings in late summer, root them into trays or small pots and pot up in spring. Alternatively, dig up the plants in early autumn, cut back to a few centimetres/inches and pot up. A frost-free greenhouse is also the ideal place to house slightly tender patio shrubs, such as cordyline palms.

◁ USE POTS OF *ornamental plants like fuchsia and begonia to add a colourful edging to a greenhouse border planted with food crops. Keep pests under control – whitefly can be a nuisance.*

WINTER AND EARLY SPRING DISPLAYS

After clearing away summer crops such as tomatoes, a cold greenhouse can be used through the winter to house a range of plants. Pot-grown Christmas rose (*Helleborus niger*) and camellias flower earlier inside and their blooms cannot be spoilt by wind or sharp frosts. Use ivies with coloured primulas, ranunculus, polyanthus and early spring bulbs to create a colourful display on the staging. You can also grow hardy annual flowers in pots or collect the

• *see also:* GREENHOUSE CROPS p270

◁ AN ENTHUSIAST'S *greenhouse, set up specially for cultivating tender plants. Note the max./min. thermometer for checking the correct temperature is maintained at all times. The floor has been damped down for extra humidity.*

▽ WHEN HEATED *greenhouse space is available, make full use of it for propagating your own plants. Cuttings rooted in late summer occupy little bench space in winter.*

221

earliest-flowering alpines, such as many saxifrages and dwarf bulbs. Use the roof space for overwintering pelargoniums in hanging baskets or plant baskets up in early spring and suspend them from the greenhouse roof until the frosts are over.

GROWING SPRING BULBS IN POTS

Choose firm, plump, healthy bulbs. Plant them so that their 'noses' are just showing (there is no need to plant them at the same depth as you would in the ground) and close together, almost touching, for a good display. Water lightly, then place in a cool, dark place so the bulbs can form roots: use a shed, garage or the space beneath an oil tank; if it is warm, shoots will appear too soon.

When the leaves appear, move into a cold or frost-free greenhouse, keeping them in light shade for a few days to accustom them to the light gradually. Give just enough water to keep the compost moist, without making it too wet; feed fortnightly with weak liquid tomato feed. After flowering, tip the bulbs out of their pots and plant the entire clump in the garden.

SPECIALIST COLLECTIONS

❖

After cultivating a mixed collection of plants, many greenhouse gardeners develop a taste for one particular group of plants – perhaps cacti, fuchsias, pelargoniums or giant-flowered exhibition begonias – and wish to specialize in them. You can then set up the greenhouse to cater to their needs, perhaps buying specialist equipment like blinds, heaters or fans.

Pond care

Ponds provide a soothing environment for people and a valuable habitat for garden wildlife. They also present a unique opportunity to grow a fascinating range of plants that could not easily be accommodated elsewhere. Ponds need regular maintenance to keep them looking their best.

222

◁ **DUCKWEED** *consists of two tiny leaves that float on the water's surface, with short, trailing roots. It multiplies rapidly, forming mats that smother the pond. Skim them off with a fish net.*

INTRODUCING PLANTS

The start of the growing season is the time to add new plants to the pond. Most 'marginal' plants such as water iris (*Iris laevigata*), marsh marigold (*Caltha palustris*) and pickerel weed (*Pontederia cordata*) need positioning so they have 7.5cm (3in) of water over the top of their pots. Stand them on shallow planting shelves round the edge of the pond. Water lilies need deeper water, 15–45cm (6–18in) depending on the variety. Large varieties are in any case too invasive for normal garden ponds; choose dwarf kinds, which also prefer shallow water.

Always buy water plants grown in baskets, and sink them into the pond slowly; stand them on bricks if needed to achieve the correct depth. Floating aquatics such as water lettuce, water hyacinth or water chestnut add variety but are not winter-hardy, so they will need to be re-introduced annually.

It is essential to include oxygenating plants (submerged water weeds) if you keep fish in the pond; they are not grown in baskets, but root themselves into the silt at the bottom of the pond. Canadian pondweed is the most popular kind; being evergreen, it releases oxygen into the water even in winter, besides providing shelter for fish.

DIVIDING WATER PLANTS

Established water plants will need dividing every few years, when they become congested. Lift the planting baskets out of the pond and remove the old plants. Divide in the same way as for garden perennials, then discard the old growth from the centre of the clump and replant one healthy division taken from the edge. Line the basket with hessian or with fine plastic mesh sold for this purpose, then fill with special aquatic compost or ordinary soil that has not been treated with fertilizer. Put pebbles on top of the compost to weigh it down, and replace the basket carefully in the pond.

◁ **A FOUNTAIN** *brings the sound of moving water to a garden. Variegated iris are good plants for small ponds and enjoy being splashed by water.*

• *see also:* POOLS AND OTHER WATER FEATURES p50; PLANTS FOR POOLS p158; MARGINALS AND BOG GARDEN PLANTS p160

△ CANADIAN PONDWEED *is a vigorous and invasive water plant but it is the only one that is evergreen and does not die off in winter. It is therefore an essential ingredient to keep water oxygenated if you have fish. Thin out excess growth several times during the summer.*

DEALING WITH MURKY WATER

Green or murky water is a common problem with new ponds and often also affects established ponds temporarily in spring while aquatic organisms reach their own balance.

The problem normally resolves itself within a few months. It helps to keep the water clear if you use a mixture of marginals and enough water lilies or other floating plants to shade half the water surface. A small underwater pump will also help clear murky ponds by aerating the water and filters can remove some algae. A wad of organically grown barley straw sunk in the water sometimes keeps the water clear as will chemical products, available from garden centres or aquatic suppliers.

BLANKET WEED
❖

Blanket weed is a type of algae, forming fibrous strands that build up into thick, cottonwool-like masses, choking the pond. It is liable to get out of control where nitrogen fertilizer leaches into the pond from the surrounding garden and where there are too few marginal and other pond plants. Remove blanket weed regularly by hand or insert the tip of a cane into the mass, twirl it round and lift out. If removed often enough, blanket weed slowly reduces the nitrogen levels in a pond and the growth of weed becomes less of a problem. It makes a good compost ingredient.

◁ TOP UP THE *water level of ponds weekly in summer. If you see fish gasping at the surface in hot weather, this indicates oxygen shortage. Spray the water surface with a fine shower from the hose as this gets air into the water fast.*

SUMMER CARE

○ All forms of water weed spread rapidly and will need regular thinning in summer: simply pull out handfuls, shaking out fish fry and tadpoles. Put waste weed on the compost heap.

○ When working in the garden, take care not to allow fertilizers or chemicals in or near the pond as these can kill fish or encourage the growth of algae.

○ In hot weather, top ponds up regularly with ordinary tap water – water levels can drop 2.5–5cm (1–2in) per week. (If this happens all year round, you should suspect a leaking pond liner.)

○ Leave a pump running to add extra oxygen to the water in summer, as fish tend to suffer in hot weather.

223

AUTUMN/WINTER CARE

○ Stop feeding fish once the weather turns cooler and they become less active, otherwise unused food will decompose and pollute the pond.

○ Remove dead or dying foliage from marginal plants and take out floating aquatics, such as water hyacinth, that are not frost-hardy. These can be over-wintered in jars of pond water on a bright windowsill indoors, or discarded.

○ Cover the pond with netting to prevent fallen leaves contaminating the pond and to keep out herons, which take fish from garden ponds in winter. Clear dead leaves from the netting frequently.

Growing in containers

Containers filled with tender plants make eye-catching displays on a patio. But tubs, pots and troughs are also a convenient way to grow plants in all sorts of situations where there is no soil, turning paved courtyards, terraces and even steps into oases of colour. The beauty of containers is that they are mobile so you can move them to wherever some interest or a splash of colour is needed.

224

△ **MAKE THE MOST OF** *containers to create a garden in places that are totally without soil. Mix tall pots with hanging baskets and pots on plinths.*

TYPES OF CONTAINER

Terracotta pots are the traditional favourite and come in all shapes and sizes but, being porous, the plants in them dry out fast. Frostproof terracotta is less likely to crack if used outside in winter. Glazed ceramic pots, some decorated with oriental designs, are colourful and look especially good teamed with flowers that coordinate with the pot colour. Plastic containers are the most economical; cheap plastic becomes brittle when exposed to sunlight over several years, but the high-quality ones are more durable. Wooden containers such as tubs or half barrels last longest if lined with black polythene before use – be sure to cut matching drainage holes in the plastic liner.

POTTING COMPOST

You can use any type of potting compost in containers. Soil-based kinds are heavier, so they provide greater stability for tall or top-heavy plants, whereas on a roof garden, where weight is a consideration, you would

△ **PLANT POTS,**
planters and troughs can be bought in plastic, terracotta, timber and ceramic in an immense range of styles, shapes and sizes. Avoid mixing too many different kinds together as the effect will be bitty.

▽ **IN A LARGE**
container, you can almost create a potted flower bed; pack in the plants for best display.

• *see also:* PLANTS FOR SUMMER CONTAINERS p152; WINTER AND SPRING CONTAINERS p154; UNUSUAL CONTAINER PLANTS p156

SUMMER CARE

DRYING OUT is the biggest risk for plants in containers, so check regularly and water as often as necessary to keep the compost moist. In midsummer, watering may be needed daily – twice daily for small containers – but take care not to overwater at the start of the season, while growth is slow.

FEED CONTAINERS once a week from late spring to late summer. Liquid tomato feed is ideal for any flowering plants: dilute to half or quarter normal strength, depending on plant vigour. This can be used in addition to slow-release fertilizer for real show-stopping displays.

DEAD-HEADING is vital for plants grown in containers, as they are on show all the time. Do this twice weekly all summer to keep plants tidy and flowering well.

PLANTING UP CONTAINERS

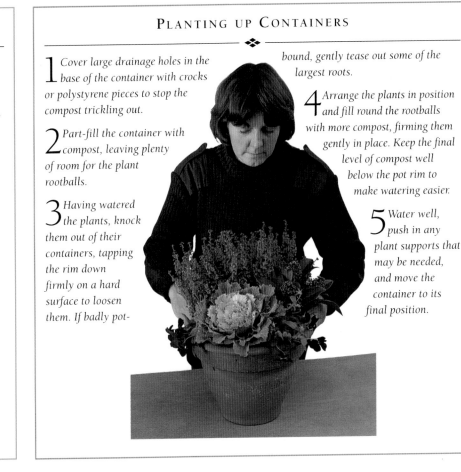

1 Cover large drainage holes in the base of the container with crocks or polystyrene pieces to stop the compost trickling out.

2 Part-fill the container with compost, leaving plenty of room for the plant rootballs.

3 Having watered the plants, knock them out of their containers, tapping the rim down firmly on a hard surface to loosen them. If badly pot-bound, gently tease out some of the largest roots.

4 Arrange the plants in position and fill round the rootballs with more compost, firming them gently in place. Keep the final level of compost well below the pot rim to make watering easier.

5 Water well, push in any plant supports that may be needed, and move the container to its final position.

do better to use a soilless compost. To make the routine care of container plants easier, mix water-retaining gel crystals and slow-release fertilizer granules into the compost before planting up, following the maker's instructions carefully.

SUMMER PLANTS FOR CONTAINERS

Containers for summer displays may be planted after the last frost or, if you have space in a frost-free greenhouse, they can be planted up to six weeks earlier and displays allowed to mature before they can safely be put outside. Use any reasonably compact kinds of bedding plant or half-hardy perennials such as fuchsia, pelargonium, gazania or felicia. A combination of trailing plants, such as lobelia, with upright plants like begonia and bushy subjects like pelargonium, makes a good display. Group several similar pots together and follow a distinct planting theme to create an eye-catching container garden.

WINTER AND SPRING DISPLAYS

When the summer bedding is over, shortly before the first frosts, empty and replant containers for winter and spring colour. There is no need to replace the compost as winter plants prefer it low in nutrients. Remove all spent plants and their roots, and if necessary top up the container with more compost. Replant with spring bulbs, winter-flowering pansies, or spring bedding such as polyanthus, primulas or wallflowers. Foliage plants like ivies or euonymus can be added as fillers. Alternatively, to avoid the risk of plants being damaged during a severe winter, you can wait until spring; buy spring bedding such as ranunculus or forget-me-nots and plant into containers when already flowering for immediate impact.

Place winter and spring containers in a sheltered spot and prevent any waterlogging by raising them up on bricks or pot feet. In early summer, when winter and spring flowers are over, remove the plants and completely replace the compost, ready for summer bedding.

Year-round containers

Bedding plants need replacing in summer and autumn to keep containers colourful all year round but hardy evergreen plants make ideal permanent candidates for containers. Choose compact kinds of shrub, conifer, ivy, phormium and hardy palms for best effect. Some deciduous plants, such as hostas and clematis, also make excellent container subjects.

POTS AND POTTING COMPOST

Instead of growing a mixture of plants in a single container, as with summer schemes, use only one specimen shrub per large pot for year-round interest or plant a group of herbaceous plants such as hostas in a wide container. Plastic or wooden containers are most durable for outdoor use in winter; if using terracotta or ceramic pots, choose frost-resistant kinds to prevent cracking in cold weather (contrary to popular belief, they do not protect the plants in them from freezing).

Soil-based composts are the most suitable for plants that will remain in the same pots for several years as they retain nutrients better than peat- or coir-based mixes. If you are growing lime-hating plants, such as azaleas or camellias, use ericaceous compost. Add water-retaining gel crystals and slow-release fertilizer to the compost when planting up; reapply the fertilizer every spring by making holes in the compost with a pencil and trickling it down.

226

WINTER CARE

- Containers may need occasional watering even in winter since walls and fences often deflect rainfall.

- Raise pots up on bricks or 'pot feet' to prevent waterlogging.

- Avoid feeding after late summer as this would encourage soft growth, easily killed by frost.

- Shrubs left outside for winter may need tying to trellis for stability in windy weather.

- During prolonged frosty conditions it is vital to prevent containers from freezing solid as this can kill plant roots. Either lag pots with insulating material such as bubble plastic or plunge them up to their rims in garden soil and loosely drape plants with horticultural fleece. If space is available in a greenhouse, sunroom or enclosed porch, plants will be safe there. Do not leave them for more than a few days in a dark shed, however.

AUTOMATIC WATERING SYSTEMS

To care for containers more easily, consider installing an irrigation system. The type of scheme employed in a greenhouse, whereby each pot is provided with its own drip pipe, can be used out of doors, with pots either connected to a water butt or linked by hose to a mains tap. If these are left in place all the time, watering can be done at the turn of a tap – or you can install a water computer to switch on and off for you. The advantage of this system is that you do not need to make any special arrangements at holiday times.

◁ **A PAIR OF** *potted evergreens either side of the door provides a formal year-round welcome, while flowering shrubs like the witch hazel* (Hamamelis mollis) *create a seasonal display.*

• *see also:* UNUSUAL CONTAINER PLANTS p156; WATERING YOUR GARDEN p184

△ **FOR A SHADY SPOT,** Fatsia japonica *and ivies make a good container team. The fatsia flowers in winter, when little else is in bloom.*

MATURE CONTAINERS

Most slow-growing plants can be left in the same container for three to five years before they need repotting, provided they are in soil-based compost and receive regular feeding. Simply remove the top layer of compost every spring and replace it with fresh (this also removes any moss or liverwort that may be growing on the surface of the compost). If plants outgrow their container or their growth declines, you will need to repot them sooner. For most plants, the best time to do this is spring, at the start of the growing season, although spring-flowering plants such as dwarf rhododendron are best left until immediately after flowering. Carefully remove plants (if they are too big for the container, plant them out in the garden), refill the tub with fresh compost and replant with either the original plants or with new ones.

▷ **EXOTIC PLANTS** *like agave and Chusan palm* (Trachycarpus fortunei) *can be grown outside in summer (in very mild regions, all year round). If frost threatens, bring the pots under cover.*

PERMANENT PLANT SUBJECTS

Compact evergreen shrubs such as hebe, euonymus, choisya and rosemary make ideal subjects for large containers or you can use potted topiary specimens clipped from bay or box. Architectural plants such as *Fatsia japonica* and phormium look especially striking when isolated in pots and in mild areas you can use slightly tender, architectural evergreens like the Chusan palm (*Trachycarpus fortunei*) and cordylines, as they will survive outside in winter. Lime-hating shrubs such as dwarf rhododendrons, camellia and pieris make good tub specimens and, where the garden soil is unsuitable, this is often the only way to grow them, using ericaceous compost. Some striking deciduous plants are perfect for pots, including Japanese maple, hostas (which are easier to protect from slugs in pots), heucheras and clematis grown up obelisks. Shade clematis by growing other plants around the pot, to keep their roots cool and moist. Conifers also look good in containers, provided they can be prevented from drying out: if this happens their foliage goes brown and does not recover.

◁ **IN A SUDDEN** *frost, use old newspapers for emergency lagging. Once compost freezes solid, plant roots are unable to take up moisture and even the hardiest plants can die.*

227

Growing in hanging baskets

Hanging baskets are the perfect way to display trailing plants and to bring a splash of colour to walls, doorways and porches. You can follow a display of summer annuals by winter and spring bedding. As they are surrounded by air on all sides, baskets tend to dry out quickly, but hanging them in a sheltered spot and giving them frequent attention are the secrets of success.

△ **VARIEGATED HEBE,** *trailing ivies and winter pansies form the basis of a winter basket.*

228

TYPES OF BASKET

Traditional wire baskets look wonderful, although their open-weave sides mean that the contents dry out fast; when the compost is bone dry, water runs straight through, making it difficult to wet again. Wire baskets need to be lined before they can hold compost; moss is the favourite material as plants can still be grown through the sides of the basket. Various flexible fabric or plastic linings can be bought and black polythene can also be used, though these are less natural looking: cut holes in the sides for planting through. Solid-sided hanging baskets are also available, made of plastic, terracotta or ceramic, some with built-in water reservoirs. Though easier to look after, they can only be planted at the top.

THE BEST PLANTS

Trailing plants such as lobelia, petunia, ivy-leaved pelargonium and trailing fuchsia make the most obvious candidates but plants with a naturally lax, bushy habit, like impatiens, laurentia and brachycome also look good in hanging baskets. Annual climbers such as *Thunbergia alata*, morning glory (*Ipomoea*) and dwarf sweet peas make good basket subjects too; tie some stems round the sides, leaving others to climb up the supporting chains.

WINTER AND EARLY SPRING BASKETS

These only succeed in a really well-sheltered spot or if baskets can be moved under cover in bad weather. After summer flowers are over, empty

◁ **AS SUMMER BASKETS** *have a long growing season, you can cultivate sensational displays like this. The secret lies in starting early, with good plants, then keeping them well-fed, watered and regularly dead-headed. Choose old favourites like fuchsia, petunia and pelargonium for a prolific display.*

• *see also:* PLANTS FOR SUMMER CONTAINERS p152; WATERING YOUR GARDEN p184

the basket and replant with winter-flowering pansies or, for a more weatherproof scheme, a mixture of ivies, winter-flowering heathers, euonymus and santolina; dwarf bulbs like crocus, iris or daffodil can be included. If you wait until spring you can plant primroses, violas or polyanthus in flower, with ivies for foliage 'trails'.

EDIBLE BASKETS

A hanging basket by the back door makes a handy place to grow herbs or a mixture of salad leaves such as sorrel, purslane, American land cress, rocket and cut-and-come-again lettuces. Or choose compact, trailing varieties of tomato, miniature cucumber or strawberry, giving each crop its own basket. Watering and feeding are crucial, but slugs are less of a problem than at ground level, and crops can easily be protected from birds by draping with netting or a crop-protection fleece.

△ **FOR A SOPHISTICATED** *scheme, go for plenty of coloured foliage with hints of flower. This basket holds coleus, helichrysum,* Heuchera *'Palace Purple' and* Verbena *'Peaches and Cream'.*

ROUTINE BASKET CARE

❖

- Watering: check hanging baskets daily, and give enough water to keep the compost moist. In summer, when the basket is full of roots, water both morning and evening.

- If wire baskets get so dry that water runs through them, lift down and soak in a bowl of water overnight.

- Special pulley devices are available to make watering easier by lowering the baskets for watering, as well as extension arms for hoses that reach up into high baskets.

- Feeding: regular feeding is vital to keep plants growing and flowering well in a small amount of compost. Use high-potash liquid tomato feed once or twice a week; apply at half strength until plants fill the basket.

PLANTING A LINED WIRE BASKET

❖

1 *Place the fibre liner inside the basket and cut to size if it overlaps round the edge. Part-fill with potting compost mixed with water-retaining gel crystals and slow-release fertilizer granules. Push small plants in through the overlapping sections of the liner, so they make a ring halfway up the basket sides. (Or line the basket with wads of moss.)*

2 *Fill the basket to the rim with more compost, firming lightly to settle it round the roots of the first row of plants. Then plant a second layer in the overlapping sections of the liner, pushing the plants in from the outside of the basket. Choose plants that contrast in form and colour with the previous ones for a more interesting display.*

3 *Finally, plant the top of the basket; you could either use more bedding plants or choose climbers or, as in this case, a single, large plant, which will form a striking centrepiece when the plants round the sides grow up to fill out the arrangement. Water well and hang in position. You could sink a plastic-bottle 'funnel' in the middle for easier watering.*

Raising plants from seed

Growing your own plants from seed is extremely satisfying and one of the cheapest ways to add new stock to the garden. No special equipment is needed – you can even use a windowsill indoors – but, as you become more adventurous, you will find that a heated electric propagator in the greenhouse provides perfect conditions for growing more challenging plants or for producing seedlings in quantity.

△ **A COLD FRAME** is *a useful extra alongside a greenhouse for hardening off all kinds of frost-tender plants for a few weeks before they can be safely planted outside.*

230

PROVIDING THE RIGHT CONDITIONS

Check the back of the seed packet or a leaflet on germination requirements (available free with your order from some mail-order seed firms) for precise instructions about individual seeds. Seeds vary mainly in the optimum temperature for their germination; plan sowings so that those needing similar heat go into the propagator together.

Some seeds, such as lettuce, require light to germinate, in which case do not put these in an airing cupboard and cover them thinly with vermiculite instead of seed compost. Other seed, such as primula, must be kept continuously moist and fail if allowed to dry out at all: it can be helpful to stand these on moist capillary matting.

SOWING SEED

Have clean trays and pots and a fresh bag of seed compost ready. Use 8cm (3½in) pots for small quantities of seed and half trays for larger amounts; square pots make the best use of propagator space. Fill them loosely with compost then level the top by running a flat-edged wooden block over it. Tap the container down gently to consolidate the compost and firm lightly with a presser. Water thoroughly and allow to drain. If sowing very fine, dust-like seed, sprinkle a thin layer of vermiculite over the surface of the compost and sprinkle

△ **SOW SEEDS VERY THINLY** *over the surface of the prepared seed tray. Overcrowded seedlings are more likely to succumb to fungal infections and in any case will be drawn up and leggy. You could mix seed with silver sand first.*

SOWING TIPS
❖

- Never let seeds dry out after sowing; if partly germinated, this can kill the embryo and the seeds will never come up.

- Storing seed: keep unopened packets in a cool, dry place out of direct light – do not leave in the greenhouse. Fold over the top of part-used packets and reseal with tape; put in an airtight container with a sachet of silica gel crystals. Keep in a cool place, like a refrigerator.

• *see also:* DEVELOPING A PRODUCTIVE GARDEN p258

the seed thinly over it – there is no need to cover them. For medium-sized seeds, such as lettuce or tomato, sprinkle thinly and barely cover with sifted seed compost or vermiculite. Put on a propagating case lid, specially made to fit over a standard seed tray.

△ **PRICK OUT** *seedlings when big enough to handle but before they grow enough to get tangled together. Prick them into fresh trays of compost, spacing them about 2.5cm (1in) apart. Pot up singly when they fill the tray with roots.*

Space out larger seed like peas or beans 2.5cm (1in) or more apart and push into the compost till just buried. Large seed can also be sown singly in small, individual pots.

PRICKING OUT

When seedlings are large enough to handle (usually when the first true leaf unfolds, after the initial pair of seed leaves), loosen their roots using a pencil point or dibber and lift them out carefully. Handle the seedlings by their leaves, not by the stem – if this is bruised, a seedling often dies. Space seedlings out into trays of fresh seed compost, 2.5cm (1in) or more apart, depending on their vigour. Large seedlings are best transferred into small, individual pots at this stage.

Return freshly pricked out seedlings to the propagator or other warm, enclosed conditions out of direct sun and accustom them gradually to cooler conditions.

GROWING ON YOUNG PLANTS

Once the seedlings are established in trays or small pots, stand them on the greenhouse staging to grow until they are big enough to plant out. If you stand them on capillary matting, by simply wetting the matting regularly the containers will stay evenly moist without being over-watered. After four weeks, the nutrients in the original seed compost will be exhausted, so start weekly liquid feeding as well, using a small can. Never leave feed on the foliage as young plants may scorch. Protect from slugs and other pests, and ensure plenty of ventilation whenever possible to prevent fungal disease. Keep

the plants in good light, but shaded from strong, direct sunlight.

HARDENING OFF

Before planting outdoors, all plants – not just tender ones – need to be hardened off to accustom them gradually to lower temperatures and fluctuating outdoor conditions. To do this, stand the plants outdoors on fine days, bringing them in at night, then start leaving them out on cooler or breezier days as well, until after two to three weeks they are ready to be planted outside. If you have a cold frame, move plants from the greenhouse to the cold frame, leaving the lid on at first but start opening the lid on fine days until eventually it is left off all the time. Begin hardening off frost-tender bedding and vegetables like sweetcorn three weeks before the last expected frost, and do not plant out until after that date.

231

▽ **HARDY ANNUALS** *and vegetable seedlings like lettuces and cabbages can be sown in mid-spring and raised entirely in an unheated cold frame.*

Propagating by cuttings

Rooting cuttings is the fastest way to grow plants for the garden, provided you have access to suitable parent plants. Use this method to increase the stock of favourite plants in your own garden, to root tender perennials for overwintering and to obtain new plants from those in friends' gardens.

△ **PUT A PLASTIC** *bottle or bag over the top to maintain humidity round the cuttings, unless you are using succulent, furry or silver-leaved plants that prefer dry air.*

232

SOFTWOOD CUTTINGS

This type of cutting can be made at any time during the growing season from the soft tips of new shoots. It is best to take them near the start of the growing season, in early summer when the new shoots are young, although they are also used in late summer to propagate half-hardy perennials for overwintering as rooted cuttings.

SEMI-RIPE CUTTINGS

Often known as heel cuttings, these are taken by twisting or tearing a complete young side shoot away from the parent plant, which often leaves a small 'heel' of skin at the base of the cutting. The very base of the cutting has a small amount of slightly woody tissue, darker in colour

than the soft tissue at the tip of the shoot. Tidy the base with a sharp knife, removing torn skin and cutting cleanly below a leaf joint at the very base of the stem, leaving the woody tissue intact. About 10cm (4in) up from this, cut the tip of the shoot off just above a leaf joint. Take semi-ripe cuttings from midsummer onwards, when the plants have had time to grow side shoots.

BASAL CUTTINGS

These are commonly used to propagate herbaceous plants in spring. When new shoots appear from the crown of the plant, wait till they are a few centimetres

△ **HARDWOOD CUTTINGS** *need no special facilities: simply put prepared cuttings into a slit trench made by pushing a spade back and forth in deeply cultivated soil containing plenty of fine organic matter to create a V-shape. Firm them in using your heel along each side of the row.*

◁ **TO MAKE** *a softwood cutting, cut 10cm (4in) from the tip of a young shoot, remove the leaves from the bottom half of the shoot and cut off cleanly just below a leaf joint, using a sharp knife. Dip the cut end in hormone rooting powder, then push each cutting into a pot of seed compost and water in.*

△ JERUSALEM SAGE *(Phlomis fruticosa) roots easily from any type of cutting; for quickest results, take softwood cuttings in midsummer and root in a pot on a shady windowsill indoors.*

rooting powder specially formulated for hardwood cuttings. Make a slit trench in a well-cultivated but vacant area of the garden (such as a corner of the vegetable plot) and, if the soil is heavy, trickle 2.5cm (1in) of sharp sand into the bottom. Push the cuttings in vertically, 30cm (12in) apart, and firm the soil back round them, closing the trench. Water in. Expect them to take a year to root well enough to be moved.

high, then cut shoots 7.5–10cm (3–4in) long. The base of the cuttings will usually be pale-coloured, where light has been kept from the stem by the mulch, by nearby shoots or by the remains of last year's stems. Then treat as for softwood cuttings. Sometimes, entire shoots can be detached from the parent plant with a few small roots already formed; known as 'Irishman's cuttings', these can be potted singly but treat them as cuttings until they are well rooted.

LEAF CUTTINGS

The leaves of some stemless house plants, including African violet, *Begonia rex* and streptocarpus, can be rooted. Remove a whole leaf, complete with leaf stalk, choosing one that is young but full-sized. Push the leaf stalk into a pot of seed compost till the leaf rests on the top.

When rooted, a cluster of young plants forms at the base of the leaf. When these are about 2.5cm (1in) high, tip them out of the pot, divide them up and pot singly. The leaves of *Begonia rex* can also be laid flat on a tray of compost, with the veins in the back nicked in several places and the leaf staked to the compost with cocktail sticks. If kept humid, a young plant will form at each nick.

HARDWOOD CUTTINGS

Use this method in late autumn to propagate shrubs such as roses, willows, philadelphus, weigelas and dogwoods. Cut woody shoots from the base of the current year's growth, trim cleanly below a leaf joint (only the scar will be visible) and remove the tip to leave the cuttings 20–30cm (8–12in) long. Dip the base into a hormone

233

Other means of propagation

There are several ways of propagating plants other than by seed and cuttings. Subjects that have a clump-forming habit are best divided, which gives several new plants straight away. Plants that naturally produce offsets or runners grow their own rooted 'pups', which need only to be potted when they are big enough to move. And for some difficult plants that need special facilities to root from cuttings, layering is the simple alternative.

DIVISION

Dividing clumps is the fastest way to propagate plants like grasses and bamboos, herbaceous perennials including hostas and hardy cranesbills, and some house plants such as maidenhair fern. The safest time to divide most subjects is in spring, at the start of the growing season, when the new plants can start growing away at once. Tough perennials like Michaelmas daisies can, however, be divided in autumn and bearded iris should be divided six weeks after flowering.

To divide a plant, knock it out of its pot or dig it up from the garden, and separate it into several smaller clumps. Prise the roots apart by hand, or use a knife or spade. Throw away the old woody material from the centre of the clump and replant the healthy young divisions from round the edge, after improving the soil in which they are to grow with organic matter and fertilizer.

OFFSETS

Plants such as aloes, bromeliads and agaves naturally surround mature plants with small replicas of themselves, which grow from underground shoots or leaf axils. When offsets are recognizable as independent young plants with expanded foliage, the best way of removing them is to dig up the plant, or remove it from its pot, and separate the offsets carefully with your fingers, along with as much of their own roots as possible. Then pot them singly. Some plants, such as tolmeia, produce offsets from the leaves of the adult plant; in this case, wait until they grow roots naturally then pot them up, or alternatively peg a leaf down to a pot of compost while still attached to the parent; separate only when well rooted.

RUNNERS

Some plants, such as strawberries, produce runners that rather like horizontal stems with baby plants

△ **TO LAYER** *a rhododendron, make a long, sloping cut part-way through a young stem, 30cm (12in) from the tip, and hold it open by wedging in a matchstick. Bury it in well-prepared soil, pegging it down, and leave for a year or more.*

growing at the end of them. These 'pups' root naturally where they are deposited by the extending runner, and in time form a large mat round the parent plant. Individual, rooted runners can be dug up and transplanted; however, in the case of strawberries, it is best to sink pots of seed compost alongside the parent plants and peg runners into them using wire hoops, so that the young plantlets root into the pots. When they are well-rooted, detach them from the parent and grow them on separately until they are big enough for planting.

△ **HARDY CRANESBILLS** *like this* Geranium *'Johnson's Blue' are quickly propagated by digging up and dividing the parent plant in early spring.*

• *see also:* PROPAGATING BY CUTTINGS p232

234

△ MOST HERBACEOUS PLANTS *spread slowly to form clumps but after three to five years start to die in the middle. This is the time to dig them up and divide them, replanting only the youngest pieces.*

AFTERCARE FOR NEW PLANTS

❖

• Keep young plants out of direct sun, in humid air and at an even temperature, watering them only lightly for a week or two after propagating so that they acclimatize gradually to their new conditions.

• Nip out the growing tips of young plants when potting them to encourage bushy growth.

• Start feeding newly propagated plants four to six weeks after potting, as all the nutrients in the compost will then be exhausted.

LAYERING

This is the best means of propagating camellia, rhododendron, magnolia and similar plants that do not root well from cuttings. It can be done at any time of year except winter, though spring is the best season. Choose a flexible, young branch that can be pulled or bent down to ground level, and prepare the soil where it touches the ground by digging in sharp sand and well-rotted organic matter. Make a long, sloping cut towards the shoot tip, going only about a third of the way through the stem, at a convenient point in the underside of the branch, and wedge the cut open with a matchstick. Dust with rooting hormone, and bury that section of the stem 5–7.5cm (2–3in) deep in the improved soil. Hold firmly in place with two strong wire hoops, one each side of the cut, or with a large stone. Tie the shoot tip to a cane to train it vertically. Wait at least a year, until strong new growth is visible and the plant resists when tugged, indicating that it is well rooted. Then dig up and replant elsewhere.

AIR LAYERING

This technique is mainly used for hard-to-root house plants such as ficus. Instead of taking the stem down to the ground, place moist compost round a stem and hold it in place by binding thin polythene around it. Use the equivalent amount of compost to that held in a 10–15cm (4–6in) pot. Make a sloping cut through part of the stem, prop it open and treat with rooting powder, as for outdoor layering. With air layering, it is evident that the shoot has rooted when roots can be seen round the edge of the plastic. When this happens, cut through the stem just below the roots, and pot the young plant up. Air layering is sometimes recommended for outdoor shrubs but it is not really practical as the compost dries out too quickly and can heat up or freeze, according to the weather.

▷ STRAWBERRIES *produce runners that root naturally in soil. Peg them down into pots of compost and detach when well-rooted.*

Pruning tools

Pruning, trimming and training are not only essential to maintain a tidy garden, but are some of the most creative aspects of gardening, giving you an opportunity to control growth and determine the size, shape and habit of your shrubs. It is vital to have the correct tools for the job and to keep them sharp and in good condition. Secateurs are the basic pruning tool, but more specialized equipment is available for other cutting jobs round the garden.

△ BUY GARDEN SHEARS
of good quality and keep the blades clean and sharp so they will cut cleanly without tearing.

236

CHOOSING THE RIGHT PRUNING TOOLS

❖

Secateurs come in a range of sizes and weights, so try several before buying. If possible, use them to cut through branches to see if the handles fit your hand and that the spring is not too powerful for your grip. If too heavy, they will be tiring to work with for any length of time. Some secateurs are specially designed for left-handed use. Choose a model that is appropriate for the type of pruning your garden requires – there is no need to buy heavy-duty secateurs or loppers if you have only a few small trees. Buy the best quality you can afford, as good tools last longer and work better during their life.

SECATEURS

Secateurs are for pruning and cutting woody stems up to 1cm (½in) in diameter; they come in two distinct types. Bypass secateurs have two opposing blades, rather like heavy-duty scissors, which glide past each other; they are often thought to give more precision cutting. Anvil secateurs have a single blade that cuts against a flat plate, more like slicing down on to a board.

This action can cause slight crushing or bruising of plant stems, which you would not want when taking woody cuttings for propagation, for instance. However, when old or slightly blunt, they give a cleaner cut than bypass secateurs in the same condition. A ratchet version of anvil secateurs makes cutting easier for people with weak or arthritic hands.

◁ A FOLDING PRUNING SAW (top) is *not much bigger than secateurs (anvil, above and bypass, left) but will deal with tree branches. Tools with bright handles are less easily lost when put down in the garden.*

LOPPERS

Long-handled, heavy-duty cutters are available in various styles for tough pruning of thick or out-of-reach branches. Long-handled loppers resemble croppers, but with secateur blades that will slice through branches 5cm (2in) or more in diameter. Some manufacturers supply long-handled extensions to which specially adapted secateurs and pruning saws can be fitted for tackling tall trees without having to use a ladder; the same handles can then be used with a fruit picking net.

SNIPS

Halfway between scissors and secateurs, snips are intended for lightweight jobs such as dead-heading and cutting flowers, as an alternative to picking them with your fingers. They are also handy for trimming and tidying plants on which it is inappropriate to use shears, perhaps for large-leaved topiary plants such as bay (*Laurus nobilis*), where shearing would cut some leaves in half. Flower gatherers are a variation of snips, where a secondary blade grasps the flower stem after cutting, preventing it from dropping to the ground.

• *see also:* TRIMMING HEDGES p200; WHY PRUNE? p238; SPECIAL PRUNING NEEDS p240

◁ TRIMMED
TREES *such as these*
potted standard
bays make a good
formal feature.
Maintain their
shape by pruning
them lightly several
times during the
growing season.

PRUNING SAW

These are special saws with narrow
blades, good for getting in and out
between closely spaced branches. Fairly
coarse teeth make much lighter work of
sawing green wood than a fine-toothed
carpentry saw. Small, folding pruning
saws are also available that fit into a
pocket. Use a pruning saw for
branches that are too thick to cut with
secateurs; a saw can be used for material
several centimetres thick as well as for
cutting down saplings or small trees.

GARDEN SHEARS

Shears are used for various clipping
jobs: trimming short lengths of hedge
such as dwarf box edgings,
for trimming topiary shapes, and for
dead-heading shrubs like heathers and
lavender after flowering. Two-handled
hedging shears are the most convenient
for general use, but sheep shears –
which only need one hand – are handy
for small areas of fine trimming and
the dead-heading of dwarf
flowering hedges.

▽ SINGLE-HANDED SHEARS
(*shown here*) *or sheep shears*
are ideal for precision-trimming
topiary like this box spiral.

USING SECATEURS

○ Hold secateurs or loppers firmly in
your hand with the larger blade
uppermost, and position them at 90°
to the stem you are cutting or, on
plants with alternate growing buds,
at a more sloping angle.

○ Use with a scissor action to produce
the cleanest cut.

○ Do not twist the secateurs from side
to side or tug at a tough stem, as this
only tears the fibres of the stem,
making it harder to cut through and
damaging the plant.

○ Instead, bend the branch slightly
downwards, away from the blades,
to open the cut up a little, making
it easier to slice through.

237

CARING FOR
YOUR TOOLS

○ Wipe the blades with a damp cloth
and a little washing-up liquid after
use to remove sap, which makes the
cutting surfaces sticky and prevents
a good cut next time.

○ Leave secateurs with the
blades open to dry thoroughly
before putting them away.

○ Wipe blades over with an oily
rag before prolonged storage,
and keep in a dry environment
to prevent rusting.

○ Some secateurs are dismantled
for sharpening; others can be
sharpened using a long, narrow
sharpening stone. Sharpen regularly
to avoid tearing the bark or
damaging plant tissues.

▷ LONG-HANDLED LOPPERS *allow you*
extra purchase when cutting thick branches.

Special pruning needs

Certain groups of deciduous flowering shrubs and climbers need regular pruning to improve their display and these include some of the most popular garden plants: roses, clematis, wisteria and hydrangea. Without pruning, the flowers of these plants may be lost among excess leafy growth or may be produced so high up that they can only be seen from an upstairs window. In pruning these plants, the aim is to control their size yet encourage free flowering.

△ **PRUNE HYBRID CLEMATIS** *in late winter/early spring, cutting all the stems off close to ground level. Also use this method to rejuvenate overgrown species of clematis, such as C. montana.*

240

PRUNING ROSES

If unpruned, roses become tall and woody and carry few flowers, mainly at the top of the plants, where they cannot be enjoyed.

• Prune **modern bush roses** in mid-spring, after the worst frosts are over. Cut plants back to 30–45cm (12–18in) above ground level, pruning strong stems back least and weak ones most to even out growth (hard-pruned stems grow away strongest).

• Prune **shrub roses** and old-fashioned roses after flowering, by removing the dead flowerheads plus about 20cm (8in) of stem.

• Do not prune **shrub roses** that have good hips as this will stop them being produced.

• Prune **climbing roses** when all their flowering is finished (some varieties flower twice in summer, others only once), cutting back side shoots to within 8–10cm (3–4in) of the main framework of branches tied out over the wall.

• Shorten the main branches of **climbers** to keep them within their allotted area.

• Prune **ramblers** after blooming to cut flowered stems back to their junction with a strong, new shoot. This will produce replacement stems that will carry next year's flowers.

• Remove all weak, diseased, damaged or congested stems entirely.

PRUNING CLEMATIS

If unpruned, clematis eventually grow big and tangled, with bare bases to their stems; the flowers of some

◁ **CLIMBING AND RAMBLER ROSES** *look superb trained over a pergola. Annual pruning keeps them free-flowering and vigorous.*

• *see also:* SELECTING CLEMATIS p146; CHOOSING AND USING ROSES p148; GROWING CLIMBERS p208

▷ **WISTERIA AND CLEMATIS** *produce prolific flowering displays when correctly pruned; if left, they can be disappointing and even, in the case of wisteria, a nuisance.*

varieties grow so high up they cannot be enjoyed. Since clematis vary in pruning needs from one variety to another, always keep the nursery label as this includes pruning instructions, or copy them on to the back of the plant label for easy reference. If you do not have the nursery label, consult a specialist guide book before pruning to ensure you prune each type correctly.

• Prune hybrid clematis varieties that flower at the tips of their shoots (these flower in mid- to late summer) in late winter or very early spring: cut them down to a pair of new buds close to ground level.

• Other hybrid varieties, which flower on short side shoots grown in the current year, are best left unpruned (these are varieties that start flowering in early summer). If overgrown, cut back hard in early spring; they will still flower but at a later time.

• Clematis species, such as *C. montana*, do not normally need pruning; if overgrown, cut them back hard in early spring and train the new stems into place.

PRUNING WISTERIA

Left unpruned, wisterias will grow into enormous, straggling vines, choked with vigorous twining stems produced at the expense of flowers.

• Start by training a framework of main stems out over the area to be covered and tie in place.

• Each year, in midsummer, cut back the new shoots growing from the main branches (these are green, as against the brown skin of older shoots) to about 15–20cm (6–8in) from the main stems.

• In midwinter, go over plants again and shorten to about 2.5cm (1in) the side shoots that grew from these stubs at the end of the summer. This encourages the formation of twiggy 'spurs', from which the flowers grow.

PRUNING HYDRANGEAS

Do not dead-head these shrubs after flowering; if the dead flowerheads are left on all winter they act as umbrellas, sheltering the young shoots beneath them from severe weather.

• Prune hydrangeas in mid-spring, cutting them off just above a young shoot to remove dead flowerheads plus a few centimetres of stem.

• Do not prune mophead or lacecap hydrangeas too hard, or cut off shoots with a fat green bud at the tip, as these are the stems that will flower in the current year.

• Varieties of *Hydrangea paniculata*, however, can be pruned hard to encourage shoots to grow from the base.

▷ **RESIST THE** *temptation to dead-head your hydrangeas after flowering or prune too hard in spring: both will spoil next year's flowering.*

THE CORRECT CUT

○ Use sharp secateurs to make a clean cut and always cut just above a leaf joint or growth bud, as the next young shoot will grow out from here.

○ On plants such as roses, that have alternate growth buds, make an angled cut, sloping it slightly away from the bud side of the shoot.

○ Prune above a bud that is pointing in the direction in which you want the new shoot to grow. Cut to outward-facing buds to make a dense bush grow more open in habit; and cut to an upward-facing bud to make a droopy plant grow more strongly upright.

○ On plants that have opposite buds, like hydrangea, make a straight cut just above a strong pair of buds or shoots, taking care not to damage them. If you want to encourage growth in one direction only, remove the unwanted bud or shoot after making the cut.

○ Delay pruning for a few weeks if cold weather persists in spring, as pruning encourages the production of vigorous new shoots whose growth is very soft and can be killed by late frost.

○ When clematis, wisteria or climbing roses are grown informally, rambling through trees, no pruning is necessary.

241

Dealing with pests and diseases

Vine weevil

A garden is a haven for a wide variety of insect life, much of which is a great asset to the gardener. Only a small number of species are harmful to plants and where chemicals are not used indiscriminately these will be controlled naturally by beneficial predators. To reduce the risk of attack by pests and diseases, buy healthy plants and practise good garden hygiene. If it becomes necessary to use chemical insecticides or chemical forms of disease control, treat only affected plants and take precautions to avoid harming beneficial creatures such as bees.

242

IDENTIFYING GARDEN PESTS

A huge range of insect and other pests can attack plants in the garden, making ornamental plants unsightly and edible crops less palatable. Pests can also threaten the lives of plants by weakening them or by spreading viral disease. Since it is much easier to keep plants free from pests than to nurse them back to health after serious damage has been done, it is worth learning to recognize the most common enemies and check for them regularly.

Described below are the insects and other pests that regularly attack garden plants. The various methods of control are explained in more detail on the following pages.

Greenfly (aphids) are small, wingless insects found on the tips of shoots and buds and the undersides of leaves, both outdoors and in the greenhouse; the name greenfly is misleading as aphids can also be pink, cream or brown. Control by hand by washing aphids off leaves or tips, or spray with selective aphicide. Many natural predators control aphids, including lacewings, ladybirds, hoverfly and blue tits.

Vine weevil adults are brown beetles 1cm (⅜in) in length whose long snouts bite scalloped notches round the edges of evergreen leaves such as rhododendron; their larvae are fat, white, C-shaped grubs that live in soil, feeding on the roots of cyclamen, primulas and other plants, both in pots and in borders. Control by hand or use biological control nematodes.

Brassica whitefly are like tiny white insects; they resemble the glasshouse whitefly but live outdoors on brassica

crops like cabbages as well as on weeds of the same family. They are fairly resistant to chemical sprays, so the best remedy is to cover plants with fleece.

Slugs are a familiar, slimy pest that rasp soft tissues from plants, leaving characteristic lacy holes. Offenders can often be caught red-handed by torch-light at night, but on bright days they hide away in cool, dark places to avoid drying up. The most effective, though expensive, remedy is biological control in the form of nematodes. Water on to the soil over whole borders during the warmer months, especially round plants most at risk, such as hostas. Use slug pellets sparingly and hide them under broken pots to protect pets and birds.

Snails cause similar damage to that of slugs but will climb woody stems and walls to reach soft plant material, making nematodes ineffective; hunt out groups hibernating in wall-niches in winter and destroy, or use pellets with care.

◁ **ALL GREENFLY** *are females and produce live young, ready to feed immediately – and within a few days the young greenfly can also lay young.*

Woodlice

Lily beetle

Woodlice are grey creatures 5mm (½in) long that roll up into balls when disturbed. They feed on decaying vegetation and as such are beneficial to compost heaps. They may, however, take weak seedlings or attack plants already damaged by other causes, especially in greenhouses. Good hygiene, keeping the garden free from dead vegetation and debris, is the best remedy.

Earwigs are slender creatures, 2.5cm (1in) long, with a pair of pincers at the rear end. They bite holes in flower petals, especially of exhibition-type blooms such as dahlia and chrysanthemum. Good garden hygiene is the best remedy or you could make old-fashioned earwig traps, placing upturned plant pots stuffed with scrunched-up newspaper on top of canes among plants. Empty daily and destroy pests. Earwigs do some good in the garden by feeding on greenfly.

Millipedes are slow-moving, black, pencil-shaped creatures with many legs moving in 'waves' along the body; they feed on plants. Avoid introducing them to the garden by checking new plants for passengers and physically remove any you see.

Lily beetles are small, bright red beetles infesting lilies and related plants; the larvae resemble dark, slimy bird droppings and eat foliage. They are a relatively new pest in warmer areas. Physical removal is the best remedy; chemicals are not very effective against them.

Leaf miners are small, cream torpedo-shaped larvae that tunnel inside leaves, creating wiggly white tunnels between the upper and lower surfaces of leaves. Pick off affected leaves by hand. Spraying systemic insecticide may help deter adults laying eggs if done early in the season.

Codling moth larvae are the maggots inside apples. As an alternative to regular preventative spraying, codling moth traps may be hung in fruit trees in early summer, using one for every five or six trees – these lure adult male codling moths to sticky paper by using pheromone scent, killing the males and preventing the females being fertilized and laying eggs.

GREENHOUSE PESTS

Red spider mites are minute, light brown or orange, dust-like insects causing a mottled appearance to leaves. Fine webbing may be evident. High humidity deters them, so damp down greenhouses by spraying paths with water on warm days. Alternatively, use pesticide sprays or introduce the predatory mite *Phytoseiulus* to control them naturally.

Whitefly, which resemble tiny white moths, can be found on the undersides of greenhouse plants, taking to the air in white clouds when disturbed. Control by regular chemical sprays or introduce the predatory, parasitic wasp, *Encarsia formosa*. Avoid overcrowding plants and ventilate the greenhouse well.

Thrips are minute flies whose larvae live inside plants and cause tiny silvery speckles on foliage. Use dilute systemic insecticide, drenching compost and spraying plants with the solution.

◁ **HOLD A LEAF** *up to the light to locate a leaf miner; squeeze the larva between your fingers to kill it.*

243

Sciarid (mushroom fly) are tiny black flies hovering round compost heaps and pots of plants (especially those growing in peat-based compost); their larvae are tiny white 'worms' in the compost. Springtails are similar but their larvae jump when pots are watered. To control, drench compost with spray-strength systemic insecticide.

PEST CONTROL TECHNIQUES

Various methods, both natural and biological, can be used to control pests though it is always preferable to prevent any infestations in the first place by buying healthy plants and practising good garden hygiene. Chemical pesticides are useful as a last resort, although nowadays there are plenty of 'green' alternatives.

244

△ **USE STICKY TRAPS** in the greenhouse to snare pests like whitefly; for best results, suspend just above favourite plants like fuchsias and disturb plants occasionally to set insects flying.

Manual forms of control

Some pests can be kept at bay by hand, without resorting to using insecticides, and this should always be the first means to try. Slow-moving, non-flying insects like aphids are easily wiped off the leaves and tips of shoots, for example. Individual caterpillars may be picked off plants by hand and you can make old-fashioned slug traps by sinking saucers of beer in among plants. In the kitchen garden you can pinch out the tips of broad beans to deter blackfly and prune out the webs of tent-forming caterpillars from fruit trees.

Using natural predators

It is vital to know which the natural predators of various plant pests are, to avoid destroying them by mistake.

Natural predators include insectivorous birds like blue tits as well as shrews, frogs and toads, carnivorous beetles, centipedes, spiders and hoverfly and lacewing larvae. Both the larvae and adults of some flying insects, like ladybirds, feed on greenfly, and several wasp species parasitize plant pests such as caterpillars by laying their eggs inside the body; the larvae then destroy the pest. To encourage natural predators into the garden, first stop using chemicals; you could also make a pond and leave plant debris round the edge of the garden to protect spiders in winter.

Biological control

Many common pests can now be controlled by using specially introduced predators and parasitic insects. The secret of their success is

to use them at the right time. Under glass, use *Phytoseiulus* (a predatory mite) to tackle red spider mite and *Encarsia formosa* (a small wasp that parasitizes whitefly) in spring: a warm greenhouse is vital. These predators are supplied by post and released immediately to control infestations.

Two kinds of microscopic nematode (beneficial eelworms) are available to tackle slugs and vine weevils. Both kinds are mixed with water and applied via a fine rose on a watering can to the open soil around plants, to greenhouse border soil or, for vine weevil, to individual pots of plants at risk of attack, such as cyclamen or primulas. Use in spring when the temperature of the soil has risen above 10°C (50°F), and

PHYSICAL BARRIERS

❖

Barriers are mainly used to protect fruit and vegetables from pest attack; the barrier can take a variety of forms.

- Susceptible plants such as brassicas or rows of carrots may be covered with a very fine mesh net through their growing life to prevent insects from reaching them; the mesh is supported by hoops of wire, tied loosely round individual plants, or laid over rows and dug into shallow trenches along the edges.

- Netting is often used to cover fruit cages to stop birds picking the fruit

and similar structures can be used to screen vegetable plots from pigeons or butterflies.

- Grease bands are sometimes put around the trunks of fruit trees in winter to protect them from crawling pests. Pest-control 'glue' may be applied round the rim of tubs to deter slugs and snails.

- Fitting a collar (cardboard disc) snugly round the base of brassica stems will prevent the female cabbage root fly from reaching the soil to lay her eggs.

DISEASE IN GARDEN PLANTS

Plant diseases due to fungus, bacteria or virus cause a wide range of different symptoms and can severely check the growth of mature plants or kill young ones. Garden hygiene and good cultural practices are the best ways to prevent disease but there are several means of control to tackle the various problems caused by disease.

Common diseases

A great number of different diseases can attack plants, though relatively few are common in gardens. Some affect only particular plants. The diseases described below are those most likely to be seen in gardens from time to time; the majority are easily prevented or controlled, often without resorting to chemicals.

ensure that the soil is moist. Beneficial nematodes are unlikely to survive the winter outside in the garden, and even under glass they usually die out due to the interruption in their food supply, so it becomes neccesary to reapply them every year.

Using chemicals

Where there is no alternative to spraying with chemicals, choose products that control only the target pest, for instance selective aphicides that kill greenfly and blackfly without harming beneficial insects or bees that also feed on the plant. Check the manufacturer's label carefully. Most pesticides in fact kill a wide range of pests, so use them in the late evening, after bees have left the garden. Spray on a windless day and wear protective clothing such as gloves and goggles. Avoid spraying open flowers, or plants that are either under stress due to lack of water or suffering from disease.

For small gardens and occasional use, buy ready-mixed chemical products in

their own sprayer-bottles and use just what you need each time. This works out much more cheaply than buying concentrated products for which you need a separate sprayer and have to make up larger quantities than you need, wasting the rest.

Do not dispose of unwanted 'neat' chemicals down the drains – contact your local council for advice on where to put them. If you have small amounts of diluted chemicals left over after spraying, dispose of them by watering them down further and spraying the solution over vacant ground. Rinse out the sprayer after use and dispose of the rinsings over empty ground, in the same way.

Powdery mildew

Grey mould

Powdery mildew resembles a floury residue on the upper surfaces of plant leaves or stems, especially of roses and vines, in late summer. It usually occurs when plants are short of water: irrigate thoroughly during dry spells to help prevent it. To treat, spray with an appropriate fungicide.

Grey mould (botrytis) shows as fluffy, grey, mouldy patches on leaves, stems or dead flowerheads, usually on dead tissue or following an injury. Since it is encouraged by high humidity, ventilate the greenhouse regularly; good garden hygiene also helps to reduce its incidence. Spray with an appropriate fungicide.

Black spot is seen on rose foliage in the form of round black patches, which may spread until the leaves are almost covered; it can lead to premature leaf drop. Some rose varieties have a natural resistance, so grow these if you want to avoid spraying. Otherwise, spraying every two weeks with a suitable fungicide through the growing season is the only means of prevention. Gather and burn fallen leaves in autumn and spray bare stems and the soil beneath plants with a winter wash.

Black spot

Rust causes rusty orange or reddish pustules on leaves, particularly those of roses, pelargonium and leeks. Remove affected leaves if the infestation is light and spray regularly with a suitable fungicide to prevent outbreaks getting worse. Combined rose fungicides against rust, mildew and black spot often include an aphid killer too. Burn badly affected plants.

Rust on rose foliage

Honey fungus affects mainly woody plants, including hedges, which can die suddenly or sicken and die more gradually. The disease is mainly spread between plants by black 'bootlaces', which are sometimes found under the bark or in the soil, and in autumn golden toadstools may appear round the plant. In areas where honey fungus is prevalent, have dead tree stumps winched out so they cannot act as a source of infection. When planting into infected soil, surround new plants with a 60-cm (2-ft) deep polythene collar sunk into the ground round them to prevent infection by bootlaces.

Root rots cause the roots or necks of plants to rot away. Early symptoms include sudden wilting, followed by the rapid death of the plant, or reddish tints to the foliage of heathers and conifers, which fail gradually over time. Root rots are worst where the soil is poorly drained. Prevent harmful soil organisms building up to problem levels by not planting the same type of plant in the same place for successive years; use a crop rotation system on vegetable plots.

Damping off causes seedlings to collapse, as though their stems have been bent over close to the base, and rapidly die. It may be due to various cultural problems, such as unclean seed trays, propagator or growing medium, or can be caused by overcrowding or growing conditions that are too

cold or dark. Watering with a suitable fungicide may help but improving the growing conditions is the best solution.

Clematis wilt affects newly planted clematis, whose stems and leaves suddenly wilt, then turn brown as if scorched. If the affected stems are cut away, new growth often resprouts from the base, provided the clematis was originally planted deeply, with the rootball 10–15cm (4–6in) below the surface of the soil. Varieties of *Clematis viticella* appear immune.

Virus diseases cause a range of symptoms, most commonly mottled or streaked leaves and in some cases streaked flower colour. Affected plants grow poorly and the yields of vegetable plants or fruit bushes and canes are gradually reduced. Viruses are mainly transmitted between plants by aphids or other sap-sucking insects, so control these pests to limit the spread of viruses. Even virus-free plants are eventually affected, due to transmission by insects or on hands but they give good yields for some years before this happens. There is no cure; affected plants must be destroyed.

Physiological disorders
A huge range of strange symptoms that appear in plants, such as 'blind' shoots, blotchy fruit and discoloured leaves, are due to physical causes rather than insect infestation or disease. Extreme conditions such as drought or waterlogged soil, excessively high or low temperatures or humidity, and poor light or sun-scorch are common causes. Hail, wind, frost, scorching sun and weedkiller can also cause physical symptoms. The damage suffered cannot be reversed but new

◁ HONEY FUNGUS *affects shrubs and hedges and is spread below the bark. It may manifest itself in autumn as yellow toadstools round the base of the plant.*

conditions and much more likely that plants grow poorly and look sick due to shortage of a whole range of nutrients. This happens on impoverished soil when plants are not fed regularly, especially on soil with a very high or low pH, where nutrients are chemically 'locked up'. The solution is to remedy the growing conditions.

DISEASE CONTROL

As with pest control, various measures can be adopted, escalating in their seriousness from manual to chemical forms.

247

THE PREVENTION OF DISEASE

❖

• Keep aphids under control because sap-sucking insects spread viral disease between plants in their saliva. Cover fruit bushes and vegetable crops with fine nets as an alternative to spraying.

• Use a garden disinfectant product to clean pots, seed trays and other propagation implements to reduce the risk of spreading disease.

• Buy seed and potting composts in quantities that can be used up quickly; re-seal the neck of the bag between uses to exclude airborne disease organisms.

• Clean knife or secateur blades with bleach or disinfectant from time to time when either propagating or pruning plants.

• Burn badly diseased plants to prevent organisms spreading; never put diseased material on to the compost heap or use diseased plants for propagation.

---

growth generally returns to normal once growing conditions are improved. Prune out damaged stems to improve the plant's appearance.

Nutritional disorders

Deficiency symptoms vary according to which elements are in short supply. With a nitrogen shortage, plant leaves are typically pale green and slightly stunted, with red or orange glints. Plants suffering from phosphate deficiency have bluish leaves with purplish or bronzy tints. A shortage of potash shows up as brown edges or brown spots on leaves. Chlorosis, caused by lack of iron, makes the leaves look yellow; this is a common problem, most often seen on lime-hating plants grown on chalky soil. It is unusual for a single nutrient to be deficient in garden

Manual forms of control

Check your plants regularly so problems can be detected early. If disease affects only a few leaves, pick them off by hand and burn to prevent spores spreading the disease. Make it a habit to remove dead leaves and flowerheads, and prune out dead stems or tips of shoots when you see them, as these are the first sites that disease organisms will invade. Protect plants from physical bruising or breakage as damaged tissues are susceptible to being infected by disease.

Cultural control

Meticulous garden hygiene, ensuring freedom from debris and weeds, and good growing conditions make for strong, healthy plants that are better able to withstand disease than weak specimens. In vegetable plots, practise

crop rotation to prevent a build-up of root disease in the soil. Check new plants for tell-tale disease symptoms and reject any unhealthy ones.

Chemical control

Regard spraying with chemicals as a last resort. It is effective mainly against fungal disease; few products tackle bacterial diseases and none treat viruses. Most fungicides work against several different fungal diseases so you need not identify the precise problem; read the label first, however. Follow the guidelines given for insecticides in the Safe Use of Chemicals box on the previous page.

Weeds and weeding

A weed is any plant growing in the wrong place and usually weeds are rampant species of wildflower that invade gardens by wind-borne seed, animal or bird vectors, or through roots or seed in manure. Invasive garden plants can themselves become weeds, due to excess seeding or spreading roots. The secret of a weed-free garden is never to let weeds get out of control: there are techniques for tackling even the most stubborn species.

IDENTIFYING COMMON WEEDS

Most common weeds, like groundsel and nettles, are well known to gardeners, but anything out of the ordinary can usually be identified by looking it up in a book of wildflowers. Otherwise, take a specimen to a garden centre or horticultural society to be looked at by someone more expert.

Annual weeds

Annual weeds are those, like groundsel, that flower, set seed and die in one year but others, such as bitter cress, produce several generations of seed each year. Neglected ground contains thousands of dormant weed seeds and when soil is cultivated they are brought to the surface and exposed to light, enabling them to germinate. Control by regular hoeing, hand weeding, mulching or use of contact weedkillers before flowering, so they cannot set seed.

Perennial weeds

Perennial weeds such as nettles and ground elder behave like herbaceous plants, dying down in autumn and reappearing the following spring. Small clumps may be dug up, but well-established colonies, especially of spreading perennials like couch grass and bindweed, are best treated with translocated weedkiller. When growing among cultivated plants, 'spot treat' individual weeds by spraying or painting with weedkiller. Regular hoeing also works, given time, by frequently cutting off new growth, eventually weakening the plant.

Woody weeds

Woody weeds like sycamore seedlings and brambles grow fast and are hard to dig out, on account of their deep roots. Dig out seedlings while young but cut off well-established plants close to ground level and treat the resulting vigorous new growth with brushwood killer. Protect nearby plants.

COMMON PROBLEM WEEDS

Bindweed, a vigorous, twining plant with large, white, trumpet-shaped flowers, spreads by thick, white, brittle underground roots – new plants are readily propagated if these are broken by digging. When plants first emerge above ground in spring they form a rosette before climbing: treat at this stage with translocated weedkiller and repeat when regrowth appears. Cut off scrambling stems among shrubs at ground level: leave the stems to die, after which they are easier to untangle. Treat new growth at ground level as it emerges.

Couch grass is a wiry grass that spreads by thin white underground rhizomes. Small clumps may be dug out but all root must be removed. Spray larger areas with translocated weedkiller and wait until the foliage turns brown before removing debris, to ensure the roots are dead. Clear heavily infested sites by covering whole areas with thick black polythene or old carpet to cut out light. Leave in place for at least a year.

Creeping buttercup

Horsetail

248

△ **BINDWEED** *has deceptively pretty white trumpet flowers but if left unchecked it soon spreads to form a dense cover that will smother cultivated plants, such as this artichoke.*

Creeping buttercup is a low, spreading, rosette-like buttercup with plantlets at the ends of runner-like stems (like strawberry runners). It has a tough root system from which the top of the plant snaps off when pulled but the remains regenerate quickly. Spot-treat rosettes with weedkiller and prevent runners rooting by early weeding. Never put on the compost heap.

Celandine is a pretty spring wildflower with yellow, buttercup-like blooms and low rosettes of deep green foliage. Plants die down in early summer, leaving clusters of tiny, fragile bulbils underground. Digging breaks up clusters and distributes bulbils even more widely through the soil – they are too small to remove by hand. Water foliage with contact weedkiller before flowering. One treatment will usually be effective.

Ground elder has short, upright growth with characteristic elder-bush type foliage and flat white heads of flowers; it spreads by strong underground stems and roots. Digging is ineffective as broken root fragments propagate new plants. Spray young growth with translocated weedkiller in spring and retreat each time new shoots appear. Or grass over the area and cut regularly to prevent regrowth. It may take several years to eradicate strong colonies.

Horsetail is a primitive plant related to the fossilized remains of the giant horsetail, found in coal seams; new growth resembles asparagus tips from which tall, ferny foliage develops later. The roots can penetrate huge distances. Do not try to dig out as damaged roots regrow. Weedkillers are not very effective against horsetail, so mow it out of lawns, hoe borders regularly to weaken it, use path weedkiller on gravel or paving and try systemic herbicides on vacant land or among shrubs.

Wild ivy can damage loose mortar in walls and unstable fences with its penetrating aerial roots and smother shrubs and hedges with its shoots. If large quantities build up in the heads of old trees, this can increase their wind resistance enough to bring them down on stormy nights. Remove ivy seedlings while young and pull out climbing stems from the base of hedges regularly. To remove established ivy from trees, cut through the base of stems near ground level; when the foliage turns brown, the stems are easier to strip off. Ivy stumps can be treated with brushwood killer to prevent regrowth. Though not a parasite on other plants, ivy uses them for support as it climbs and can smother small plants.

249

Ground elder

THE KITCHEN GARDEN

❖

THERE ARE MANY good reasons for raising vegetables, fruit and herbs in the garden, not least the sensuous pleasure of contemplating them in all their orderly profusion, knowing they will ultimately end up on the plate.

Growing your own produce provides you with choice, giving you the chance to taste vegetables fresher and with more variety, colour and flavour than any you might buy. Fruit and vegetables in the shops are inevitably limited to a few easily managed varieties, compared with the inspiring range of unusual, exotic or old-fashioned crops available to tempt the kitchen gardener. You could choose to grow a large quantity of a favourite crop, for freezing or sheer self-indulgence, or prefer to have a little of everything, well spaced out for continuity all season. How you tend your plants is a further option: you might decide to grow 'organically', without depending on chemical treatments, to be sure that what you eat has had no unwanted additives.

Do not be daunted by the prospect of managing a kitchen garden. Most crops can be grown successfully with the same basic skills used elsewhere in the garden. Nor do you need a huge area of ground – a few strawberries or summer lettuces can be tucked in a fertile corner, parsley or carrots grown beside a path beneath a neat espalier apple, and climbing vegetables such as runner beans and outdoor cucumbers trained vertically to save space.

253

Andi Clevely

ANDI CLEVELY

Designing a kitchen garden

Few gardeners have any choice about where to create a kitchen garden and, as most sites are less than perfect, it is important to know how to assess and improve the selected plot. Bear in mind that integrating food crops with other plants around the garden can sometimes be easier than keeping them separate and hidden from view.

254

△ WHERE THERE *is enough room in the garden, vegetables are traditionally grown in parallel rows, accessible both for cultivation and for harvest.*

MAXIMIZING THE SPACE

❖

Fences and walls, including those of the house itself, offer extra space for growing crops: bush and tree fruits may be trained on walls, as can tall or climbing vegetables such as beans, peas, tomatoes and cucumbers. Most crops will thrive in pots and other containers, making it possible to assemble a collection of vegetables, herbs and fruit in a courtyard or even on a balcony.

PROVIDING SHELTER

Exposure to wind can have an adverse effect on crops, even light breezes reducing yields while strong winds stunt or damage plants. Many gardens are enclosed by fences, hedges or walls and these usually provide adequate shelter. Where crops are likely to be exposed, it is a good idea to protect them with a windbreak such as a hedge, perhaps of gooseberries or some other fruit, or an open fence on which climbing crops can be trained. Temporary or seasonal screens of sweet peas, Jerusalem artichokes, sweetcorn or raspberries are also effective.

ASPECT

Most crops like maximum sunlight for fast, healthy growth although some sensitive vegetables appreciate light shade in midsummer. Make sure any screen does not cast too much shade. The branches of overhanging trees can often be thinned to admit more sunlight, while excessively tall hedges may need to be reduced in height, for these cast shade and also confine still air on cold nights, turning a low-lying garden into a frost pocket. When designing your kitchen garden, note those areas where frost remains longest or which walls receive the most sunlight, and allocate crops where they are best suited.

△ WEATHER CONDITIONS *can be fickle, especially in late spring, and tender vegetables like marrows benefit from cloche protection after planting out.*

see also: DESIGN CONSIDERATIONS p18; PRUNING AND TRAINING FRUIT p278; PRODUCTIVE CONTAINERS p280

△ TRY GROWING CROPS *informally in beds, combining and dispersing them with flowers.*

COPING WITH SLOPES

❖

Gardens are not always conveniently level, but this need not be a disadvantage when growing food crops: sloping sites are often less prone to frost, for example, and may also expose crops to more beneficial sunlight. Steep slopes can be difficult to cultivate, however, unless you divide them into a series of level terraces; alternatively, plant rows across the slope to prevent soil erosion by heavy rain.

THE LAYOUT

Crops may be grown in rows right across the cultivated area, but many gardeners prefer to divide the kitchen garden into small beds, arranged as squares edged with boards or bricks, or as long, narrow beds about 1.2m (4ft) wide so that the centre may be reached from each side without treading on the soil. Every system has its benefits and advocates, and part of the adventure of growing

your own is experimenting with various options. Allow for paths of a practical width that lead to all areas of the garden. You will need access to water, whether from a mains tap or rainwater stored in a tank or water butt, and you will probably find a utility corner necessary, preferably nearby, for a compost heap and toolshed.

PERENNIAL CROPS

When designing a kitchen garden, plan the positions of permanent crops first. Fruit trees and bushes are often used to define the layout, but other crops remain in the same place year after year, such as asparagus, globe artichokes, rhubarb and perennial herbs. Most annual vegetables move to fresh soil each season to avoid pest and disease problems.

▷ THE IDEAL WIDTH *of access paths depends on their use: 30cm (12in) is enough between herb beds but 90cm (3ft) may be needed for the comfortable passage of a laden wheelbarrow.*

The ornamental kitchen garden

There is great satisfaction to be found in straight, disciplined rows of crops, but vegetables, fruit and herbs can also be used as imaginative design elements of the mixed border or flower garden. Among them you will discover glorious colours and shapes to rival those of many purely ornamental plants.

△ COLOURFUL, *frilled lettuces grow with nasturtiums, onions and borage in timber-edged beds.*

256 ▷ EXPLOIT THE *ornamental qualities of food plants by growing them in a geometric pattern of formal beds, defined by low box hedges.*

THE BENEFITS

Medieval gardeners regarded crops as decorative in addition to being utility plants, and it was only the advent of the horse-hoe that established straight lines and wide spacings. If you abandon the hoe-a-row philosophy, you will find yields actually increase when plants are grown close together in small beds, their foliage touching and suppressing weeds as well as shading the soil. Pests and diseases often fail to find crops when they are integrated with other flowering plants, and it is easy to tuck just a few plants here and there, making up a cosmopolitan community that offers a little of everything.

DESIGN IDEAS

Several traditional garden styles can be adapted for the ornamental kitchen garden. **The potager** is a formally planned layout in which geometric beds are edged with dwarf vegetables or salad crops, then filled with flowers and crops arranged like summer bedding around a tall centrepiece. **The cottage garden** is an easy, informal patchwork of fruit, flowers and vegetables, combined in an apparently artless style that makes maximum use of every corner. Or you can borrow from **the grand kitchen garden** style in which straight paths divide the area into equal-sized beds, usually four to accommodate traditional rotation schemes, edged with flowers for cutting and enclosed with trained fruit trees.

In an existing garden you could start by introducing a fruiting variety wherever you want a small tree or shrub, or erect a cane wigwam of purple-

• *see also:* BASIC CULINARY HERBS p284

◁ **LETTUCES GROW** *companionably with flowering annuals such as marigolds. Wedge-shaped beds, edged with rope tiles, are separated by a framework of gravel paths.*

podded peas or scarlet-flowered runner beans over untidy areas where bulb foliage is dying down. Sage and rosemary make exciting path-side shrubs, while annual crops can be combined with summer bedding – dwarf beans with geraniums, for example, or wallflowers with dwarf curly kale. A cordon-trained pear or thornless cut-leaf blackberry will clothe a pillar as prettily as a climbing rose, while paths may be edged with alpine strawberries, dwarf broad beans, mat-forming herbs like thyme and marjoram, or a mixture of carrots, parsley and dwarf bulbs.

THE VERTICAL DIMENSION

Many crops can be trained upwards. Fences and walls are often neglected, and yet their intensive use will sometimes double the potential of a small plot. Most fruits can be trained on fences and walls, including the walls of the house itself, and tall peas, beans, cucumbers, trailing squashes and outdoor tomatoes all benefit from the support and reflected warmth there. Thornless blackberries and loganberries, together with grape vines, can be trained on tripods, pillars and pergolas, or will scramble happily over an arbour shading a garden seat. These all occupy minimal space and cast so little shade that other vegetables and herbs may be grown at their base.

CONTAINER GARDENS

Although often seen as a substitute for open ground cultivation, containers extend both the cropping area and the decorative potential of any garden. Pots and tubs of herbs or salads can be clustered together on hard-surfaced areas, beside steps and doors for easy access or as ornamental groups on a patio; they are particularly useful for half-hardy crops that can be moved under cover when frost threatens. Half-barrels and other large containers may be planted with fruit trees or climbing crops, underplanted with a mixture of dwarf herbs and trailing bedding plants.

VEGETABLES IN THE BORDER

❖

Vegetable crops merge happily into flower borders if you place them according to their height.

FRONT OF BORDER: dwarf plants can be grown in rows or groups in front of all the others. Lettuces, beetroot and radicchio add colour and decorative leaf form that contrasts with ferny carrots and parsley.

MID-BORDER: asparagus, salsify and scorzonera are ideal here as flowering or foliage plants. Use rhubarb, Swiss chard and orache (mountain spinach) for eye-catching colour, combined with red Brussels sprouts and curly kale.

BACK OF BORDER: reserve space for tall crops such as globe artichokes, sweetcorn and herbs such as lovage, fennel and angelica, combined with tall peas and climbing beans on cane wigwams.

257

MAKING SPACE FOR FRUIT

❖

Trained fruits are the perfect choice where decorative highlights are needed, perhaps in the centre of a border or at the intersection of paths. Standard gooseberries and redcurrants make handsome individual features, while apples and pears (*right*) trained as cordons, espaliers and fans can flank paths or frame a gateway, especially if allowed to arch gracefully over the path. Try using rows of cordon-trained soft fruit as fruiting fences within the garden, or 'step-over' apples (single espaliers), 38–45cm (15–18in) high, as an edging to beds.

Developing a productive garden

You do not need green fingers to be sure of raising tasty crops. If you start with good-quality seeds and give healthy young plants the right spacings and the routine care they need, the plants will do the rest, especially if you concentrate on feeding the soil to improve its fertility.

△ **USEFUL AIDS** *to productivity include a fruit cage to keep birds off and a greenhouse for early sowings.*

◁ **ORGANIC MATTER** *can be added to the soil as garden compost. Make sure it is well rotted down before using.*

258

IMPROVING THE SOIL

Plants are only as good as the soil they grow in. Their roots prefer a moist, friable and fertile environment, and the more you can do to provide these conditions, the better your crops will be. Light, sandy soils are naturally friable but they need the addition of plenty of humus in the form of garden compost or well-rotted manure to keep them moist. The same materials will open up the texture of sticky, clay soils, allowing plant roots to penetrate deeply and use the nutrients. Fork in organic materials in autumn, or simply spread them on the surface of bare ground or between rows as a protective mulch. The addition of lime can also improve some soils (*see box, right*).

PLANTING

Transplant outdoors while plants are still young, about six weeks after sowing and when fully hardened off by being gradually acclimatized to outdoor temperatures over a period of 10–14 days. Make sure both plant and soil are moist. Then, using a trowel, dig out a hole large enough to take the rootball comfortably. Replace the soil over the rootball, firm into place and water the surrounding levelled soil; in dry weather, water the plant in the open hole and allow it to drain before refilling with soil. If the plants are large enough, mulch straight after planting to conserve moisture. Catch-cropping and inter-cropping (*see next page*) helps maintain a continuous supply of salads and vegetables.

• *see also:* DIGGING AND IMPROVING YOUR SOIL p180; MAKING COMPOST p182; FEEDING PLANTS p186

GENERAL CARE

Weeding Cultivated plants suffer in competition with weeds, which are more vigorous. Keep young crops weed-free until their foliage suppresses rivals by hoeing, mulching and weeding.

Watering Soaking plants thoroughly is more use than an occasional sprinkle. Leafy crops need regular watering, but other kinds benefit more from watering at critical times such as flowering or fruiting.

Feeding If the soil has been well-prepared with compost or manure, supplementary feeding will be needed only by the greediest crops. Choose a general (balanced) fertilizer for routine use, a nitrogen-rich feed for stimulating leaf growth after winter and a high-potash feed to improve flower and fruit quality.

KEEPING PLANTS HEALTHY

Pests and diseases are a natural part of garden life and cannot be kept at bay all the time. Problems are rarely serious if you take precautionary measures, such as using good-quality seeds and plants, choosing naturally resistant varieties, keeping the soil in good heart and clearing and destroying infected material promptly. Avoid the excessive use of chemicals that kill natural allies as well as pests. Use an environmentally friendly insecticide and fungicide.

PROTECTING CROPS

Cloches, cold frames or a greenhouse will extend the normal growing season by up to a month at each end, and will improve the quality of winter-hardy crops. Use cloches to warm the soil initially, to hasten germination and to

△ **A COLD FRAME** *is invaluable to overwinter, force or harden off plants ready for planting out. In summer it will provide extra growing room.*

protect growing plants from frost; in autumn they help ripen late crops or keep them growing for longer. A cold frame can be used for the same purpose, and also for hardening off crops before planting them out.

259

SOWING INDOORS

❖

You can make an early start and retain greater control over later batches of plants by sowing in fresh seed or multi-purpose compost in pots under cover.

1 *Fill the pot or tray with compost and level the top, then tap or lightly firm to settle the contents; water and allow to drain. Sow sparingly on the surface and cover with a thin layer of compost (use vermiculite if light needed to germinate). Cover with glass or plastic; keep warm.*

2 *When the seedlings are large enough to handle, hold each one carefully by a leaf and transplant, singly, to small pots or 5cm (2in) apart in trays of compost; water in and keep shaded for a few days.*

3 *Alternatively, sow direct in small pots or cell trays (modules), large seeds singly and others in small pinches.*

SOWING OUTDOORS

❖

Before sowing direct into the ground, prepare a seedbed by forking out any weeds, dressing the surface with 60g per sq m (2oz per sq yd) general fertilizer, then raking to produce a fine level tilth that is free of stones.

1 *Using a taut line or the edge of a board as a guide, inscribe a straight channel (drill) at the correct depth for the seeds. Water the drill first in dry weather.*

2 *Either sprinkle the seeds sparingly along the full length of the drill or space a small group of seeds at a measured distance apart.*

3 *Carefully cover the seeds with fine soil, gently tamping and watering this into place, and label the row. Protect with netting if birds are a problem.*

Home-grown salads

Freshness and variety are essential for a well-made salad, and you can ensure both qualities by raising your own salad crops. A host of flavours, colours and leafy delights may be gathered from a small bed throughout the season and, with the help of cloches, fleece or a cold frame, this profusion can be extended year-round.

△ **RADISHES CAN BE GROWN** *as a catch-crop between rows of lettuce.*

LETTUCE

Different varieties come in attractive guises. Butterheads (Bib lettuces) are soft-textured and grow faster than upright cos (romaine) varieties; crispheads (icebergs) enjoy plenty of water and sunshine; while loose-leaf kinds may be cut repeatedly from an early age. Red, brown and frilled lettuces add tempting colour and form to the salad bowl.

Cultivation

Sow little and often, 1cm (½in) deep in rows 15cm (6in) apart and thin seedlings to 15–23cm (6–9in) apart according to variety. Keep weed-free, water as required and feed two or three times during growth. Start harvesting early as batches usually mature together, about 8–12 weeks after sowing, and may then deteriorate quickly. Either gather a few leaves at a time from loose-leaf kinds, or cut complete plants down to a 2.5cm (1in) stump to allow for regrowth.

RADISHES

Summer varieties with small red, white or bicoloured roots mature in just three to four weeks and need frequent sowing for continuity. Larger Japanese (mooli) types and winter radishes are sown after the longest day for use three months later. Special low-temperature varieties may be grown under glass in winter.

Cultivation

Sow thinly, 1cm (½in) deep in short rows 15cm (6in) apart, every two weeks outdoors and four to six weeks in autumn and winter under glass. Thin seedlings to 2.5–7.5cm (1–3in) apart while still small. Water regularly for fast growth; crops on well-prepared soil need no feeding. Harvest summer kinds as soon as they are large enough, mooli varieties when 15cm (6in) long. Leave winter varieties in the ground and use as needed.

SALAD ONIONS

Often known as spring onions, these non-bulbing varieties can be available almost all year round and add a savoury flourish to salads. They like fertile conditions and may be grown as an edging to beds.

Cultivation

Sow every three to four weeks in spring and summer, 1cm (½in) deep, in rows 20cm (8in) apart or as 7.5-cm (3-in) wide bands 15cm (6in) apart; thin seedlings to 2.5cm (1in) apart. Sow in late summer for spring use, and cover

◁ **LETTUCE IS AN** *easily grown crop, with a range of enticing varieties. Frilly-leaved kinds are good value and stay usable over a long season.*

260

see also: Developing a productive garden p258; Greenhouse crops p270; Saving space with mini-vegetables p272

crops with cloches over winter. Weed regularly and water when dry. Harvest as soon as large enough, starting with the biggest thinnings, then pull up alternate plants, leaving the others to gain size.

OTHER SALAD CROPS
Many leaf crops can be used in varying amounts to enliven salads: these are just a few of the more popular kinds.

Chicory
Refreshingly bitter, crisp leaves in loose, round heads or tight, conical chicons. Red-leafed radicchio and green sugar-loaf chicory are grown in the same way as lettuce. Witloof chicory is sown in late spring, in rows 15cm (6in) apart, thinned to 20cm (8in) apart in the rows.

Red-leaf chicory 'Prima Rosa'

Dig up the roots in autumn, trim off the leaves, plant in pots and force in warmth and total darkness to produce blanched chicons.

Corn salad
Sometimes called lamb's lettuce (*Valerianella locusta*), this is a mild leaf crop sown in late summer for winter and spring use. Sow in drills 15cm (6in) apart and thin seedlings to 10cm (4in) apart; transplant thinnings to a cold frame or greenhouse for protection.

Land cress
An easily grown substitute for watercress, land or American cress is sown in spring for summer use, and in late summer for picking over winter. Grow 15cm (6in) apart each way and keep moist at all times. Plants self-seed and produce seedlings that may be transplanted.

Summer purslane
Portulaca oleracea has succulent, tangy leaves that may be cut or picked repeatedly over a long period. Sow by broadcasting seed in early summer in a warm, sunny position, thin seedlings to about 5cm (2in) apart and harvest as a cut-and-come-again crop.

CUT-AND-COME-AGAIN
❖

Most leafy salad vegetables can be grown as seedling crops, sown in strips or patches at close spacing. Harvest the plant tops with scissors when about 8cm (3in) tall, working across the patch gradually and leaving 2.5-cm (1-in) high stumps to regrow for a further two or three cuttings. Surplus lettuce, chicory and endive seeds can be blended to make your own salad mixture.

TIPS FOR SUCCESS

LETTUCE
○ Site summer lettuces in light shade, but choose an open, sunny position at other seasons.
○ Keep consistently moist, but do not overwater.
○ Seeds become dormant in hot weather; make summer sowings in the afternoon and cover with damp newspaper for 24 hours to keep cool.
○ Mulching plants on dry soils prevents them from bolting to seed early.

RADISHES
○ Radishes are brassicas, so do not grow where there is club-root disease.
○ Roots grow best in a bright position, but midsummer crops will appreciate light shade.
○ If plants run up to flower, leave them to produce their edible seedpods.
○ Watch out for slugs and flea beetles attacking seedlings.

261

SALAD ONIONS
○ Grow parsley nearby as a traditional deterrent against onion fly.
○ Sow very early crops under glass in modules, a few seeds to each cell.
○ Spring- and summer-sown crops take about eight weeks to mature, over-wintered plants 30–36 weeks.
○ Choose a hardy variety for late-summer sowings.

CATCH-CROPPING AND INTER-CROPPING
Maintain a continuous supply by sowing fast-maturing crops such as radishes, corn salad, land cress and turnips wherever ground is likely to be empty for a few weeks before or between other crops. Alternatively, allow similar crops to take advantage of the space between rows of slow-growing vegetables while their plants are still small. Use these empty spaces to sow seedlings for transplanting later, or to grow young plants on for a few weeks.

Growing peas and beans

High in protein and delicious when harvested fresh from the garden, peas and beans of all kinds are decorative vegetables that are typical of the kitchen garden in summer. They are good for the soil too, because bacteria in their roots draw nitrogen from the air and leave it in the ground for later crops to use.

△ **COLOURED VARIETIES** *of bean, such as these golden waxpods, are as prolific as plain green kinds and look attractive when served.*

▽ **PEAS AND DWARF BEANS** *enjoy the same soil preparation and can be grown side by side, the peas supported on canes and string to aid rapid growth and easy picking.*

262

PEAS

Round-seeded varieties are hardy and used for autumn or late winter sowings, whereas the sweeter, wrinkled kinds are sown from spring onwards. Ordinary peas produce fat green or purple pods filled with seeds for shelling, but some have flat (mangetout) and cylindrical (sugar-snap) fibreless pods that are picked young and eaten whole.

Cultivation

Sow 4–5cm (1½–2in) deep and 7.5cm (3in) apart in strips 23cm (9in) wide, in deeply dug and well-manured ground; spread lime on the surface if the soil is acid. Firm the soil after sowing and net against birds. Support when the first tendrils appear, with canes and netting or twiggy sticks that match the variety's height. Weed regularly and mulch when about 15cm (6in) high. Water in dry weather, especially when plants carry flowers or pods; harvest pods before they become large and fibrous. After cropping, cut plants at ground level and leave the roots to decay.

BROAD BEANS

Easy, prolific and reliably hardy, these are the first summer vegetables in most gardens. Both the young green, white or red seeds and also the immature pods are eaten. There are tall or short varieties, some robust enough to sow in autumn for the earliest crops.

Cultivation

Make two or three monthly sowings from late winter onwards, burying the large seeds 5cm (2in) deep and 23cm (9in) apart each way in well-dug, well-manured soil, limed if acid; also sow in mid- to late autumn for overwintering, or start seeds in pots under glass in midwinter. Mulch plants to prevent soils drying out, and support tall varieties with stakes and string. Water if necessary while plants are flowering and cropping. Start harvesting pods for cooking whole when about 7.5cm (3in) long, two to three weeks later for shelling.

RUNNER BEANS

With their vivid scarlet blooms, these are perhaps the most ornamental beans. They crop very heavily on fertile soils where their roots are always cool and moist. Provide strong support for the heavy top growth.

△ **RUNNER BEANS** *were first grown as colourful annual climbers rather than productive vegetables and are ideal to train over an archway.*

see also: THE ORNAMENTAL KITCHEN GARDEN p256; DEVELOPING A PRODUCTIVE GARDEN p258; GREENHOUSE CROPS p270

◁ **CLIMBING BEANS**
sown into these degradable whalehide pots can be planted out without any root disturbance.

FRENCH BEANS

Both dwarf and tall, twining kinds are grown for a number of purposes: pods may be eaten whole or sliced, or can be shelled for their seeds, either fresh (flageolets) or for drying (haricot beans). Pods are flat or cylindrical in various colours, often dramatically speckled.

Cultivation

Either sow direct outdoors about a month before the last frosts or start seeds in small individual pots under glass. Dig and manure the ground thoroughly before sowing seeds or planting out young plants. Give support in the form of canes, arranged either in rows or in the form of a wigwam. Water the plants twice-weekly from the time the flowers first open.

Cultivation

Sow in pots under glass or outdoors in rich, deeply dug soil three to four weeks before the last frosts. Sow 4–5cm (1½–2in) deep, spacing climbers as for runner beans and dwarf kinds 23cm (9in) apart each way or every 10cm (4in) in rows 45cm (18in) apart. Grow on like runner beans. Start picking before the seeds are prominent in the pods and repeat every three to four days.

TIPS FOR SUCCESS

PEAS
○ Sow maincrop and mangetout varieties once or twice in spring, early kinds every 3 weeks for succession.
○ For earliest pickings, start hardy varieties outdoors in late winter under cloches or in pots in a cold frame.
○ Peas like cool conditions, so keep moist and give midsummer crops light shade.
○ Space seeds carefully: peas dislike overcrowding.

BROAD BEANS
○ Pinch off the tips of main stems when the first pods have formed to hasten maturity and deter blackfly.
○ Sow dwarf varieties up to late summer in cool shade for a late crop.
○ Save surplus seeds for sowing as a green manure crop in spare ground.
○ In cold gardens cover autumn sowings with cloches or fleece.

RUNNER BEANS
○ Runner beans cannot stand frost, so make sure pot-grown plants are hardened off before planting out.
○ In clean, fertile ground, plants can grow in the same place each year with permanent supports.
○ Dwarf varieties, or tall kinds kept pinched back to 45cm (18in) high, need no supports but benefit from a straw mulch to keep pods clean.
○ Grow with a few sweet peas to improve the beans' chances of pollination.

FRENCH BEANS
○ Harvest lasts for 6–8 weeks, so make two or three further sowings of dwarf kinds for continuity.
○ Earth up stems and support dwarf varieties with twiggy sticks to keep crops clean.
○ For haricot beans, leave the pods on the plant until brown, hang up complete plants to dry, then shell out the seeds for storing.

263

SUPPORTING CLIMBING BEANS

❖

Sturdy support is essential for the lush top growth. Use 2.5m (8ft) canes or treated 5 x 5cm (2 x 2in) timber set firmly in the ground and tied securely at the top for stability. Proprietary fittings are available for securing the tops of wigwams and also for joining the canes in short rows, sometimes with built-in watering arrangements.

Start harvesting when beans are about 15cm (6in) long and check every two to three days for further pods.

Sow seeds 5cm (2in) deep and 15–20cm (6–8in) apart at the foot of each supporting cane.

Mulch with straw or well-rotted garden compost after germination or planting, to conserve moisture.

Growing root crops

The most popular root crops for garden cultivation are beetroot, carrots, parsnips and potatoes. They give good yields from a small area and share a preference for light, open, well-cultivated soil, which their roots can penetrate with little effort, together with a reasonable degree of fertility.

BEETROOT

As well as the familiar round red beetroot, varieties may have white or yellow flesh and flattened, barrel or tapering shapes. Fast-maturing 'baby' beet and large maincrop storing varieties are available, although many can be used for both purposes.

Cultivation

Sow 2cm (¾in) deep in rows 23cm (9in) apart for early varieties, maincrops 30cm (12in) apart. Thin

▽ **A GOOD CROP OF BEETROOT** *will result if the seedlings are thinned at an early stage, up to 15cm (6in) apart for the largest roots, but less for 'baby beets'.*

to 10–15cm (4–6in) apart; alternatively space plants 15cm (6in) apart each way. Weed at first, then mulch with garden compost or grass clippings; water every two to three weeks in dry weather. Pull early roots when 5cm (2in) across. Lift maincrops in autumn, twisting off the foliage; store in dry sand or compost.

CARROTS

Varieties with small, sweet roots are useful for both early and successional sowings; large maincrop kinds for storing. Choose varieties according to the time of year crops are required.

Cultivation

Sow thinly, 1cm (½in) deep in rows 15cm (6in) apart, every two to three weeks from spring until midsummer. Keep moist but not waterlogged; weed carefully until seedlings have two or three true leaves, then mulch with compost or grass clippings. Thin several times to leave plants finally about 7.5cm (3in) apart. Pull as soon as large enough; maincrops may be over-wintered under straw on light soils, or dug in autumn and stored in dry sand.

PARSNIPS

These sweet winter roots are hardy and remain in the ground until they are

△ **FRESHLY HARVESTED PARSNIPS** *have a sweet flavour. They can be left in the ground until they are required, without deteriorating.*

needed. Seeds have a limited lifespan and should be bought fresh each year.

Cultivation

Make a single sowing in spring, 1cm (½in) deep, in rows 30cm (12in) apart, either as pinches of seed 15cm (6in) apart or continuously; thin to leave single seedlings at this spacing. Water, weed and mulch as for carrots. Harvest roots as required from autumn onwards.

AVOIDING CARROT FLY

❖

- Hide carrot rows as intercrops among onions.

- Grow resistant varieties.

- Surround plants with a 45cm (18in) high screen of polythene or fleece.

- Avoid releasing the irresistible carrot scent by sowing sparsely to make thinning unnecessary; or soak plants thoroughly after thinning.

- Sow in mid-spring and midsummer when fly populations are lower.

264

See also: DEVELOPING A PRODUCTIVE GARDEN p258; SAVING SPACE WITH MINI-VEGETABLES p272

POTATOES

Maincrop varieties are useful pioneers for new ground; early kinds occupy less space and yield welcome crops of new potatoes from early summer onwards.

Cultivation

Six weeks before planting, lay seed tubers in trays to 'chit' (produce short green sprouts). Starting in early spring, plant first earlies 10–15cm (4–6in) deep, every 30cm (12in), in rows 45–60cm (18–24in) apart; follow in mid-spring with other varieties, 38cm (15in) apart in rows 75cm (30in) apart. Earth up growing plants for frost protection and to avoid green tubers. Water every two to three weeks. Start lifting earlies when the flowers first open, later kinds when the top growth turns brown. Store in boxes or paper sacks in a dark, frost-free place.

EARLY ROOT CROPS

For very early beetroot and carrots, sow in cell trays or modules under glass for planting out in spring after hardening off. Choose early varieties, round-rooted in the case of carrots, and sow a pinch

▷ **EARTH UP POTATO PLANTS** *by raking soil up into a neat ridge. Earth up all varieties in early summer when plants have made 20cm (8in) of growth, leaving the top 5cm (2in) exposed.*

△ **A HOME-MADE 'POGO'** *potato planter helps you make planting holes 10–15cm (4–5cm) deep.*

(six to eight carrot seeds, two or three beetroot capsules) in each cell. Germinate in warmth, then grow in a cooler place until large enough to plant out as unthinned clusters. Space a little further apart than usual.

TIPS FOR SUCCESS

BEETROOT
- Soak seeds in water for an hour to improve germination.
- Monogerm varieties reduce the need for thinning by producing a single plant.
- Start sowing a month before the last frosts; repeat every 4 weeks until midsummer.
- Small roots need 8–12 weeks to mature, maincrops 14–16 weeks.

CARROTS
- Sow a fast-maturing variety in late winter or early spring under cover, and again in early autumn to extend the season.
- Make early and late outdoor sowings in warm, sheltered positions.
- Early varieties take 7–10 weeks to mature, maincrop 10–16 weeks.
- On heavy or stony soils, grow round or short-rooted varieties.

PARSNIPS
- Sow on a still day because seeds are papery and light.
- Warm soils with a floating mulch if sowing before mid-spring.
- Avoid hoeing too near the plants – damaged roots are prone to canker.
- Mark rows with canes in autumn before the foliage dies down.

POTATOES
- First earlies take 12–14 weeks to mature, second earlies 15–18 weeks, maincrops 18–22 weeks.
- Always plant healthy tubers, certified disease-free.
- Adding plenty of compost or well-rotted manure improves yields.
- Choose varieties carefully: some are more resistant to pests, disease or drought than others.

265

The cabbage family

The brassica group is a varied race of leaf and stem vegetables, all enjoying rich, moist soil that is firm and alkaline. If these conditions are satisfied, you can be certain of high-quality crops all year round, especially in winter when other vegetables may be scarce.

Cauliflower ready for harvesting

CABBAGES

Round-headed or pointed, green or red, plain-leafed and savoy, there are cabbages to suit every taste; they are sown at various times of year according to their type. For garden use, choose fast-growing, compact varieties that stand for a long time without deterioration.

Cultivation

Sow 2.5cm (1in) deep where plants are to grow or in a nursery bed for transplanting; thin to 7.5cm (3in) apart. When about six weeks old transplant firmly to final positions in good light. Plants may also be raised in pots and modules under glass. Space spring

▽ FOR THE BEST CROPS *of solid Brussels sprouts, plants such as 'Oliver', shown here, need wide spacing in firm ground. Cover the plants with netting to foil hungry pigeons.*

CLUBROOT
❖

This root disease is perhaps the most serious ailment of brassicas. As a preventive, always lime the soil before planting any variety, and do not grow brassicas in the same place two years running. If you have clubroot, try growing plants in pots for as long as possible, so that they have a headstart when finally planted out.

---

cabbages 25cm (10in) apart each way, summer/autumn varieties 38–45cm (15–18in) apart and winter kinds 50cm (20in) each way. Keep the soil moist (mulching helps), and check regularly for pests such as caterpillars, aphids and whitefly; net against birds if necessary. Harvest as required, leaving 5–7.5cm (2–3in) stumps to resprout a further crop of small, leafy cabbages.

BRUSSELS SPROUTS

This hardy crop does not occupy much room if you choose a compact F1 hybrid and harvest the leafy plant tops when the lowest sprouts are just half-formed. Early, maincrop and late varieties extend the season from late summer to early spring.

Cultivation

Sow under glass in late winter or in a nursery bed outdoors in spring, 1cm

(½in) deep, and treat as for cabbages. Transplant finally when about 15cm (6in) high, 50–60cm (20–24in) apart each way and firm in. Feed at midsummer, but not afterwards, and support leaning stems with stakes. Start picking when lowest sprouts are large enough; remove leaves up to the level picked. In a cold winter, dig up complete stems and hang upside down under cover for picking.

CAULIFLOWERS

Cauliflowers are the greediest vegetable and a test of any gardener's skill: grow them in very well-manured soil and water regularly for best results. Green, yellow and red varieties are available, as well as the traditional white kinds and there is also a perennial form which makes a tall, branching bush.

Cultivation

Sow summer varieties in early spring, others a few weeks later, under glass or outdoors, as for Brussels sprouts. Water before and after transplanting to 45–60cm (18–24in) apart each way in rich, well-limed soil. Harvest while heads are still firm and tight; in cold weather

See also: THE ORNAMENTAL KITCHEN GARDEN p256; DEVELOPING A PRODUCTIVE GARDEN p258; SAVING SPACE WITH MINI-VEGETABLES p272

266

△ RED- OR CURLY-LEAFED *brassicas make an attractive contribution to decorative planting schemes.*

TIPS FOR SUCCESS

CABBAGES
○ F1 hybrids are often more uniform in size, with some pest or disease resistance.
○ If space is limited, concentrate on winter kinds, which are usually the most welcome.
○ Explore oriental brassicas for interesting shapes and flavours, but do not sow too early or they may bolt.

BRUSSELS SPROUTS
○ If space is short, transplant between rows of early potatoes.
○ Set young transplants with their lowest leaves at ground level.
○ Hard sprouts need very firm soil, so tread back any stems loosened by wind or frost.
○ The leafy tops are edible when picked as tasty 'greens'.

CAULIFLOWERS
○ In small gardens, grow mini-cauliflowers 15cm (6in) apart each way for individual servings.
○ Mulching helps keep the plants consistently moist.
○ Break some of the outer leaves to cover maturing heads and protect them from frost or sunshine.
○ Start cutting while heads are small, as crops often mature simultaneously.

BROCCOLI
○ Plants tolerate lower fertility than other brassicas, and are an easy alternative to cauliflowers.
○ The fastest varieties take 10–11 weeks to mature, others a month longer.
○ Choose a warm position for the earliest crops and provide light shade for summer sowings.
○ Sow an early variety in late summer and transplant to a cold frame for spring use.

267

dig up plants and hang upside down in a cool place for up to three weeks.

BROCCOLI

The spears of cauliflower-like florets make broccoli (calabrese) a popular crop, easily grown in the garden if you choose a fast-maturing F1 hybrid. Many produce secondary side shoots after the main head is cut.

Cultivation

Sow little and often in succession from early spring to midsummer. Sow in groups of two to three seeds in modules under glass or outdoors, 23cm (9in) apart each way to avoid any root disturbance; thin to a single seedling. Water regularly and mulch. Harvest the central head while still tight, feed with nitrogenous fertilizer and cut resulting side shoots when 10cm (4in) long.

SPROUTING BROCCOLI AND KALE

❖

These popular brassicas provide succulent pickings of green, white or purple shoots early in the year. Sow in a nursery bed in spring for transplanting in summer 45–60cm (18–24in) apart. The young shoots start forming in late winter and may be cut over a long season.

Extending the choice

There is no end to the range of vegetables you can try. Apart from the main salad, cabbage, root, and pea and bean groups, several other important crops deserve consideration if you decide to expand the variety of fresh produce you grow.

△ **RAISE MARROWS** *from seed in small, individual pots under glass. Made from newspaper, these pots are degradable in soil.*

BULBING ONIONS

An essential vegetable for any kitchen and easily grown if you plant sets (immature bulbs already several weeks old). They tolerate poor soil, give a flying start to the season and often mature earlier than plants from seed.

Cultivation

Choose a site manured for a previous crop, or fork in plenty of compost and firm well. Plant sets with a trowel, every 7.5–10cm (3–4in) in rows 25–30cm (10–12in) apart, leaving their tips at soil level; start maincrop sets in early spring, over-wintered kinds in mid-autumn.

Weed regularly (take care when hoeing as their roots are very shallow), water in dry weather and feed at monthly intervals. Start harvesting when bulbs are large enough. For storing, wait until tops die down, fork up and spread in the sun to dry; keep in a cool, frost-free place.

◁ **A POPULAR AND HARDY** *member of the onion family, leeks are undemanding plants that may be tucked in wherever there is space. Their foliage casts little shade over nearby plants.*

GARLIC

An increasingly popular vegetable, garlic is very hardy and trouble-free to grow. Start in autumn because plants need several weeks at low temperatures if they are to make good bulbs.

Cultivation

Prepare the ground as for bulbing onions. Separate bulbs into cloves, and plant single cloves, point upwards, 15–20cm (6–8in) apart each way in holes 7.5cm (3in) deep. Alternatively, pot bulbs up individually and keep in a cold frame until they can be transplanted in spring. Water in dry weather and keep weed-free. When the leaf tips turn yellow, fork up bulbs and suspend or spread out to dry in the sun. Store in a frost-free, dry place.

LEEKS

Whether grown as fat, short-stemmed plants or pencil-slim mini-leeks, this undemanding crop can be available for up to eight months of the year. There are early, mid-season and late varieties, although their seasons of use overlap.

Cultivation

Buy plants in early summer, or sow in a nursery bed outdoors in spring, 1–2cm (½–¾in) deep, and thin seedlings to 4cm (1½in) apart. Plant out when about 15–23cm (6–8in) high with two or three strong leaves, spacing them every 15cm (6in) in rows 30cm (12in) apart.

△ **DRY GARLIC** *and maincrop onions thoroughly, then store bulbs in an airy place to keep them sound for as long as possible.*

See also: THE ORNAMENTAL KITCHEN GARDEN p256; DEVELOPING A PRODUCTIVE GARDEN p258; SAVING SPACE WITH MINI-VEGETABLES p272

Either plant on the surface, or for a longer blanch make holes 15cm (6in) deep with a dibber and drop a seedling in each; fill the hole with water to settle plants. Water if dry and feed once or twice up to late summer. Harvest as soon as they reach a usable size.

MARROWS AND COURGETTES

The squash family also embraces other summer kinds such as custard and spaghetti squash, and winter types that include pumpkins and edible gourds for storing. All are grown in the same way as marrows and courgettes.

Cultivation

Plants are not hardy, so start them in pots under glass a month before planting out. Sow seeds on edge, singly, 2.5cm (1in) deep in small pots. Dig a hole for each plant, 30cm (12in) deep and wide, and half-fill with decayed manure or garden compost; top up with soil, leaving a depression for watering. After the last frosts, plant in the centre of the depression. Water lavishly every week when flowering starts, and mulch to conserve soil moisture. Pinch out tips of trailing

△ GOLD COURGETTES *are as tasty as the more familiar green varieties and make an ideal crop for home cultivation.*

△ LEEKS HAVE BEEN GROWN *through a mulch of newspaper. A light mulch will also keep onions moist, but the bulbs should be exposed to sunlight as soon as they ripen.*

varieties when about 60cm (24in) long. Start to gather courgettes when about 10cm (4in) long with the flower still attached; cut other squash when large enough.

STORING SQUASHES
❖

Harvest pumpkins and other winter kinds before the autumn frosts, ideally when their stems start to dry out. Cut each fruit with a long piece of stem, and cure the skin for two weeks in warm sunshine, outdoors or under glass; when the skin is hard and sounds hollow if tapped, the squash is ready to store, on a shelf or suspended in netting in a warm, airy place.

TIPS FOR SUCCESS

ONIONS
○ Watering or feeding maincrop onions after midsummer may shorten their storage life.
○ Use split, thick-necked and flowering bulbs first as these do not keep well.
○ Some gardeners alternate rows of onions and carrots to confuse invading carrot root fly.

GARLIC
○ Garlic prefers light soil, so work plenty of grit into heavy ground.
○ Plants often flower, but this does not affect their storage life.
○ Viruses can cause yellow leaf markings: infected bulbs are still safe to eat, however.
○ Save bulbs from a healthy crop for replanting the following year.

LEEKS
○ Sow earlier crops in late winter, under glass in trays or modules.
○ For a longer blanch, draw soil up the stems as they develop.
○ Early varieties are not hardy and should be used before winter.

MARROWS AND COURGETTES
○ Grow trailing marrows under sweetcorn plants for ground cover.
○ Marrows and pumpkins planted on the top of completed compost heaps revel in the extra fertility.
○ Increase marrow yields by cutting smaller fruits for immediate use, leaving the last few to ripen for storing.
○ Tying courgette stems to vertical stakes as they grow improves air circulation and reduces mildew.

269

Greenhouse crops

In temperate climates where the seasons are unpredictable, a greenhouse can ensure success with crops that need more warmth than might be available outdoors. Under glass, crops such as dwarf French beans, winter lettuces and strawberries can be raised to maturity out of season. In the summer, four cold-sensitive vegetables are particular favourites for growing bags, pots and greenhouse borders: these are tomatoes, cucumbers, peppers and aubergines.

Plum tomatoes 'Super Roma'

TOMATOES

Although many varieties of tomato may be grown outdoors in a good year, early heavy yields are more predictable under glass. Choose an indoor variety described as short-jointed to ensure the maximum number of fruit trusses in a limited space.

Cultivation

Plants may be bought or started from seed, sowing them at about 18°C (65°F) in midwinter for growing with heat, and in early spring for unheated greenhouses. Sow thinly in pots and just cover with compost for pricking out later, or sow two seeds in a 7.5cm (3in) pot and remove the weaker seedling. Keep warm and evenly moist, and pot on if necessary. Plant out tomatoes when the first cluster of flower buds is visible. Water and feed regularly, remove the side shoots from tall (cordon or indeterminate) varieties, and support on canes or strings. Pinch out growing tips two leaves beyond the fourth or fifth flower truss. Harvest fruits when fully coloured, removing lower yellow leaves at the same time. Clear out the old stems at the end of the season.

CUCUMBERS

Indoor varieties of cucumber need high temperatures and humidity to produce their heavy crops of slim, tender fruits. All-female types are easiest to grow, because others need daily checking to remove male flowers and so prevent fertilization (this results in a bitter flavour).

▷ CUCUMBERS
grown under glass can produce heavy yields.

Cultivation

Buy plants in late spring or sow seeds individually in early spring, 1cm (½in) deep in 7.5cm (3in) pots and germinate at 26°C (80°F). Move on into 11cm (4¼in) pots and provide a thin cane

◁ WITH THEIR EXTENSIVE
root system, tomato plants need to be grown in tubs or generous-sized pots to ensure maximum yields.

POPULAR GROWING METHODS UNDER GLASS

❖

POTS: 23cm (9in) is the smallest practical size of container; use a rich, soil-based compost (for example, John Innes No 3).

GROWING BAGS: Plant two or three tomato or cucumber plants (three of peppers or aubergines) in each bag. For heavier crops use two growing bags, one sitting above the other, with the plastic cut out underneath each plant to encourage deeper rooting.

SOIL BORDERS: Dig in plenty of well-rotted compost or decayed manure before planting, and change or sterilize the soil each year to prevent the spread of infection from one crop to the next.

270

See also: DESIGNING A KITCHEN GARDEN p254; DEVELOPING A PRODUCTIVE GARDEN p258; SAVING SPACE WITH MINI-VEGETABLES p272

TRAINING PLANTS

❖

Tie cucumbers or cordon varieties of tomato to upright canes or gently twist their stems around strings suspended from the greenhouse roof. If you have only a few plants, space them out and allow two low side shoots to grow, one on each side, to form further stems that can be trained at an angle from the main plant. Bush tomatoes need no training; use short twigs or canes to support laden branches.

for training the main shoot. Keep warm and in a moist atmosphere. When plants have 8–10 leaves, plant out and train upwards as for tomatoes. Feed every two weeks and pinch out the growing tip when the main shoot reaches the roof; pinch out side shoots two leaves beyond a female flower (look for the tiny cucumber at its base). Cut fruits as soon as they are large enough.

PEPPERS

Both sweet and hot chilli peppers can be grown in the same conditions as for tomatoes, trained on canes or wires to keep them tidy. Surplus fruits can be dried in warmth for winter use.

Cultivation

Buy plants in late spring or sow in early spring in the same way as for tomatoes,

Aubergine 'Asian Bride'

in a temperature of 20–25°C (68–77°F); grow the seedlings on at 12–15°C (54–60°F). Pot on as necessary in soil-based compost. Plant in late spring, and water and feed with tomato fertilizer regularly. Tie main stems to canes or strings, pinching out the growing tips of sweet peppers when about 38cm (15in) high; chilli peppers can be trained as cordons up to about 1.5m (5ft). Gather fruits when they are fully coloured.

AUBERGINES

A popular crop with heavy, waxy, highly ornamental fruits that may be purple, white or maroon/white striped. Grow several plants because each will set only four to five full-sized fruits.

Cultivation

Grow as for peppers, keeping the seedlings at 15–18°C (60–65°F). Plant in mid- or late spring, support plants with canes and pinch out the growing tip when about 30cm (12in) high. Dampen down the greenhouse regularly during flowering, and when five fruits have formed, remove any further side shoots and flowers. Feed with tomato fertilizer every time you water. Harvest fruit when fully coloured and still shiny.

TIPS FOR SUCCESS

TOMATOES

○ Too much water or fertilizer and too little sunshine can all dilute the flavour of the fruit.

○ Always use a tomato or high-potash fertilizer as excessive nitrogen produces leaves rather than fruit.

○ Check regularly for pests such as aphids, whitefly and red spider mite.

○ Help flowers to set fruit by tapping the supporting canes or strings and damping the surroundings on a warm, sunny day.

○ Ripen green fruits at the end of the season by spreading them in a box with a ripe apple or banana.

CUCUMBERS

○ When planting in a border, set plants on a mound of soil for good drainage.

○ Cucumbers need much more humidity than tomatoes, so keep them apart in the same greenhouse.

○ Make sure no fruits are overlooked and left to turn yellow, as cropping may then cease.

○ Use clean compost, pots and labels to avoid fungal diseases, and ventilate in hot weather.

PEPPERS

○ Watch out for aphids, whitefly and red spider mites: spray as necessary.

○ Harvesting sweet peppers while still green encourages the production of more fruits and a higher overall yield.

AUBERGINES

○ Start plants earlier than peppers if possible, because crops take five months to mature.

○ Protect young plants against fluctuations in temperature, especially on cool nights.

271

Saving space with mini-vegetables

Fist-size cauliflowers and carrots no larger than a little finger are part of a revolution in attitudes to food crops. The emphasis is changing from monster crops to compact varieties planted close together so that a tiny patch can yield a whole range of fresh, more delicately-flavoured, miniature vegetables.

△ **COMPARED TO** *demanding, full-sized cauliflower plants, mini-varieties produce firm, individual portions from a small plot.*

THINK SMALL

The basic methods of cultivation are the same as for normal vegetables, with one essential difference: compact growing varieties are planted closer together, giving a high density of small plants that are harvested while still young. Many mature faster than their larger relatives, which permits a quick turnover of vegetables and the chance to grow more in succession. This method is ideally suited to cultivation in small beds, with plants arranged in compact groups to produce a patchwork of varied crops at different stages of maturity.

THE GROUNDWORK

The total yield from a small plot managed in this way over the whole season is quite large, so fertile soil is essential. Work in plenty of garden compost, well-rotted manure or a proprietary concentrated manure when preparing the ground at the start of the season, and again after

272

MINI-PLANTS AND MINI-PRODUCE

It is important to distinguish between normal varieties (for example, leeks) that tolerate close spacings, yielding smaller produce but taking the usual time to mature, and mini-vegetables (some lettuces, turnips and dwarf kale), bred to make small plants at high density, often maturing earlier. There are also baby varieties that are grown in the normal way but yield miniature produce: baby sweetcorn, tiny Brussels sprouts and small-seeded broad beans are popular examples.

◁ **WITH THEIR NATURALLY** *compact and upright habit, small cos lettuce varieties such as 'Little Gem' are the perfect option for high-density planting schemes.*

• *see also:* BASIC CULINARY HERBS p284

GUIDE TO SPACING AND RATE OF GROWTH

VARIETY	SPACING (within rows)	SPACING (between rows)	TIME TO MATURITY	SIZE AT MATURITY
Beetroot 'Pronto'	2.5cm (1in)	15cm (6in)	12 weeks	5cm (2in) across
Cabbage 'Minicole', 'Protovoy' (savoy)	15cm (6in)	15cm (6in)	12–20 weeks	from 8cm (3in) across
Calabrese 'Trixie'	15cm (6in)	15cm (6in)	10–12 weeks	8–10cm (3–4in) diam.
Carrot, Amsterdam or Nantes type	1cm (½in)	15cm (6in)	10–12 weeks	finger-thickness
Cauliflower 'Dominant', 'Idol'	13cm (5in)	15cm (6in)	15 weeks	8cm (3in) diam.
Kale 'Showbor'	15cm (6in)	15cm (6in)	14–16 weeks	30cm (12in) high
Kohl Rabi 'Logo'	2.5cm (1in)	15cm (6in)	10 weeks	4–5cm (1½–2in) across
Leek 'King Richard'	1cm (½in)	15cm (6in)	12–14 weeks	2cm (¾in) thick
Lettuce 'Little Gem', 'Tom Thumb'	15cm (6in)	15cm (6in)	8–12 weeks	15cm (6in) diam.
Parsnip 'Gladiator'	8cm (3in)	15cm (6in)	20 weeks	2.5–5cm (1–2in) thick
Potato 'Rocket', 'Swift'	25cm (10in)	25cm (10in)	12 weeks	5cm (2in) across
Turnip 'Tokyo Cross'	2.5cm (1in)	15cm (6in)	7–8 weeks	2.5–5cm (1–2in) across

273

clearing one crop to make way for the next. No extra fertilizer should be necessary, but a compost mulch round young plants helps sustain fast growth and can be forked in between crops to improve soil fertility and structure.

THE PLAN
Start early by making the first sowings under glass in pots or modules, cluster-sown where appropriate, and planting these out under cloches or fleece. At planting time start another batch in the same way for succession; this ensures that the ground is never empty, because there is always another sowing waiting to follow on. Plant or sow (crops such as parsnips must be sown direct) in rows or

blocks at close spacings (see box above), siting similar-sized crops next to each other so that none competes unfairly for light. Keep the ground evenly moist to promote the fast, consistent growth essential for success.

WHICH VEGETABLES?
Many normal varieties can be grown closer together than usual to give smaller produce: maincrop onions produce medium-sized bulbs at 4cm (1½in) apart, for example; early potatoes can be spaced as close as 25cm (10in) apart each way; and slender types of carrot grow happily 5cm (2in) apart each way. Special varieties have also been developed that are naturally small at maturity and these

are often the best choice where space is limited or only a few vegetables are needed. When harvesting any variety, start by using every alternate plant, leaving the others to continue growing.

△ **ROUND CARROT** *varieties may be sown and grown in clusters and quickly produce juicy, bite-sized roots at close spacing.*

Growing tree fruits

Where there is room for a specimen tree in the garden, the various types of tree fruit (or 'top fruit') offer produce as well as decorative beauty. Most kinds can also be trained in ornamental forms to create space-saving screens, dividers or garden features, especially if grown on dwarfing rootstocks.

Apples in storage

APPLES

Perhaps the most popular of all tree fruits, this is also the easiest to grow if you choose a regional variety suited to your district and type of soil. Where possible, grow at least two varieties that flower at the same time to ensure good pollination.

Cultivation

Dig and manure the ground well, and make sure it is free-draining. Plant a bare-root tree while dormant, or a container-grown specimen any time the soil is workable. Make a planting hole large enough to take the rootball comfortably, burying it at the same depth as the previous soil mark, and stake or support securely. After planting, and every spring thereafter, spread a 5cm (2in) mulch of decayed manure around the tree or feed with general fertilizer at 70g per sq m (2oz per sq yd). Keep weed-free and water young trees every 10–14 days in dry weather. Young fruitlets naturally thin themselves in early summer, but any clusters remaining should be thinned to one or two fruits. Pick fruits as soon as they part easily from the branch: early varieties should be consumed as

◁ **PRUNED AS A** *mophead standard for a formal lawn feature, this 'James Grieve' dessert apple demonstrates the adaptability of tree fruit.*

soon as they are ripe; later varieties can be stored in a cool, frost-free place, in boxes or perforated polythene bags.

PEARS

These need a warmer position than apples but often thrive on poorer soils. As pears flower a few weeks earlier, avoid frosty sites or train trees on a warm wall. Most varieties need a pollination partner nearby in order to set well.

Cultivation

Prepare the ground and plant in the same way as for apples. Trees benefit from a high-nitrogen feed in spring, at a rate of 105g per sq m (3oz per sq yd), followed by a mulch of decayed manure. Thin in early summer, as for apples. Start harvesting as soon as the first varieties turn colour, testing each fruit to see if it comes away easily; most varieties need to be stored for a few weeks to finish ripening (test if they are ready by gently pressing the stalk end).

PLUMS AND GAGES

These succulent fruits are plentiful after a mild spring but are occasionally spoilt by late frosts. The best varieties are sweet and melting, especially gages, which deserve the warmest position, preferably against a warm wall; damsons, on the other hand, are very hardy and may be grown as hedge trees or windbreaks.

• *see also:* FEEDING PLANTS p186; THE ORNAMENTAL KITCHEN GARDEN p256; DEVELOPING A PRODUCTIVE GARDEN p258; PRUNING AND TRAINING FRUIT p278

Cultivation

Grow in full sun with protection from frosts. Prepare, plant and cultivate in the same way as for apples, and feed with nitrogen every spring (*see Pears, above*). Thin fruits after the natural midsummer drop, and support laden branches that might break. Harvest fruits when they part easily with their stalks, especially before heavy rain, which can cause ripening fruits to split; use immediately, freezing or bottling any surplus.

CHERRIES

Dessert (sweet) varieties are very choice, but you will need to protect them from birds; culinary (acid) varieties are less popular with birds and are easier to grow in shady gardens. The two types are pruned in different ways. Choose a dwarfing rootstock and a self-fertile variety if you are growing a single tree.

Cultivation

Prepare, plant and cultivate in the same way as for apples (above). Add plenty of compost or manure to light soils, and choose a sunny position for sweet cherries; full sun or light shade for acid kinds. Fruits do not need thinning.

PEACHES, NECTARINES AND APRICOTS

◆

These flower very early and succeed only where springs are frost-free and summers warm and sunny. Try growing one in the greenhouse, or against a warm wall where it can be covered with a curtain of polythene sheeting against frost and also peach leaf curl disease. Fruits need rigorous thinning to 15cm (6in) apart for good size (as shown); varieties are self-fertile but may need hand-pollination in a cold season.

Harvest as soon as they are ripe and before they split, picking or cutting complete with stalks. Use immediately and freeze or bottle the surplus.

◁ MOST PEAR

varieties enjoy heat and summer sun and training a pear tree as a fan against a warm wall will ensure good crops in a cool garden.

TIPS FOR SUCCESS

APPLES
○ Avoid diseases by choosing resistant varieties rather than treating problems when they arise.
○ Prop up heavily laden branches to prevent breakage.
○ Grow grass right up to the stem of vigorous, established trees to control their growth.
○ Growing single cordons enables you to build up a collection of apple varieties in a small space.

PEARS
○ Gather up young fruitlets that fall early, as these often contain pests.
○ Good drainage is very important, although pears are also less drought-tolerant than apples.
○ Pears do not ripen all together: trees will need picking over several times.
○ Pears need less pruning than apples and tolerate harder pruning back.

PLUMS AND GAGES
○ Even self-fertile varieties crop more heavily with a compatible pollinator that blooms at the same time.
○ Only prune when trees are actively growing, as wounds then heal quickly.
○ Train as fans, not cordons or espaliers.
○ 'Pixie' is a dwarf rootstock to consider.

CHERRY
○ Prune during active growth to avoid disease problems.
○ Water copiously and regularly in a dry season, especially wall-trained trees.

POLLINATION
○ If you can grow only one variety of a tree fruit, choose a self-fertile kind.
○ Most varieties (including self-fertile ones) crop better with a pollinating partner, another variety that flowers at the same time and, in the case of plums and cherries, which belongs to a compatible group. Consult an informative catalogue before buying.

277

Pruning and training fruit

Most soft and tree fruits will give a crop of some kind if left to develop unchecked from one season to the next. However, pruning and training are valuable methods of controlling growth. They help to create plants that are healthier, more attractive and, above all, consistently give heavy yields of high-quality produce.

△ **CORDON-TRAINED PEARS** *make efficient use of a wall or fence and allow different varieties to be grown for cross-pollination.*

DEFINITIONS

Pruning involves the removal of all surplus or misplaced growth, partly to maintain size but also to stimulate later development in a particular way – changing direction, for example, or encouraging fruit rather than leaf buds.

Training is the complementary art of steering this growth in ways that suit the type of plant and its position, with the aim of improving both its appearance and its yield. While the same basic principles are involved in creating all trained forms (see panel), in practice the ultimate shape you want will determine how they are applied.

BUSHES

This is an easy and productive shape to form and maintain, although it can occupy a lot of space in a small garden. Standards and half-standards are simply bushes on single, straight stems of varying heights. A young bush should have three to five main branches, which will develop if the main stem of a one-year-old tree is pruned back after planting. Shorten these branches by half in winter to produce secondary branches. The following winter, select the best seven or eight shoots as the permanent branches, and shorten them by half again. Thereafter, tip these main branches each winter, and shorten side shoots to three to five buds to maintain shape.

CORDONS

A cordon is a single-stemmed apple, pear, gooseberry or redcurrant, grown upright or at an oblique angle of about 45°; multiple cordons have two or more parallel stems, each formed and pruned in the same way. Tie the leader (main stem) to a strong cane or stake, leaving

278

△ **ACID CHERRY VARIETIES,** *such as 'Morello', are ideal candidates for fan-training on a wall.*

ROOTSTOCKS

❖

Most tree fruit varieties are grafted on to rootstocks of known vigour, so the eventual tree's size is predictable: this can reduce the amount of pruning needed to maintain trained form, and helps trees adjust to different soil conditions. Each fruit has its own types of rootstock, which can range from very vigorous to very dwarfing. Names and types vary between countries: check in a good catalogue to ensure that you are choosing the right kind for your region and site.

• *see also:* FEEDING PLANTS p186; WHY PRUNE? p238; THE ORNAMENTAL KITCHEN GARDEN p256; DEVELOPING A PRODUCTIVE GARDEN p258

△ **ESPALIERS ARE** *space-saving forms that allow top fruits such as apples to be trained productively in narrow beds or beside paths.*

PRUNING TIPS

Keep bushes goblet-shaped, with open centres formed by removing any branches that grow inwards.

On wall-trained fruit, cut out any misplaced shoots growing towards or away from the wall before they are too big.

Do not try to grow tip-bearing apple varieties as cordons, fans or espaliers.

Always use sharp tools, think carefully before pruning any stem, and cut to a bud facing in the direction you want its shoot to grow.

Train fruit securely on strong stakes (and on wires where appropriate); check ties regularly to make sure they are not too tight.

it unpruned until it reaches full height; then prune the same way as new side shoots. Shorten these in midsummer to four or five leaves, and prune further the following winter to one or two buds.

ESPALIERS

These are trained trees, with single upright main stems and pairs of straight branches (arms) arranged in tiers 38–45cm (15–18in) apart and running in opposite directions on horizontal wires. Most espaliers have two, three or four pairs of arms, but the low-growing form called a 'stepover' tree has one pair about 38cm (15in) above ground.

Start training an espalier by planting a one-year-old maiden and cutting its stem just below the bottom wire. From the several shoots then produced, train the topmost one vertically, and the next two to each side at an angle of 45°. The following winter, lower these two side branches to the bottom wire and tie them securely; cut the main stem just below the next wire. Repeat each year until the top wire is reached. Each side arm is then trained and pruned like a cordon (*see above*).

FANS

The fan is a decorative form ideal for many fruits, but most often used for plums, peaches and cherries. Start training in the same way as for an espalier, but leave the first two side branches tied in at an angle, shortening

SUMMER AND WINTER PRUNING

Pruning in mid- and late summer benefits all fruits trained in restricted forms – such as cordons, fans and espaliers – by redirecting their growth into developing fruiting spurs and buds, and so increasing overall yields. Winter pruning applies to all fruit, and is used to remove dead and diseased stems, limit size and control shape. To avoid exposing wounds to disease, stone fruits such as plums, cherries and peaches are winter-pruned in early spring, when the buds first start to burst.

279

them in late winter to about 45cm (18in) long. During the summer, tie in the strongest four or five shoots that form on each arm, spreading them out evenly like the ribs of a fan. Late the following winter, shorten these by one-third to produce further side branches for tying in to create the main framework.

Fruiting side shoots are produced on these branches and pruned according to the type of fruit. Treat apples, pears and sweet cherries in the same way, by forming permanent spurs (*see cordons above*). With plum, peach and acid cherry, cut out the side shoots after fruiting to make way for new shoots.

Productive containers

High-quality produce can be harvested fresh from a backyard, a terrace or a balcony – indeed, anywhere there is no open ground – if you grow your crops in pots. From apple trees and runner beans in half-barrels to small strawberry pots and parsley pigs, container cultivation adds a decorative element to the garden as well as yielding satisfying rewards.

△ **ALPINE STRAWBERRIES**, *with their trailing growth and decorative appearance, can be as effective as summer bedding for a trough or box.*

VEGETABLES

Most vegetable crops may be grown in pots, including early potatoes forced out of season or runner beans trained on a wigwam of canes and surrounded with yellow courgettes. Cucumbers, peppers and tomatoes all crop well in 30cm (12in) pots stood against a warm wall, especially if you plunge the base of the pots in a growing bag for extra rooting volume – in this way a row of tomatoes can be arranged along the side of greenhouse or shed.

BUSH AND TREE FRUIT

In a large container, 38cm (15in) or more, decoratively trained fruit such as standard gooseberries or a weeping apple can make impressive features for a permanent position. Top fruits must be grafted onto very dwarfing rootstocks to limit their growth, although there are genetically dwarf varieties of peaches and other fruits; it is even possible to assemble a mini-orchard of cordon or columnar apples in pots. Fig trees have vigorous roots that support excessive leaf growth unless restrained, and these crop well in a half-barrel or large planter.

BASIC CULTIVATION

Choosing containers

A pot must be the right size for the plant. Some short-term crops, such as basil or leaf lettuce, can remain in 13–15cm (5–6in) pots throughout their growth, whereas other plants need more

◁ **PROVIDED SUPPORT** *is given, tall plants such as runner beans or tomatoes can be grown in large, heavy containers filled with soil-based compost for stability.*

BLUEBERRIES IN POTS

❖

Blueberries (*Vaccinium* spp.) hate lime in the soil, and must be grown in containers if the soil is not naturally acid. They are attractive bushes, often turning fiery shades of copper and orange in autumn. Plant each bush (you will need at least two for cross-pollination) in a tub of ericaceous or lime-free compost and water regularly with rainwater in summer. Net plants against birds as soon as the fruit starts ripening in late summer. Thin some of the older stems from mature bushes in winter and shear lightly to shape in spring.

• *see also:* FEEDING PLANTS p186; THE ORNAMENTAL KITCHEN GARDEN p256; DEVELOPING A PRODUCTIVE GARDEN p258; BASIC CULINARY HERBS p284

◁ THE AMOUNT OF compost in a growing bag is limited, so start plants off in large pots and stand one bag on top of another to increase the rooting volume.

room as they develop: remember that undersized pots cramp growth, while roots in too large a pot can rot in a quantity of stagnant soil. Ornamental pots such as strawberry towers may be adapted for other crops, such as leaf lettuces or a collection of thymes. Generous-sized containers, such as half-barrels and tubs, will accommodate a variety of larger vegetables and also trained fruits (on dwarfing rootstocks where appropriate). Make sure that all containers have adequate drainage holes in the bottom.

Good growing habits

After buying a potted plant, gently knock it out of the container: if its roots are winding around the rootball, pot it on straight into the next size of

▷ FIGS CROP more heavily if their roots are restricted in a pot. Container cultivation also allows figs to be moved indoors in a cold winter.

container. Cover the bottom with a generous drainage layer (pebbles, broken clay pots or crushed stones), and use a good potting compost, preferably soil-based for stability; this may be mixed with some garden soil if it is clean and fertile. Stand all containers where plants receive optimum light, warmth and shelter, bearing in mind that pots are portable features and can be moved according to the season and the maturity of the contents. Growing

tender plants in containers allows you to move them around to follow the sun or to avoid frost, as was traditional with citrus fruits kept in large, square Versailles boxes.

When grown in pots, plants need more frequent watering and you should check them regularly – daily watering will be required in hot weather but less often in shade or winter. A month or so after potting, start feeding every week with a dilute, balanced fertilizer and turn containers occasionally to encourage even growth.

EARLY STRAWBERRIES

❖

Perpetual strawberry varieties in pots can be forced into an early harvest in a warm, sheltered place, with a later crop following outdoors in the autumn. Pot up rooted runners in 9cm (3½in) pots in summer and keep outdoors, potting them on as they develop, either individually into 13cm (5in) pots or several plants together in towers or stacking pots to save space. In late winter, bring under glass to force early blooms; after fruiting, move outdoors and feed to encourage an autumn crop.

281

Planning a herb garden

Whether you grow just a few basic herbs or collect all possible varieties, culinary herbs are essential kitchen-garden accessories. Each contributes unique fragrance and beauty to its surroundings, and will add supreme flavour to dishes and salads when they are gathered fresh from the garden.

CHOOSING A SITE

For best results, choose a position in full sun with shelter from cold, drying winds. Easy access is important: a site near the kitchen door would be ideal for a small herb collection. A larger, well-stocked herb garden can be an ornamental feature, with shaped beds of plants, paths and perhaps a seat. A bed 1.2m by 1.8m (4ft by 6ft) will easily accommodate basic *bouquet garni* herbs (parsley, thyme, sage, marjoram and bay), with mint, chives and tarragon: arrange with the taller plants in the centre or at the back. Where space is limited, grow your herbs in containers on a sunny patio or balcony.

Larger herb gardens need to be planned on paper, so draw a scale plan first. Decide on the shape, remembering that simplicity is a virtue, and include paths for access. Square or circular beds provide a disciplined outline for the varied plant shapes, although a relaxed cottage garden arrangement can be pleasing. Choose the herbs you know and use, adding others if there is space.

PREPARATION AND CARE

Mark out your plan on the ground. Dig over the site, working in plenty of garden compost or bought bagged compost; add gravel or grit to heavy soils for improved drainage. Fork out all perennial weeds, as these are hard to remove after planting. Beds can be edged with boards, bricks

◁ **IN THIS POTAGER STYLE** *herb garden, a pot of lemon balm forms the centrepiece to geometric beds planted with silver thyme, purple sage, marjoram, tarragon and bay.*

• *see also:* BASIC CULINARY HERBS p284; MAKING A HERB COLLECTION p286

◁ **CHOOSE A SUNNY SITE** *for a herb garden. This new one, backed by a protective wall, has square, timber-edged beds with paths of bark chippings.*

or tiles, and paths finished with bark, gravel or a suitable hard surface.

Sow or plant new herbs in spring, although container-grown plants can be introduced at any time. Place perennial herbs first, as these provide a permanent framework, then position annuals and biennials among them, aiming for a satisfying balance of shapes and sizes. Site special herbs prominently – silver or grey plants where they catch the sun, aromatic sage or rosemary where it will be brushed in passing. Water in after planting, and on light soils mulch with compost or bark (on heavy ground use gravel or grit to aid drainage).

Leafy herbs need regular watering, whereas woody perennials and seed-bearing plants require very little. Trim perennials annually after flowering, and cut back herbs such as mint in summer to stimulate further young foliage. Cut down and clear away all dead growth in late autumn.

RESTRAINING INVASIVE HERBS

Herbs such as tarragon and most mints spread vigorously by underground runners and will threaten neighbouring plants unless restrained. Surround with a barrier of slates buried vertically in the ground, or plant in a bottomless bucket buried to its rim. A large plastic bag with a perforated base, filled with soil and buried just out of sight, is a good substitute.

SPECIAL USES

Herbs can be used as design elements around the garden. Sweet bay may be trained as topiary or as an ornamental tree, while closely planted rosemary makes a classic hedge. Use mat-forming herbs such as marjoram, thyme and pennyroyal for edging or plant in paving joints to make an aromatic path.

▽ **MANY HERBS** *are naturally prostrate or bushy and eventually sprawl informally over the edges of beds. Here, bright green parsley softens the angularity of paving slabs.*

HARVESTING HERBS

Harvesting herbs regularly helps to keep plants neat and shapely, so gather leaves and shoots as required. For drying, freezing and other forms of preservation, pick them on a dry morning during or just before flowering, when their flavour is most intense. Spread out or hang up stems to dry in warm shade, or freeze the leaves immediately.

283

Basic culinary herbs

Cookery enthusiasts consider five classic herbs essential for flavouring many dishes: bay, marjoram, parsley, sage and thyme; they are often combined together as a bouquet garni. They are all easy to grow and will form the nucleus of any herb collection.

△ **A WINDOW BOX** *makes an excellent miniature herb garden, offering convenient pickings of rosemary, sage and thyme.*

▽ **PURPLE-LEAVED SAGE,** *tall angelica and feathery bronze fennel are combined with other decorative plants like alchemilla, alliums, iris and French lavender.*

BAY (*Laurus nobilis*)

An evergreen Mediterranean tree growing up to 6m (20ft) high, with tough, glossy leaves. It is usually grown as a bushy shrub or clipped into simple topiary shapes such as mophead standards. Slightly susceptible to frost, especially while young, bay can be grown in a container and brought under cover in winter.

Grow in well-drained soil or soil-based potting compost, in full sun with shelter from cold winds. Feeding is unnecessary, but plants benefit from occasional watering in dry weather. Trim to shape in early summer and again in autumn for formal topiary. Propagate by cuttings of side shoots, taken with a heel of old wood.

Harvest leaves at any time for immediate use or drying in darkness.

MARJORAM (*Origanum*)

Highly decorative shrubby herbs up to 60cm (2ft) high, reasonably hardy if grown in full sun and well-drained soil. Pot marjoram (*O. onites*) is very hardy, with a milder flavour than sweet marjoram (*O. marjorana*); oregano or wild marjoram (*O. vulgare*) is very pungent and available in many ornamental forms.

Grow in dry, warm soil, with a little lime if known to be acid. Trim hard in late autumn, and lift one or two plants for use indoors in winter. Propagate by sowing in early spring under glass, by division in spring or autumn, or from cuttings in summer.

Harvest fresh at any time, or gather shoots just before flowering for drying slowly in darkness.

△ **BAY TREES** *are traditionally grown in terracotta pots, where young plants can be clipped and shaped to use as formal ornaments.*

See also: PROPAGATING BY CUTTINGS p232; THE ORNAMENTAL KITCHEN GARDEN p256; DEVELOPING A PRODUCTIVE GARDEN p258; PLANNING A HERB GARDEN p282

284

Marjoram (Origanum vulgare 'Gold Tip')

Parsley (Petroselinum crispum)

Thymes, including golden and variegated forms

PARSLEY (*Petroselinum crispum*)

A leafy biennial, usually grown as an annual, the common curly kinds make dense, decorative plants 30cm (12in) tall; the flat-leafed French or Italian kind has a stronger flavour and can reach 60cm (2ft) high.

Grow from seed, sown thinly outdoors in rich, moist soil, in late spring and again in late summer for succession over winter; seedlings are often slow to appear. Thin to 15–23cm (6–9in) apart, and keep well-watered at all times. Earlier crops may be started under glass in pots. Transplant a few late-summer seedlings to pots or a greenhouse border for winter use. Harvest sprigs as needed, and cut whole plants before they flower for freezing in bags or in ice cubes.

SAGE (*Salvia officinalis*)

Large, handsome bushes with subtle leaf colours, as much at home in a flower border as in the herb garden. Plants are easily grown but resent wet conditions in winter, so work plenty of grit into heavy soils before planting. Pineapple sage (*S. rutilans*) is tender and best grown under glass, where its scarlet flowers appear in winter.

Grow in fertile, well-drained soil, in full sun with shelter from cold winds. Clip annually to shape after flowering, and renew plants after four to five years before their stems become bare. Propagate plain green forms from seeds sown outdoors in spring, all kinds from 8cm (3in) summer cuttings of side shoots pulled off with a heel.

Harvest leaves and shoot tips at any time, or just before flowering for drying in warm shade.

THYME (*Thymus*)

There are many different thymes for various purposes: the upright common thyme (*T. vulgaris*) is perhaps best for culinary use, while the many forms of creeping wild thyme (*T. serpyllum*) are neat, mat-forming plants for edging or growing in between paving slabs, and also for collecting in thyme pots and other containers.

Grow in full sun, in dry, well-drained soil with low fertility; add plenty of grit to heavier soils for good drainage. Trim several times in spring and summer, especially straight after flowering, to keep plants dense and neat, and replace after four or five years. Propagate by seed or division in spring, by cuttings from side shoots in summer, or by layering in autumn.

Harvest the leaves and tips of shoots as needed to use fresh, or just as the flowers open for drying.

CULTIVATION TIPS

285

- In cold areas, the willow-leaved bay (*L. nobilis* f. *angustifolia*) often proves a little hardier than the common form.

- Marjoram makes an ideal plant for edges, joints in paving and for hanging baskets.

- Seeds of parsley often fail because of drought; hasten germination by soaking seeds in warm water over-night, and keep the soil consistently moist until seedlings appear.

- Red-, purple- and gold-variegated forms of sage make attractive pot plants, but are less hardy than the plain green kinds.

- Plant upright varieties of thyme 10–15cm (4–6in) apart and clip regularly to make a dwarf hedge around a small herb bed.

THE GARDENER'S CALENDAR

❖

THE KEY TO SUCCESSFUL GARDENING is doing the right thing at the right time, so over the following pages I have set out to provide topical tips and advice through the seasons. Whether you are planning a new garden from scratch or developing an established one, by referring to this guide each week you can plan out what needs to be done, then sow, plant, prune, propagate and cultivate to get the best out of your garden.

To help you find the advice you need, the seasonal jobs are divided up to cover the different areas of the garden, from flower border and kitchen garden to lawns, pond and greenhouse. In addition, major seasonal activities are covered in more detail, along with a checklist of jobs to keep your garden problem-free and your plants growing strongly. New gardeners will find this practical guide especially useful, keeping them up-to-date with all the major tasks around the garden, while experienced gardeners can use it more as a reminder.

Why not keep your own personal gardening diary, recording the plans and projects you undertake, keeping notes on crop yields and plant performance, and noting all the plants, materials and equipment you buy. This will quickly build into a complete picture of your own garden, to which you can refer back for guidance each year. The best way to learn about gardening is, quite simply, to have a go, so turn these pages to find out what you could be doing in your garden every day of the year.

289

ADAM PASCO

Early Spring

Everything moves up a gear as winter steps into spring, with much to put in place for the coming season. Try and plan out your work, especially seed sowing and propagation plans, setting yourself weekly targets and noting them in a gardening diary.

THE FLOWER GARDEN

Snowdrops Lift and divide congested clumps while still in leaf. This stage is often referred to as being 'in the green', and whole clumps can be carefully lifted, teased apart, and individual bulbs replanted at a wider spacing but at the same depth as before. This is also a good time to buy new snowdrops from specialist growers.

Perennial planting As soon as soil conditions are warmer, this is a good time to plant up new herbaceous beds with perennials. Plant them in groups to create the best effect. It helps to plan the border on paper first, checking the height and spread of individual plants in an encyclopedia so that taller types can be planted at the back, with shorter subjects at the front.

Pruning shrubs On many shrubs the previous season's growth should be pruned back close to its base, to within 2.5cm (1in) of the point it developed from last year. Shrubs that can be pruned now include *Hydrangea paniculata*, *Buddleja davidii* and *Caryopteris x clandonensis*. Large and unshapely plants of *Brachyglottis* 'Sunshine' can be pruned hard, or old stems shortened back to new side shoots. *Leycestaria formosa* also responds well to hard pruning.

Soil preparation Rake over and prepare sites for sowing hardy annuals later in the season.

Protection Be prepared to protect the new shoots and developing foliage of tender shrubs and trees from frost and freezing winds. Keep old net curtains or large sheets of fleece handy to spread over and wrap round plants at risk. These include Japanese maples, romneya, caryopteris, ceratostigma, paulownia, some ceanothus, and tender wall plants like *Cytisus battandieri*.

PLANTING FOR SUMMER COLOUR

❖

LILIES Plant lily bulbs outside where you want them to flower or in pots for planting out later. Many shorter types, especially scented ones, are ideal for patio tubs.

GLADIOLI Plant corms at intervals over the coming months to extend their flowering season. On light soil and in mild areas they can be planted now, but delay planting for a few weeks in colder, wetter areas.

DAHLIAS Tubers can be planted directly outside as the weather gets warmer. Dig out a large hole, spread out the tuber, then cover with about 10cm (4in) of soil or compost. Protect any emerging shoots from frost by covering with straw or fleece.

ROSE PRUNING

❖

Most bush roses, especially hybrid tea and floribunda varieties, require an annual prune in early spring. This prevents bushes becoming very woody and bare at the base, encouraging strong new shoots to develop each year which carry flowers. Start pruning by removing all dead or diseased stems completely, using loppers to remove portions of old wood. Then look at the size and shape of the bush, and prune out crossing or badly positioned stems. Remove unproductive old stems to make space for the new shoots. Finally, shorten all the existing shoots: in most cases they can simply be shortened by about a third to a half, remembering that weak shoots should be pruned back harder than strong ones, as this results in more vigorous new growth. Always prune to just above a bud, using the natural characteristic of shoots to control the resulting shape of the bush: each new shoot will grow out in the direction in which its bud is pointing.

CUTTING DOWN TO SIZE

❖

The colourful stems of willows and dogwoods have brightened the winter garden, but these now need pruning hard to encourage a flush of new shoots. Stooling is a pruning technique that keeps vigorous shrubs within bounds where space is limited. All stems are pruned right down to their base, using secateurs or loppers, and although this might look drastic you will soon see a flush of new shoots sprouting out from the woody stubs, providing stems clad in foliage for summer interest and wands of coloured bark next winter.

As well as many shrubby varieties of cornus and salix, other shrubs that can be kept compact and respond well to hard pruning include purple hazel, whitewash bramble, Cotinus coggygria and golden-leaved elder. Stems of the summer-flowering Buddleja davidii should also be pruned hard down to a woody framework at their base.

Flowering shrubs like the perennial lavatera also benefit from hard pruning. Cut away old growth on perennials like the Russian sage (Perovskia), and trim back cotton lavender (Santolina).

RAISING NEW SHRUBS BY LAYERING

❖

Many shrubs can be propagated by the simple technique of layering a low branch to the ground. At the point the branch touches the ground, dig out a hole and improve the soil with gritty compost. Make a cut about 2.5cm (1in) long about a third of the way into the stem and towards the shoot tip. Hold the slit open with a matchstick, and dab with hormone rooting powder. Bury in the hole, covering with more gritty compost, water well and hold in place with a large stone or paving slab. Hold the shoot tip upright by tying it to a cane. Keep the soil watered during dry weather. This layered shoot can take a year, or even longer, to root well, at which time it can be separated from its parent and grown separately. Shrubs that can be propagated by branch layering during spring include arbutus, evergreen azalea, berberis, camellia, chimonanthus, magnolia, gaultheria and rambling roses. Rhododendrons are easily layered until early autumn, while clematis can be layered during summer.

291

THE KITCHEN GARDEN
Vegetable crops

Seed sowing As soon as soil conditions are suitable start sowing crops outside. These should include parsnips, broad beans, onions, beetroot, carrots, kohl rabi, leeks, peas, radish, mangetout, spinach and turnips.

Onion sets Plant out sets to their required spacing, usually about 10–15cm (4–6in) apart along the row, with rows about 20cm (8in) apart, to allow for hoeing and weeding.

Asparagus New crowns will soon be available to plant. Choose a vigorous male variety which will not run to seed and plant in deeply cultivated soil. Spread out the roots over a ridge of soil so the crown is planted 5cm (2in) deep.

Shallots Finish planting out shallots in well-drained soil in a sunny site.

Potatoes Plant out early varieties. Seed potatoes will have been chitted on a windowsill, so should have several little shoots sprouting from them.

Salad crops Ensure a regular supply of salads to harvest each week by sowing little and often. The key is to sow a short row of lettuce, radish, salad leaves, spring onions and other crops every week or fortnight, which results in a continuity of crops to harvest through the summer. Sow unusual salad leaves like purslane and salad rocket.

Brassica crops Sow seed of several brassicas in a nursery bed. When the seedlings are large enough to handle, transplant them to their final positions at the proper spacing. Types to sow now include Brussels sprouts, calabrese and summer and autumn cabbage. Sow summer cauliflower under cloches and transplant seedlings from earlier sowings.

Seakale Plant new crowns in spring. Grow plants for a couple of years, feeding them regularly, before they are large enough to cover in winter to form blanched shoots.

Comfrey patch Plant a patch of comfrey in a bright, sunny corner of the kitchen garden. The leaves make an excellent addition to the compost heap, may be spread over the soil round crops as a mulch, or can be used to make a liquid feed. The variety 'Bocking 14' is the most productive comfrey.

Herbs Divide large clumps of chives, separating them into smaller portions to replant. In pots in cold greenhouses or frames sow parsley, sage, chives, dill, lemon balm, sorrel and many others. If you have a heated propagator, sow more tender herbs like basil, coriander, fennel and borage, growing them on in pots ready for planting out in summer.

Fruit crops

Planting Complete planting of new fruit trees and bushes as soon as possible, particularly bare-rooted plants which should always have their roots soaked well before planting.

Strawberries Cover rows with tunnel cloches to encourage earlier flowering and fruiting. Remember to open the

---

MULCHING FOR A BETTER GARDEN

❖

A thick layer of compost or similar material spread over the soil helps to suppress annual weeds and conserve moisture. Some mulches break down more quickly than others, being taken down by worms to improve the soil. Others provide an attractive surface and ornamental finishing touch.

WHAT TO USE A wide variety of materials can be used, in particular home-made compost and leafmould, or rotted farmyard manure and mushroom compost. Garden centres sell bark and cocoa shell products by the bag, but larger quantities are available in bulk.

HOW TO MULCH Be generous, spreading a mulch at least 7.5–10cm (3–4in) thick to prevent weed growth. For low-maintenance borders, cover the site with a weed barrier membrane, plant through this into the soil, then cover the membrane with a bark or cocoa shell mulch.

---

sides each day when in bloom, to allow access for bees and pollinating insects.

Gooseberries Finish winter pruning, shortening long side shoots and removing congested stems to create open-centred bushes; this provides better air circulation, reducing mildew disease and making picking easier.

Mulching Spread mulches generously along rows of raspberries and round fruit trees and bushes.

Feeding Continue sprinkling sulphate of potash and general feeds round your fruit, including strawberries.

Peaches and nectarines Keep potted trees in a cold greenhouse until later in spring or early summer to protect the flowers from frost.

Fruit trees in lawn Keep grass trimmed away from the base of trees growing in grass, as this can compete for moisture and nutrients. Maintain a clear area about 60–90cm (2–3ft) wide round the trunk, covering the soil with a mulch of compost.

Outdoor vines Complete pruning before vines start into growth.

Pest and disease control Be ready to spray newly emerging leaves with pesticides or fungicides to prevent problems arising this year. Choose products carefully, always following the manufacturer's instructions, and avoid using when plants are in flower as pollinating insects could be harmed.

Frost warning Protect the blooms on cherries, currants and early-flowering fruit from damaging frost.

LAWN CARE

Moss control Where thick moss is spreading across the lawn, apply a chemical moss killer then thoroughly

---

rake out the dead moss. Improve surface drainage by hollow spiking the lawn to help prevent the problem recurring.

Cutting grass It is still too early to start regular mowing in most areas, but if the weather is very mild and dry, try running the mower over the lawn with blades set high to tidy its appearance.

Lawn edges Re-cut worn or damaged lawn edges. If the edges are in a poor state, aim to replace them with new turf. Alternatively, cut back into good grass using a board and grass cutter to form a clean new edge. Various edging strips are available to put in place to protect edges. Where border plants tumble over the grass, consider putting a row of bricks round the edge as a cutting strip for the plants to spread over. Cut back any invasive plants.

Raking and scarifying As the weather warms up, scarify lawns thoroughly, either by hand using a lawn rake or with a powered model. This removes all the debris that accumulates at the soil surface, including moss. Bare patches can be re-seeded later in spring.

POND CARE

Pumps In mild districts, bring pumps out of store and place back in ponds to drive fountains, waterfalls and other moving water features.

Pond heaters Floating electric pond heaters can be removed once the weather warms up and the risk of thick ice developing has passed.

Plant care Any marginal plants that have grown too large can be lifted and divided, replanting in smaller groups. Remove invasive plants and thin out any which have become too vigorous for your pond.

Pond weed Keep blanket weed under control, scooping out regularly with a net to prevent it smothering floating plants.

New planting Buy new aquatic plants such as water lilies, iris, sedges and reeds, planting them in aquatic baskets and positioning them on bricks at the correct depth below the water surface.

IN THE GREENHOUSE

Peaches With peaches, nectarines and apricots now coming into bloom, protect wall-trained plants on cold nights under a screen of netting or fleece. Bees and other pollinating insects may not be around, so do the job for them by gently dabbing flowers with a soft brush, and transferring pollen from one flower to another. Water if the soil is dry, making sure fruit never goes short of water during the flowering period.

Fuchsias Pinch out the tips of new

SOWING VEGETABLES IN THE GREENHOUSE

Several tender crops can be raised from seed now, but they need to be sown in pots or trays and kept in a warm, heated propagator to germinate. These include tomatoes, aubergine, peppers (capsicums) and cucumbers. Most will need to be grown in a greenhouse throughout their life, but some varieties can be planted outside in early summer, preferably under cloches at first, to produce crops later in the year. Celery, celeriac and varieties of squash can be raised under glass for planting out later.

---

shoots once they have produced two or three pairs of leaves. This encourages branching and a better shaped plant which will carry more flowers. Train up single stems of vigorous, upright varieties to form standards.

Chrysanthemums Continue taking cuttings from new shoots developing on overwintered plants, or buy new stock from specialist growers. Cuttings should be about 5cm (2in) long, and rooted in pots of compost in heated propagators maintained at around 13°C (55°F).

Bedding plants Many varieties of half-hardy summer bedding plants can be sown in heated propagators now. Check the back of seed packets for details.

Seedlings Prick out seedlings from earlier sowings, spacing them out in large seed trays or planting them individually into small pots.

Damping off disease Some seedlings can collapse and die from damping off. Take steps to prevent the disease by always using clean pots and fresh compost, by sowing thinly and watering with fungicide solution. Never overwater and remove propagator lids to improve ventilation when seeds have germinated.

Primulas Sow a tray of *Primula obconica* to raise flowering pot plants.

Keeping cool Damp down the floor of the greenhouse in the morning on warm days to increase humidity, opening doors and vents to prevent temperatures rising too high. Remember to close them again in the evening.

Abutilon Prune back large plants grown under glass over the winter to encourage strong growth from the base.

Cacti and succulents Repot large plants during spring in very gritty, loam-based compost. Most prefer terracotta pots, which also provide extra stability.

EARLY-SPRING CHECKLIST

❏ Lift, divide and replant large, congested clumps of established perennials every three or four years.

❏ Cover soil in the kitchen garden with polythene or cloches to keep it dry and to warm it up for early sowings.

❏ Pick off the dead flowerheads from spring-flowering bulbs like daffodils and tulips. Scatter fertilizer round each clump.

❏ Cover rhubarb with large pots or buckets to exclude light and force an earlier crop.

❏ Pick off dead flowerheads of winter and spring bedding plants.

❏ Buy in supplies of pots and compost for early sowing and potting. Store bags of compost in the greenhouse so it is already warm for seed sowing.

❏ Open the lids on cold frames each morning to improve ventilation, closing them again each evening.

❏ Control the growth of vigorous spreading herbs, like mint, by cutting back large clumps or by growing them in pots.

❏ Once potted bulbs grown in the home are past their best, plant them outside and give them a liquid feed.

❏ Instead of using cold water from the mains, always leave a full can of water in the greenhouse to take the chill off it before use.

❏ Watch out for slugs and snails which can damage seedlings and the soft new shoots on perennials, especially hostas. Use slug pellets if the problem is severe.

293

Mid-Spring

Spring gardens are full of life, vigour, flowers, fresh growth, and a promise of even better to come. Bulbs and blossom steal the show, but the surging growth of new grass indicates a need for regular attention from now on. Seed sowing under glass keeps us busy and the resulting burgeoning trays of seedlings are a testament to the productivity of this season.

THE FLOWER GARDEN

Gladioli Plant corms in succession from now until the end of spring to extend their flowering season. Place them about 10cm (4in) deep and the same apart, planting in groups of one variety for best effect.

Phormiums Pull off the dead outer leaves, wearing gloves and goggles for protection. Divide congested clumps.

Dahlias Plant sprouting tubers deeply in mild districts, but delay planting tubers by a few weeks in cold areas. Do not plant out young dahlia plants raised from cuttings until all risk of frost has passed.

Sweet peas Plant out young sweet peas raised from autumn sowings. Pinch out the shoot tip if they have not started to branch naturally. Sow seeds at the base of canes or other vertical supports to grow up for later flowers.

Pampas grass Divide large and congested clumps, or plant out new ones as border features.

Agapanthus Plant bulbs in groups in large pots, or directly outside in warm and sheltered borders.

Bulbs Sprinkle fertilizer or liquid feed round established drifts of winter- and spring-flowering bulbs like aconites, snowdrops, crocus and narcissus.

Chrysanthemums Continue potting up rooted cuttings, and plant out well-rooted chrysanthemums once they have been hardened off in a cold frame.

Division Many clump-forming and spreading perennials like Russian sage (*Perovskia*) and chrysanthemum can be divided now. Discard the old central portions and replant the young outer pieces in groups.

Indoor bulbs Once pots of bulbs have finished flowering, plant them outside and water well with a liquid feed.

Tubs and containers Remove winter insulation wrapped round patio tubs. Move back containers of shrubs and permanent planting from their sheltered winter homes to their usual positions. Stand containers on pot feet or bricks to ensure good drainage.

SUPPORTING BORDER PLANTS

Many tall or lax-growing flowering perennials will need support to keep them upright and prevent them collapsing on neighbouring plants if they get caught by the wind. Now is the time to consider how they will be supported over the summer. Simple garden canes, topped with rubber caps to prevent eye injuries, are cheap and effective, as are twigs of hazel and other trees. Metal support frames placed over clumps now allow the stems of the perennial to grow up through its criss-cross structure to gain support. Green plastic-coated frames blend into the border far better than bare metal ones.

SOWING ANNUALS

A wide range of hardy annuals can be sown directly outside in borders wherever you would like them to flower this summer. Choose a range of varieties to suit a colour theme, and sow each variety in a separate block, with taller subjects towards the back and lower ones grouped along the front of the border. Always sow in rows to distinguish germinating seedlings from weeds. Rake over the site, mark out areas for each variety, then take out seed drills 15–20cm (6–8in) apart. Sow sparingly, cover with soil and water in. Thin once seedlings have germinated.

THE KITCHEN GARDEN
Vegetable crops

Peas Sow peas and mangetout outside. For a continuity of crops aim to sow at monthly intervals until summer, sowing in bands about 15cm (6in) wide and 5cm (2in) deep. Give tall varieties canes or twigs for support.

Potatoes Plant out maincrop potato varieties. Draw earth up round the stems of newly emerging early varieties every week, and cover with fleece to protect from frost.

Onion sets Plant out as soon as the soil is prepared, spacing them 10–15cm (4–6in) apart in rows about 20cm (8in) apart, allowing room for weeding.

Celery Prepare trenches for planting out young plants raised under glass.

Herbs Several herbs can be sown at this time, including parsley, fennel, dill, coriander, marjoram and thyme.

Broad beans Sow a crop now to harvest in the autumn.

Lettuce Start sowing a short row of lettuce every other week to ensure a regular supply of salad leaves through the summer.

Sprouting seeds A wide range of salad seeds can be sprouted in jars on the kitchen windowsill to use fresh in salads. These include alfalfa, fenugreek, mung beans, rape salad and even chick peas and green lentils. Put a few seeds in a jam jar, rinse with water, then cover the top with muslin and leave upside down to drain. Repeat rinsing and draining daily. Seedlings soon sprout and will be ready to eat in a few days. Set up the number of jars and quantities needed for your family requirements.

Carrots Sow under cloches or outside for small salad carrots, or later for maincrop varieties. Sowing sparingly at

intervals along the row avoids the need for thinning, which can attract carrot root fly. Covering rows with fleece after sowing, buried along the edges, also prevents attack from carrot root fly. A few varieties, like 'Sytan' and 'Flyaway' also claim resistance to this pest.

Crops to sow indoors Sow beetroot, carrots, radish, kohl rabi, lettuce, spring onions, peas, spinach, swede and turnip, and brassicas like sprouting broccoli, kale, cabbage and Brussels sprouts in seed trays.

To sow in pots Sow courgette, marrow, squash, tomato, sweetcorn and French beans in pots indoors. In warm districts some crops can also be sown outdoors, under cloches.

Fruit crops

Strawberries Cover the rows of crops with tunnel cloches, opening the sides each day to allow access for pollinating insects to reach the early flowers as soon as they open.

TRANSPLANTING TIPS

❖

Transplant young seedlings of cabbages and other brassicas sown in seed beds earlier in the year. Choose an overcast day if possible, and water plants well the day before. Lift carefully with a hand fork and transplant to well-prepared soil at their correct spacing where they will grow to maturity. Always firm soil round brassica roots. Water in well and place a collar of old carpet underlay round the stem of each to prevent female cabbage root fly gaining access to lay her eggs.

MID-SPRING PRUNING TASKS

❖

HEATHERS Trim back the dead flower heads on winter-flowering heathers with shears, just cutting into green shoots to shape and tidy the plants. Be careful not to cut back too far into old wood which will not generate new shoots.

FORSYTHIA As soon as flowers have faded, prune back flowering shoots. Trim forsythia hedges with powered hedge cutters, or remove individual shoots with secateurs to create a neat, balanced shrub.

CONIFERS AND TOPIARY With new growth starting and weather improving, give decorative clipped hedges, conifers and topiary the first clip of the year.

FLOWERING CURRANTS To control their size and vigour, varieties of ornamental currant (ribes) need pruning after flowering to remove the old flowered stems and promote new growth that will carry flowers next spring. Prune about a third of stems back hard to encourage new growth from the base, and lightly trim the flowered portion from the rest.

PRUNING SHRUBS Many shrubs flower on shoots produced this year. If they look tall and untidy after the winter they can be pruned hard now to encourage new growth from below. These include hardy fuchsias, *Hydrangea paniculata*, romneya, ceratostigma and caryopteris. Some can be pruned back to a slightly larger framework of stems from where new shoots will develop. On shrubs like *Buddleja davidii* and *Leycestaria formosa* leaving stems of differing lengths will result in a taller, tiered display of flowers.

295

MID-SPRING MAINTENANCE

❖

❏ Move young plants from greenhouses and windowsills into cold frames to get them gradually used to cooler outside conditions before planting out.

❏ Hoe borders regularly to kill germinating weed seedlings and dig up emerging perennial weeds.

❏ Sprinkle a generous handful of fertilizer round every flowering shrub, raking it into the soil surface if possible.

❏ Apply a residual weedkiller to gravel paths and drives.

❏ Spread a mulch of bark or compost round shrubs and fruit bushes to suppress weed growth and conserve soil moisture.

❏ Plant up troughs with alpine plants to enjoy this spring.

❏ Keep vegetable plots tidy, removing leaves and debris that could encourage slugs and snails. Dig up and destroy old brassica plants that could be harbouring the grubs of cabbage root fly.

Raspberries New canes will be growing now. Remove any coming up between rows or in paths, and thin out the rest to leave them spaced about 15cm (6in) apart.

Peaches Thin out heavy crops on fan-trained trees under glass.

Pruning plums Avoid pruning plums and cherries in winter as this can spread disease. Now their sap is rising and they are starting into growth, prune to remove dead and damaged shoots, thin congested growth and tie in new shoots.

Mulching Spread a mulch of compost around fruit trees and bushes to conserve soil moisture and keep down the weeds.

Feeding Sprinkle fertilizer round trees and bushes and rake into the soil.

Disease control Mildew diseases attack apples, gooseberries, currants and other fruits. Planting disease-resistant varieties is one way to avoid them, but protect susceptible varieties by spraying with a systemic fungicide.

Frost protection Keep netting or fleece handy to cover fruits in flower on cold nights to protect them from frost.

Greenfly control To reduce the spread of greenfly by ants on fruit trees, wrap a sticky collar round the trunk and stake.

LAWN CARE

Mowing Begin a weekly mowing regime, collecting all the cuttings as you mow. Keep the blades set quite high at the start of the season, lowering it a little at a time as grass growth increases over the weeks.

Feeding Apply a high-nitrogen lawn feed to all grass areas to get growth off to a good start. Water in granular formulations if it does not rain.

Seeding and patching Thin and worn areas of lawn can be seeded or over-sown to thicken up growth. Scratch over the area with a rake, sprinkle with seed, cover with a thin layer of potting compost, and water well. Small patches can be covered with a piece of clear polythene, pegged in position, to keep birds off. Remove as soon as the grass has germinated.

Weeding Dig out problem weeds like daisies, dandelions and buttercups.

Scarifying Use a tined rake or powered scarifier to rake out moss and thatch that has accumulated deep down in the lawn near the soil surface.

Moss Treat areas of moss with a moss killer, then rake out the dead moss. Take steps to improve soil drainage and relieve compaction by forking over the lawn with a hollow-tined aerator. Brush sharp sand or grit down into the hollow cores to produce drainage channels.

POND CARE

Tidy-up Collect dead stems or foliage from pond or marginal plants, scooping them out of the water with a small net if necessary. Take care not to damage butyl-lined ponds.

Feeding plants Push fertilizer pellets down into the compost of established

STARTING A NEW LAWN

❖

With damper weather and regular showers in spring, this is a good time to raise new lawns from seed or to lay turf. Always prepare the site well, ensuring the area is free from weeds. Once you have dug over the soil, consolidate by walking over it on your heels, raking it level and mixing in fertilizer. Sow seed at the stated rate but no thicker, as sowing too thickly results in weak, congested growth that is prone to disease.

Keep off a newly sown or laid lawn until well established, although you will need to give it an occasional cut with the mower blades set quite high. Ensure the grass never goes short of water in the period while it is establishing.

water lilies and other aquatic plants growing in baskets.

Pumps and fountains Pumps stored in the garage over winter can be placed back in ponds now. Replace old filters and attach to fountains and waterfalls.

Filtration systems Run a pond filtration system, such as those containing ultra-violet lights, to kill algae and purify the water. These are simple to install and are an effective way of keeping pond water clear.

Water lilies Divide large plants now. Lift the whole aquatic basket from the pond, remove the water lily, and cut into sections with a knife. Make sure each piece has shoots and roots attached. Replant into baskets of fresh aquatic compost and cover this with a layer of gravel. Gently lower back onto their shelf in the pool.

IN THE GREENHOUSE

Shading Temperatures can soar under glass on hot days, so put up shading blinds and screens, or apply shade paint to the outside of the glass.

Ventilation Open vents each morning, closing them again in the evening. On very hot days also leave the door ajar to provide extra ventilation.

Cold protection If frost is forecast, cover plants on staging with sheets of fleece or sheets of newspaper for extra protection from cold, removing them in the morning.

Seedlings Continue pricking out seedlings as soon as they are large enough to handle.

Cuttings Take cuttings from new growth of dahlias, fuchsias and many house plants, including leaf cuttings from saintpaulia and *Begonia rex*.

Potting on Always choose a pot just one size larger when potting on, leaving an extra 1cm (1/2in) or so of fresh compost round the rootball. Always use the same type of compost as before, keeping plants growing in a loam-based compost in loam, for instance.

Primulas Sow seed of several primulas which can be grown as pot plants, including *Primula obconica*, *P. kewensis* and *P. sinensis*.

Growing bags Plant cucumbers, peppers and early tomatoes into growing bags in heated greenhouses.

Nerines Continue watering and feeding nerines growing in pots for a few more weeks before reducing the watering to allow the leaves to die down. Give plants a complete rest over the summer, leaving them in a warm position under the greenhouse staging.

Plants by post As soon as young plants are delivered, open boxes, water any dry plants and stand in good light. Contact the nursery if plants were damaged in the post. Pot up as soon as possible.

GREEN MANURES TO SOW
❖

Where space in a border will remain vacant for anything from a few weeks to a few months, sow a green manure crop which will grow to produce fresh, leafy growth that can be chopped up and dug in to improve the soil. Some green manures also have nitrogen fixing bacteria in nodules in their roots which take nitrogen from the air, and make this available to following crops for them to feed on. It is always preferable to plant young plants into soil improved with green manures, as the decaying vegetation can inhibit seed germination. If sowing crops, leave at least a month before sowing. Green manures to choose from which fix nitrogen include tares, trefoil, fenugreek, clover and lupins. Those that don't include fast-growing mustard, phacelia and buckwheat.

297

CHOOSING THE BEST PLANTS
❖

To ensure that you always buy the very best plants, observe these rules when visiting the nursery or garden centre.

1. Aim to shop at the end of the week when stocks of fresh plants are in place for the weekend. You are more likely to get personal advice if you shop during the week when it is quieter.
2. Check that plants look strong, healthy, vigorous and well shaped.
3. The compost should be moist. Never buy plants that have dried out.

4. Check that thick roots are not growing through the bottom of the pot, which is a clear indication that an old plant has become pot-bound.
5. Avoid plants with a thick layer of moss or weeds growing on the surface of the compost.
6. Check that plants have no visible signs of pests or diseases.
7. Make sure plants are labelled with a variety name and cultural instructions.
8. Try to choose plants that come with a money-back or replacement guarantee.

Late Spring

There is hardly a moment to spare this season, with plants to propagate from cuttings for summer displays and vegetable crops and salads to sow outside. Mowing, trimming, weeding and planting all form part of the weekly action plan, and with warmer weather boosting new growth, all plants will benefit from a good feed and more regular watering.

THE FLOWER GARDEN

Plant supports Use canes to support the developing stems of herbaceous perennials, particularly floppy ones like peonies and tall subjects like delphiniums. Either stake individual stems and flower spikes, or surround a clump with several canes. Join them together with garden twine and place eye protectors on the tops of canes.

Feeding Give all acid-loving garden shrubs, like rhododendrons, azaleas, pieris and camellias a feed with a fertilizer formulated specifically for them, such as iron sequestrene, to prevent leaves turning yellow. All spring-flowering bulbs will benefit from a liquid feed. Apply fertilizer round conifers, perennials, established shrubs and along the base of hedges.

Seed sowing In a nursery bed, sow seeds of wallflowers and forget-me-nots and of biennial flowers like honesty and Canterbury bells. These can be transplanted to their flowering position later in the year. Towards the end of spring sow nasturtiums outside.

Forking borders Regularly spike over border soil with a fork to relieve compaction and remove weeds. Fork in a general fertilizer round established plants at the same time.

Perennials Spread a layer of well-rotted compost round perennials. Watch out for slugs and snails, removing any you find, or use a chemical control.

Hardy annuals Continue sowing directly into borders wherever you would like them to flower. Thin out seedlings from earlier sowings to their desired spacing.

Frost protection Many summer bedding plants are frost-tender, so do not plant outside until the all risk of a late frost has passed. Make sure plants have been hardened off by gradually acclimatizing them to outdoor conditions. Open cold frames fully each day, or move plants out of the greenhouse for the day, taking them back in again every evening.

Euphorbias Prune out old flower stems in late spring to provide more space for the developing stems. Wear gloves, as the sap of euphorbias is a skin irritant.

Hellebores It is useful to leave the old flowers on some hellebores, like *H. niger* and *H. orientalis* to allow them to self-seed. On others like *H. argutifolius*, however, the resulting seedlings come up like weeds, so remove flowerheads before they spill their seed.

Dividing plants Lift and divide primulas, polyanthus and forget-me-nots now. Dig up whole plants and tease them apart, ready for planting in a nursery bed to grow on to a larger size before planting out later in the year.

298

MOVING SPRING BULBS

❖

We run the risk of congestion in flower borders as spring-flowering bulbs are still growing strongly in the positions in which summer bedding will soon be planted. Do not be too hasty in cutting off the foliage from bulbs, which is needed to help them build up reserves for next spring. Leave the foliage intact for at least six weeks after flowering, longer if possible, and never tie in knots.

After six weeks, cut off the leaves at soil level. Leave deeply planted bulbs in place, allowing bedding to be planted on top without harming the bulbs. Lift shallow-planted bulbs in clumps with as much root and soil as possible and heel in, in a quiet corner of the garden. Water with a liquid feed and allow to die down naturally before lifting, cleaning and storing in a cool place for summer.

LATE-SPRING PRUNING

❖

❏ Once flowering has finished, cut all the stems of flowering almond (*Prunus triloba*) right down to their base to encourage new growth.

❏ Prune broom (*Genista*) after flowering to shape the plants and prevent them growing lanky, shortening the stems but never cutting back into old wood.

❏ Tie in new growth of wall-trained pyracantha to their supports, and prune out any unwanted shoots that are developing directly into or away from the wall.

Dahlias Harden off rooted cuttings, ready to plant out when risk of frost has passed. Prepare planting sites by digging in plenty of compost, and hammer tall, thick stakes in position ready for training and supporting tall varieties.

Climbing plants

Planting Finish planting out sweet peas, and tie in new growth. Plant out annual climbers raised under glass at the end of this season, positioning them near fences, trellis or other supports for them to cling to and climb.

Training Tie in new growth and flower stems on clematis, directing their stems into areas where you would like blooms. Tie in the new shoots of honeysuckle and climbing roses, particularly those trained over arches or pergolas, so that they hang down gracefully.

Rose care

Feeding Sprinkle a generous handful of rose fertilizer round the base of all roses. Hoe shallowly into the soil surface if possible, taking care not to harm roots, or simply water well before covering with a mulch of compost.

Pests Look out for signs of greenfly on the shoot tips which can damage new leaves and growth. Rub off by hand or spray with a soap-based insecticide.

Diseases If your rose varieties are susceptible to mildew, black spot and rust, try picking off leaves showing signs of infection to prevent it spreading. Alternatively, start a regular spray programme, using a rose fungicide.

Standard roses Check supports are sound, and replace if damaged or unstable. Loosen ties which could be damaging the stem. Replace if worn.

THE KITCHEN GARDEN
Vegetable crops

Mangetout Continue sowing mangetout peas in shallow trenches about 15cm (6in) wide and 5cm (2in) deep, spacing the seeds about 7.5cm (3in) apart across the area. Cover with soil, firm it down and water in the seeds. Provide twiggy supports for taller-growing varieties.

Asparagus Cut spears as they develop, using a long knife to sever them well below the soil surface.

Rhubarb Continue pulling rhubarb regularly and water clumps during very dry weather to encourage new growth.

Broad beans Pinch out the tips of broad bean stems to remove the soft growth which blackfly find so attractive.

Potatoes Complete planting of maincrop varieties. Earth up stems of early varieties to increase yields.

Brussels sprouts Transplant young plants raised from earlier sowings to their final permanent rows, leaving about 60cm (2ft) between plants.

Planting out When all risk of frost has passed, plant out tender crops like outdoor tomatoes and ridge cucumbers, celeriac and celery raised under glass.

Seed sowing Once all risk of frost has passed, sow runner beans, dwarf French beans, ridge cucumbers, courgettes and sweetcorn outside. Cover with cloches until crops are well established. Sow beetroot, spinach, Chinese cabbage, winter cauliflower, New Zealand spinach, calabrese, cauliflower, chicory, endive, kohl rabi, lettuce, spring onions, peas, radish, swedes, turnips and chicory.

Fruit crops

Strawberries Spread straw along rows and under swelling strawberry fruits to keep them off the soil, reducing the risk of attack by slugs and getting covered in soil. Pick fruits from early strawberries growing under cloches.

SEASONAL SOWINGS

❖

To ensure a continuity of cropping for the longest season possible, it is important to make several sowings at intervals during spring and early summer. Many crops, especially salads, can be sown little and often to produce sufficient crops to meet family needs. Lettuce, radish, spinach, turnips and salad leaves may be sown fortnightly. Sow in short rows, perhaps only 60cm (2ft) long, of each variety, to grow the crops you need. With other crops, like maincrop peas and kohl rabi, two or three sowings at monthly intervals will be adequate.

CROPS IN GROWING BAGS

❖

Even where space is very limited, a number of crops can be grown in compost-filled growing bags. Traditionally used in greenhouses for tomatoes, they can be used to grow virtually any crop, including peppers, cucumbers, aubergines, strawberries, salads or herbs, all of which can be planted in an unheated greenhouse now. Growing bags are also useful for balcony and roof gardens. To make watering easier, stand the bag on a gravel tray and cut several slits in the base of the bag to carry wicks to take water from the reservoir to the compost. Remember that growing bags contain little fertilizer, and from about a month after planting, crops will need a weekly liquid feed. Keep the reservoir permanently topped up with water. Tie developing plants to frames, strings or other supports.

HANGING BASKETS AND CONTAINERS

❖

If you have a greenhouse or a conservatory, try to plant up containers and baskets with summer bedding early in the season. This allows small plants to get established and reach a larger size before being put into their permanent home for the summer months.

A wide variety of half-hardy bedding plants and tender perennials – like fuchsias, pelargoniums and argyranthemums – will now be available at garden centres, in addition to trailing begonias and other flowers. Be generous when planting containers, choosing large pots and putting in plenty of plants to create the most impressive displays. Mix a slow-release fertilizer into the compost at planting time to feed your containerized plants for several months.

Raspberries Tie in new growth and thin congested canes to leave them spaced about 15cm (6in) apart along the row. Hoe off any raspberry suckers growing up between the rows.

Gooseberries Thin fruits, using the crop for cooking. Remove every alternate fruit along stems, leaving more room for remaining ones to swell and develop. Keep spraying against powdery mildew if this is a problem.

Suckers Remove suckers on fruit trees growing up from their rootstocks.

Mulching Spread a thick layer of garden compost round fruit trees and bushes to conserve soil moisture.

Fan-trained fruits Regularly tie in branches of fan-trained fruit trees like peach, nectarine, plum, cherry and damson, extending the fan framework to cover a wall or fence.

Outdoor grape vines Pinch out the tips of all side shoots growing from the main rod framework once they have started developing flower trusses. Tie shoots in to their supports.

Bird control Cover fruit cages with netting, or drape netting over fruit bushes and strawberries to keep birds away from developing fruits.

Disease control Continue a regular spraying programme with a suitable garden fungicide to control powdery mildew, apple scab and other diseases.

Codling moth control Hang pheromone traps in apple trees from late spring to attract and catch the male codling moth. Remember to replace the pheromone capsule after a few weeks, when it has become exhausted.

LAWN CARE

Cutting height Gradually lower the height of the blades on your mower as grass growth gets stronger. Start by cutting this season at a height of about 2.5cm (1in), and lower the blades progressively over the coming weeks to a height as low as 1.25cm (½in) for fine-quality lawns.

Feeding Apply lawn feed in some form. Quick-acting liquid feeds which are high in nitrogen can be applied with a watering can, or slow-release granular feeds applied evenly with a wheeled lawn spreader.

Moss control Renovate lawns that are full of moss and dead grass. Apply a moss killer, then thoroughly rake out the dead moss and the accumulated debris by hand or by using a powered lawn rake.

Repairs Areas where grass growth is very thin can be over-sown with grass seed, raking it into the soil surface and covering with a fine sprinkling of compost. Small patches can be covered with clear polythene, pegged down to keep the birds off until the grass seed has germinated.

Lawn weeds Dig out individual weeds by hand, or treat large areas of spreading weeds with a herbicide specially formulated for lawns.

POND CARE

Water lilies This is a good time to divide large plants. Lift baskets from their pond shelf, empty the contents and divide clumps up into individual portions, each with root and shoot attached. Replant into fresh aquatic compost and gradually lower back onto their shelf in stages as the plant grows.

Green algae Filamentous algae soon spread through ponds, covering the surface and strangling plants. Remove regularly by twisting onto a stick or rake, adding this to the compost heap. Take care not to damage butyl liners.

New plants Add oxygenating plants to ponds to improve the quality of the water. Plant deep-water aquatics like water hawthorn (*Aponogeton*), water lilies (*Nymphaea*) and floating heart (*Nymphoides*).

General advice Top up water levels whenever necessary. Use a small net to scoop out accumulated debris or remove floating duckweed.

IN THE GREENHOUSE

Fuchsias Pinch out the shoot tips to encourage branching. Remember that while this helps form bushier plants it does delay flowering.

Grape vines Carefully thin out large bunches with finely pointed scissors, removing small or damaged grapes. Pinch out the tips of long shoots a few leaves beyond developing bunches.

Begonias Tubers started into growth earlier in the year can now be potted up individually into 15cm (6in) pots.

Vine weevil Be vigilant for any signs of adult or larval damage from vine weevil, and treat compost in pots and borders by drenching with a biological pest control nematode if any are found.

Watering Most plants are demanding more water now, so check those in the greenhouse daily. Add liquid feed weekly.

Cuttings Select non-flowering shoots of new growth on hydrangeas to use as cuttings. Take cuttings of alpines. Pot on any cuttings that rooted earlier.

Seedlings Prick out seedlings once large enough to handle, and pot on rooted cuttings and young plants.

Shading Prevent greenhouses getting too hot on bright days by shading the glass on the south side and the roof, in particular, with shade paint, netting or roller blinds. Open doors and ventilators each morning, or fit automatic vent openers. Keep heaters on stand-by to use on cold nights.

Hardening off On warm days, move pots and trays of bedding plants, dahlias, chrysanthemums, and tender vegetables outside or into frames to harden them off and acclimatize them to outside conditions.

Cucumbers Pinch out the tips of side shoots two leaves beyond developing fruits. Stop any side shoots not carrying flowers once they have reached a length of about 60cm (2ft). Remove the main shoot tip when it reaches the roof. Feed cucumbers regularly.

Tomatoes Tie leading shoots to canes or supports each week, and pinch out side shoots, which can grow at each leaf up the stem. Tap flowers daily as they open to encourage pollination and a better fruit set. Never let plants go short of water, and feed twice weekly with a high potash tomato fertilizer.

Bulbs at rest Reduce watering of pots of nerine, lachenalia, veltheimea and freesia to allow them to die down for a summer rest. Stand under the staging.

LATE-SPRING MAINTENANCE

❖

❑ Pick off the faded flowers from camellias, rhododendrons, azaleas and magnolias.

❑ Trim privet hedges regularly to keep them tidy and well shaped.

❑ Support the developing flower stems of tall lilies, and use canes to support gladioli in exposed gardens.

❑ Hoe regularly on dry days to prevent weed seedlings getting established.

❑ Apply a long-lasting weedkiller to gravel paths and drives.

❑ Treat the new growth of emerging perennial weeds with herbicide.

❑ Be considerate of birds that may be nesting in hedges or shrubs.

❑ Watch out for greenfly or other pests on shrubs, and treat if required.

❑ Finish planting perennials, watering in with a liquid feed.

❑ Keep rock gardens and alpine containers tidy, cutting off dead flower stems when they are over.

❑ Repair damaged edges to lawns.

❑ Keep newly purchased plants in a quarantine area of the greenhouse for a few days in case they are carrying pests.

301

Chrysanthemums Keep potting on cuttings and young plants into larger sized pots as their roots grow. To encourage well-branched plants to form, pinch out the shoot tips. The number of shoots retained to flower depends on the variety being grown.

Early Summer

Everything is growing strongly now, including the weeds, and the priority is to get everything planted up ready for the summer displays and crops. As temperatures increase so does the need for daily watering, so find time while relaxing in your garden each evening to potter round the plot with a watering can.

THE FLOWER GARDEN

Summer bedding Complete planting out of tender bedding plants, either in pots and containers or directly in borders, watering them in with a solution of liquid feed.

Training climbers Tie in to walls, trellis and supports the new growth of climbers and shrubs like honeysuckle, roses, clematis and *Solanum crispum*.

Cuttings Plant out chrysanthemums and dahlias raised from cuttings, giving each a strong stake to support the flower stems as they grow. Pinch out the main shoot tip on early-flowering chrysanthemums to encourage them to produce well branched plants.

Canna lilies Plants grown in pots in the greenhouse can be planted outside, providing taller growing accent plants within summer bedding displays.

Layering shrubs Raise new plants of cytisus, deciduous azaleas, magnolias and other shrubs by layering low-growing shoots of young growth to soil level. Keep soil round shoots layered earlier in the year constantly moist.

Supporting Continue tying flower spikes to canes on tall-growing perennials, like delphiniums.

Spraying roses Rose varieties which always succumb to mildew or black spot should be sprayed with a suitable fungicide at regular intervals throughout the summer. Replace disease-prone roses with new disease-resistant varieties in the future. Where greenfly are also a problem, apply a combined insecticide and fungicide.

Disbudding roses For extra-large rose blooms, perhaps for cutting or for exhibition, remove any buds developing at the side of the main terminal bloom on each shoot.

Feeding Sprinkle granules of a general fertilizer round flowering plants and shrubs. Hoe into the soil surface and water in if the weather remains dry. Alternatively, give plants a generous soaking with liquid feed every fortnight.

Clematis Prune large and overgrown *C. montana* after flowering, cutting back hard to encourage new growth.

KEEPING A RECORD
❖

Take photographs of your garden each month to develop a detailed record of your borders for future reference. These can be used to identify gaps in displays and help you remember the flower colours, size and habit of neighbouring plants so that you can be sure of ordering new plants that will fit in with your colours and enhance your planting scheme.

PRUNING SHRUBS
❖

• *Prune late spring- and early summer-flowering shrubs like philadelphus, weigela, pyracantha, ceanothus, kerria,* Berberis darwinii, *escallonia and deutzia immediately after flowering.*

• *Although pruning is not needed every year, it encourages new growth from the base and prevents shrubs becoming tall but bare at the bottom.*

• *A system of renewal pruning can be used for many shrubs, cutting out about one in three shoots to promote fresh new shoots to grow up and replace them.*

• *On wall-trained shrubs, tie in new shoots to support wires or trellis. Remove shoots growing directly away from, or straight into, the wall. Healthy new shoot tips of many shrubs can be used as cuttings.*

• *After pruning, give shrubs a generous soaking with liquid feed and cover the soil round them with a mulch.*

THE KITCHEN GARDEN
Vegetable crops

Beans Plant out runner beans or dwarf French beans raised in pots in the greenhouse, or sow directly outside for a later crop.

Potatoes Draw soil up round the stems to encourage them to root into this ridge of soil and develop a larger crop. Sprinkle a general fertilizer along the rows, mixing this into the soil as earthing up proceeds.

Outdoor cucumbers Plant out ridge cucumbers in cold frames. In warmer regions they can often be grown successfully outside.

Planting out Plant out leeks, self-blanching celery, marrows, courgettes, squashes and pumpkins.

Tomatoes Both bush and cordon tomatoes can also be planted out now risk of frost has passed. Tie cordon tomatoes to thick stakes standing at least 90cm (3ft) tall. Train these up as a single stem, removing their side shoots, while bush tomato varieties can be left to scramble over the ground unchecked.

Broad beans Pinch out the soft tips of broad bean plants to reduce the risk of attack by blackfly.

Chicory Sow chicory as soon as possible, growing roots that can be lifted and potted next winter to raise chicons.

Salad sowings Sow a few seeds of salad crops like lettuce, radish and salad leaves every fortnight during summer.

Crops to sow Other crops to sow now for a late harvest include endive, swede, beetroot, carrots, chicory, marrow, kohl rabi, purslane, New Zealand spinach, swede, sweet corn, Chinese cabbage, turnip and cauliflower. Thin out seedlings from earlier sowings to their final spacing.

Fruit crops

Bird control Cover gooseberries, currants, strawberries and soft fruits with netting to keep birds away. Weave a cane into the base edge of the netting and peg down to the ground to prevent birds getting underneath.

Strawberries Spread a straw mulch along strawberry rows just under the foliage and developing fruits to keep them off the soil.

Gooseberries Pick small gooseberries to thin out heavy crops, leaving the remaining fruits well spaced out along the branches to continue growing to a larger size. Use these small, immature fruits for cooking.

Thinning apples Apple trees may have set a very heavy crop. Some of these will fall naturally, but you can help by picking off malformed, damaged or diseased fruits, or those showing signs of pest attack.

Plums Thin out fruit to leave them spaced about 5–7.5cm (2–3in) apart.

EARLY-SUMMER PLANT PROPAGATION

- *Lift and divide congested clumps of flag iris after flowering. Dig up the whole clump, cutting away old or damaged pieces of rhizome, and replant healthy individual flags into newly enriched soil. Keep the rhizome resting at the soil surface so that it can bake in the sun. In exposed sites the leaves, or flags, may be reduced in size.*
- *The soft new growth to be found on many shrubs makes ideal material for softwood cuttings. These will quickly root in a heated propagator or greenhouse. Try taking cuttings from hydrangea, cotoneaster, weigela and philadelphus among many others.*
- *Propagate only from healthy non-flowering shoots. Most root better if the cut end is dipped in a hormone-rooting compound which usually also contains a fungicide to prevent rotting. Or dip cuttings in a fungicide solution.*
- *Individual cuttings can be placed in small pots of moist, gritty compost. Cover pots with clear polythene bags, held in place with an elastic band. Once roots can be seen growing through the bottom of the pot, remove the bag.*

EASIER CROP WATERING

- *Marrows, courgettes, pumpkins and squashes can be planted outside now. Make a slight hollow in the ground to plant into, mounding the soil up round the young plant in a ring so that water poured into this depression runs directly to the roots.*
- *With outdoor tomatoes and other plants with a high demand for water, sink an empty 7.5–10cm (3–4in) plastic pot into the soil next to each plant. Watering straight into the pot directs water to the plant roots instead of just wetting the soil surface.*
- *Add a high-potash tomato fertilizer to the water once a week throughout the summer. Cover the soil surface round plants with a mulch of garden compost both to conserve moisture and to prevent the growth of weed seedlings.*

303

CHOOSING THE BEST PLANT FOOD

❖

Visit any garden centre and you will be faced with a vast array of fertilizers and plant foods, so how do you choose the right one? To start with, remember that plants need three main foods to grow and flourish. These are nitrogen, phosphorous and potassium, often referred to on the side of the packet as NPK. A number next to each letter indicates their respective proportions in the fertilizer. Nitrogen is needed for leaves and vigorous growth, phosphorous for root development, and potassium for the formation of flowers and fruits.

Consider what you want from each plant, and then choose a fertilizer offering the best balanced diet. For instance, for luscious lawn growth in spring and summer you should choose a food high in nitrogen, but when it comes to flowering pot plants or fruit bushes, plants will need plenty of potassium, or potash. To make life easier, many manufacturers have formulated fertilizers for specific uses, like lawns, shrubs, ericaceous plants, tomatoes and so on. Always use them at exactly the rate described on the packet.

HOME COMPOSTING

❖

Virtually all garden waste can be recycled into compost, along with old vegetables, fruit, peelings and egg shells from the kitchen. If possible, invest in two compost heaps, so that while one is rotting down fresh material can be added to the other. A totally enclosed bin with a lid is far better than an open one with slatted sides. Aim to mix together a variety of materials as they are added to the heap. Avoid putting in thick layers of lawn mowings, for instance, which can form a soggy mass. Add a little at a time between layers of clippings and other waste. Shred thick and woody material before composting. Mix a biological compost activator into the heap to speed up the composting process, and make sure the material never dries out.

Figs Tie in the shoots of fan-trained figs growing against warm walls. Pinch out the tips of all side shoots once they have produced five leaves.

Raspberry beetle If you have found small maggots in fruits in the past, consider spraying fruitlets with a suitable insecticide now to control the pest. Also spray blackberry, loganberry and other cane fruits. Control aphids, too, which spread debilitating viruses.

LAWN CARE

Mowing Cut lawns at least once a week now grass is growing strongly, and twice a week for a better finish on fine lawns.

Clippings Recycle grass cuttings, composting them in a bin or using them as a mulch round trees and bushes.

Length of cut If the weather is very dry, leave grass longer than normal to help it withstand drought.

Watering Do not waste water on your lawn by leaving lawn sprinklers running. Recycle your domestic water, pouring bowls of washing-up or bath water onto the lawn.

Lawn weeds Dig out or spot-treat individual weeds, like dandelions. Badly weed-infested lawns may need treating more thoroughly with a liquid or granular weedkiller. Remember to water the area if rain does not occur within a few days of application.

Feeding Feed grass with a high-nitrogen lawn feed. Liquid formulations are often quicker to apply than powders and get straight to work, while some granular formulations have a longer-lasting action to feed grass all season.

Lawn mowers If your mower is not cutting efficiently, adjust or sharpen the blades, or have the mower serviced.

POND CARE

General advice Top up water levels as they fall in hot weather. Use a child's small fishing net to scoop out duckweed and filamentous algae. Tidy the pond margins regularly, to prevent dead flower stems and leaves accumulating, and falling into the water.

Plant cover It is essential to achieve the right balance in a garden pond. Aim to cover about a half to two-thirds of the surface area with floating plants, like water lilies. Plant more aquatics in baskets now if this is necessary to achieve better cover.

Wildlife safety Make sure you place a small ramp into steep-sided, formal pools and water features so that small mammals, like hedgehogs, can climb out if they accidentally fall in. Informal ponds that have been made using a liner can be left with a pebble beach along one edge instead.

IN THE GREENHOUSE

Keeping cool Open greenhouse doors and vents each morning to keep temperatures down, but close them at night. Hang shade netting or blinds over the south side of greenhouses, or paint with shading paint.

Feeding Continue feeding plants in pots and growing bags at least once a week. It is sometimes better to use a liquid feed at half-strength twice a week to ensure plants in containers never go short of nutrients.

Cuttings Take cuttings from coleus, fancy-leaf begonias, African violets and other house plants. Also propagate fuchsias and Regal pelargoniums.

Pinks Take cuttings of non-flowering shoots about 10cm (4in) long, pushing several into small pots of compost.

Begonias Pot on tuberous begonias and support tall plants with canes. Feed begonias and gloxinias regularly.

Seed sowing Sow flowering pot plant varieties of *Primula malacoides*, *Primula sinensis*, calceolaria and cineraria.

Whitefly under glass Hang yellow sticky cards in the greenhouse or conservatory to trap whitefly. Release the parasitic wasp (*Encarsia*) as soon as whitefly are seen, to prevent the problem getting out of hand.

PEST CONTROL

Aphids Heavy infestations of greenfly may need treating with a soap-based spray or insecticide.

Slugs and snails Collect any slugs or snails you find in a jar of salt water to kill them. These pests often come out in the cool of an evening, and can be spotted by torch light. Alternatively, sprinkle slug pellets sparingly round plants and seedlings at risk of attack, or sink containers filled with old beer into the soil almost to their rims to catch slugs.

Codling moth Replace pheromone capsules in codling moth traps hanging among apple trees.

GROWING TREES AND SHRUBS IN TUBS

❖

Both evergreen and flowering shrubs and small trees, like Japanese maples, make perfect subjects for patio tubs. They are mobile, so displays can be varied, and plants taken with you when you move home.

Choose large containers at least 35cm (14in) across and the same depth, making sure they have drainage holes in the base. Add a layer of crocks before filling with a soil-based compost. However, for acid-loving shrubs like camellias and blueberries, use an ericaceous compost. Plant, leaving a

5cm (2in) gap between compost level and the top of the pot to make watering easier. Shrubs will require almost daily watering at the height of summer, plus a liquid feed each week. Stand pots on bricks or feet to improve drainage.

Fruit trees can also be grown in large tubs. Choose compact varieties of peach, cherry, plum, apple and other fruits specially recommended for this purpose, often grown on a dwarf rootstock. If you only have space for a single tree, choose a self-fertile variety, otherwise a pollinator will be needed.

EARLY-SUMMER MAINTENANCE

❖

❏ Pinch out side shoots of sweet peas being grown as cordons.

❏ Pick off the dead flowerheads from rhododendrons and azaleas.

❏ Sow seed of wallflowers in a corner of the garden to transplant in autumn, planting them with bulbs for flowers next spring.

❏ Support gladioli in exposed gardens by tying their foliage and the developing flower spikes loosely to canes inserted alongside each plant.

❏ Hoe or hand-weed paths and borders regularly. Treat perennial weeds with a systemic weedkiller.

❏ Mark the position of spring-flowering bulbs when their foliage dies down or is removed, so that they will not be damaged by careless digging.

❏ Save any rain that falls in water butts to use on the garden. Give extra water to plants growing at the base of walls where the soil can remain very dry despite rain.

❏ Cut overgrown *Clematis alpina* and *C. macropetala* back hard once flowering is over.

❏ Cut down early-flowering perennials like delphiniums, lupins and nepeta to tidy the plants and hopefully encourage a second flush of bloom later in the year.

❏ Pinch out the tips of trailing plants in hanging baskets to make them branch out. Pick off dead flowers every few days.

❏ Raise biennials and perennials by sowing now, in pots or in a nursery bed. Plant out in the autumn.

305

Midsummer

At the height of summer, when garden displays reach a crescendo, take time to learn from your own successes and from those of friends and neighbours. Consider dead-heading and watering as pleasurable routines to be savoured, in order to prolong the flowering season, but look ahead to preparations for the seasons to come.

THE FLOWER GARDEN

Bedding plants Dead-head plants in baskets, containers and borders every few days to keep them tidy and productive. Allowing them to set seed looks messy and results in an early end to your flower display.

Autumn-flowering bulbs Buy bulbs to plant now for autumn blooms. These include colchicums, autumn crocus, sternbergia, *Nerine bowdenii* and *Amaryllis belladonna*.

Sweet peas Remember to water regularly, and either pick flowers or remove dead seedheads to ensure that plants continue to flower.

Heathers Spread a fresh mulch of compost or bark round heathers.

Philadelphus When flowering is over, prune out a proportion of the oldest and weakest shoots and prune to improve the shape of the shrubs.

Dahlias Support new growth, which can be easily damaged in strong winds, and feed with a liquid fertilizer.

Blue hydrangeas Water regularly with a solution of colourant to ensure blue varieties remain blue next season, and to encourage pink ones to turn blue where soil conditions are not naturally acid.

Iris Finish splitting congested clumps of bearded iris.

Roses Trim back stems that have finished flowering to a point just above a leaf. This encourages the formation of new growth which carries a late flush of bloom. However, do not prune back varieties that form colourful autumn hips.

Pruning wisteria Tie in long shoots of new growth to continue developing wisteria's framework. Take the main growth upwards, then along wires so that the flowers can drape from these in tiers. In midsummer, prune back all side shoots to about 15–10cm (6–8in) of the main stem. These same shoots will be shortened still further in winter to about 5cm (2in). This twice-yearly pruning encourages flowering spurs to form along the main shoots.

Care of wisteria Keep well watered during any dry periods in summer and feed established wisteria with a high-potash liquid feed at regular intervals to promote flowering. Always buy a named variety of wisteria, never an un-named seedling. Plants can take several years to establish and flower.

ROSE SUCKERS

Keep an eye out for rose suckers growing on rootstocks from below ground level. Excavate the soil to find the point of origin and pull cleanly away; suckers can re-grow if simply cut off with secateurs. Cut any suckers growing on the stems of standard roses neatly away with a knife. Avoid hoeing too deeply round roses as damage to the roots encourages suckers to form.

RAISING NEW LILIES

Propagate new lilies from scales now, carefully lifting bulbs after flowering and removing a few healthy plump outer scales before replanting. Wash in a fungicide solution before placing in clear polythene bags of moist vermiculite to develop. When roots and small bulbs can be seen on each scale, pot up individually and place in a cold frame to grow on for a year before planting in a nursery bed. It will take about three years for bulbs to reach flowering size. Some varieties develop bulbils at each leaf up their stem. When these are plump and come away easily in your hand they can be picked off and planted shallowly in pots or seed trays like large seeds to grow on.

306

CUTTING HEDGES

Most hedges need only a single cut in mid- to late summer. If you time it right, any new growth forming will produce a neat-looking hedge for the winter. Hedges to prune over the coming weeks include beech, hornbeam, thorns like hawthorn, and conifers such as thuja and Lawson cypress. Yew can be cut a little later. All the above plants should be cut with shears or hedge trimmers. The exception is laurel, whose shoots are best cut individually with secateurs to prevent leaving unsightly large, torn leaves which die back.

More regular trimming is required to keep some formal hedges and topiary looking neat and pristine. Box, privet and Lonicera nitida *need cutting more often, from late spring onwards, to maintain a well-shaped formal hedge. Give the final cut in late summer so that further growth ripens and hardens before the onset of cold weather.*

To ensure a level top and an even cut, run a length of string between two canes at either end of the hedge, joined by a string set at the desired height: use this as a guideline to cut up to. With tall hedges, taper the sides slightly as you cut, leaving the base a little wider than the top to allow more light to reach the hedge. Spread a large sheet along the base of the hedge to collect prunings, then shred and compost them.

Propagating plants

Cuttings Propagate a wide range of tender perennials from cuttings now, including argyranthemums, coleus, osteospermum, fuchsia, pelargonium and felicia. Root into small pots, or strike several cuttings to a larger pot and divide once rooted. These will produce well-rooted young plants in 7.5cm (3in) pots to keep through the winter.

Layering Bend shoots of honeysuckle, wisteria or passion flower down to the ground, slit the stem, dust with rooting powder and bury this portion of the stem in the soil. Hold in place with a large stone and do not let the soil dry out. Tie the shoot tip to a cane. Layered shoots take about a year to root well.

Shrubs Take soft and semi-ripe cuttings using non-flowering shoots of shrubs such as cotinus, potentilla, ivy, hydrangea, spiraea, rosemary, weigela, pyracantha, hypericum, honeysuckle, philadelphus, cotoneaster and ceanothus as well as hedging plants.

Roses Many varieties grow easily from shoot cuttings. Produce cuttings about 30cm (12in) long by trimming below a leaf joint at the base, removing lower leaves, and trimming above a leaf at the top to remove the soft shoot tip. Insert to about half their depth in slits in the soil, and leave to root and develop until the following autumn when you can lift and transplant them.

Carnations To raise new plants, layer non-flowering side shoots. First improve the soil with compost, then bend shoots down to the soil. Make a small diagonal slit through a joint, peg down to hold firmly in place, cover with compost and water in. Keep moist until rooted, when a young plant can be dug up, detached from the parent and planted out.

TASKS FOR MIDSUMMER

❑ When water is scarce at the height of summer, give priority to soft fruits and vegetables, where watering can significantly increase your yields.

❑ Never let hanging baskets and containers go short of water; add a high-potash liquid feed to the water every week.

❑ Consider setting up an automated system connected to the tap to make watering easier, enabling you to control the time and duration of irrigation with a computerized tap timer.

❑ Keep on top of both annual and perennial weeds. Regularly hand-weed borders and hoe the soil between plants during dry weather to create a dust mulch.

❑ Apply mulches of compost over the soil to prevent the germination of annual weed seedlings. Use contact or non-residual weedkillers only if all other methods of weed control have failed.

❑ Wipe aphids off leaves by hand or use soap-based sprays.

❑ Pick fresh herbs regularly to dry or to freeze.

❑ Visit rose nurseries to see new varieties in bloom, and order now for autumn delivery and planting.

❑ Compost all your kitchen and garden waste, mixing shredded prunings and other material with lawn cuttings. Add an activator to boost decomposition. Empty compost bins, mix the contents and re-fill them to make the best garden compost.

Camellias Take cuttings of new shoots of camellias, rooting them in gritty compost in a covered propagator.

Hibiscus Pull off non-flowering side shoots with a heel of bark. Trim with a knife and insert into pots of free-draining compost. Place in a shaded frame to root.

Blackberry Bend the tips of new shoots down to soil level and bury in pots of compost. These can be tip-layered to root and form new plants.

PRUNING SOFT FRUIT

❖

Gooseberries and red and white currants can be summer pruned now. Prune back all side shoots to five leaves from the main stem, leaving the main shoot tips unpruned. This encourages fruiting spurs to develop on a framework of stems. Shorten the side shoots on cordon-trained fruits in the same way.

Blackcurrants are pruned differently, as they need to form new shoots from the base rather than develop fruiting spurs on a permanent stem framework. Prune out about a quarter of the oldest and weakest stems down to their base immediately after fruit has been picked. This makes room for new, young stems.

THE KITCHEN GARDEN
Vegetable crops

Lettuce Pick while young and tender, cutting every alternate one in a row to leave others more space to develop. Sow weekly to ensure continuity of harvest.

Endive Sow now for autumn crops.

Runner beans Never let plants go short of water. Pick over several times a week to ensure no beans are left to get tough.

Potatoes Dig up second earlies when their tops start to die, but keep maincrop varieties watered, spraying with fungicide to prevent blight.

Brassicas Transplant cabbage, Brussels sprouts and other brassicas from seed beds to their final position and spacing.

Onions Hoe between rows to remove weeds. Keep well watered. Harvest Japanese onions planted last autumn.

Shallots Lift shallots when ripe, laying them on the soil surface to dry before cleaning for storage.

Swedes A final sowing can still be made in midsummer. Cover rows with fleece to protect from flea beetle.

Parsley Sow a row now to produce leaves for picking during the autumn.

Leeks Plant out leeks raised from seed once they are the thickness of a pencil.

Crops to sow This is the time to sow lettuce, spinach, beetroot, radish, endive, spring cabbage, kohl rabi, peas, turnips, chard, salad leaves and Chinese cabbage.

Fruit crops

Strawberries Trim off the foliage to just above the crowns after fruiting, and remove unwanted runners. Rake away old straw.

Figs Shorten the laterals on established figs to just five leaves.

Raspberries Continue thinning out crowded new canes, pruning unwanted canes down to soil level to leave the remaining ones about 15cm (6in) apart. Cover rows of summer-fruiting raspberries with netting to keep the birds away. Pick fruits regularly to enjoy them at their best.

Apples Thin out heavy crops, picking off small, damaged or infected fruits to give the remaining ones more room to develop. Aim to leave fruits spaced about every 10–15cm (4–6in) along the branches.

Cane fruit Once you have picked crops of loganberries, Tayberries and other cane fruits, cut their old fruited canes to the ground. Tie in all the new canes that have formed this year to support wires, spreading them out evenly.

Plums Thin out very heavy crops or support heavily laden branches with props to prevent them breaking under the weight of the crop.

PRUNING APPLES AND PEARS

❖

While winter pruning helps control the size, vigour and shape of fruit trees, pruning from mid- to late summer encourages the development of fruiting spurs along the branches. The flowers that will open next spring start forming within buds later this summer, so shorten all side shoots on apple and pear trees to just five leaves, or about

15cm (6in), from their base. Trim any shoots developing from these back to just one leaf, or about 2.5cm (1in). This is particularly important on trained forms of fruit tree, such as those growing as fans, cordons and espaliers, to maintain both their shape and their productivity. Leave shoot tips unpruned to extend the framework of the tree.

LAWN CARE

Mowing Cut every week, or more often if you have time. Collect grass cuttings, mixing them with other material on the compost heap, or use them as a mulch round fruit trees.

Feeding Feed pale lawns with a high-nitrogen liquid feed to green up the leaves and boost growth. If other lawn problems exist, consider applying a triple-action lawn feed, weed and mosskiller instead.

Watering Keep lawns watered during dry spells, recycling washing up and bath water on the lawn. If water is in short supply, and drought threatens, leave the grass longer as it will cope better with periods of water shortage.

Edging Trim edges after mowing. Cut a new edge if they get worn or damaged.

Spiking Spike heavily compacted areas with a fork to relieve compaction.

POND CARE

Blanket weed Remove the long strands of blanket weed that invade ponds in summer by pushing a long stick into the water and twisting it out.

Topping up As water evaporates during the summer, top up the level of ponds and water features with a hosepipe.

Filters Clean pump filters regularly to ensure they do not get clogged up with algae. Install an ultra-violet unit in the pipework to the pump to kill water-borne algae as they pass through.

Pruning Selectively cut away leaves or shoots from very vigorous water lilies and aquatic plants to prevent them smothering their neighbours. Dead-head bog plants and pick off any damaged leaves to stop debris falling into the water.

PEST CONTROL UNDER GLASS

❖

❏ Examine plants each week for signs of pests, picking them off or treating at once if any are found.

❏ Introduce the small parasitic wasp, *Encarsia formosa*, to the greenhouse if whitefly are present. Refrain from using any chemicals either before or after their introduction or these beneficial predators may be killed by chemical residues.

❏ Damp down greenhouse floors each morning or mist lightly over plants to increase humidity which deters red spider mite attack. If infestation is getting severe, introduce the predatory mite *Phytoseiulus persimilis*.

❏ Water pots of compost with a solution of nematodes for the control of vine weevil grubs.

IN THE GREENHOUSE

Ventilation Open doors and vents daily or control by fitting automatic vent openers. Re-apply shading paint to help reduce high temperatures.

Cuttings Continue taking cuttings of hydrangeas and other plants. Pot up any rooted cuttings taken earlier.

Tomatoes Remove side shoots and tie main stems to supports. Pick ripe fruits as they form and remove leaves below the lowest truss to improve the air circulation. Check watering daily, as intermittent watering can result in split fruit. Feed every week.

Cucumbers Harvest fruits regularly. Continue pinching off the tips of side shoots two leaves beyond a female flowers. Remove male flowers.

SAFETY IN THE GARDEN

❖

❏ Always wear thick gloves when handling roses or thorny plants.

❏ Place eye protectors on top of canes and pointed plant supports.

❏ When using nylon line trimmers, wear goggles and clothing with long sleeves and trousers, to protect the eyes from stones and debris thrown up during use, and the skin from irritants in plant sap.

❏ Wear strong shoes or boots when digging or mowing the lawn.

❏ Never leave garden tools lying on the ground; they can be a hazard.

❏ Choose cloches and frames covered with unbreakable polycarbonate or clear plastic rather than glass.

❏ Always plug electric garden tools into residual current circuit breakers. Never touch a cut or damaged cable unless the power supply has been switched off.

❏ Keep pets and children out of the garden if power tools or pruning equipment is being used.

❏ If young children visit your garden, be aware of potentially harmful plants, like laburnum. Try to avoid growing poisonous plants if possible.

❏ Use chemicals sparingly. Read the label before use, and always follow the manufacturer's instructions to the letter.

Melons Pollinate female flowers, easily identified by a swelling behind the bloom, by dabbing with pollen from a male bloom. Support developing fruits in small nets attached to the greenhouse frame to hold their weight.

Late Summer

It is a good idea to simply relax at this time, although so many plants are looking their best and vying for your attention with colour and fragrance. Enjoy the simple pleasure of pottering in the late-summer garden, with pruners to hand for regular dead-heading to keep the display looking its very best. Look to the future by taking choice cuttings.

THE FLOWER GARDEN

Bulbs Plant out bulbs of colchicums, sternbergia, autumn crocus and the Madonna lily (*Lilium candidum*).

Perennials Cut off the old flower spikes of early-flowered perennials, like delphiniums, polemoniums, lupins and foxtail lilies (*Eremurus*).

Everlasting flowers Pick dried flowerheads and seedheads from a range of plants. Annuals like limonium and helichrysum are at their best, as are seedheads of poppies, nigella, lunaria, moluccella, eryngiums and a range of grasses. Hang upside down in bunches in a dry, airy room.

Supports Late-flowering perennials like chrysanthemums and Michaelmas daisies are growing taller by the day and getting more top-heavy as their flowers develop. Check plant supports are in place, adding more canes and string to ensure they hold up and cannot be flattened by wind and rain.

Hedges Trim back laurel hedges using secateurs to remove complete shoots. Also cut privet, beech, hornbeam, yew, box and holly. Most conifer hedges can be given their single cut of the year at the end of late summer.

Sweet peas Untie the stems of cordon-trained sweet peas which have reached the tops of their supports. Lower stems to the ground and re-tie the tips to provide new canes for them to climb.

Dahlias Pick dahlias regularly and continue tying in stems to their supports. Maintain regular liquid feeding. Trap earwigs that can damage flower buds, especially on dahlias, in upturned pots full of straw or crumpled newspaper on top of short canes. Empty out daily and destroy earwigs.

Camellias Camellias will be forming flower buds now to bloom next spring, so ensure they never go short of water or their buds can drop prematurely.

Roses Prune rambler roses when their flowering is over.

THE KITCHEN GARDEN
Vegetable crops

Harvesting Pick crops regularly to keep plants productive, particularly on courgettes and beans. Pick sweet corn while cobs are sweet and tender. Raise large marrows selected for storage up onto bricks to keep in the sun to ripen and harden their skins.

310

PROPAGATION PLANS

❖

❑ **Choose healthy stems of new growth on ramblers and other roses to use as cuttings. Remove the soft growth at the tip to prepare cuttings about 30cm (12in) long, removing lower leaves, and inserting to about two-thirds of their length in a slit of soil in a sheltered part of the garden. Keep watered.**

❑ **Take cuttings of shrubs like lavender, choosing non-flowering side shoots. Others to try include aucuba, berberis, ceanothus, lonicera and philadelphus.**

❑ **Peg down non-flowering shoots of carnations into the soil to root. Water regularly. Cut off and plant separately when well rooted.**

❑ **Collect stem bulbils from lilies. Plant in trays to grow on over the next few years to flowering size.**

❑ **Penstemons can be raised from cuttings. Place individually into 7.5cm (3in) pots and cover with a clear bag until rooted.**

Watering Water crops as regularly as possible to increase yields, especially runner beans and others carrying fruits and pods. Maincrop potato yields will increase considerably if watered now.

Celery Never allow celery to get dry at the root. Keep watered and earth up trench varieties to blanch their stems.

Tomatoes Pinch out the tops of outdoor tomatoes, as any further flowers developing now will not form ripe fruit before autumn.

Blanching Cover a few endive plants with plates to blanch their leaves.

Sowing Sow hardy varieties of winter lettuce outside or in frames. Sow winter spinach. Enjoy tasty turnip tops this autumn by sowing a few now.

Ordering Order onion sets and garlic for autumn planting.

Fruit crops

Strawberries Tidy up strawberry beds, cutting off unwanted runners, and trimming all the foliage down to the crown with shears. Transplant strawberry runners rooted in pots or plant up new beds with healthy plants obtained from a specialist grower.

Tree fruits Water apples, pears and other fruits to help increase their size. Pick early-ripening apple varieties like 'Redsleeves', 'Discovery', 'Epicure' and 'George Cave' which can be eaten straight from the tree.

Bird protection Cover cherries and autumn-fruiting raspberries and blackberries with nets, or hang reflective scarers in trees to keep birds away.

Plums Once fruit has been picked, prune back side shoots to three leaves, and cut out dead wood. Do not prune shoots needed to extend the framework.

LAWN CARE

Mowing Continue regular mowing to keep lawns looking smart, and trim the edges each week.

Spiking Spike lawns with a hollow-tined aerator, sweeping up the soil cores left on the lawn surface. Brush sand or gritty compost into the holes.

Repairs Repair damaged lawn edges, and patch up worn areas. Spot-treat individual weeds with a herbicide or dig out by hand.

New lawns Prepare sites for sowing or laying lawns in early autumn.

IN THE GREENHOUSE

Watering Keep crops in pots and grow bags, like tomatoes, peppers and cucumbers, well watered. Never allow their compost to get dry; feed weekly.

Keeping cool Ventilate daily to keep temperatures down, opening doors in addition to roof and side vents. Close on cool nights.

Propagation Take cuttings of tender perennials like fuchsias, pelargoniums and argyranthemums now, to produce well-rooted plants that will survive the winter. Pot up the rooted cuttings.

Cyclamen Sow cyclamen seed to raise indoor flowering pot plants. Water dormant plants towards the end of summer to bring them back into growth.

Gloxinias Reduce watering of gloxinias when they have finished flowering. Once their foliage has dried, pick off and store tubers for the winter.

Hyacinth Plant prepared bulbs in bowls, keeping to one variety per bowl to ensure they flower uniformly.

Bulbs Plant freesia, lachenalia and early narcissus, like 'Paperwhite'.

FRUIT PRUNING
❖

❏ Finish summer pruning apple trees.

❏ Remove old fruited canes of summer raspberries completely, cutting them off at soil level. Tie in and space out the remaining canes of new growth, which will fruit next summer.

❏ Give old blackcurrant bushes their annual prune, removing about a quarter of the oldest branches to make room for new growth.

❏ Prune out shoots of peaches and nectarines that carried fruit. Train in the new shoots to their supports, pinching off any side shoots growing from these.

❏ Summer prune damsons and gages after the fruit has been harvested, removing all fruited wood.

❏ Prune off shoot tips on gooseberries badly infected by powdery mildew.

311

LATE-SUMMER CHECKLIST
❖

❏ Collect seed from a range of flowers. Some can be saved and stored for future use and others, like foxgloves and aquilegia, sown freshly by scattering around to fill gaps in borders.

❏ Pot up a few clumps of parsley, cutting off their leaves to encourage fresh growth for winter use.

❏ Water pots of nerines to encourage growth and autumn flowering.

❏ Regularly dead-head flowers in hanging baskets and tubs.

❏ Order spring-flowering bulbs for autumn planting.

❏ Pick fresh herbs to dry or chop and store in ice cubes in the freezer.

❏ Sow hardy annual flowers in pots now to flower early next year.

❏ Remove suckers developing from the roots of roses and other fruiting and ornamental trees.

❏ Prune lavender bushes if this was not completed last season.

Early Autumn

After a relaxing summer it is time for a new surge of activity in the autumn garden. It is an exciting time because, as we finish collecting the produce and clearing away the remains of one season, we start putting plans in place for the next. The first bulbs can already be planted to flower next spring.

THE FLOWER GARDEN

Tender perennials Lift plants from summer bedding displays, clean off dead flowers and leaves, then pot them up and bring into the greenhouse or home for the winter.

Sweet peas Sow seed in pots in autumn, and overwinter plants in a cold frame to plant out next spring. These plants will flower earlier than those sown outdoors in spring.

Moving shrubs Overgrown or badly positioned shrubs and conifers can be transplanted to a better site now. Thoroughly prepare the new planting site, digging compost deeply into the soil. Very large shrubs could lose quite a lot of roots during the process, so prune out some of the oldest top growth to help them survive.

Rose care Finish pruning out all shoots from rambler and climbing roses that carried flowers as soon as they have faded. Remove suckers from round bush roses, or any growing from the stems of standards.

Pruning perennials Cut down faded and dying flower stems from border perennials, tidying up the plants but leave as much foliage as possible. Collect, wash and store away plant supports no longer needed.

Dahlias Tie tall flower stems to supports the prevent wind damage. Continue cutting blooms for the home.

Hardy annuals In mild regions hardy annuals can be sown outside in autumn instead of delaying until spring. Sow where you would like them to flower. Varieties to choose include calendula, nigella, godetia, eschscholzia, larkspur, candytuft, annual alyssum, Shirley poppies, scabious and limnanthes.

Anemones Plant tubers of anemone 'De Caen' and 'Saint Brigid' at intervals to extend their flowering next spring.

SPRING BEDDING

❖

Clear areas of summer bedding now getting past its best to make room for spring bedding, which can be planted out as soon as space becomes available. All old plant remains can be lifted, chopped up and composted. Early planting allows the bedding to settle, establish new roots, and develop bushy plants before the onset of winter. For best effect, base your spring displays on a single colour theme, choosing varieties which flower for a long period. These could include wallflowers, pansies, sweet Williams, primulas, polyanthus, forget-me-nots and others. To add a second tier of colour, and extend the flowering season still further; underplant bedding with taller tulips to grow up through them in matching or contrasting colours.

BUYING AND PLANTING BULBS

❖

A wide range of spring-flowering bulbs can be planted now, including crocus, hyacinth, muscari, iris and daffodil. Most should be planted directly in borders where you would like them to flower. Extend the season of interest of your winter patio tubs into spring by the addition of bulbs, as well as planting bulbs in pots and bowls for indoor displays.

Choose bulbs which look healthy, with no signs of rot or mould, and which are firm to the touch. Bulbs are graded by size, larger bulbs costing more but producing better blooms. As a general rule, plant so that bulbs are covered by at least twice their depth in soil. Most garden centres sell only a limited range of bulbs, but a greater variety is available by mail-order.

312

Dutch iris To follow on from spring bulbs, plant blocks of Dutch iris in sunny positions, setting them about 7.5cm (3in) deep by 15cm (6in) apart. These flower in early summer.

New planting Early autumn is a good time to plant evergreen shrubs, conifers or hedging plants, like laurel. Warm soil conditions encourage root growth and establishment before winter.

Carnations Side shoots layered to the soil in summer should now have rooted, and can be detached from the parent and planted in a new site. Alternatively, lift and pot up into 10cm (4in) pots. Keep in a frame for the winter to plant out next spring.

THE KITCHEN GARDEN
Vegetable crops

Onions Lift onion crops now, easing each bulb up with a fork to break its roots, then leaving to dry on the soil surface for a day before collecting. Lay in the greenhouse to dry fully before cleaning and storing in a shed or garage.

Watering Continue watering outdoor crops like tomato, beans and courgettes to encourage more fruits and pods to form and ripen.

Spring cabbage Plant out at close spacing. From early spring, harvest every other cabbage, leaving more space for the remaining ones to develop. Plant in shallow trenches so that soil can be pulled up round the stems for extra support as they grow.

Lettuce Sow hardy winter varieties of lettuce under cloches or in the borders of a greenhouse.

Celery Continue wrapping trench varieties of celery with newspaper, then draw earth up round the stems to blanch them ready for cutting in late autumn.

Turnip tops Make a sowing of turnips now for cutting as green turnip tops later in the year.

Potatoes Keep the foliage of maincrop varieties free from potato blight disease until ready to harvest, using regular fungicide sprays. If blight appears, cut all the foliage off right away to prevent the disease spreading to the tubers. Continue harvesting early varieties as required for the kitchen.

Outdoor tomatoes Strip off both ripe and unripe fruits from outdoor plants before they are damaged by an early frost or blight. Alternatively, lift the entire plants and hang them in the greenhouse for the remaining fruits to ripen under cover.

Root crops Carefully lift maincrop carrots and beetroot before autumn rain causes the roots to swell and split. Cut off the foliage and store healthy crops in boxes between layers of almost dry sand or compost. These keep in good condition for several months under frost-free conditions.

Endive Cover a few plants each week with plates to blanch them for use in salads. Complete blanching takes about two weeks. Upturned flower pots can also be used, but cover holes with a tile to exclude light. Take precautions against slugs and snails.

Leeks Continue blanching leeks, covering plants with tubes of cardboard or drainpipe.

Harvesting Pick crops at their best including marrows, runner beans, ridge cucumbers, spinach, sweet corn, radish, beetroot and salads. In cold districts complete harvesting before the end of this season.

EARLY-AUTUMN PROPAGATION

DIVIDING PERENNIALS Those gardening on light soils can lift and divide congested clumps of perennials during autumn, replanting healthy portions of young growth into enriched soil, but discarding old and unproductive portions. If your soil is heavy, delay dividing perennials until spring.

SAVING SEED Collect seed from hardy annuals, perennials and other flowers. Many, like aquilega, produce masses of seed which can be sprinkled directly onto the soil and raked in where you would like new plants to grow. Once collected, dried and cleaned, store seed in individual envelopes labelled with variety name in a sealed box. Keep in a cool place.

ROSES Take hardwood cuttings from roses, choosing healthy stems of the current season's growth. Trim below a leaf joint at the bottom, stripping off the lower leaves and cutting away the soft tip to just above a leaf to produce a cutting about 30cm (12in) long. Insert into slits in the soil outside filled with sharp sand or grit and leave to root and develop for about a year before transplanting.

LAVENDER Whole shoots of lavender can be used as cuttings now, pulling shoots away from the main stem with a heel. These can be rooted directly into gritty soil outside or in a cold frame.

OTHER SHRUBS Hardwood cuttings can be taken now, many with a heel, and rooted in gritty soil in a cold frame or under cloches. Shrubs to try include privet, laurel, holly, aucuba, berberis, phlomis, potentilla, griselinia, rosemary and many conifers. Keep soil moist at all times.

313

EARLY-AUTUMN MAINTENANCE

❖

❑ Cut down border perennials now past their best.

❑ Collect up, clean and store away canes and plant supports.

❑ Dig up and compost old summer bedding plants.

❑ Be ready to net ponds to prevent autumn leaves blowing in.

❑ Cut down any marginal plants round pools that are dying back.

❑ Plant spring-flowering bulbs in pots and containers.

❑ Save seed from flowering plants.

COLLECTING LEAVES

❖

All autumn leaves can be collected and composted into leafmould for use as a mulch, a soil conditioner or for mixing with potting compost. Garden vacuums are useful for collecting leaves, and some models shred them as they collect, speeding up their decomposition. On lawns, use a rotary lawn mower with blades set high to gather and shred leaves. Small quantities can be mixed with other garden waste and put on the compost heap, but large quantities of leaves are best stacked in leaf bins, or kept in black plastic sacks, with their tops tied, and a few air holes punched in the sides. Add a leaf compost activator to speed up decomposition, which should take from 6–12 months, depending on the type of leaf.

Fruit crops

Strawberries Well-rooted runners in pots can be planted out to form new beds. Healthy certified new stock should also be available to buy. Water well until established. Clear up strawberry beds, removing unwanted runners and hoeing between rows.

Peaches Continue pruning to remove all shoots that have carried fruit, then tying in new shoots to replace them.

Apples Harvest early-ripening varieties like 'Discovery', 'Beauty of Bath' and 'Blenheim Orange', and eat while crisp and at their best.

Cane fruits Prune all old fruited canes from hybrid cane fruits and loganberries at soil level. Tie in the new canes produced this year, spacing them out evenly. These will carry a crop of fruit next summer.

New fruit Order new trees and bushes to plant later this autumn and winter.

Cherries Cut out dead wood from fan-trained cherries. Prune back all side shoots previously shortened in summer to just three buds, and tie in growth.

Raising new gooseberries

Propagate new bushes by taking hardwood cuttings from healthy plants before their leaves drop. Take stems of the current season's growth and remove the soft tip to leave a cutting about 25cm (10in) long. Remove all buds except the top three or four, so that the resulting bush has a head of branches on a clean stem. Cover an area of soil with black polythene, pushing the cuttings down through it to about half their depth. Alternatively, insert in slits in the soil with grit in the base, firming soil back round them with your boot.

LAWN CARE

Sowing a new lawn This is an ideal time to sow a new lawn into soil prepared during the previous season. Be sure it has been well firmed and allowed to settle before levelling. Sow evenly, marking out the area and scattering seed in both directions, then raking it into the soil surface. Water the area if it does not rain, and ensure the soil remains moist until germination is complete, within two to three weeks. Use netting or scarers to keep birds away. Refrain from walking over the new lawn. Trim only lightly, with mower blades set high, when the growth is about 4–5cm (1½–2in) long.

Over-sowing Where grass growth is very thin and sparse, over-seed now with a suitable grass seed mixture. Cut the lawn, then rake the surface to remove debris. Sprinkle with seed, sweeping it into the surface. On small areas, cover with a fine layer of compost.

General care Continue regular mowing, raking off dead grass and any debris that has accumulated deep down in the lawn over the summer.

Feeding Apply an autumn lawn food to encourage good root growth and to strengthen the grass for the coming winter.

POND CARE

Plant division Lift and divide large marginal plants, or those growing in bog gardens. Cut up or pull apart, ensuring that each piece being replanted has a portion or root and shoot attached.

Primulas Plant out hardy primulas raised from seed or divisions.

Leaf netting Get ready to cover pools with netting to keep out fallen leaves.

IN THE GREENHOUSE

Cyclamen Sparingly water potted cyclamen that were dried off for the summer to encourage them back into growth. Pick off early flowers to ensure a good display later.

Freesias Plant pots of prepared freesia corms to use for displays or cut flowers.

Lachenalia Bulbs should be available for planting in pots now. Any saved from last year can be knocked out of their old containers and repotted in fresh compost.

Cuttings This is your last chance to take cuttings of geraniums and fuchsias which will root well in small pots to be kept through winter. Continue taking cuttings from impatiens, coleus, tradescantia, heliotrope, African violets, begonias and other plants.

Hardy annuals Sow pots of hardy annuals, like calendula and zinnia, for colourful displays in cold greenhouses and porches.

Clean-up Once old crops in pots and growing bags are past their best, pick any remaining produce. Cut down plants and take all the debris to the compost heap.

Cleaning glass Wash shade paints from the outside of the glazing, and clean all glass thoroughly inside and out to remove dirt and algal growth. This ensures maximum penetration of light during winter.

Heaters Make sure greenhouse heaters are in good working order, and paraffin or bottled gas supplies in stock.

Bulbs in bowls Plant early-flowering bulbs, including prepared hyacinths, in pots or bowls. Use bulb fibre or seed compost, planting so that the tips of the bulbs lie at the surface. After watering, place in a cool, sheltered position for the bulbs to root. Bring indoors only when shoots have developed to about 5–7.5cm (2–3in) long.

Begonias Reduce watering and allow the top growth on begonias and gloxinias to die down.

Achimenes Lay pots of hot water plant on their side so that the foliage will die down and compost dry out. Rhizomes can be left in the dry compost for the winter, or tipped out, cleaned and stored in envelopes.

Watering As nights get cooler and plant growth slows down in autumn, gradually reduce the quantity and frequency of watering. Allow compost to almost dry out between waterings, and stand pots on greenhouse staging instead of on moist capillary matting.

Chrysanthemums Bring late flowering varieties in pots into the greenhouse in case flower buds get damaged by frost.

Potting Complete potting up plants or cuttings early in autumn to ensure plants get established before winter.

Cutting the cost of greenhouse heating

Insulation Line the inside with bubble polythene to double glaze it and reduce heat loss. Hang a curtain of polythene across the doorway. Use thick sheets of white polystyrene to line the north side, especially under the staging.

Sealing draughts Mend poorly fitting doors and vents, sealing over low-level vents completely with clear polythene.

Broken glass Replace cracked panes.

Storage heaters Place dustbins filled with water under greenhouse staging to act as storage heaters. These warm up during the day, releasing their heat at night. This warm water can be used for watering plants.

WINTER POTS AND BASKETS

❖

Empty tubs, baskets and window boxes of summer bedding past their best, and replant to provide winter interest. Include a balance of hardy shrubs along with a few winter- and spring-flowering bedding plants and dwarf bulbs. Good shrubs include winter-flowering heathers, variegated euonymus, gaultheria and dwarf conifers. Cover the edges with trailing ivies, which can be pegged to the sides of baskets for complete cover.

Be generous when planting to produce an instant, mature look. Water well and then check regularly, at least twice a week. Winter pots will not require weekly feeding, but occasional liquid feeds in late winter and early spring will boost growth. Raise tubs off the ground on bricks to improve drainage.

STORING SUMMER BULBS

❖

- *Dig up bulbs and corms of non-hardy varieties to store in a dry and frost-free place over winter. Packing them in dry compost helps insulate them and prevents dehydration.*
- *Lift gladioli corms carefully, keeping named varieties separate. Cut foliage down to within 2.5cm (1in) of the corm, clean off any soil and pick off small cormlets to store separately in envelopes.*
- *Lift and dry begonia tubers and bulbs of canna lilies and eucomis and treat in a similar way.*

Mid-Autumn

Autumn colours transform the garden, changing almost daily as the foliage on deciduous trees and shrubs puts on a final show before falling. With bulb planting yet to be completed and the end-of-season clear-up in progress, there is still plenty to keep the gardener busy.

THE FLOWER GARDEN

Sweet peas Sow in deep containers in cold frames. Sow several per pot and either thin to leave the strongest or leave to plant out in groups.

Tulips Plant bulbs now, setting them up to 15–20cm (6–8in) deep where you want them to naturalize.

Spring bedding Plant out wallflowers, forget-me-nots, primulas, polyanthus, bellis, pansies and other bedding plants for spring flower displays. Many can be interplanted with spring bulbs which will grow up among them.

Planting This is a good time to plant shrubs, conifers and hedging. Soil conditions are still warm, so roots will grow to get plants established before the onset of winter.

Dahlias Lift tubers as soon as the foliage has been blackened by frost. Clean off soil, cut back stems, and stand upside down to drain water from them. Label, then store in boxes of compost.

Rambler roses Finish pruning as soon as possible, removing all old stems.

THE KITCHEN GARDEN
Vegetable crops

Harvesting Finish picking ripened marrows and bring in for winter storage. Pick all remaining outdoor tomatoes and tender crops. Lift potatoes, clean them and store in paper sacks in a frost-free place. Lift carrots and beetroot and store in boxes of compost.

Peas Sow a row of hardy peas and cover with cloches. Broad beans can also be sown now.

Brussels sprouts Pick off yellowing leaves and harvest when large enough.

Celery Finish earthing up trench celery to blanch the stems.

FLOWER BORDER CARE

❏ Cut down all dead flower stems on herbaceous perennials, and tidy borders to remove foliage and plant remains; compost this material. Leave late-flowering perennials.

❏ Divide congested perennials and herbs, like bergamot and lady's mantle, from mid- to late autumn, or delay until spring.

❏ Collect plant supports and canes to store for winter.

❏ Fork over the soil between plants in established borders to loosen the surface; remove weeds, then spread on a layer of well-rotted compost.

PREPARING FOR THE COLD WEATHER

Cooler days and even colder nights signal a timely warning of frost risk. Move all tender plants, especially tender perennials and shrubs like pelargoniums, fuchsias, cordylines and marguerites, to the shelter of a frost-free greenhouse. Lift and pot up those enjoyed during the summer in flower borders, and bring under cover as soon as possible.

Asparagus Cut all ferny shoots right down to soil level.

Cauliflowers Bend outer leaves over curds to prevent them discolouring.

Artichokes Finish harvesting globe artichokes before cutting down their tops. Cut back screens of Jerusalem artichokes to about 30cm (12in) from the ground once the leaves turn brown, and dig up the crop as required. Cover with a mulch to protect over winter.

Garlic Plant individual cloves of a hardy variety during autumn, spacing them about 15cm (6in) apart. Choose an open, sunny and free-draining site.

Herbs Pot up parsley, chives and other herbs for winter use, and keep on a sunny windowsill. Plant a few roots of mint in shallow trays and bring into a warm greenhouse to force fresh shoots to use over the coming months.

Digging Remove old crops, clear the ground and dig compost or manure into the soil. Leave heavy soil rough-dug so frost can penetrate to help break it down.

Fruit crops

Cherries Prune out fruited stems from 'Morello' and other varieties.

Cuttings Take hardwood cuttings from healthy bushes of gooseberries and currants, using shoots of the current season's wood.

Blackberries Prune all canes that have carried a crop of fruit back to ground level and tie new shoots produced this year in their place.

Blackcurrants Finish pruning old bushes, removing about a quarter of the oldest branches.

Strawberries Clean and tidy established strawberry beds, removing weeds and any runners growing between rows.

Harvesting and storing Continue to pick apples and pears as each variety ripens. Damaged fruits should be eaten or cooked right away; store only healthy fruits. Check crops in store regularly for signs of deterioration.

Grease bands Wrap grease bands round the trunks of apples, plums and cherries to catch the winter moth as she climbs to lay her eggs.

LAWN CARE

Leaves Collect up dead leaves as soon as they fall.

Raking Rake and scarify lawns to remove thatch and accumulated debris.

Spiking Improve drainage and relieve surface compaction with a hollow-tined aerator, filling the cores removed with sharp sand or grit.

Top-dressing Spread a layer of gritty loam-based compost over lawns.

Repairs Build up hollows over several months with thin layers of compost; mend damaged lawn edges.

IN THE GREENHOUSE

Watering Reduce watering now to suit the demands of each plant. It is far better to water individual pots in saucers than to use self-watering benches of capillary matting. Keep the atmosphere as dry as possible.

Protection Bring pots of tender bulbs and perennials into the greenhouse for the winter. Canna lilies, eucomis and many other bulbs die down completely, so require no water over winter.

Cuttings This is your last chance to take cuttings of argyranthemum, penstemon and other perennials.

Chrysanthemums Bring potted late-flowering varieties under glass before frost strikes. Keep the greenhouse well ventilated and check watering each day.

Begonias Refrain from watering tuberous begonias, gloxinias and achimenes to allow foliage to die down.

Fuchsias Reduce watering over winter, but never allow the compost to dry out completely. Wrap pipe insulation round the stems of standard fuchsias.

Old crops Remove old crops and growing bags once pickings diminish.

Young plants Finish potting on rooted cuttings and seedlings. Pinch out the tips of schizanthus and other plants to encourage well-branched, bushy growth.

Heating Get ready to clean glass and fix up bubble insulation. Check that heaters are working efficiently.

POND CARE

Marginals Cut down marginal plants as their foliage dies back for the winter.

Netting Stretch net over ponds to prevent leaves blowing in; anchor it down tightly round the edges. On small formal ponds, make a frame covered with netting to fit right over the pond. Remove once all leaves have fallen.

Winter storage Remove pumps and filters. Clean well before storing.

Heating Float a pond heater on fish ponds, especially those made from concrete, to prevent thick ice forming on the surface. This expands to crack ponds and can trap harmful gases.

MID-AUTUMN MAINTENANCE

❏ Sprinkle fertilizer over areas to be planted up this autumn.

❏ Move shrubs found to be growing in the wrong place, or to relieve congestion in packed borders.

❏ Empty and wash out water butts, before replacing them to collect winter rain.

❏ Order fruit trees, bushes, roses and shrubs to plant out over winter. Where possible, choose newer, disease-resistant varieties.

❏ Check all tree stakes and ties. Replace loose and damaged ties, and loosen any which are too tight.

❏ Continue taking hardwood cuttings of roses and shrubs like cornus, willow, buddleja and ribes.

❏ Propagate hedging varieties of conifers from cuttings, using shoots of the new growth. Root directly into gritty soil in a cold frame.

❏ Throw a net over a branch carrying holly berries to keep the birds away and keep this to cut for indoor decorations.

❏ Order farmyard manure and compost required for soil conditioning and mulching.

Late Autumn

There is still much to be done in the autumn garden, with ground to prepare and new shrubs, roses and hedging to plant. Removing old crops and tidying at the end of one season makes the garden ready to plan for the next.

THE FLOWER GARDEN

Agapanthus Move pots to a cold greenhouse or frame for the winter.

Chrysanthemums Once late-flowering varieties have finished blooming they can be dug up, labelled and stored in boxes. They can be encouraged into growth in late winter to form cuttings.

Hedging For the best value hedge, plant bare-rooted deciduous shrubs like beech and hawthorn.

Buddleja Shorten tall stems by half to reduce wind rock, but wait until spring before pruning back hard.

Jasmine Take heel cuttings of winter jasmine and root in pots in a frame.

Rock gardens Pick off leaves that have fallen on alpine plants, and give a final weed by hand. Replenish gravel mulches round alpines.

Soil preparation When weather allows, dig over and prepare soil for new planting.

Planting Continue planting trees, shrubs, roses, conifers and hedging.

Bulbs Finish planting up tulips and other spring-flowering bulbs. Lift dahlias, cannas, gladioli or other tender bulbs for storage under dry and frost-free conditions.

Roses Check stakes and ties on standard roses. Collect and destroy fallen leaves infected with black spot. Shorten long stems and top growth on standard roses to reduce wind rock.

THE KITCHEN GARDEN
Vegetable crops

Peas Sow hardy varieties in well drained soil, covering with cloches for extra protection.

Brussels sprouts Pick crops which are large enough from the bottom of the stem upwards and remove yellowing and fallen leaves.

Bean trench Dig out a trench where next summer's runner bean crop will be grown, and fill the base of it with leaves, compost, old crops, weeds and kitchen waste over the winter. Cover with soil in spring before planting the beans.

Chicory Lift chicory roots, plant in pots, then place in the greenhouse covered with upturned pots to force tasty chicons.

Jerusalem artichokes Cut down the tops and carefully dig out of the soil, cleaning and storing in paper bags in a similar way to potatoes.

Root crops Lift and store beetroot, turnips, salsify and scorzonera in boxes of compost. Parsnips can also be stored, or left in the soil. However, they can be attacked by soil pests, and are difficult to harvest if the ground freezes.

Crops in store Check vegetables in store for signs of rot or deterioration, and use crops while at their best.

318

PLANTING ROSES
❖

Bare-rooted roses should be arriving in garden centres or will be available by mail-order. Plant at any time from now until late winter, preparing the soil well, removing weeds and adding plenty of compost and fertilizer. Avoid planting new roses on a site where roses have grown for many years unless fresh soil and compost have been added. In addition to choosing for colour and fragrance, choose varieties offering good natural resistance to disease.

DEVELOPING A NEW VEGETABLE PLOT
❖

This is the ideal time to prepare a new plot, digging over the site deeply while adding large quantities of well-rotted compost or manure. Grass can be dug in, turning it upside down in the base of a trench then covering it with soil to prevent re-growth. Plots dug early can be left rough so that the frost and winter weather helps break down large lumps, and birds can forage for soil pests.

Fruit crops

New planting Prepare the soil for planting new fruit trees and bushes. Place orders to ensure early delivery to complete planting before next spring.

Supports Check post and wire supports, and replace any which are loose or damaged. Put up new supports ready for planting young raspberries and cane fruits.

Pruning Start winter pruning on apples and pears to shape trees, thin out congested growth and remove damaged branches. On neglected, overgrown trees, remove complete branches to open up the head and let in more air and light.

Grape Vines Prune out fruited canes as soon as the leaves have fallen.

Fruit in store Check regularly: use the best fruits but remove any starting to rot.

LAWN CARE

Mowing Cut grass if weather remains warm and dry, and trim the edges.

Repairs Mend any damaged edges and patch up worn areas of lawn.

Spiking Spike lawns with a hollow-tined aerator, and brush grit into the holes to improve drainage.

Top-dressing Spread a thin layer of gritty compost over the lawn surface.

Care of mowers Service mowers before putting them into winter store. Sharpen the blades, clean well, then wipe all metal surfaces with an oily cloth. Store in a dry and frost-free place, covered with an old sheet.

IN THE GREENHOUSE

Bulbs in pots When shoots are about 5cm (2in) tall, move potted bulbs from frames to a cool greenhouse to develop

---

TENDER PLANTS

❖

Move all tender plants to a sheltered site for the winter. Those growing in containers can be moved to a cold greenhouse or provided with frost-free conditions if these are required. Others growing in borders, like some fuchsias, or climbers growing up against walls should be given extra protection, covering the soil round their base with straw, bracken or a thick mulch of bark. Slightly tender wall-trained shrubs or fruits like figs can have straw packed round them, held in place with netting.

---

in full light, ready to bring indoors.

Hippeastrum Pot up large bulbs into 15-20cm (6-8in) pots. Soak the dry roots until they become plump, then plant bulbs to half their depth and place in a warm position to develop.

Watering Growing conditions are now much cooler and damper, so use water sparingly. Try not to wet plant leaves. The compost of many plants, like pelargoniums, can be allowed to dry out almost completely for the winter.

Cyclamen Keep in cool conditions and water sparingly from below. Feed every week with a liquid fertilizer.

Heating Check heaters daily, and use a max–min thermometer to ensure they are not set too high, wasting heat. Make sure the greenhouse is well insulated, but ventilate freely on warm days.

Propagators Small collections of tender plants and rooted cuttings can be over-wintered in a heated propagator. These are far cheaper to run than heating an entire greenhouse.

LATE-AUTUMN CHECKLIST

❖

- ❏ Collect ripe berries and fruits from shrubs, clean to remove seed and sow in pots to raise new plants.
- ❏ Sweep up and collect leaves to keep the garden tidy and remove overwintering sites for slugs.
- ❏ Spread compost or manure over borders to be dug.
- ❏ Wash cloches and cold frames inside and out.
- ❏ Clean and store flower pots and seed trays.
- ❏ Collect, clean and store canes and plant supports in a dry shed.
- ❏ Empty compost bins, sieving out well-rotted material to use while winter digging. Throw the remaining material back into the bin, mixing in a compost activator.
- ❏ Clean garden furniture and store under cover.
- ❏ Move ceramic pots and any which are not frost-proof into the greenhouse for winter.
- ❏ Cover cold frames with old carpet or extra insulation on cold nights.
- ❏ Order mail-order seed catalogues.

319

POND CARE

Plants Cut down marginal plants and remove dead leaves or flower stems from aquatic plants.

Netting Use a net to remove leaves and plant debris from the water.

Storing Remove pumps and filters and clean before storing away for winter.

Heating Float a pond heater in fish ponds to prevent ice forming.

Early Winter

With the arrival of winter, day- and night-time temperatures drop, so check that you have done all you can to protect tender plants and any crops in store. The shorter days mean less hours to work outside, but give more time for planning.

THE FLOWER GARDEN

Roses Prune tall hybrid tea roses slightly to remove old flower stems and any dead or diseased wood.

Standard roses Reduce top growth to reduce damage from wind rock, but leave full pruning until early spring.

Perennials Finish cutting dead perennials down to soil level and tidy flower borders to remove plant debris that could harbour slugs, snails and other pests. Add it to the compost heap.

Wisteria Prune wisteria, shortening all side shoots back to about 2.5cm (1in), or two buds, from the main branch framework.

Borders Fork over bare patches between plants to relieve soil compaction, working garden compost into the soil as you go.

Mulching Spread straw or a bark mulch over the crowns of slightly tender plants, and round the base of tender climbers to provide extra protection from cold.

Planting Plant bare-rooted trees, shrubs and roses into well-prepared soil.

Propagating ivy Peg some low-growing ivy stems down to soil level to root and form new plants. Once well-rooted, detach from the parent plant and transplant elsewhere.

Holly If branches carrying berries will be needed as festive decorations, cover with nets as soon as possible to keep hungry birds away.

New features This is a good time to plan and construct new features, like rock gardens and ponds.

Shelter Build screens to protect newly planted conifers from cold winds.

Storing Regularly check bulbs, corms and tubers in store and remove any that show signs of rot. Ensure conditions are cool, dry and frost-free; dust with sulphur powder to prevent rotting diseases.

TAKING HARDWOOD CUTTINGS

❖

Increase stocks of shrubs and fruit by taking hardwood cuttings. Choose healthy stems, remove the tip and cut into sections about 30cm (12in) long. Push these to about two-thirds of their depth into gritty, free-draining soil. Suitable plants to try include cornus, salix, forsythia, ribes, roses, gooseberry and currants. In most cases these will root directly into soil in sheltered areas outside, but they can be covered with frames or cloches for extra protection. Basal heat from a propagator in the greenhouse will also speed up rooting.

320

MONEY-SAVING TIPS

❖

❑ Re-use old flower pots and seed trays, scrubbing them clean inside and out, then soaking them in a solution of disinfectant.

❑ Clean, oil, sharpen and service your tools. Keep an oily rag handy to clean the blades and handles of tools before storing them for the winter. Spray metal surfaces with light oil to prevent them rusting.

❑ Install new water butts to the down pipes from the house, garage or greenhouse to save water from winter rains. If you pay for water on a meter this will save you money. Remember to empty and wash out existing water butts to remove accumulated dirt.

THE KITCHEN GARDEN

Digging Provided the soil is not frozen, carry out winter digging. Remove any old crops, clear weeds and dig in plenty of garden compost or rotted manure. Every third year dig a little deeper, forking the soil to a depth of at least 30–45cm (12–18in) to break up any compaction.

Soil testing Use a soil test kit or meter to check the acidity or alkalinity of your soil (the pH). Use this figure to determine whether the soil requires treating with lime to make it more alkaline or sulphur powder to make it more acid, aiming to produce a neutral soil preferred by most crops.

Vegetable crops

Onions Sow onion seed in pots or trays in the greenhouse for the biggest crops.

SUPPORTING CLIMBERS

❖

Tie climbers and wall shrubs into their supports to prevent them from being battered and damaged in winter winds. Use thick plastic-coated wire or plant ties to attach stems at regular intervals to wall trellis. Or fix horizontal wires at 30–45cm (12–18in) intervals up the wall and train climbing plants to these. With climbers trained against fences and trellis, check that the woodwork is in good condition. If it needs treating with preservative, some climbers can be untwined now so that timber treatments can be applied, then re-tied when dry.

Asparagus Prepare beds for planting new asparagus in late winter or early spring. Order one-year-old crowns from a reliable mail-order supplier.

Brassicas Draw soil up round the stems of Brussels sprouts and other brassicas for support.

Protection Cover brassicas and other winter crops at risk from bird attack with netting or cloches. These can also provide extra protection for hardy peas, broad beans and other crops.

Celery Protect hardy trench celery with straw until ready to harvest.

Harvest Lift and store swede and turnip for winter use.

Herbs Keep tender herbs cropping for longer by covering with cloches. Pot up a few roots of mint to grow an early crop either on the windowsill or in a cold frame.

Fruit crops

Fruit trees Plant fruit trees and bushes, choosing new, disease-resistant varieties where possible. Family fruit trees, where several varieties are grown as different branches on one tree, are a good choice for small gardens.

Rhubarb Place forcing jars over clumps of rhubarb and seakale to encourage early stems for picking.

Pruning Winter prune apple and pear trees to control their shape and vigour, removing weak, damaged, crossing or congested branches, and any showing signs of canker or disease.

Grape vines Prune outdoor grape vines.

IN THE GREENHOUSE

Perennials Check pelargoniums, fuchsias, argyranthemums and other overwintering plants, removing any dead or yellowing leaves.

Vines Prune greenhouse vines when all leaves have fallen and vine is dormant. Brush off loose bark that could be harbouring pests.

Chrysanthemums Cut down the tops of pot-grown late-flowering chrysanthemums to their base. Store in a greenhouse or cold frame.

Protection Bring potted peaches and nectarines under cover to reduce the spread of peach leaf curl disease.

Insulation Insulate greenhouses with bubble polythene or other materials.

Heating Check heaters daily to ensure they are working efficiently. Monitor, using a max–min thermometer.

Cleaning Clean empty greenhouses, scrubbing down the frame and staging and cleaning the glass inside and out.

EARLY-WINTER MAINTENANCE

❖

❏ Scoop leaves and dead plant debris out of ponds.

❏ Tie string round upright-growing yew and conifers to prevent snow distorting their shape by pulling down branches.

❏ Write off for seed catalogues and place orders for potatoes, onion sets and shallots.

❏ Collect any remaining fallen autumn leaves, particularly if they are smothering alpines and border plants.

❏ Empty mature compost heaps and use the compost when winter digging.

❏ Treat timber posts, trellis and fencing with preservative now that many plants are dormant. Repair or replace loose or damaged fence panels.

❏ Thoroughly brush paths and steps to remove moss and slime.

❏ Make sure the water supply to outside taps has been turned off to prevent pipes bursting in the cold. Lag taps and pipework.

❏ Check tree stakes and ties and replace any that are loose, worn or damaged.

❏ Hard frosts can lift the soil, so firm down round newly planted stock.

❏ Feed birds, especially in freezing weather, and put out fresh water each day. Hanging feeders close to fruit trees and roses encourages the birds to forage on their stems for overwintering pests.

REMEMBER: *Avoid walking on frosted or waterlogged lawns.*

321

Mid-Winter

Long evenings indoors provide time to plan for the coming season and to place orders for plants and seed. There are still plenty of jobs to tempt you outside on bright days and, with the bare bones of the garden exposed, this is a good time to plan any major changes to the design and to move structures and plants around.

THE FLOWER GARDEN

Planting Continue planting trees, shrubs, hedging and roses.

Protection Use cloches to protect alpine plants outside from damage by winter cold and rain, or cover individual plants with a sheet of glass supported on wood or wire legs.

Bulbs Plant lilies in patio pots, keeping them in the greenhouse to develop.

Borders Be careful not to damage any emerging bulbs when forking over border soil.

THE KITCHEN GARDEN
Vegetable crops

Beans Enrich soil with compost where beans are to be grown.

Celery Prepare celery trenches, digging in plenty of garden compost.

Potatoes and onions Buy seed potatoes, shallots and onion sets. Sow onions in a heated propagator.

Warming up Cover soil needed for early sowings with cloches to warm it.

Rhubarb Place forcing jars over clumps of rhubarb and seakale.

Chicory Dig up chicory roots, pot up and cover to force chicons to develop.

Protection Bend large outer leaves over cauliflower curds to protect from cold and frost.

Storage Use fruit and vegetable crops in store; discard any showing signs of rot.

Fruit crops

Planting Plant fruit trees and bushes, choosing disease-resistant varieties where possible.

COLD-WEATHER CHECKLIST

❖

❑ Firm soil which has been raised by frost back round plants.

❑ Knock snow from the branches of trees and shrubs to prevent damage.

❑ Lag garden taps and turn off the mains water supply to prevent pipes from freezing.

❑ Avoid walking on lawns or pruning fruit trees if covered in frost.

❑ Do not let ice form on the surface of concrete pools as it can expand and damage the sides.

❑ Move tender plants or shrubs in containers to a sheltered site.

❑ Wrap sacking or bubble polythene round terracotta and ceramic containers to prevent them from freezing, or move them into a greenhouse.

TAKING ROOT CUTTINGS

❖

Now is the time to take root cuttings from oriental poppies, acanthus, verbascum, Primula denticulata, *Phlox* paniculata, *brunnera, anchusa, eryngium, gaillardia, romneya, rhus and many other plants. Either lift entire clumps or excavate soil from the edges to expose the roots. Cut off a few thick and healthy roots, using a straight cut. Most root cuttings are inserted vertically into pots of gritty compost; it is important that you keep this straight-cut end uppermost. Cut the sections of root about 2.5–5cm (1–2in) using a slanted cut, indicating that this end is inserted downwards.*

Several root sections can be put in a small pot, but the very fine roots of some perennials are best spread over the soil surface and covered with a thin layer of compost. Place in a frame or unheated greenhouse, and pot on individually once new shoots have started to develop.

322

MOVING SHRUBS

❖

Shrubs that have outgrown their allotted space, or which simply do not fit into the planting scheme, can be moved in this dormant season. Prepare the site to which the shrub will be moved, digging over the soil deeply and mixing in compost. To lift the shrub, use a spade to cut a circle of soil round it about 45–60cm (18–24in) from the stem. Excavate a trench of soil outside this circle, and start cutting inwards and under the shrub's roots to loosen it completely. Ease a sheet of polythene or sacking under the rootball and tie firmly in place, then drag or lift the shrub to its new site. Replant, firming soil round the rootball, then water thoroughly. Before moving a very large shrub, prune out about a quarter of the oldest branches to reduce the plant's overall size and its subsequent demand for moisture.

Pruning Prune old canes on autumn-fruiting raspberries down to soil level. Complete winter pruning of fruit trees, removing congested branches and pruning out damaged or diseased wood. Prune mature blackcurrant bushes, removing a quarter of the oldest branches at their base to encourage the production of healthy new growth.

Protection Make a polythene tent to prevent rain falling on wall-trained peaches and to reduce attack by peach leaf curl. Support the clear polythene on a framework of wooden battens, making sure you allow air in the sides and base for ventilation.

IMPROVING YOUR SOIL

❖

❏ Dig over borders and vegetable plots or start cultivating new ground to prepare it for planting. Avoid digging soil which is waterlogged or frozen.

❏ Cover areas still to be dug with a sheet of polythene to keep off rain and snow, ensuring that the soil remains dry enough for digging.

❏ Improve drainage on heavy, wet soils by mixing in generous quantities of gravel or sharp grit. All soils benefit from digging garden compost or well-rotted manure into the top layer.

❏ On newly cultivated areas of ground try and dig down to about twice the depth of your spade or fork to really break up the soil below. Thoroughly dig in compost at the rate of about one barrowload to the square metre (square yard), as this will feed the worms, increase the humus content and improve the soil's drainage.

IN THE GREENHOUSE

Protecting Bring container-grown shrubs like camellias into a cold greenhouse for extra winter protection.

Sowing Sow seed of slow-maturing half-hardy summer bedding plants, like verbenas, pelargoniums and begonias, in heated propagators.

Cuttings Take cuttings from greenhouse chrysanthemums.

Rhubarb Dig up crowns of rhubarb from the garden, place in pots in the greenhouse and cover to force early stems for picking.

Grape vines Prune greenhouse vines while completely dormant, and clean off dry bark from their rods.

Pruning Winter prune climbers and shrubs like passiflora and bougainvillea.

Watering Water plants only sparingly during cool weather.

Cleaning Give greenhouses a thorough clean, washing the glass inside and out and scrubbing the framework and staging with disinfectant to remove dirt and overwintering pests.

Heating Check that heaters are in good working order and fuel levels high enough to last the night.

MID-WINTER MAINTENANCE

❖

❏ Paint fences and trellis with timber preservative.

❏ Clean and tidy garden sheds.

❏ Wash and sterilize flower pots and seed trays, then stack ready to use.

❏ Inspect bulbs and tubers in store, removing any showing signs of rot.

❏ Sharpen blades on pruning tools.

❏ Send petrol mowers to be serviced.

❏ Buy in well rotted farmyard manure or mushroom compost to mulch borders and dig into soil.

❏ Bring potted bulbs into the home to flower.

❏ Clean grime and algae from patios and steps with a pressure washer, or scrub with a stiff broom.

❏ Take cuttings from conifers.

❏ Order seeds and young plants from mail-order companies.

❏ Start keeping a gardening diary and record book and update it each week.

323

Late Winter

Although the cold weather, frosts and occasional snow make this a dormant season in the garden, some plants still brave the elements to put on a show. There are also plenty of tasks to complete and projects to develop before the arrival of warmer spring weather.

THE FLOWER GARDEN

Lilies Plump, healthy lily bulbs can be planted outside or in pots to provide flowers this summer.

Heathers Trim back winter-flowering heathers as soon as the flowers have started to fade. Trim varieties of *Erica carnea* with shears each year to keep growth compact, so plants do not become straggly and bare at the centre.

Snowdrops Lift and divide congested clumps of snowdrops after flowering, but while still in leaf or 'in the green'; new plants can also be purchased for planting now and these establish far better than planting dry bulbs.

Roses Plant new roses before spring. Bare-rooted bushes are still available for purchase by mail-order, and should be planted immediately on arrival, so prepare the site for them now.

Winter jasmine Prune after flowering, shortening long old shoots to encourage new growth from lower down the plant.

Ivy Clip wall-trained ivy, pulling it back from windows and gutters. Untidy, straggly and battered old foliage can be completely clipped back with shears; although plants look rather bare for a few months, fresh new leaves soon form.

Planting Continue planting new trees and shrubs, particularly bare-rooted subjects which must be planted while they are still dormant.

PLANTS TO BUY NOW

❏ Order a wide range of summer-flowering bulbs, corms and tubers for garden cultivation, including gladioli, dahlias, anemones, freesias, tigridia, ranunculus and acidanthera. Buy tuberous begonias and gloxinias for pots.

❏ Order seedlings and young bedding plants. These will be delivered later in spring to pot up and grow on to flowering size.

❏ Choose the best seed potatoes, shallots and onion sets from garden centres or order by post.

PRUNING CLEMATIS

Several large-flowered clematis hybrids may be pruned now by shortening long shoots down to a pair of swelling leaf buds. Some varieties and vigorous species can be pruned hard back to buds at the base of the main stem. All the previous season's growth of varieties like C. tangutica and C. orientalis can be pruned back to their woody stem framework or base. Although less vigorous, C. texensis can be pruned in a similar way, to buds at the base of stems. The non-twining C. x durandii, usually grown alongside a shrub for support, sends up new shoots from below soil level. Old dead stems can be removed completely. Feed after pruning.

DIVIDING FLOWERING PERENNIALS

Some border perennials quickly spread over large areas, particularly ground-cover varieties. You may have observed how others only flower well at the edges of clumps and not at the centres, which start looking rather bare. Once every three or four years, aim to rejuvenate them by digging up complete clumps then teasing them apart or cutting with a knife or sharp spade.

Discard the old, original centre of the clump and replant the fresh outer portions in groups. Before planting, dig over the whole site well, forking in compost and fertilizer and removing all weeds. Division will be needed more regularly on the more spreading and invasive perennials, and with all subjects is best completed before new growth really gets under way.

THE KITCHEN GARDEN

Digging Continue clearing ground, digging it over and adding garden compost. The surface can be left rough for the winter weather to break down and level, or it can be raked smooth.

Vegetable crops

Peas and beans Sow hardy peas and broad beans outside under cloches. Broad beans can also be sown in pots in the greenhouse for planting out later.
Seed sowing Sow early vegetable crops like carrots, spring onions and lettuce in cold frames or under cloches.
Potatoes Start chitting seed potatoes, standing them in trays in a light but frost-free position to encourage small shoots to form, ready to plant in spring.
Parsnips Sow as soon as soil conditions allow and complete before mid-spring.

Fruit crops

Pruning Finish winter pruning apple and pear trees, removing badly placed, damaged or diseased branches.
Strawberries Bring pot-grown plants into the greenhouse to encourage early flowering and fruiting.

Gooseberries Prune gooseberry bushes later this season, shortening side shoots and removing inward-growing branches to produce an open-centred bush which makes picking the fruits easier.
Peaches Spray with a copper-based fungicide to prevent peach leaf curl.
Figs Prune out the oldest branches from fan-trained figs on walls or fences. Tie in the new growth and pack straw back round stems to protect embryo fruits.

IN THE GREENHOUSE

Insulation Make sure greenhouses are well insulated with bubble polythene and draughts have been plugged. In heated greenhouses, insulation will dramatically reduce heating costs.
Sowing Continue sowing seed of summer bedding plants in heated propagators, including begonias, ageratum, pelargoniums, nicotiana, petunia, salvia and verbena. Most require a temperature of 18–21°C (65–70°F) for good germination.
Seedlings Prick out seedlings and space in larger trays as soon as they are large enough to handle by their new leaves.

Never handle by their delicate stems which are easily crushed.
Bulbs Several bulbs, corms and tubers can be planted in the heated greenhouse now. Plant **dahlias** into trays to encourage the development of shoots to take as cuttings. Plant **begonias and gloxinias** in pots or trays in heated propagators. Plant with the rounded side down and hollow side up, just covering the tuber with compost.
Fuchsias Prune back the dead shoots on overwintered plants to their base to leave a well-shaped plant. New shoots will soon develop in a warm greenhouse.

LATE-WINTER MAINTENANCE

❏ Move patio containers to more sheltered sites during the worst weather to prevent frost damage.

❏ Keep sacking or old carpet handy to cover and insulate cold frames during very cold periods.

❏ Sprinkle sulphate of potash fertilizer round the base of fruit trees and bushes.

❏ If birds are damaging buds on fruit trees and bushes, cover with bird netting for protection.

❏ Clean and sharpen blades of pruners and garden tools. Then wipe with an oily cloth to protect from rust.

❏ Sweep paths and patios to remove any remaining autumn leaves.

❏ Wash the glass on cloches and cold frames both inside and out.

❏ Rake lawns to remove moss and thatch and to scatter worm casts that may have accumulated.

PLANTING A HEDGE

You can plant new hedges at any time during winter. Bare-rooted plants available from hedging specialists work out much cheaper for large projects than pot-grown plants. However, as they are dug up straight from the field and sold with bare roots they can be sold only while fully dormant and must be planted right away. Prepare the soil for a new hedge thoroughly as these plants will be expected to grow strongly and perform well for many years. Dig deeply, to about twice the depth of your spade, mixing in generous quantities of compost and a good handful of fertilizer per square metre (square yard). Improve the soil on either side of the line of the hedge, preparing a strip 90–120cm (3–4ft) wide to encourage the hedging plants to root into this.

V

Vaccinium 280
   V. corymbosum 157
Valerianella locusta 261
variegated evergreen shrubs 100
variegated honesty see Lunaria annua
   variegata
variegated iris **222**
variegated Italian buckthorn see
   Rhamnus alaternus
variegated leaves 132–3
vegetables 260–73
   autumn care 313, 316, 318
   containers 280–1
   greenhouses 220
   mini varieties 272–3
   sowing from seed 293
   spring care 291, 295, 299
   summer care 303, 308, 310
   winter care 320–1, 322, 325
Venus' navelwort see Omphalodes
Verbascum **123**, 322
   V. thapsus 125
Verbena
   V. bonariensis 167, **167**
   V. 'Peaches and Cream' **229**
   V. 'Silver Anne' 153
Viburnum 30, 31, **58**, **71**
   V. x bodnantense 'Dawn' 109, **109**
   V. carlesii 'Diana' 103
   V. cinnamomifolium 127
   V. davidii **79**
   V. opulus 107, **107**
   V. opulus 'Xanthocarpum' 169,
     169
   V. rhytidophyllum 59
   V. tinus 64, **64**, **67**, 99
Vinca 60
   V. minor 155
vine weevil 242, **242**, 244, 301, 309

vines 292, 321
Viola 229
   V. odorata **124**, 125
   V. x wittrockiana Universal Series
     143
   winter-flowering pansies 143,
     225, **228**
viper's bugloss see Echium vulgare
Virginia creeper see Parthenocissus
   quinquefolia
viruses 246
Vitis
   V. coignetiae 21, 43, 62, **62**, 117,
     117, 206
   V. vinifera 'Purpurea' **69**, 206

W

wake robin see Trillium cuneatum
wallflowers see Erysimum
walls 28–9
   climbers 207, 208
   fixing to 112
   planting preparation 111
   as screens 46–7
   shade 64, 112–13
   sunny 110–11
washing lines 19
water chestnut 222
water features 50–3
water figwort see Scrophularia
water forget-me-not see Myosotis
water hawthorn see Aponogeton
water hyacinth see Eichhornia
water iris see Iris laevigata
water lettuce 222
water lily 222, 297, 301
water soldier see Stratiotes
water violet see Hottonia
watering 184–5, 307

automatic systems 226
   crops 303, 310, 313
   greenhouse plants 219, 315, 319
   hanging baskets 229
   kitchen garden 259
   lawns 304, 309
weedkiller 250
weeds and weeding 90, 196, 248–9,
   250, 259, 296, 300, 304
weeping silver pear see Pyrus salicifolia
weeping willows 59
Weigela **71**, **73**, **76**, 233, 302
   cuttings 303, 307
   W. 'Florida Variegata' 133, **133**
Western red cedar see Thuja plicata
white currants 275, **275**, 308
white forsythia see Abeliophyllum
   distichum
whitebeam see Sorbus aria
whitefly 242, 243, 244, 305
whitewashed bramble see Rubus
   cockburnianus
wild marjoram see Origanum vulgare
wildflower lawns 190
wildflowers 124–5
wildlife 21, 30, 50, 51, 96, 304
willow see Salix
willow-leaved bay see Laurus
windbreaks 30, 174, 254
windy sites 168–9
winged spindle see Euonymus alatus
winter
   alpine care 217
   colour 108–9
   container displays 154–5, 225
   flower garden 142–3
   greenhouse maintenance 219
   hanging basket displays 228–9
   jobs to do 320–5
   pond care 223
   pruning fruit 279

winter aconite see Eranthis
winter iris see Iris unguicularis
winter jasmine see Jasminum
   nudiflorum
winter-flowering pansies
   see Viola
wintersweet see Chimonanthus
Wisteria 43, **43**, **71**, 207, 209
   layering 307
   pruning 241, **241**, 306, 320
   W. floribunda 'Multijuga' 117
   W. sinensis 65, **65**, 111, **111**
witch hazel see Hamamelis x
   intermedia
witloof chicory 261
wood anemone see Anemone
   nemorosa
woodlice 243, **243**
worm bins 183
wrap-around gardens 84–5

Y

yarrow see Achillea filipendula
yellow Banksian rose see Rosa
   banksiae var. banksiae 'Lutea'
yellow flag see Iris pseudacorus
yellow-groove bamboo see
   Phyllostachys aureosulcata
yew see Taxus baccata
Yucca 21, 57, **75**, **167**
   Y. filamentosa **62**
   Y. flaccida 'Golden Sword' 127,
     127
   Y. gloriosa 127

Z

Zinnia 315

ACKNOWLEDGMENTS

The producers and authors would like to thank the following for their support in the creation of this book: **Mrs P Mitchell**, **Mrs R Hills** and **Victoria Sanders** for allowing us to photograph in their gardens; **Paul Elding** and **Stuart Watson** at BOURNE VALLEY NURSERIES, Addlestone, Surrey for their advice, materials and studio; and **John Swithinbank** for all the support and encouragement he gave to Anne.

PICTURE CREDITS

KEY: t = top; b = bottom; l = left; r = right; c = centre; D = designer; G = garden

A-Z BOTANICAL COLLECTION: **DW Bevan** 183b; **Anthony Cooper** 114bl; **Terence Exley** 150bl; **Geoff Kidd** 286r; **Jiri Loun** 150t; **Robert Murray** 246b; **Sheila Orme** 283b; **Adrian Thomas Photography** 148t.

Neil Campbell-Sharp: G: Barnsley House 9l; 38l, G: Westwind 86; 94bl, G: Oare House 97t; G: Tintinhull 114br; G: Westwind 116t, 119t; G: Mrs Royd 121t; G: Applecourt, Hants 127bl; G: Tintinhull 132l; G: Pictons 140b; G: Barrington Court, Somerset 141t; 141br, G: Marwood Hill 151tl; G: Bosvigo 154br; G: Westwind 155l; G: Homecourt 162b; G: Tintinhull 163bl; 179tl, G: Champs Hill 183t; G: Westwind 184c; G: The Dillon Garden, Dublin 217t; G: Hope Scott, Malvern 220l; 233l, G: The Dillon Garden, Dublin 235tl; G: Westwind 262r.

336 ELSOMS SEEDS LTD: 272r.

GARDEN FOLIO: **Graham Strong** 46r.

Dr Phil Gates: 249r.

John Glover: G: Lime Tree Cottage 8l; G: Mereworth, Sussex 8r; G: Toad Hall 20l, G: Chelsea 1992 21b; 26bl, D: Naila Green 50r; G: Holbeach Rd, Shrops 51l; 56l, 178l, 179tr, G: The Anchorage, Kent 190r; G: RHS Wisley, Surrey 194bl; 206l, D: Jill Billington & Barbara Hunt 210b; 218r, G: Save the Children, Chelsea 1991 227tl; 233r, 244, 252, 259t, 268r, 269br, 270b, 275r, 278l, 280l, 280r, 281br.

HAMILTON PHOTOGRAPHY: **Stephen Hamilton** 37bl, 37br.

HARPUR GARDEN LIBRARY: **Jerry Harpur** G: Barnsley House, Glocs 18r; Diana Ross, London 18l; G: Chenies Manor, Bucks 188tr; D: Judith Sharpe, London 192r; G: Cobblers, East Sussex 196b; G: CJ Beresford, Stilebridge, Kent 198r; D: Sheila Chapman, Chelmsford, Essex 206r; 208tr, G: RHS Wisley, Surrey 212l; 213r, G: Home Farm, Balscote, Oxon 222b; G: Old Rectory, Sudborough, Northants 226l; D: Simon Fraser, Teddington, Middx 237t; G: Winfield House, London 239l; 239r, G: Nick & Pam Coote, Oxford 241r; D: Tessa King-Farlow 256r; Ron Simple 257b.

HOLT STUDIOS INTERNATIONAL: **Nigel Cattlin** 242l, 243 all, 245 all, 246t, 248br; **Bob Gibbons** 248bl.

HOUSE AND INTERIORS PHOTOGRAPHIC FEATURES AGENCY: **Simon Butcher** 207; **Graham Cradock** 232tl; **Sandra Ireland** 201t; **David Markson** 185; **Gilly Thomas** 241t.

Jacqui Hurst: 40br, G: Manor Farm, Lincs 54l; 137tl, 176, 215tr, G: Wreatham House 268bl.

Andrew Lawson: 28bl, 46l, 88bl, 89t, 97bc, 132r, 149t, 153bl, 154br, 154t, 161t, 163t, 164bl, 174r, 228b, 254r, G: Barnsley House 257t, 275l; 278r, 281bl, 285c, 287.

CLIVE NICHOLS GARDEN PICTURES: **David Hicks** 30r; **Clive Nichols** G: Brook Cottage, Oxon 9r; D: Jill Billington 10; 16l, G: Mill House, Sussex 16r; D: Mr & Mrs D Terry 17t; D: Jill Billington 19; D: Gordon White, Austin, Texas 20r; D: Sue Berger 21t; D: Dan Pearson 24t; D: R & J Passmore 25; G: Meadow Plants, Berks 27l; D: Christopher Masson 29; D: Claus Scheinert 31l; D: Oliva Clarke 31r; G: Coton Manor, Northants 32br; D: Jill Billington 33; D: Randle Siddeley 37t; D: Wendy Lauderdale 38tr; D: R & J Passmore 40bl; 40t, D: Vic Shanley 41l; D: Lucy Gent 41r; D: Jill Billington 43r; G: Wollerton Old Hall, Shrops 44; D: Olivia Clarke 45t; D: Jill Billington 47l; G: Butterstream, Eire 48l; D: Nigel Colburn 49l; G: Turn End Garden, Bucks 49r; D: Jill Billington 51r; G: Mill House, Sussex 52; D: Christian Wright 53l; D: E Bristo, Chelsea 1991 53r; D: Julie Toll 54r; 55t, G: Wollerton Hall, Shrops 55b; G: Greystone Hall, Oxon 58l; D: Jill Billington 58r; G: Vale End, Surrey 60; G: Mrs Glaisher, Kent 61; G: Red Gables, Worcs 186tr; G: Dower House, Glocs 214bl; 214r, D: R & J Passmore 224bl; 229tl, Wendy Lauderdale 240bl; G: Manoir Aux Quat Saisons, Oxon 260b; D: Rupert Golby, Chelsea 1995 267t; G: National Asthma, Chelsea 1993 282; 285r; **Graham Strong** 224br.

PHOTOS HORTICULTURAL PICTURE LIBRARY: 27r 88t, 91c, 94t, 115l, 117tr, 118b, 120br, 121bl, 133bc, 144br, 149bl, 150br, 151r, 152 all, 153t, 155r, 156b, 180br, 181tl, 184r, 260t.

DEREK ST ROMAINE PHOTOGRAPHY: **Derek St Romaine** 15l, 15r, G: Bonita Bulaitis, Hampton Court 1996 28cr; 30b, D: Mark Walker, Chelsea 1996; 32bl, 32tr, 34bl, D: Julie Toll, Chelsea 1996 39bl; G: Wyken Hall 45b; D: Julian Dowel & Jacquie Gordon, Chelsea 1997 47r; 57, 147t, 227br, 230t, 231r, 237bl, 249l, G: Rosemoor 258l; 258r, 269bl, 270tl, 271r, D: Matthew Bell & Noula Hancock, Chelsea 1994 284bl; 285l, 286l; **Helen Dillion** 38br.

THE GARDEN PICTURE LIBRARY: **David Askham** 122b, 266r; **Philippe Bonduel** 234bl; **Lynne Brotchie** 42l, 284br; **Chris Burrows** 145tl;

Rex Butcher 242r; **Brian Carter** 91l, 93b, 94br, 99b, 100b, 103br, 119br, 126r, 129bl, 133br, 169c, 173r, 247; **Kathy Charlton** 103bc; **Densey Clyne** 148b; **Geoff Dann** 12b, 124bc; **Jack Elliot** 114bc; **Ron Evans** 91r, 101bl, 106r, 107bl; **Christopher Fairweather**: 101br, 103t, 134bc, 159tl, 167bl; **Vaughan Fleming** 217b; **John Glover**: 56r, 92b, 94bc, 96, 97br, 98b, 105bl, 105bc, 106bl, 109b, 111bl, 112br, 116l, 119bl, 120t, 123br, 124tr, 125b, 126l, 127t, 128l, 129t, 134t, 136t, 140t, 142t, 142bl, 143tr, 145tr, 149br, 158l, 163t, 164tl, 164br, 166b, 169l, 169r, 170t, 171b, 172r, 174l, 191, 197t, 204, 251tl, 270tr, 276l, 276r; **Tim Griffith** 24b; **Gil Hanly** 265l; **Sunniva Harte** 146bc; **Marijke Heuff** 134br, 136br; **Neil Holmes** 102t, 102b, 105br, 107tl, 108t, 110bl, 122t, 141bl, 160br; **Michael Howes** 221r, 235br, 266l; **Jacqui Hurst** 119bc, 125t, 134bl, 261t; **Roger Hyan** 144bl; **Noel Kavanagh** 59; **Lamontagne** 61r, 147r, 157l, 171t; **Jane Legate** 116b, 182b; **Mayer/Le Scanff** 88bc, 92t, 123bl, 130bl, 167br, 219, 254l, 264l, 264r, 274bl; **Sidney Moulds** 139br; **Clive Nichols** 12c, 93t, 109t, 160bl, 161bl, 170br; **Marie O'Hara** 50l, 135l; **Jerry Pavia** 26tl, 97bl, 121br, 137tr, 139bl, 172bl, 175t; **Laslo Puskas** 149bc; **Howard Rice** 48r, 114t, 124bl, 126c, 130bc, 133bl, 136bl, 143tc, 146t, 146br, 158l, 159tr, 160t, 165t, 173l, 267b, 277bl; **Stephen Robson** 112tr, 218l; **Gary Rogers** 123t; **David Russel** 161br; **JS Sira** 12t, 43tl, 103bl, 105t, 111br, 113br, 124br, 128r, 130br, 137b, 139tc, 142br, 143tl, 146bl, 170bl, 190tl, 215bl; **Friedrich Strauss** 157r, 274br; **Ron Sutherland** 13, 36; **Brigitte Thomas** 35t, 39r, 42r, 110tr; **Juliette Wade** 172tl, 190bl, 212r, 255t; **Mel Watson** 28tl, 131l, 131r, 168bl; **Dider Willery** 99t; **Steven Wooster** 2, 113l, 138r.

TIM SANDALL: 288

AL TOZER LTD: 272l.

ADDITIONAL PHOTOGRAPHY: **Peter Anderson** 87r, 104l, 107r, 108b, 112bl, 112bc, 115r, 117bl, 117br, 127br, 129br, 138l, 151bl, 153br, 159b, 175b, 179bl, 179br, 180tr, 181bl, 181br, 182t, 186bl, 187r, 195tl, 216bl, 216br, 222t, 223 all, 238t, 255b, 259bl, 259bc, 259br, 261b, 262tl, 262bl, 263br, 269t, 271l, 273, 279tl, 279r, 281tl. **Steve Gorton** 1, 11t, 26tr, 26br, 34tr, 35b, 38tc, 87l, 88br, 89b, 90 all, 98t, 100t, 101tl, 104r, 106tl, 110t, 118t, 130t, 135r, 144t, 145bl, 145br, 156tl, 165b, 166t, 167tl, 167tr, 177 all, 180tl, 184l, 186tl, 188l, 188bl, 188bc, 188br, 189bl, 189br, 192l, 193 all, 194tl, 194br, 195tr, 196t, 197b, 199bl, 199bc, 199br, 200bl, 200lc, 200tr, 201br, 202r, 203bl, 208bl, 208bc, 208br, 209bl, 209r, 210t, 214tl, 221l, 224tr, 225, 226r, 227cr, 228t, 229bl, 229bc, 229br, 230bl, 230br, 231bl, 232bl, 232tc, 232tr, 236 all, 237br, 240tl, 240br, 248t, 250t, 251cr, 251br, 253 all, 263t, 263bl, 263bc, 265 all, 268tl, 274tr, 277tr, 279bl, 283t, 284t. **Matthew Ward** 11b, 14 all, 17b, 22 all, 195bl, 195br, 200cr, 201bl, 203br, 205 all, 211 all, 215tl, 234tl, 234tr, 238b, 250b.